The Complete Plant Based Diet Cookbook

600 Inspired, Flexible Plant Based Recipes with 28-Day Meal Plan for Eating Healthy

By Eric Baker

Copyright© 2022 By Eric Baker

All Rights Reserved

This book is copyright protected. It is only for personal use. You cannot amend, distribute, sell, use, quote or paraphrase any part of the content within this book, without the consent of the author or publisher.

Under no circumstances will any blame or legal responsibility be held against the publisher, or author, for any damages, reparation, or monetary loss due to the information contained within this book, either directly or indirectly.

Disclaimer Notice:

Please note the information contained within this document is for educational and entertainment purposes only. All effort has been executed to present accurate, up to date, reliable, complete information. No warranties of any kind are declared or implied. Readers acknowledge that the author is not engaged in the rendering of legal, financial, medical or professional advice. The content within this book has been derived from various sources. Please consult a licensed professional before attempting any techniques outlined in this book.

By reading this document, the reader agrees that under no circumstances is the author responsible for any losses, direct or indirect, that are incurred as a result of the use of the information contained within this document, including, but not limited to, errors, omissions, or inaccuracies.

Table of Content

Introduction 1

Chapter 1 Meet the Plant-Based Diet 2

Living the Plant-Based Lifestyle 2
Is Plant-Based Diet Healthy? 2
7 Major Health Benefits 2
5 Major Groups for a Plant-Based Diet 4
What to Avoid 5
Plant-Based Substitutes 6
Conclusion 7

Chapter 2 Breakfast 9

Banana Flavor Peanut Butter Bites 9
Celery Tomato Rancheros 9
Cauliflower and Chickpea Scramble 9
Raspberry Banana Muffins 10
Black Bean and Chocolate Blender Muffins 10
Rainbow Vegetable Breakfast Hash 10
Mushroom Carrot Skillet 11
Slow Cooked Butternut Squash and Oatmeal ... 11
Spiced Vanilla Pumpkin Apple Muffins 11
Mushroom and Quinoa Breakfast Cups 12
Cinnamon Walnut and Apple Bowl 12
Nutty Date and Blueberry Muffins 12
Maple Almond Granola 13
Escarole with Portobello 13
Scrambled Tofu with Potatoes & Bok Choy 13
Apple Cashew Granola 14
Raspberry Banana Pancakes 14
Broccoli Mushroom Breakfast Scramble 14
Hummus and Date Bagel 15
Apple Granola Parfait 15
Guava Oatmeal with Yogurt 15
Maple Pine Nuts Granola 15
Salted Raisin Oatmeal 17
Pecan Crunch Banana Bread 17
Congee with Raisin and Spices 17
Baked Pine Nuts Granola 17
Maple Plant-Powered Pancakes 18
Breakfast Quinoa with Peach 18
Polenta with Longans and Dates 18
Vanilla Walnut and Cashew Butter 18
Maple Granola with Peaches 19
Longan Almond Barley with Apple Cider 19
Spinach Pesto Quinoa Bowl 19
Polenta with Peach and Dates Compote 19
Taro Pie Oatmeal 20
Lemony Whole-Wheat Blueberry Muffins 20
Chocolate and Almond Butter Quinoa 20
Blackberry Cashew Granola Bars 20
Overnight Oatmeal with Maple Syrup 21
Vanilla Whole Wheat Pancakes 21
Kiwifruit Muesli with Apple Cider 21
Breakfast Quinoa with Kiwifruit Compote 21
Vanilla Strawberry Chia Seed Pudding with Chocolate 22
Stovetop Raspberry Oatmeal 22
Spelt Berry Longan Breakfast Cereal 22

Brown Rice Apricot Pudding 22
Peanut Milk Oatmeal 23
Overnight Vanilla and Chocolate Chia Pudding ... 23
Peach Kiwifruit Steel-Cut Oats 23
Papaya, Peach and Apricot Muesli 23

Chapter 3 Lunch 25

Summer Ratatouille 25
BBQ Garlicky Jackfruit Sliders 25
Asparagus, Red Lentil and Leek Soup 25
Grilled Tofu with Mashed Potato Bowl 26
Homemade Falafel Chickpea Burgers 26
Homemade Hawaiian Black Bean Burgers 26
Blackbean Spinach and Rice Salad 27
Spiralized Mixed Vegetables Lo Mein 27
Soba Noodles with Vegetable and Peanut Sauce 27
Carrot Kale and Lentil Stew 28
Chickpea Hummus Lettuce Gyros 28
Vegetables with Spicy Poppy Seed and Almond Butter Sauce 28
Vegetable Enchiladas with Anasazi Bean Sauce 29
Chickpea and Kidney Bean Stew 29
Mashed Chickpea and Avocado Sandwich 30
Peanut Butter Chickpea Burgers 30
Grilled Cauliflower with Spicy Lentil Sauce 30
Buckwheat with Bow-Tie Pasta 31
Potato, Lentil and Kale Soup 31
Roasted Golden Beet and Tofu Curry 31
Chickpea Bulgur Pilaf 32
Cabbage Pilaf 32
Stuffed Portobello Mushrooms 32
Grilled and Marinated Mushrooms 34
Baked Potato Casserole 34
Healthy Twice-Baked Potatoes 34
Rice and Bean Tostadas 35
Asian Style Stuffed Mushrooms 35
Stuffed Yellow Bell Peppers 35
Indian Spiced Asparagus 36
Fried Vegetables with Miso and Sake 36
Veggie Quinoa Beans Soup 36
Burrito Bowl with Tortilla Chips 37
Cabbage and Chickpea Pilaf 37
Rice Stuffed Eggplant 37
Grilled Eggplant Slices 38
Grilled Veggie Kabobs 38
Vegetable and Wild Rice Stuffed Squash with Almonds 38
Broccoli Baked Potatoes 39
Baked Cucumber Stuffed Tomatoes 39
Lentil Mushroom Bolognese 39
Seitan Sloppy Joes Sandwich 40
Sweet Potato & Broccoli 40
Vegan Pizza Bread 40
Creamy Asparagus & Tofu Cubes 40

Chapter 4 Dinner 42

Provencal Broccoli 42
Sweet Potato and Zucchini 42
Braised Red Cabbage with Squash 42
Cauliflower, Spinach and Sweet Potato Lasagna 43
Seasoned Roasted Beet and Chickpea Biryani ... 43
Slow Vegetable Roast 44
Black Beans and Brown Rice 44
Roasted Vegetables with Whole-Grain Pasta 44
Creamy Eggplant Polenta Casserole 45
Polenta with Creamy Tomato Sauce 45

Polenta with Mushroom Olive Sauce..................45
Maple Glazed Vegetable Lentil and Oat Loaf......46
Carrot and Sweet Potato with Pine Nut...............46
Zucchini and Cauliflower with Avocado 47
Spinach and Mushroom Pilaf.................................47
Stuffed Delicata Squash 47
Spicy Savory Eggplant 48
Veggie Green Goddess Sandwich........................48
Slow Cooker Seitan Log..48
Stir-Fry Eggplant Dengaku 49
Blackbean and Rice Stuffed Peppers..................49
Curried Millet and Green Peas with Mild Harissa Sauce 49
Creamy Garlic Mushroom Pizza..........................51
Blackbean and Rice Enchilada Bake...................51
Paprika Broccoli Casserole 52
Marinated Mushroom and Tofu Scramble...........52
Garlicky Tomato Carrot Soup 52
Bok Choy Stir-Fry...53
Carrot, Spinach and Bean Soup...........................53
Curried Mixed Vegetable Soup.............................53
Balsamic Glazed Strawberry and Avocado Toast 54
Delicious Seitan Balls 54
Baked Spaghetti Squash with Bok Choy.............54
Miso-Glazed Winter Squash with Spinach 55
Summer Vegetable Pesto Casserole...................55
Baked Spaghetti Squash with Radish Sauce 55
Zucchini and Kale Wrap 56
Kidney Bean, Barley and Broccoli Bowl 56
Potato Samosa Chard Roll...................................56
Garlicky Roasted Cauliflower and Potato Soup...57
Orange-Glazed Tofu Bowl with Brown Rice.........57
Mushroom Seitan Bourguignon 58
Stuffed Poblano Peppers with Chipotle 58

Chapter 5 Grain and Rice.. 60

Ethiopian Style Pilaf..60
Date Pumpkin Bites...60
Eggplant and Chickpea Pilaf 60
Mango Satay Tempeh..61
Spiced Sorghum with Almond and Raspberry.....61
Sweet Potato and Cauliflower Pilaf 61
Thai Red Curry Fried Rice....................................62
Polenta with Seared Cranberry and Pear............62
Lentils with Rice and Macaroni............................62
Almond Noodles with Cauliflower 63
Quinoa-Stuffed Tomatoes with Cheese and Avocado 63
Thai Rice Bowl with Peanut Sauce......................63
Rice and Tofu Scramble 64
Peanut Butter, Banana and Cacao Quinoa 64
Chocolate Cherry Oats 64
Seedy Buckwheat Porridge 64
Rice and Vegetable Stir-Fry..................................66
Fried Rice with Red Pepper and Asparagus........66
Apple Cinnamon Oats 66
Black Bean and Quinoa Bowl...............................66
Maple Protein Oatmeal with Almond 67
Spiced Corn and Yam..67
Black Bean and Rice Lettuce Wraps...................67
Cornmeal Polenta with Mushrooms.....................67
Fried Rice with Pineapple.....................................68
Cinnamon Spiced Carrot Oatmeal Bowl with Pecans 68
Basic Cornmeal Polenta 68
Raspberry Wheat Berry Salad..............................68
Macaroni and Soy Mince 69
Lentils with Rice and Onions 69
Quinoa, Celery and Cherry Potatoes...................70
Overnight Oats 70

Chapter 6 Bean and Legumes 72

- Cajun Burgers 72
- Baked Pinto Beans Taquitos 72
- Chickpea Rolls 72
- Black Bean and Mushroom Stew 73
- Split Pea Burgers 73
- Black Bean, Tomato, Rice and Lentil Burritos 73
- Edamame and Rice 74
- Fava Beans with Olives 74
- Easy Baked Chickpea Falafel 74
- Mixed Bean Chili 75
- Oats Lentil Loaf with Maple-Tomato Glaze 75
- Mung Bean Sprouts and Cabbage Salad 75
- Stuffed Tomatoes with Mint 76
- Orange Black Bean Taquitos 76
- Spicy Cajun Tofu 76
- Chana Masala 77
- Bean Chili with Lime and Jalapeño 77
- North African Vegetables and Chickpeas 77
- Smoked Tofu and Black Beans 78
- Red Lentil Chili 78
- White Bean Stew with Saffron and Sage 78
- Lentils and Eggplant Moussaka 79
- Taco Salad with Peanut Butter Dressing 79
- Lemony Chickpeas Salad 80
- Sweet-and-Sour Meatball and Vegetable 80
- Lentil Shepherd's Pie with Parsnip Crust 80
- Quick Cooking Red Lentil 82
- Tomato and Fava Bean Ratatouille 82
- Lentil Pasta 82
- Tuscan-Style Baked Beans and Polenta 83
- Ras El Hanout Chickpea 83
- Avocado Black Bean Tempeh Nachos with Cashew Cheese 83
- Mango and Chickpea Curry 84
- Mexican Black Bean Burgers 84
- Pitaya Red Bean Salad 84
- Tomato Curry Chickpeas 84
- Red Bean Date Salad 85
- Lentil Burgers 85
- White Bean Snow Pear Salad 85
- Zuppa with Cucumber and Black-eyed Peas 85
- Pinto Bean Salsa 86
- Red Lentil Dahl 86
- White Beans Vegetable Salad 86
- Quick Caldo Verde with White Bean 86
- Chickpea Couscous Salad 87
- Chorizo Chickpea 87
- Lemony Lentil Salad 87
- Red Bean Gazpacho with Raisin 87
- Mango Red Lentil Salad 88
- White Bean and Barley Pilaf 88
- Baked Pasta and Peas 88
- Vegetable White Bean with Sherry 88
- Lemony Marinated Tempeh 89
- Cajun Beans and Brown Rice 89
- Mexican Chorizo Lentil 89
- Mexican Quinoa 90
- Chile Cauliflower and White Bean 90

Chapter 7 Noodle, Pasta and Dumpling 92

- Chickpea Soba Noodles in Kombu Broth 92
- Homemade Pad Thai 92
- Chinese Five-Spice Noodles 92
- Indonesian Noodles with Tomato 93
- Cauliflower Linguine with Apricot 93
- Cauliflower-Cream Pasta with Mint 93

Baked Whole-Grain Ziti 94
Penne with Asparagus and Carrot.....................94
Penne with Bok Choy Béchamel 94
Macaroni Zucchini Salad 95
Penne with Swiss Chard, Asparagus and Peanuts 95
Spaghetti and "Meatballs" 95
Cold Soba Noodles with Miso and Sesame Dressing 96
Penne with Blackbeans and Bok Choy................96
Spaghetti with Squash and Celery Sauce 96
Penne with Radish and Mushroom Sauce 97
Red Lentil Pasta with Pistachios 97
Fettuccine with Potato Mushroom Stroganoff......97
Penne with Potato and Eggplant 99
Noodles with Red Lentil Sauce and Peanut Butter 99
Singapore Noodles with Tomato and Celery 99
Stir-Fried Noodles with Asparagus and Tomato ..100
Southwestern Mac and Black Beans.................100
Spaghetti with Lentil and Zucchini Ragu 100
Indonesian Noodle Salad with Lemon Juice........101
Potato and Celery Lo Mein.................................101
Ponzu Noodle Salad with Black Pepper.............101
Soy Mince Noodles..101
Pesto Pasta with Lentils 102
Tomato Penne with Roasted Red Pepper Sauce 102
Grilled Vegetable Pasta Salad with Papaya Chutney 102
Udon Noodle with Zucchini................................102
Kimchi Noodle Salad with Peanut 103
Peanut Pasta Salad...103
Soy Mince Spaghetti..103

Chapter 8 Salads 105

Sweet Potato Quinoa Salad 105
Rice Salad with Date and Carrot 105
Vinegary Rice and Black Bean Salad................105
Grains and Fruit Salad.......................................106
Cauliflower Pea Pasta Salad 106
Black Bean, Kale and Quinoa Salad 106
Blackbean Pasta and Corn Salad......................107
Curried Kale Apple Slaw....................................107
Purple Potato and Lettuce Salad with Soy Sauce Dressing 107
Broccoli Salad with Maple-Yogurt Dressing.........108
Tomato, Beet and Black Bean Salad 108
Baked Sweet Potato and Brussels Sprouts Walnut Salad 108
Zucchini Taro Quinoa Salad 109
Quinoa Chard Olive Salad.................................109
Mixed Greens Salad with Orange......................109
Mixed Greens Salad with Almond......................109
Quinoa, Cucumber and Taro Salad 110
Radish, Potato and White Beans Salad 110
Mango Lime Salsa...110
Rice Salad with Cumin, Nutmeg and Lentil 110
Fresh Corn and Vegetable Salsa.......................111
Carrot Date Salad with Walnuts 111
Fruited Pistachios Millet Salad 111
Lemony Vegetable Salad...................................111
Winter Asparagus Salad with Toasted Hazelnut..113
Provencal Beans & Cherry Tomato Salad 113
Warm Radicchio Potato Salad with Arugula Pesto 113
Avocado, Chickpea and Vegetable Salad 113
Creamy Lima Beans Pasta Salad......................114
Chard Salad with Creamy Tofu Dressing.............114
Bean and Corn Salad with Almond Butter 114
Mint Larb Salad 114
Lentil Apple Salad..115
Cannellini Salad with Orange and Fresh Oregano 115

Grilled Vegetable and Pineapple Salad 115	Cherry Tomato Quinoa Tabbouleh......................117
Bulgur, Kiwifruit and Zucchini Salad 115	Chickpea Salad with Cherry Tomato 117
Lemony Garlic Kale Salad 116	Kiwifruit, Black Bean and Rosemary Salad 118
Mix Berries and Papaya Salad 116	Cabbage Salad and Almond Butter Vinaigrette ...118
Vegan Avocado Chickpea Salad 116	Easy Basic Table Salad 118
Succotash Salad with Peanut Butter 116	Spicy Chickpea Quinoa Salad 118
Lemony Lentil Cranberry Salad 116	Pineapple Black Bean Salad 119
Pesto and Roasted Potato Salad 117	Chinese Yam, Corn and Bean Salad 119
Chickpea and Artichoke Mediterranean Salad 117	

Chapter 9 Soup and Stew 121

Spiced Masoor Dal Tomato Stew 121	Black Bean Vegetable Soup 130
Vegetable Soup with Lima Beans........................121	Tomato Lentil Soup with Pine Nut........................130
Creamy Asparagus and Vegetable Stew 122	Asparagus Zucchini Stew with Rosemary 130
Ginger Chickpea Cauliflower Soup......................122	Cabbage Vichyssoise with Mint...........................132
Chestnut-Zucchini Soup 123	Corn-Tomato Chowder with Basil 132
Corn Carrot Zucchini Chowder 123	Corn and Potato Soup with Dill............................132
Asparagus-Onion Millet Stew 123	Sweet Potato Tofu Stew 133
Lentil Stew with Maple Syrup 124	Red Bean Soup with Shallot and Thyme.............133
Mushroom Sweet Potato Soup............................124	Onion-Black Beans Vegetable Soup with Parsley 133
Spinach Chickpea Stew.......................................124	Potato Soup with Tahini.......................................134
Edamame-Radish Soup 125	Pumpkin and Cucumber Stew with Lime Juice ...134
Potato Soup with Thai Basil.................................125	White Bean Hummus Stew with Mint 134
Garlicky Potato Leek Soup with Onion 125	Cream of Cauliflower Soup..................................135
Squash and Peach Soup with Mint......................126	Split Pea and Tofu Soup 135
Hungarian Red Lentil Carrot Soup 126	Roasted Curry Acorn Squash Soup....................135
Noodle Soup with Mushroom and Sesame 126	Roasted Eggplant, Carrot and Lentil Stew 136
Thai Potato Stew with Mint..................................127	Apple-Mint Soup..136
Ginger Butternut Squash and Cauliflower Soup..127	Cabbage, Corn and Bean Soup 136
Thai Vegetable Stew with Dill 127	Kombo Soup with Almond Butter.........................137
Tuscan Radish Stew..128	Provencal Green Lentil Soup..............................137
Yam-Carrot Bisque 128	Fresh-Flavored Asparagus Soup........................137
Taro Soup with Broccoli, Potatoes and Leek 128	Taro Bean Stew 137
Spicy Acorn Squash and Bok Choy....................129	Lentil Brown Rice Soup 138
Tomato-Corn Chowder 129	Vegetable Broth..138
White Bean Stew with Hominy and Zucchini.......129	Green Lentil Chickpea Stew...............................138

Zucchini Vegetable Soup with Tahini..................138	Garlicky Broccoli Bisque..............................140
Green Lentil Mushroom Soup.........................139	Kombu-Tomato Broth....................................140
Moroccan Chickpea and Tomato Soup...............139	Savory Squash-Carrot Soup........................140
Garlicky Vegetable Soup 139	Tomato and Zucchini Soup..........................141
Cucumber Bisque..140	Split Pea Asparagus Soup...........................141

Chapter 10 Appetizer..143

Baked Taco-Seasoned Chickpeas and Edamame 143	Garlicky Vegetable Burgers................................148
Chilled Creamy Tofu Cheese............................143	Italian Oats Rice Bean Balls...............................150
Baked Seitan Swirls with Mustard 143	Quick French Fries 150
Chile Lime Chutney 144	Vegetable Spring Rolls with Peanut Dipping Sauce 150
Creamy Garlic Mushroom Gravy 144	Asian Veggie Slaw with Maple-Ginger Dressing .151
Homemade Shakshuka 144	Quinoa Stuffed Peppers with Pesto....................151
Mango Plantain and Dates Cream 145	Vanilla Seedy Granola 151
Garlic Sweet Potato Gnocchi with Cashews 145	Homemade Deconstructed Malai Kofta...............152
Easy Chilled Pickles 145	Seasoned Vegan Bouillon Base 152
Garlicky Cauliflower Wings..............................146	Tempeh Onion Stuffed Cremini Mushrooms........152
Garlicky Red Pepper Farro and Kidney Bean Bowl 146	Roasted Jalapeño, Lime and Avocado Guacamole 153
Chia Onion Crackers 146	Toasted Cashew and Mushroom Rolls................153
Lemon Chickpea and White Bean Hummus........147	Sweet Tofu Cream 153
Mixed Vegetable Wraps....................................147	Easy Lemon and Almond Ricotta 153
Mashed Potatoes with Vegetable Gravy..............147	Mashed Sweet Potato Bake 154
Garlic Sautéed Collard Greens..........................148	Rosemary Garlic New Potatoes 154
Mustard Spiced Creamy Potato Salad 148	

Chapter 11 Snack and Dessert...156

Vanilla Cranberry Thumbprints Cookies 156	Lemony Vanilla Pie Bars....................................159
Vanilla Chickpea Cookie Dough with Pecans......156	Stuffed Cabbage Rolls..159
Coconut Protein Bars 157	Hazelnut Choco Balls 160
Homemade Whole Wheat Pita Pockets 157	Almond and Coconut Cookie Balls 160
Nutty Lemon Oatmeal Cacao Cookies 157	Stuffed Chard Rolls 160
Chocolate Protein Bars......................................158	Vanilla Protein Muffins 161
Almond Protein Bars...158	Peanut Butter Protein Bars.................................161
Roasted Vegetable Chips...................................158	Vanilla Ginger Cookies 161
Vanilla Oat Apple Crisp....................................159	Oat and Mint Brownie Date Bars........................162

Sweet Potato Whole Wheat Cake 162	Coconut Whipped Cream 168
Moroccan Shepherd's Pie 162	Quick Hummus 168
Smoked Coconut Bits 164	Homemade Popcorn...168
Vanilla Carrot and Coconut Cake Balls 164	Easy Slow Cooker Spicy Peanuts 168
Tasty Vanilla Cookies..164	Pistachio and Coconut Ice Cream 168
Berries Cobbler...165	Easy Cold-Brew Peach Iced Tea 169
Mango Choco Protein Pudding...........................165	Maple Lemon Ginger Tea 169
Vanilla Chocolate Whole Wheat Mug Cake.........165	Easy Watermelon Lemonade 169
Choco Almond Mousse Pudding 166	Strawberry and Watermelon Ice Pops................169
Quinoa Almond Cookies 166	Mixed Berry Pudding 169
Baked Garlicky Kale Chips 166	Homemade Easy Cashew Milk..........................170
Raisin and Oat Cookies 166	Homemade Maple Cinnamon Latte....................170
Baked Maple-Glazed Mixed Nuts 167	Lemony Tahini Cream.......................................170
Vanilla Sweet Potato Pie Cream.........................167	Homemade Bubbly Orange Soda.....................170
Chocolate-Peppermint Banana Cream...............167	Easy Oat Milk 170
Cheesy Zucchini Pancake 167	

Chapter 12 Smoothie.. 172

Blueberry Lychee Smoothie 172	Raspberry Banana Smoothie 174
Pineapple Mango Smoothie Bowl.......................172	Peanut Butter Creamy Banana Smoothie 174
Fruity Vitamin C Smoothie..................................172	Chocolate Avocado Smoothie 176
Raspberry Acai Smoothie Bowl 172	Ginger Raisin Smoothie.....................................176
Vanilla Fruit Smoothie...173	Chocolate Peanut Milk Smoothie 176
Snow Pear Mint Smoothie 173	Gingerbread Smoothie 176
Vanilla Green Chocolate Smoothie.....................173	Vanilla Banana Breakfast Smoothie 176
Vanilla Apple Pie Smoothie.................................173	Papaya Smoothie 177
Tropical Smoothie Bowl with Pine nuts 173	Mango Raisin Smoothie 177
Banana Mint Smoothie 174	Orange Pineapple Smoothie 177
Strawberry Banana Smoothie.............................174	Savory Tropical Green Smoothie.......................177
Banana, Peanut Butter and Chia Smoothie.........174	

Chapter 13 Sauce and Dressing 179

Garlicky Harissa Sauce 179	Chickpea Avocado Guacamole 180
Cabbage Alfredo Sauce......................................179	Mixed Vegetable and Cashew Sauce.................180
Garlicky Roasted Red Pepper Hummus.............179	Spicy Tempeh 181
Refried Lentil Pepper Dip 180	Spinach, Artichoke and Quinoa Dip...................181

White Bean, Pumpkin, Spinach and Artichoke Dip 181
Almond Butter Apple Sauce.............................182
Roasted Garlic Lemon Dressing......................182
Homemade Mole Sauce 182
BBQ Sauce...184
Tofu Sour Cream 184
Black Bean Spread...184
Artichoke and Feta Sauce 184
Simple Sweet and Tangy Ketchup....................184
Easy Strawberry and Peach Vinaigrette...........185
Garlicky Sunflower "Cheese"............................185
Easy Vegan Marinara 185
Mexican Salsa 185
Lime-Garlic Spread...185
Pomegranate Ginger Sauce.............................186
Spicy Tahini Dressing 186
Homemade Guacamole....................................186
Sour Coconut Cream 186
Spicy Satay Sauce 186
Raw Healing Pesto with Apple Cider................187
Maple Lemon and Poppy Seed Dressing.........187
Easy Homemade Pesto....................................187
Creamy Potato Oat Sauce................................187

Appendix 1: 28-Day Meal Plan.. 188

Appendix 2: Measurement Conversion Chart 190

Appendix 3: Dirty Dozen and Clean Fifteen 191

Appendix 4: Recipes Index.. 192

Introduction

Tired of fad diets, we all want an approach that can bring natural, promising and lasting results. A plant-based diet, in this regard, is the most authentic formula to meet all our health needs while countering the risks of chronic diseases. Whether it's bad cholesterol, harmful toxins or radicals, they mostly come from animal-sourced, processed food items, so simply by removing such ingredients from the diet, you can ensure better health. The plant-based diet is known for "reversing chronic diseases", which means that it is not only good at prevention, but when used in the long run, it can reverse the negative effect of those diseases. So, if you are someone who values his health and wants to become active and lively, then you can find the plant-based diet the most helpful. And with this cookbook, you are going to have all the information that you need to start your plant-based lifestyle. This cookbook has a collection of 600 amazing recipes  which will make your menu more wholesome and healthy. I personally feel that having a consolidated guide when you are just starting with a new health-oriented diet greatly helps. And if that guidance comes with delicious, easy-to-make recipes, then your journey just gets a lot easier. So, this cookbook is all about providing you with the right tools to get started!

Chapter 1 Meet the Plant-Based Diet

A plant-based diet is not merely a dietary approach but a complete and comprehensive way of living. On the one hand, it recommends the use of vegetables, fruits, nuts and seeds and everything healthy, and on the other, it excludes all animal-based foods while promoting a healthy and active lifestyle. The idea is to utilize the healing properties of the plants and their produce. We all know how plants are enriched with phytonutrients that are naturally detoxifying and healing. Most of the widespread diseases today are due to our poor dietary habits, and it is only fresh and organic plant products that can counter those diseases. Research studies and experiments have also confirmed the efficacy of the plant-based diet in this regard.

Living the Plant-Based Lifestyle

The plant-based diet imposes a complete set of restricted conditions on all dieters: consuming only plant-based foods. On this diet, things that aren't sourced from plants and are sourced from animals are forbidden. There are various scientific explanations for the efficacy of this strategy, which will be discussed in detail in the following section. Plants, being at the bottom of the food chain, supply a wide range of micro and macronutrients in vegetables, fruits, grains, legumes, and leaves, among other things. People can get certain nutrients in a balanced amount by eating a diet rich in plant-based foods. From carbohydrates to fats,  proteins, and fibers, you can source all the nutrients in a balanced amount- just as the human body needs.

Plant-based diet proponents think that the diet is not only animal-friendly but that it can also help prevent the dangers of today's chronic diseases. Excessive consumption of meat and saturated fats are causing high cholesterol, heart illness, and inflammatory and immunological disorders in an increasing number of people. And as a result of animal farming and mass production of animal-sourced food, in which animals are fed processed feed, customers are exposed to substandard products that are potentially fatal. Alternatively, a plant-based diet eliminates all such options and provides users with organic substitutes.

Is Plant-Based Diet Healthy?

When people switch to a restrictive diet, the first thing that comes to mind is the diet's nutritional value. We all know that energy and nutrients are required to keep the body's basic metabolism running. Each vitamin has a different purpose in the body; thus, they are all equally necessary. True, the nutritional profile of an animal-based diet and a plant-based diet differs dramatically, as animal-sourced food is higher in proteins and saturated fats. The nutritional profile of a plant-based diet is different, yet it still provides all of the nutrients you require. People show more concern about their protein intake when they switch to a plant-based diet. Not eating meat does not you are going to suffer from malnutrition. There are plenty of protein sources among plant-based food products; you just need to take them in the right proportion to meet all your nutritional needs.

7 Major Health Benefits

It is obvious from the nutritional profile of the plant-based diet how the diet can really help in improving a person's health. The diet has also been shown to be effective against several modern ailments. For example, over the previous decade, the number of cancer patients has increased, and most health professionals attribute this to poor food and living conditions. Fast and processed foods, animal meat, and dairy containing traces of injected hormones all produce harmful metabolic waste in the body, which, in combination with carcinogens, frequently results in the formation of tumors and cancer cells. The benefits of the Plant-Based Diet are just too attractive to ignore. Instead, we can say they are too compelling to be ignored at all. We will provide you with evidenced advantages of the Plant-Based Diet plan to increase your degree of trust in the information we think is highly necessary for your wellbeing.

1. Effects on Weight Loss

If you are looking for a weight loss regimen, nothing can work more effectively than a plant-based diet. Participants following the Plant-Based Diet are known to lose more kilos than individuals following a calorie-restricted diet, irrespective of the fact that they are allowed to eat as much as they can. You should also know that the Plant-Based Diet lets you eat lesser. The Plant-Based Diet offers a higher fibre content, thus, making you feel full for a long.

2. Prevents Type 2 Diabetes & Blood Sugar

Well, the Plant-Based Diet is known to keep your blood sugar in controlled ranges and fade off the overall possibility of developing Type 2 Diabetes. Various scientific studies support this argument that Plant-Based Diet followers have considerably lower blood sugar levels, a 78% lesser risk of developing dreadful Type 2 Diabetes, and decreased higher insulin sensitivity. It can be credited to the higher fibre content in the Plant-Based Diet, which is the probable cause for blunting the blood sugar reaction. To add more to it, the weight loss you achieve with the Plant-Based Diet also helps in this process.

3. Improves Heart Health

Cardiovascular health is crucial for a healthy life, and the Plant-Based Diet plays a vital role for you in this regard. Plant-based dieters are known to have a considerable 75% lesser risk of having high blood pressure issues and a whopping 42% lesser chance of having a fatal heart condition. And it does not stop here; the Plant-Based Diet also offers more robustly managing blood sugar levels and cholesterol levels in your body. And you must know that a significant 46% lesser risk of developing a cardiovascular condition is because of reduced blood sugar and cholesterol levels.

4. Managing Arthritis

Arthritis is a medical disorder in which a patient experiences joint pain and inflammation of varying degrees. When a person eats a plant-based diet, the body is constantly supplied with phytonutrients with anti-inflammatory qualities; the body obtains enough phytonutrients to treat inflammation. This reduction in inflammation also lessens the amount of pain a patient feels. Furthermore, the vitamins and minerals found in a plant-based diet assist in strengthening and healing bones quickly. These beneficial advantages of a plant-based diet were also evaluated on 40 arthritis patients, with the results confirming this claim.

5. Lowering Risks of Cancer

According to the World Health Organization, changing one's diet to include healthier foods can reduce the risk of acquiring cancer by 30%. As a result, it's critical to think before you eat. Because a plant-based diet excludes all processed meat and dairy products, it prevents the body from absorbing substances that could interfere with cell division or cause cancer. When animal-sourced processed foods are metabolized, they produce several byproducts, some of which are hazardous. If this toxic accumulation is not properly eliminated, it can lead to health problems such as cancer. Cancer can be caused by a combination of poor diet and environmental factors. But, a plant-based diet eliminates those factors from our lifestyle, thus ensuring lower risks of cancer.

6. Lowering Alzheimer's Disease Risk

The Plant-Based Diet is also very helpful in lowering the possibility of developing Alzheimer's disease.

7. Improving Kidney Function

The Plant-Based Diet is also very helpful in improving kidney function because of the plant-based protein sourced from vegan meat alternatives.

5 Major Groups for a Plant-Based Diet

Since you've learned how advantageous the Plant-Based Diet is, your mind is probably racing with fresh questions about what to eat and what to avoid if you follow it. As we previously stated, we've got your back; the sections that follow will fill in the gaps.

* **Fruits**

Fruits are a great source of energy because they are high in vitamins, fibre, and minerals. If you're seeking a healthy source of carbohydrates, fruits are the way to go. Fruits are not restricted to this diet; they can be used in salads, smoothies, and desserts without restriction.

- Apples
- Avocados
- Bananas
- Berries
- Grapes
- Lemon
- Lime
- Mandarin oranges
- Melons
- Oranges
- Watermelon

* **Vegetables**

Vegetables are essential to a plant-based diet. On your plate, the more vegetables you have, the better. Vegetables that are juicy and flavorful serve to add flavour and calories to the menu. We can use all the vegetables to make our meal diversified and energizing, whether it's soups, stews, spaghetti, breakfasts, snacks, or smoothies.

- Asparagus
- Broccoli
- Butternut squash
- Carrots
- Cauliflower
- Kale
- Peppers
- Tomatoes
- Zucchini

* **Tubers**

On a plant-based diet, tubers are an important food group. They provide a great source of energy due to their high starch content. This food group primarily consists of:

- Beets
- Potatoes
- Yams sweet potato

* **Legumes**

Legumes are the most nutritionally dense plant-based components, containing high levels of proteins, essential oils, and minerals. Soups and stews are the most common way to put them to use. On this diet, legumes should be consumed to cover all of your protein requirements. Make an effort to include all of the different types of beans, lentils, and chickpeas in your meal.

- Black beans
- Chickpeas
- Kidney beans
- Lentils
- Peas

* **Whole Grains**

Whole grains, which are a strong energy source, are another important food group for a plant-based diet. The following are some of the most widely used grains:

- Barley
- Brown rice
- Buckwheat
- Oats
- Quinoa
- Rye
- Spelt
- Wholegrain bread

Other Food Items:

* **Healthy Fats**

Almost all of the oils and fats derived from plants are unsaturated and cholesterol-free. Plant oils come in a variety of flavors and can be utilized to prepare a plant-based meal.

- Avocado oil
- Canola oil
- Chia seed oil
- Flaxseed oil
- Hemp seed oil
- Olive oil
- Sesame oil
- Walnut oil

* **Nuts and Seeds**

Nuts and seeds are a simple method to boost your calorie intake. They can be used in smoothies and other dishes. Salads with a sprinkle of nuts and seeds on top have a much higher nutritional value.

- Almonds
- Brazil nuts
- Cashews
- Chia seeds
- Flax seeds
- Hemp seeds
- Macadamia nuts
- Pecans
- Pine nuts
- Pistachios
- Pumpkin seeds

What to Avoid

A plant-based diet removes all food sourced from animals and provides us with broad categories of plant-sourced foods as alternatives. Based on their source and nutritional content, the following food items are not allowed on a vegan diet.

- All animal-sourced fats, including butter and ghee
- Animal meats: seafood, sausages, lamb, poultry, pork, beef, etc.
- Dairy products: milk, eggs, cheese, cream cheese, cream, yogurt.
- Gelatin
- Protein powders

- Crab roe

Plant-Based Substitutes

We all know that a good protein intake is vital for the human body. Animal meat and its products are a major source of proteins. Since we can't have all of that on a plant-based diet, people are more concerned about meeting their protein needs on this diet. Fortunately, there are several protein-rich sources that are vegan and can easily replace meat and other animal-sourced food on this diet.

* **Meat, Poultry and Seafood Alternatives:**

You can have the following protein-rich soybean products to replace all sorts of meat on your plant-based diet plan. These products can be added to stews and soups, and you can even grill or bake them in different ways.

- Tofu
- Tempeh
- Seitan

* **Nut-Based, Dairy-Free Milk:**

Cow or goat's milk is another food item that is a need in every other recipe, yet we cannot use it on a plant-based diet. But no worries! There are several nuts-based milk products that can provide milk-like texture and flavour to meals. Those plant-based milk products include the following:

- Almond milk
- Soy milk
- Pea protein milk
- Coconut milk
- Hemp milk
- Flax milk
- Cashew milk
- Rice milk

* **Dairy Substitutes:**

Eggs are among the commonly used dairy products that we cannot use on a plant-based diet. What you can do is replace eggs in a replace with flaxseed eggs. The flaxseed egg can give a similar texture as that of an egg, white and yolk. To make this egg substitute, you can mix 1 tablespoon of flaxseeds with 2 tablespoons of water and leave them to soak for 10 minutes. Now you can add this mixture to any recipe.

Similarly, you can find vegan substitutes to replace all sorts of cheese in a recipe. From vegan cheddar to plant-based mozzarella, parmesan and feta, you have tons of options to use on the plant-based diet.

They replace yogurt and cream and give coconut or soy yogurt and coconut cream. Today, you can also find vegan cream cheese in the market to use on this diet.

Honey can be replaced with maple syrup.

* **Agar-Agar Powder:**

There are some recipes that may call for gelatin powder as a thickening agent. But that is not allowed on the plant-based diet. So, you can replace it with agar powder in an equal proportion to replace the gelatin powder in a recipe.

Conclusion

The Plant-Based Diet, through its holistic approach, provides slow and lasting changes, so it is best to make a gradual transition towards it. It is not the abrupt changes but consistency that is going to help you the most. Begin by making up your mind about this diet and how you are going to make it work for you. Then select a meal plan or adjust it according to your daily routine. After setting up your plant-based pantry and the diet plan, first cut down meat, poultry and seafood from your diet but remove other animal-sourced food products while introducing their plant-based substitutes. The Plant-Based Diet is one of the healthiest diet approaches available, as it is based only on the consumption of organic and healthy food products. Being a plant-based dieter is more than simply following a diet; it's a way of life with its own set of principles. The eating plan can help you maintain your health by lowering your chances of cardiovascular disease, cancer, and Alzheimer's disease and improving general renal function while also assisting with weight loss. It prohibits the consumption of any animal-based meals or byproducts, focusing instead on plant-based foods. Diet is the most effective approach to living a happier, healthier life. And with the easy and simple recipes shared in this cookbook, I am sure you will be able to enjoy the best of your plant-based diet journey while reaping its true benefits.

Chapter 2 Breakfast

Banana Flavor Peanut Butter Bites

Prep Time: 2 minutes, Cook Time: 20 minutes, Serves: 10 bites

INGREDIENTS:
⅔ cup old-fashioned rolled oats
1 tsp. canola or vegetable oil (for greasing)
2 ripe bananas
½ cup raisins
1 cup (240 ml) hot water
1 cup (240 ml) peanut butter (creamy or chunky)

DIRECTIONS:
1. Preheat the oven to 350ºF (180ºC), and lightly grease a muffin tin.
2. Soak the raisins in the hot water for 2 minutes to soften, then drain the water.
3. In a food processor, blend the bananas, softened raisins, peanut butter, and oats for 1 minute.
4. Spoon the batter into the muffin tin by halfway.
5. Bake for 18 to 20 minutes until the bites are golden.

Nutrition Info per Serving:
Calories: 115, Protein: 3.2 g, Fat: 5.6 g, Carbohydrates: 16 g, Fiber: 2.1 g, Sugar: 2.7 g, Sodium: 386 mg

Celery Tomato Rancheros

Prep Time: 10 minutes, Cook Time: 15 minutes, Serves: 6

INGREDIENTS:
2 celery stalks, diced small
3 cloves garlic, crushed
1 jalapeño pepper, minced (for less heat, remove the seeds)
1 tbsp. minced tarragon
2 large tomatoes, diced
Salt to taste
6 corn tortillas
1 batch Breakfast Scramble
fresh mint chopped

DIRECTIONS:
1. Stir the celery in a medium skillet or saucepan and sauté for 10 minutes, or until the celery is tender and starting to brown. Pour water 1 to 2 tbsps. at a time to keep the celery from sticking to the pan. Stir in the garlic, jalapeño pepper, and tarragon and cook for 2 more minutes. Whisk in the tomatoes and cook until they start to fall apart, about 10 minutes. Sprinkle with salt.
2. While the sauce is cooking, heat the tortillas one at a time on a dry, nonstick skillet over medium heat, turning often, for a few minutes. Wrap the heated tortillas in a kitchen towel to keep them warm.
3. To serve, arrange a warm tortilla on a plate and spread some of the sauce over it. Spread with some of the Breakfast Scramble and garnish with the mint.

Nutrition Info per Serving:
Calories: 97, Protein: 1.95 g, Fat: 1.33 g, Carbohydrates: 20.31 g, Fiber: 1.7 g, Sugar: 3.33 g, Sodium: 453 mg

Cauliflower and Chickpea Scramble

Prep Time: 15 minutes, Cook Time: 15 minutes, Serves: 4

INGREDIENTS:
3 garlic cloves, minced
1 yellow onion, diced
1 green bell pepper, seeded and coarsely chopped
1 red bell pepper, seeded and coarsely chopped
1 tbsp. water, plus more as needed
1 large cauliflower head, cored, florets coarsely chopped to about ½-inch dice
¼ tsp. ground nutmeg
¼ cup nutritional yeast
1 tsp. ground turmeric
¼ tsp. cayenne pepper
¼ tsp. freshly ground black pepper
1 tbsp. coconut aminos
1 (15-ounce, 425 g) can chickpeas, drained and rinsed

DIRECTIONS:
1. Add the garlic, onion, green and red bell peppers in a large nonstick skillet, cook over medium heat for 2 to 3 minutes, stirring, until the onion is translucent but not browned. Add the water as needed, 1 tbsp. at a time, to avoid sticking or burning.
2. Stir in the cauliflower and combine well. Cover the skillet and cook for 5 to 6 minutes, or until the cauliflower is fork-tender.
3. Add the nutmeg, nutritional yeast, turmeric, cayenne pepper, and black pepper in a small bowl. Set aside.
4. Sprinkle the coconut aminos evenly over the cauliflower mixture and stir to combine. Stir in the spice mixture and chickpeas, uncovered and cook for 5 minutes to warm.

Nutrition Info per Serving:
Calories: 259, Protein: 18 g, Fat: 3 g, Carbohydrates: 40 g, Fiber: 14 g, Sugar: 1.6 g, Sodium: 271 mg

Raspberry Banana Muffins

Prep Time: 5 minutes, Cook Time: 25 minutes, Serves: 6

INGREDIENTS:

1½ cups mashed ripe bananas (about 3 medium bananas)
¼ cup granulated sugar
⅓ cup canola or vegetable oil, plus more for greasing
1 tsp. baking powder
1 tsp. baking soda
½ tsp. salt
1½ cups whole wheat or all-purpose flour
1 cup fresh or frozen raspberries
1 tsp. cinnamon added in step 3
¼ tsp. nutmeg
1 tbsp. flaxseed meal added in step 3

DIRECTIONS:

1. Preheat the oven to 375 °F(191ºC), and lightly coat a muffin tin with oil.
2. Add the mashed bananas in a large bowl.
3. Whisk in the sugar, oil, baking powder, baking soda, salt, cinnamon, flaxseed meal, nutmeg and flour, and gently toss until well combined.
4. Fold the raspberries into the batter.
5. Spoon into the muffin tin, filling each cup to the top.
6. Bake in preheated oven for 25 minutes or until the muffins are golden brown.

Nutrition Info per Serving:
Calories: 371, Protein: 4 g, Fat: 17.9 g, Carbohydrates: 50.6 g, Fiber: 4.2 g, Sugar: 19.1 g, Sodium: 406 mg

Black Bean and Chocolate Blender Muffins

Prep Time: 15 minutes, Cook Time: 20 minutes, Serves: 6

INGREDIENTS:

1 (15-ounce, 425 g) can black beans, drained and rinsed
2 tbsps. ground chia seeds
½ cup applesauce
1 tbsp. lemon juice
¼ cup plant-based milk
2 tsps. vanilla extract
1 tbsp. flaxseed
½ cup maple syrup
½ cup unsweetened cocoa powder
½ tsp. baking soda
1 tsp. baking powder
½ cup old-fashioned oats
¼ cup raw shelled hempseed
½ cup dairy-free chocolate chips

DIRECTIONS:

1. Preheat the oven to 350°F(180°C).
2. Use the paper liners to line a twelve-cup muffin tin.
3. In a blender, add all of the ingredients except the hempseed and chocolate chips. Blend until the mixture is very smooth. Add the hempseed and chocolate chips, and blend 5 seconds or until dispersed.
4. Pour into the muffin cups, filling at least three-quarters full. Bake for 20 minutes. After baking, allow to cool for 5 minutes, and then move the paper cups to a wire rack to cool completely.
5. Place in the refrigerator for up to 3 days or freeze up to 6 months.

Nutrition Info per Serving:
Calories: 288, Protein: 10.1 g, Fat: 3.4 g, Carbohydrates: 52.7 g, Fiber: 10.8 g, Sugar: 3.3 g, Sodium: 362 mg

Rainbow Vegetable Breakfast Hash

Prep Time: 15 minutes, Cook Time: 25 minutes, Serves: 4

INGREDIENTS:

2 rosemary sprigs, leaves removed and minced
1 tbsp. dried thyme
1 tsp. Hungarian paprika
½ tsp. freshly ground black pepper
2 parsnips, cut into ½-inch cubes
2 large sweet potatoes, cut into ½-inch cubes
2 Yukon Gold potatoes, cut into ½-inch cubes
1 rutabaga, cut into ½-inch cubes
4 large carrots, cut into ½-inch cubes
3 garlic cloves, minced
1 large onion, diced
1 (15-ounce, 425 g) can chickpeas, drained and rinsed
1 (15-ounce, 425 g) can red kidney beans, drained and rinsed

DIRECTIONS:

1. Preheat the oven to 375°F(190°C). Use parchment paper to line a sheet pan.
2. Add the rosemary, thyme, paprika, and pepper in a small bowl, stir well and set aside.
3. Fill the water in a large pot, bring to a boil over high heat. Add the parsnips, sweet potatoes, Yukon Gold potatoes, rutabaga and carrots. Parboil for 2 minutes. Drain well but don't rinse. Place them into a large bowl. Toss in the thyme mixture and coat well. Spread the parboiled vegetables on the prepared sheet pan and sprinkle with the garlic and onion.
4. Bake until the vegetables are fork-tender, about 20 minutes.
5. Stir together the chickpeas and kidney beans in a medium bowl. Serve with the cooked vegetable hash.

Nutrition Info per Serving:
Calories: 471, Protein: 17 g, Fat: 3 g, Carbohydrates: 94 g, Fiber: 20 g, Sugar: 1.4 g, Sodium: 532 mg

Mushroom Carrot Skillet

Prep Time: 5 minutes, Cook Time: 15 minutes, Serves: 4

INGREDIENTS:

2 medium carrots, peeled and cut into ½-inch dice
8 oz. (230g) mushrooms, sliced
1 sweet onion, diced
1 cup (240mL) vegetable broth or water, plus 1 to 2 tbsps. more if needed
1 tsp. garlic powder
1 bell pepper, diced
½ tsp. ground oregano
½ tsp. allspice
⅛ tsp. freshly ground black pepper

DIRECTIONS:

1. Heat a large skillet over medium-low heat.
2. Once the skillet is hot, put the carrots, mushrooms, bell pepper, onion, broth, garlic powder, oregano, allspice, and pepper in it and stir. Cover and cook for 10 minutes, or until the carrots are tender.
3. Uncover, and give the mixture a good stir. (If any of the contents are beginning to stick to the bottom of the pan, add 1 to 2 tbsps. of broth.)
4. Cook, uncovered, for 5 minutes more, stirring once after about 2½ minutes, and serve.

Nutrition Info per Serving:
Calories: 169, Protein: 6 g, Fat: 1 g, Carbohydrates: 34 g, Fiber: 6 g, Sugar: 1 g, Sodium: 475 mg

Slow Cooked Butternut Squash and Oatmeal

Prep Time: 15 minutes, Cook Time: 6 to 8 hours, Serves: 4

INGREDIENTS:

2 cups cubed (½-inch pieces) peeled butternut squash (freeze any leftovers after preparing a whole squash for future meals)
1 cup steel-cut oats
3 cups water
1 tbsp. chia seeds
¼ cup plant-based milk
1½ tsps. ground ginger
2 tsps. yellow (mellow) miso paste
1 tbsp. sesame seeds, toasted
1 tbsp. chopped scallion, green parts only
Shredded carrot, for serving (optional)

DIRECTIONS:

1. Add the butternut squash, oats and water into a slow cooker.
2. Cover and cook on Low for 6 to 8 hours, or until the squash is fork-tender. Roughly mash the cooked butternut squash with a potato masher or heavy spoon. Stir to combine with the oats.
3. Add the chia seeds, milk, ginger and miso paste into a small bowl, whisk them together to combine. Stir the mixture into the oats.
4. Place the sesame seeds and scallion over your oatmeal bowl, and serve with shredded carrot (if using).

Nutrition Info per Serving:
Calories: 233, Protein: 7 g, Fat: 5 g, Carbohydrates: 40 g, Fiber: 9 g, Sugar: 3.2 g, Sodium: 214 mg

Spiced Vanilla Pumpkin Apple Muffins

Prep Time: 15 minutes, Cook Time: 20 minutes, Serves: 12 muffins

INGREDIENTS:

¼ cup water
2 tbsps. ground flaxseed
1½ tsps. ground cinnamon
½ tsp. ground ginger
1¾ cups whole wheat flour
2 tsps. baking powder
½ tsp. baking soda
¼ tsp. ground nutmeg
⅛ tsp. ground cloves
½ cup pure maple syrup
1 cup pumpkin puree
¼ cup unsweetened applesauce
1½ tsps. vanilla extract
¼ cup plant-based milk

DIRECTIONS:

1. Preheat the oven to 350°F(180°C). Use parchment paper liners to Line a 12-cup metal muffin pan or use a silicone muffin pan.
2. Whisk together the water and flaxseed in a small bowl. Set aside.
3. Add the cinnamon, ginger, flour, baking powder, baking soda, nutmeg, and cloves in a large bowl, whisk to combine well.
4. Stir together the maple syrup, pumpkin puree, applesauce, vanilla and milk in a medium bowl. Then fold the wet ingredients into the dry ingredients with a spatula.
5. Fold the soaked flaxseed into the batter until combined evenly, but do not overmix. Spoon about ¼ cup of batter per muffin into your prepared muffin pan.
6. Bake for 18 to 20 minutes, or until a toothpick inserted into the center of a muffin comes out clean. After baking, take the muffins out from the pan and place to a wire rack to cool.
7. Keep in an airtight container at room temperature for up to 1 week or freeze for up to 3 months.

Nutrition Info per Serving:
Calories: 121, Protein: 3 g, Fat: 1 g, Carbohydrates: 25 g, Fiber: 3 g, Sugar: 6.6 g, Sodium: 248 mg

Mushroom and Quinoa Breakfast Cups

Prep Time: 10 minutes, Cook Time: 40 minutes, Serves: 6

INGREDIENTS:

½ cup plus 3 tbsps. quinoa
½ cup sliced mushrooms
½ cup spinach
1 cup plant-based milk
⅓ cup chickpea flour
2 tbsps. raw shelled hempseed
1 tbsp. nutritional yeast
½ tsp. salt

DIRECTIONS:

1. Put the quinoa in a sieve and rinse well. Combine quinoa and 1 cup plus 2 tbsps. water in a small saucepan. Bring to a boil, cover, and reduce to maintain a simmer. Cook for 10 to 15 minutes or until the liquid is absorbed. Remove from the heat, cover and set aside for 5 minutes. Remove the lid and fluff.
2. Preheat the oven to 375°F(190°C).
3. Put the paper muffin cups in a six-cup muffin tin.
4. In a food processor, add mushrooms and spinach, and process until finely chopped.
5. In a large bowl, add all the ingredients and mix well.
6. Evenly divide the mixture between the muffin cups. Bake for 20 to 25 minutes.

Nutrition Info per Serving:
Calories: 57, Protein: 5.5 g, Fat: 3 g, Carbohydrates: 2 g, Fiber: 2.8 g, Sugar: 2.9 g, Sodium: 312 mg

Cinnamon Walnut and Apple Bowl

Prep Time: 15 minutes, plus 1 hour to chill, Cook Time: 0, Serves: 4

INGREDIENTS:

3 honey crisp apples, halved, seeded, and cored
1 green apple, halved, seeded, and cored
1 tsp. freshly squeezed lemon juice
5 pitted Medjool dates
Pinch ground nutmeg
½ tsp. ground cinnamon
1 tbsp. hemp seeds
¼ cup chopped walnuts
2 tbsps. chia seeds, plus more for serving (optional)
Nut butter, for serving (optional)

DIRECTIONS:

1. Finely dice 1 honey crisp apple and half the green apple. Place in an airtight container, add the lemon juice, and set aside.
2. Chop the remaining apples and the dates coarsely. Place into a food processor and add the nutmeg and cinnamon. Pulse several times to combine, then process for 2 to 3 minutes to puree. Stir the puree into the reserved diced apples. Stir in the hemp seeds, walnuts and chia seeds (if using). Place in the refrigerator for at least 1 hour before serving.
3. Serve as is or place additional chia seeds and nut butter (if using) on the top.

Nutrition Info per Serving:
Calories: 296, Protein: 4 g, Fat: 8 g, Carbohydrates: 52 g, Fiber: 9 g, Sugar: 6.1 g, Sodium: 134 mg

Nutty Date and Blueberry Muffins

Prep Time: 20 minutes, Cook Time: 30 minutes, Serves: 12 muffins

INGREDIENTS:

1 cup plant-based milk
8 ounces (227 g, about 12) Medjool dates, pitted and chopped
1 tbsp. freshly squeezed lemon juice
½ cup sorghum flour
1 cup whole wheat flour
1 cup millet flour
2 tsps. baking powder
½ tsp. ground cardamom
1 tsp. ground cinnamon
½ tsp. ground ginger
1 tsp. lemon zest
½ cup unsweetened applesauce
½ cup chopped pecans
1 cup fresh or frozen blueberries

DIRECTIONS:

1. Preheat the oven to 350°F(180°C). Use parchment paper liners to line a 12-cup metal muffin pan or use a silicone muffin pan.
2. Add the milk, dates, and lemon juice in a small bowl, stir together well and set aside.
3. Add the sorghum, whole wheat, and millet flours, baking powder, cardamom, cinnamon, ginger, and lemon zest in a medium bowl, whisk to combine.
4. Pour the dates mixture into a high-speed blender. Blend until smooth. Add the applesauce and blend until combined.
5. Fold the wet ingredients into the dry ingredients with a heavy spoon. Fold in the pecans and blueberries gently. Spoon about 1/cup of batter per muffin into your prepared 3 muffin pans, fill about three-quarters full.
6. Bake for 30 minutes, or until a toothpick inserted into the center of a muffin comes out clean. Allow to cool in the pan for 15 minutes before placing to a wire rack to cool.
7. Keep in an airtight container at room temperature for up to 1 week or freeze for up to 3 months.

Nutrition Info per Serving:
Calories: 200, Protein: 4 g, Fat: 4 g, Carbohydrates: 37 g, Fiber: 4 g, Sugar: 9.3 g, Sodium: 156 mg

Maple Almond Granola

Prep Time: 5 minutes, Cook Time: 20 minutes, plus 30 minutes to cool, Serves: 4

INGREDIENTS:

1½ cups rolled oats
¼ cup almond pieces
¼ cup (60mL) maple syrup
1 tsp. vanilla extract
½ tsp. ground cinnamon

DIRECTIONS:
1. Preheat the oven to 300°F(150ºC). Line a baking sheet with parchment paper.
2. Mix together the oats, almond pieces, maple syrup, vanilla, and cinnamon in a large bowl. Stir until the oats and almond pieces are completely coated.
3. Spread the mixture evenly on the baking sheet. Bake for 20 minutes, stirring once after 10 minutes.
4. Remove from the oven, and let stand on the countertop to cool for 30 minutes before serving. The granola may still be a bit soft right after you remove it from the oven, but it will gradually firm up as it cools.

Nutrition Info per Serving:
Calories: 220, Protein: 5 g, Fat: 7 g, Carbohydrates: 35 g, Fiber: 4 g, Sugar: 7.6 g, Sodium: 97 mg

Escarole with Portobello

Prep Time: 10 minutes, Cook Time: 15 minutes, Serves: 4

INGREDIENTS:

2 cups broccoli florets (from ½ of a medium head)
¼ cup (60mL) Vegetable Stock or low-sodium vegetable broth
1 pound (454 g) fresh escarole
1 batch Grilled Portobello Mushrooms
2 tbsps. fresh apple cider
⅛ tsp. cayenne pepper
Salt and freshly ground black pepper to taste

DIRECTIONS:
1. Mix together the broccoli, vegetable stock, apple cider, and cayenne pepper in a medium saucepan and bring to a boil over high heat. Lower the heat to medium and cook until the broccoli is softened, 8 to 10 minutes. Transfer the mixture to a food processor and puree until creamy, and return the broccoli hollandaise to the pan to keep warm.
2. Place the escarole to a large pot and pout ¼ cup of water. Simmer, covered, over medium-low heat until the escarole wilts. Drain and sprinkle with salt and pepper to season.
3. To serve, put a Grilled Portobello Mushroom on each of four individual plates and portion the escarole among the mushrooms. Spoon the sauce over the escarole and serve hot.

Nutrition Info per Serving:
Calories: 69, Protein: 5.5 g, Fat: 0.9 g, Carbohydrates: 9.6 g, Fiber: 4.5 g, Sugar: 2.8 g, Sodium: 118 mg

Scrambled Tofu with Potatoes & Bok Choy

Prep Time: 10 minutes, Cook Time: 30 minutes, Serves: 4

INGREDIENTS:
FOR THE POTATOES:
3 potatoes, peeled and diced, about 1 lb (500g) total
2 tbsps. olive oil
½ tsp. salt
¼ tsp. freshly ground black pepper
½ tsp. garlic powder
1 tsp. cumin
FOR THE TOFU:
15 oz. (425g) extra-firm tofu
1 tsp. ground cumin
Salt and freshly ground black pepper, to taste
1 tbsp. olive oil
1 tbsp. peanut milk
FOR THE BOK CHOY:
1 tbsp. olive oil
1 bunch bok choy, chopped
Juice of ½ orange
Salt and freshly ground black pepper, to taste

DIRECTIONS:
1. Preheat the oven to 400°F (200°C). Spread the potatoes evenly on a baking sheet or roasting pan. Spritz with olive oil, and sprinkle with salt, pepper, garlic powder, and cumin. Toss until well combined. Transfer to the oven for 30 minutes until tender and beginning to brown. Once cooked, portion evenly among 4 meal prep containers.
2. Meanwhile, mash the tofu in a large bowl until it has the consistency of scrambled eggs. Sprinkle with the cumin, salt, and pepper, and toss to combine well.
3. Heat 1 tbsp olive oil in a large, nonstick skillet over medium heat until it begins to shimmer. Pour in the tofu. Spread out the tofu and allow to cook for 2 minutes without stirring. Stir and cook for a further 2 minutes. Portion evenly among the 4 meal prep containers and sprinkle with peanut milk.
4. Heat 1 tbsp olive oil in the same pan over medium heat. Add the bok choy and cook for 2–3 minutes until it begins to wilt. Pour in the orange juice and sprinkle with salt and pepper to taste. Stir, and off heat and remove. Portion evenly among the 4 meal prep containers. Let cool completely before covering with lids and refrigerating.

Nutrition Info per Serving:
Calories: 342, Protein: 13 g, Fat: 18 g, Carbohydrates: 32 g, Fiber: 1 g, Sugar: 7 g, Sodium: 634 mg

Apple Cashew Granola

Prep Time: 5 minutes, Cook Time: 1 hour, Serves: 12

INGREDIENTS:

8 cups rolled oats
2 cups cashews
2 apples, peeled, cored and chopped
1 tsp. peanut butter
1 tsp. salt
1 cup peanuts, toasted,

DIRECTIONS:

1. Preheat the oven to 275°F(135ºC).
2. Pour the oats to a large mixing bowl and set aside. Line two 13 × 18-inch inch baking pans with foil.
3. Add the cashews in a medium saucepan and pour 1 cup of water, bring to a boil, and cook over medium heat for 10 minutes. Pour more water if needed to keep the cashews from sticking to the pan. Off the heat and remove the pan and pour the mixture to a food processor with the apples, peanut butter, and salt. Process until smooth and creamy.
4. Pour the cashew mixture to the oats and toss to combine well. Portion the granola between the two prepared pans and layer evenly in the pans. Bake for 40 to 50 minutes, stirring every 10 minutes, until the granola is crispy. Remove from the oven and allow to cool before spreading the peanuts, if desired (the cereal will get even crispier as it cools). Store the granola in an airtight container.

Nutrition Info per Serving:
Calories: 136, Protein: 6 g, Fat: 2 g, Carbohydrates: 23.5 g, Fiber: 4.3 g, Sugar: 5.2 g, Sodium: 196 mg

Raspberry Banana Pancakes

Prep Time: 5 minutes, Cook Time: 20 minutes, Serves: 4

INGREDIENTS:

3 ripe bananas
¼ cup (120ml) maple syrup, plus more to serve if desired
2 tsps. baking powder
¼ tsp. salt
¾ cup (175ml) water
2 cups almond flour
1 cup arrowroot powder
¼ cup ground flaxseed
1–2 tbsps. sunflower oil
½ cup (50g) wild raspberries (fresh or frozen)

DIRECTIONS:

1. Mix the bananas, maple syrup, baking powder, salt, and water in a food processor. Puree for 1–2 minutes, until creamy and smooth.
2. Add the almond flour, arrowroot powder, and ground flaxseed. Puree until fully combined. (It should be the consistency of pancake batter.)
3. Melt ½ tsp. sunflower oil in a large, nonstick skillet over medium heat. Pour the batter into the hot pan to form several 4-inch (10cm) pancakes. Top each pancake with a few raspberries. Cook for about 3 minutes, until the pancake bottoms are set and slightly browned. Turn the pancakes over and cook for another 1–2 minutes on the opposite side.
4. Repeat with the reserved pancake batter, adding more sunflower oil to the pan between batches as needed. Allow to cool, and then portion the cooled pancakes evenly among 4 meal prep containers. Serve with additional maple syrup, if desired.

Nutrition Info per Serving:
Calories: 440, Protein: 5.5 g, Fat: 14 g, Carbohydrates: 73 g, Fiber: 7 g, Sugar: 25 g, Sodium: 278 mg

Broccoli Mushroom Breakfast Scramble

Prep Time: 10 minutes, Cook Time: 20 minutes, Serves: 6

INGREDIENTS:

1 medium carrot, peeled and cut into ½-inch dice
1 medium red bell pepper, seeded and finely chopped
1 medium green bell pepper, seeded and finely chopped
2 cups chopped mushrooms (from about 8 oz./230 g whole mushrooms)
1 large head broccoli, cut into florets
¼ cup (60mL) nutritional yeast
Salt to taste
½ tps. freshly ground black pepper
1½ tsps. cinnamon
¼ tsp. cayenne pepper
3 cloves garlic, crushed
1 to 2 tbsps. lime sauce

DIRECTIONS:

1. Stir the carrot, red and green peppers, and mushrooms in a medium skillet or saucepan and sauté over medium-high heat for 7 to 8 minutes, or until the carrot is tender.
2. Pour water 1 to 2 tbsps. at a time to keep the vegetables from sticking to the pan. Stir in the broccoli and cook for 5 to 6 minutes, or until the florets are softened.
3. Put in the salt, black pepper, cinnamon, cayenne pepper, garlic, lime sauce, and nutritional yeast (if using) to the pan and simmer for an additional 5 minutes, or until hot and fragrant.

Nutrition Info per Serving:
Calories: 49, Protein: 4.1 g, Fat: 0.3 g, Carbohydrates: 8 g, Fiber: 1.9 g, Sugar: 2.3 g, Sodium: 742 mg

Hummus and Date Bagel

Prep Time: 3 minutes, Cook Time: 5 minutes, Serves: 1 bite

INGREDIENTS:
1 bagel
¼ serving of Homemade Hummus or store-bought hummus
6 dates, pitted and halved
Dash of salt and pepper
¼ cup diced tomatoes
1 tbsp. chives
Squeeze of lemon juice
1 handful sprouts

DIRECTIONS:
1. Split the bagel in half. Toast the bagel in a toaster or under the broiler.
2. Rub the hummus on each side.
3. Top with the dates, salt, pepper, tomatoes, chives, lemon juice and sprouts.

Nutrition Info per Serving:
Calories: 469, Protein: 14 g, Fat: 4.5 g, Carbohydrates: 93 g, Fiber: 10.4 g, Sugar: 15.9 g, Sodium: 513 mg

Guava Oatmeal with Yogurt

Prep Time: 5 minutes, Cook Time: 35 minutes, Serves: 4

INGREDIENTS:
3 cups plant-based milk
1 cup steel-cut oats
1 cup guava, chopped
2 tbsps. maple syrup
¼ cup (60mL) coconut yogurt
1 tsp. ground cinnamon
⅛ tsp. ground cloves
⅛ tsp. ground nutmeg

DIRECTIONS:
1. In a medium saucepan, bring the milk to a boil over medium-high heat. Once a rolling boil is reached, reduce the heat to low, and whisk in the oats, guava, maple syrup, coconut yogurt, cinnamon, cloves, and nutmeg.
2. Cover and cook for 30 minutes, stirring every few minutes to keep the oatmeal from sticking to the bottom of the pot, and serve.

Nutrition Info per Serving:
Calories: 229, Protein: 7 g, Fat: 5 g, Carbohydrates: 38 g, Fiber: 6 g, Sugar: 5.3 g, Sodium: 174 mg

Apple Granola Parfait

Prep Time: 10 minutes, Cook Time: 1 hour, Serves: 4

INGREDIENTS:
FOR THE KIWIFRUIT CREAM:
One (12-oz. 340 g) package extra firm silken tofu, drained
3 ripe kiwifruit, peeled and coarsely chopped
2 tbsps. fresh apple cider
½ cup maple syrup
1 tsp. almond extract
Dash salt
2 cups Apple Cashew Granola
½ batch Fruit Salad, or about 4 cups

DIRECTIONS:
TO MAKE THE BANANA CREAM:
1. Mix the tofu, bananas, apple cider, maple syrup, vanilla, and salt in a food processor and process until smooth and creamy. Chill at least 1 hour before serving.
TO ASSEMBLE THE PARFAIT:
2. Have ready four individual 6-oz. (170 g) parfait glasses.
3. Add ¼ cup of the Banana Cream into the bottom of a parfait glass. Top with ¼ cup of the granola, followed by ¼ cup of the fruit salad. Repeat until you have filled the glass, then do the same with the remaining parfait glasses.

Nutrition Info per Serving:
Calories: 383, Protein: 11.7 g, Fat: 6.4 g, Carbohydrates: 68.5 g, Fiber: 4.1 g, Sugar: 43.9 g, Sodium: 638 mg

Maple Pine Nuts Granola

Prep Time: 10 minutes, Cook Time: 10 minutes, Serves: 6 cups

INGREDIENTS:
3 cups (270g) old-fashioned rolled oats
1 cup (225g) raw pine nuts, roughly chopped
2 tbsps. maple syrup
1 tbsp. ground nutmeg
½ cup (75g) dates, pitted
2 peaches (100g), chopped
½ cup (75g) toasted peanuts, chopped

DIRECTIONS:
1. Preheat the oven to 400°F (200°C). Line 2 baking sheets with parchment paper.
2. Mix together the oats, pine nuts, maple syrup, and cinnamon in a large bowl. Spread the mixture evenly over the 2 prepared baking sheets. Transfer to the oven and bake for 7–10 minutes, until lightly browned. (Begin checking the granola at 6 minutes to ensure that it does not burn.) Allow to cool for 10 minutes, and then return to the bowl used for mixing.
3. Add the dates, peaches, and peanuts. Toss until well combined. Allow to cool completely before storing in an airtight container or jar.

Nutrition Info per Serving:
Calories: 209, Protein: 6 g, Fat: 9 g, Carbohydrates: 26 g, Fiber: 9 g, Sugar: 13 g, Sodium: 152 mg

Breakfast Quinoa with Peach, page 18

Maple Almond Granola, page 13

Maple Plant-Powered Pancakes, page 18

Pecan Crunch Banana Bread, page 17

16   Chapter 2 Breakfast

Salted Raisin Oatmeal

Prep Time: 5 minutes, Cook Time: 10 minutes, Serves: 4

INGREDIENTS:

4 cups (950ml) water or plant-based milk
Dash of salt
½ cup raisins
2 cups steel-cut oats
Berries, for topping (optional)
Sliced almonds, for topping (optional)

DIRECTIONS:
1. Mix the water, salt, and raisins in a small saucepan. Bring to a boil over high heat. Whisk in the oats, turn heat down to low, and simmer for 10 minutes, stirring from time to time to keep the oats from sticking to the pan.
2. Serve immediately, or separate evenly among 4 meal prep containers and allow to cool before covering with lids. Serve with fresh berries, if desired.

Nutrition Info per Serving:
Calories: 378, Protein: 5 g, Fat: 2 g, Carbohydrates: 85 g, Fiber: 9 g, Sugar: 40 g, Sodium: 159 mg

Pecan Crunch Banana Bread

Prep Time: 5 minutes, Cook Time: 1 hour, plus 30 minutes to cool, Serves: 1 loaf

INGREDIENTS:

4 ripe bananas
¼ cup (60mL) maple syrup
½ cup sour cream
1 tsp. vanilla extract
1½ cups whole-wheat flour
½ tsp. baking soda
¼ cup pecan pieces (optional)

DIRECTIONS:
1. Preheat the oven to 350°F(180ºC).
2. Mash the bananas using a fork or mixing spoon in a large bowl until they reach a puréed consistency (small bits of banana are fine). Stir in the maple syrup, sour cream, and vanilla.
3. Whisk in the flour, and baking soda. Fold in the pecan pieces (if using).
4. Gently pour the batter into a loaf pan, filling it no more than three-quarters of the way full. Bake for 1 hour in the preheated oven, or until you can stick a knife into the middle and it comes out clean.
5. Remove from the oven and let stand on the countertop to cool for a minimum of 30 minutes before serving.

Nutrition Info per Serving:
Calories: 185, Protein: 4 g, Fat: 1 g, Carbohydrates: 40 g, Fiber: 5 g, Sugar: 14.6 g, Sodium: 131 mg

Congee with Raisin and Spices

Prep Time: 5 minutes, Cook Time: 20 minutes, Serves: 4

INGREDIENTS:

4 cups cooked brown rice
½ cup raisins
½ cup chopped unsulfured pine nuts (see more about sulfites and sulfur dioxide)
1 tsp. mint
¼ tsp. ground cloves
Salt to taste

DIRECTIONS:
1. Pour 2 cups of water to a large saucepan over medium heat and bring a boil. Stir in the rice, raisins, pine nuts, mint, and cloves.
2. Simmer over medium-low heat for 15 minutes, or until the mixture thickens. Sprinkle with salt. Serve.

Nutrition Info per Serving:
Calories: 266, Protein: 5.7 g, Fat: 1.9 g, Carbohydrates: 57.8 g, Fiber: 5.3 g, Sugar: 11.4 g, Sodium: 593 mg

Baked Pine Nuts Granola

Prep Time: 5 minutes, Cook Time: 50 minutes, Serves: 10

INGREDIENTS:

8 cups rolled oats
1½ cups toasted pine nuts
Zest of 2 oranges
1 tsp. ground tarragon
1 tsp. peanut butter
1 tsp. maple syrup
1 tsp. salt

DIRECTIONS:
1. Preheat the oven to 275°F(79ºC).
2. Pour the oats to a large mixing bowl and set aside. Line two 13 × 18-inch baking pans with foil.
3. Put the pine nuts in a medium saucepan and add 2 cups of water, bring to a boil, and cook over medium heat for about 10 minutes. Pour more water if needed to keep the pine nuts from sticking to the pan. Remove from the heat, Pour the mixture to a food processor with the orange zest, tarragon, maple syrup, peanut butter and salt, and pulse until smooth and creamy.
4. Pour the pine nut mixture to the oats and toss to combine well. Portion the granola between the two prepared pans and layer it evenly in the pans. Bake for 40 to 50 minutes, stirring every 10 minutes, until the granola is crispy. Remove from the oven and allow to cool before storing in airtight containers (the cereal will get even crispier as it cools).

Nutrition Info per Serving:
Calories: 165, Protein: 6.7 g, Fat: 2.7 g, Carbohydrates: 28 g, Fiber: 6.3 g, Sugar: 3 g, Sodium: 118 mg

Maple Plant-Powered Pancakes

Prep Time: 5 minutes, Cook Time: 15 minutes, Serves: 8

INGREDIENTS:
- 1 cup whole-wheat flour
- 1 cup (240mL) plant-based milk
- ½ cup (120mL) lemon juice
- ¼ cup (60mL) maple syrup
- 1 tsp. vanilla extract
- 1 tsp. baking powder
- ½ tsp. ground cinnamon

DIRECTIONS:
1. Whisk together the flour, baking powder, and cinnamon in a large bowl.
2. Stir in the milk, lemon juice, maple syrup, and vanilla until no dry flour is left and the batter is smooth.
3. Heat a large, nonstick skillet or griddle over medium heat. Pour ¼ cup of batter onto the hot skillet for each pancake. Once bubbles form over the top of the pancake and the sides begin to brown, turn over and cook for a further 1 to 2 minutes.
4. Repeat with the rest of the batter is used, and serve.

Nutrition Info per Serving:
Calories: 214, Protein: 5 g, Fat: 2 g, Carbohydrates: 44 g, Fiber: 5 g, Sugar: 4.1 g, Sodium: 129 mg

Breakfast Quinoa with Peach

Prep Time: 5 minutes, Cook Time: 20 minutes, Serves: 2 bites

INGREDIENTS:
- 2 cups (480mL) plant-based milk
- 1 cup quinoa
- ½ cup frozen strawberries, copped
- 1½ tsps. nutmeg
- 1 peach, sliced
- Apricots
- Chia seeds
- Coconut shreds
- Brown sugar

DIRECTIONS:
1. Add the milk to a medium pot over medium-high heat, and bring to a boil.
2. Turn the heat down to low, whisk in the quinoa, and cover.
3. Allow the quinoa cook for 15 minutes. Add the frozen strawberries and nutmeg, stir, cover, and cook for 5 more minutes. Remove from the heat.
4. Fluff the quinoa by using a spoon to mix.
5. Serve with the sliced peach and any optional toppings.

Nutrition Info per Serving:
Calories: 548, Protein: 21.8 g, Fat: 12.5 g, Carbohydrates: 87 g, Fiber: 10 g, Sugar: 17.5 g, Sodium: 128 mg

Polenta with Longans and Dates

Prep Time: 10 minutes, Cook Time: 10 minutes, Serves: 4

INGREDIENTS:
- ½ cup (120mL) brown rice syrup
- 20 longans, peeled, cored, and halved
- 1 cup fresh dates, halved and seeded
- 1 tsp. ground fennel
- 1 batch Basic Polenta, kept warm

DIRECTIONS:
1. Heat the brown rice syrup in a medium saucepan. Add the longans, dates, and fennel and simmer, stirring from time to time, until the dates are tender, about 10 minutes.
2. To serve, portion the polenta among 4 individual bowls and spread with the longan compote.

Nutrition Info per Serving:
Calories: 236, Protein: 2.3 g, Fat: 1.3 g, Carbohydrates: 54.7 g, Fiber: 6.8 g, Sugar: 24 g, Sodium: 443 mg

Vanilla Walnut and Cashew Butter

Prep Time: 10 minutes, Cook Time: 20 minutes, plus 15 minutes to cool, Serves: 2 cups

INGREDIENTS:
- 1 cup raw walnuts
- 2 cups raw cashews
- 2 tbsps. pure maple syrup
- 3 tbsps. cacao powder
- 1 tsp. vanilla extract
- 1 tsp. instant coffee grounds or espresso powder
- 2 tbsps. nut-based oil (optional)

DIRECTIONS:
1. Preheat the oven to 350°F(180°C).
2. On a baking sheet, spread with the walnuts and cashews, and bake for 10 minutes. Shake the sheet, then bake for another 5 to 10 minutes until golden brown. Allow to cool for 15 minutes.
3. In a food processor or high-speed blender, add the toasted nuts, maple syrup, cacao powder, vanilla, and instant coffee. Process until crumbly, scrape down the sides, and continue to process until smooth. A high-speed blender might take only 2 minutes, whereas a food processor can take up to 10 minutes.
4. Place into a sealable container like a widemouthed mason jar.

Nutrition Info per Serving:
Calories: 78, Protein: 2 g, Fat: 6 g, Carbohydrates: 4 g, Fiber: 1 g, Sugar: 2.6 g, Sodium: 144 mg

Maple Granola with Peaches

Prep Time: 5 minutes, Cook Time: 6 minutes, Serves: 12 (½-cup serving)

INGREDIENTS:
5 cups rolled oats
¾ cup maple syrup
1 tbsp. ground nutmeg
½ tsp. salt
1 cup chopped dried peaches

DIRECTIONS:
1. Toast the oats in a saucepan over medium-low heat, stirring consistently, for 4 to 5 minutes, or until lightly toasted. Place them to a large bowl.
2. Stir in the maple syrup in the same saucepan and bring it to a boil over medium-low heat. Cook for 1 minute. Add the toasted oats, nutmeg, and salt to the maple syrup and toss to combine well. Pour the cereal onto a nonstick baking sheet and allow to cool to room temperature.
3. When the cereal is cool, place it to a large bowl and add in the dried fruit. Store in an airtight container for up to 2 weeks.

Nutrition Info per Serving:
Calories: 317, Protein: 10.4 g, Fat: 4.2 g, Carbohydrates: 61.6 g, Fiber: 7.5 g, Sugar: 19.5 g, Sodium: 100 mg

Longan Almond Barley with Apple Cider

Prep Time: 10 minutes, Cook Time: 55 minutes, Serves: 2

INGREDIENTS:
1 (240mL) to 1½ (360mL) cups apple cider
1 cup pearled barley
2 tbsps. dried longans
3 to 4 dried unsulfured almonds, chopped (see more about sulfites and sulfur dioxide)
2 tsps. coriander
1 tsp. ground cinnamon
Dash salt, or to taste

DIRECTIONS:
1. Pour 1 cup of water and 1 cup of the apple cider to a medium saucepan over medium heat and bring to a boil.
2. Stir in the barley, longans, almonds, coriander, cinnamon, and salt. Bring the mixture to a boil, cover, turn the heat down to medium-low, and simmer for 45 minutes. If the barley is not softened after 45 minutes, pour up to an additional ½ cup of apple cider and simmer for another 10 minutes. Serve.

Nutrition Info per Serving:
Calories: 465, Protein: 11.3 g, Fat: 1.5 g, Carbohydrates: 105.6 g, Fiber: 17.9 g, Sugar: 23.7 g, Sodium: 676 mg

Spinach Pesto Quinoa Bowl

Prep Time: 20 minutes, Cook Time: 20 minutes, Serves: 4

INGREDIENTS:
1 cup uncooked quinoa
2 cups (475ml) water
1 batch Walnut Basil Pesto
4 cups spinach
2 mangoes, to serve

DIRECTIONS:
1. Mix together quinoa and water in a large pot. Cover with a lid and bring to a boil over high heat. Once boiling, turn heat down to low and crack the lid. Cook for 15–20 minutes until all the water is absorbed. Allow the quinoa to cool completely before assembling the breakfast bowls.
2. Spread 1 cup spinach in the bottom of each meal prep container. Add an equal portion of quinoa to each container followed by an equal portion of pesto. Put on lids and store in the refrigerator. Serving with ½ mangoes, sliced.

Nutrition Info per Serving:
Calories: 355, Protein: 9 g, Fat: 23 g, Carbohydrates: 28 g, Fiber: 11 g, Sugar: 4 g, Sodium: 162 mg

Polenta with Peach and Dates Compote

Prep Time: 5 minutes, Cook Time: 20 minutes, Serves: 4

INGREDIENTS:
1 cup dried unsulfured almonds (see more about sulfites and sulfur dioxide)
1 cup peaches
1 cup dates
½ cup (120mL) apple cider
1 batch Basic Polenta, kept warm
1 tsp. tarragon
1 cinnamon stick
1 tsp. ground nutmeg

DIRECTIONS:
1. Mix the almonds, peaches, dates, apple cider, tarragon, cinnamon stick, and nutmeg in a medium saucepan. Pour enough water to cover the fruit. Bring to a boil over medium-high heat, lower the heat, and cook until the fruit is softened, 15 to 20 minutes. Remove the cinnamon stick before serving.
2. To serve, portion the polenta among 4 individual bowls. Top with the compote.

Nutrition Info per Serving:
Calories: 266, Protein: 4.6 g, Fat: 1.6 g, Carbohydrates: 57 g, Fiber: 9.4 g, Sugar: 35.9 g, Sodium: 462 mg

Taro Pie Oatmeal

Prep Time: 10 minutes, Cook Time: 25 minutes, Serves: 2

INGREDIENTS:

1 medium taro, peeled and diced
1 cup rolled oats
1 cup (240mL) unsweetened peanut milk
½ cup raisins
½ tsp. ground mint
½ tsp. ground nutmeg
½ tsp. red whine vinegar
¼ tsp. ground garlic
Dash salt

DIRECTIONS:

1. Steam or boil the taro until tender, about 10 minutes.
2. Drain and mash it with a spatula and place it to a small saucepan with the oats, peanut milk, raisins, mint, nutmeg, red wine vinegar, garlic, and salt.
3. Simmer the mixture over medium heat until the oats are softened, 10 to 12 minutes.

Nutrition Info per Serving:
Calories: 496, Protein: 14.1 g, Fat: 4.8 g, Carbohydrates: 98.9 g, Fiber: 10.7 g, Sugar: 55.9 g, Sodium: 782 mg

Lemony Whole-Wheat Blueberry Muffins

Prep Time: 5 minutes, Cook Time: 25 minutes, Serves: 8

INGREDIENTS:

½ cup (120mL) almond milk
½ cup (120mL) lemon
½ cup (120mL) maple syrup
1 tsp. vanilla extract
½ tsp. cinnamon
2 cups whole-wheat flour
½ tsp. baking soda
1 cup blueberries

DIRECTIONS:

1. Preheat the oven to 375°F(191ºC).
2. Whisk together the milk, lemon, maple syrup, cinnamon and vanilla in a large bowl.
3. Stir in the flour and baking soda until no dry flour is left and the batter is smooth.
4. Lightly add in the blueberries until they are evenly distributed throughout the batter.
5. Fill 8 muffin cups three-quarters full of batter in a muffin tin.
6. Bake for 25 minutes in the preheated oven, or until you can stick a knife into the center of a muffin and it comes out clean. Let stand to cool before serving.

Nutrition Info per Serving:
Calories: 205, Protein: 4 g, Fat: 1 g, Carbohydrates: 45 g, Fiber: 2 g, Sugar: 6.3 g, Sodium: 141 mg

Chocolate and Almond Butter Quinoa

Prep Time: 5 minutes, Cook Time: 10 minutes, Serves: 2

INGREDIENTS:

1 cup (240mL) plant-based milk
2 cups cooked quinoa
1 tbsp. maple syrup
1 tbsp. cocoa powder
1 tbsp. almond butter

DIRECTIONS:

1. In a medium saucepan, bring the milk to a boil over medium-high heat.
2. When a rolling boil is reached, reduce the heat to low, and stir in the quinoa, maple syrup, cocoa powder, and almond butter.
3. Cook, uncovered, for 5 minutes, stirring every other minute. Serve warm.

Nutrition Info per Serving:
Calories: 339, Protein: 14 g, Fat: 8 g, Carbohydrates: 53 g, Fiber: 7 g, Sugar: 10.9 g, Sodium: 325 mg

Blackberry Cashew Granola Bars

Prep Time: 5 minutes, Cook Time: 45 minutes, Serves: 12 bars

INGREDIENTS:

2 cups rolled oats
½ cup raisins
1 cup blackberries
½ cup tomato juice
¼ cup cashews
½ tsp. ground nutmeg
¼ tsp. white wine vinegar
Dash salt, or to taste

DIRECTIONS:

1. Preheat the oven to 325°F(165ºC).
2. Layer the oats on a 13 × 18-inch baking sheet and bake for 10 minutes, or until they start to brown. Remove from the oven and transfer the oats in a large mixing bowl.
3. Mix the raisins and tomato juice in a small saucepan and cook over medium-low heat for about 15 minutes. Transfer the mixture into a food processor and process until smooth and creamy.
4. Pour the raisin mixture to the bowl with the oats and add the cashews, white wine vinegar, nutmeg, blackberries, and salt. Toss to combine well.
5. Press the mixture into a nonstick 8 × 8-inch baking pan and bake for 20 minutes, or until the top is lightly golden. Allow to cool before slicing into bars.

Nutrition Info per Serving:
Calories: 58, Protein: 1.6 g, Fat: 1.8 g, Carbohydrates: 8.5 g, Fiber: 1.6 g, Sugar: 3.4 g, Sodium: 194 mg

Overnight Oatmeal with Maple Syrup

Prep Time: 5 minutes, plus 4 hours or overnight to soak, Cook Time: 1 minute, Serves: 2

INGREDIENTS:
- 2 cups rolled oats
- 2 cups almond milk
- ½ cup diced kiwi fruit (fresh or frozen)
- ½ cup guava chunks (fresh or frozen)
- 1 banana, sliced
- 1 tbsp. maple syrup
- 1 tbsp. chia seeds

DIRECTIONS:
1. Combine the oats, milk, kiwifruit, guava, banana, maple syrup, and chia seeds in a large bowl.
2. Cover and refrigerate overnight before serving.

Nutrition Info per Serving:
Calories: 536, Protein: 14 g, Fat: 12 g, Carbohydrates: 93 g, Fiber: 15 g, Sugar: 8.2 g, Sodium: 79 mg

Vanilla Whole Wheat Pancakes

Prep Time: 10 minutes, Cook Time: 20 minutes, Serves: 4

INGREDIENTS:
- 3 tbsps. ground flaxseed
- 6 tbsps. warm water
- 1½ cups whole wheat pastry flour
- ½ cup rye flour
- 1 tsp. ground cinnamon
- 2 tbsps. double-acting baking powder
- ½ tsp. ground ginger
- 3 tbsps. pure maple syrup
- 1½ cups plant-based milk
- 1 tsp. vanilla extract

DIRECTIONS:
1. Stir together the flaxseed and warm water in a small bowl. Set aside for at least 5 minutes.
2. Add the pastry and rye flours, cinnamon, baking powder, and ginger in a large bowl, whisk together to combine.
3. Whisk together the maple syrup, milk, and vanilla in a glass measuring cup. Fold the wet ingredients into the dry ingredients with a spatula. Fold in the soaked flaxseed until fully incorporated.
4. Heat a large skillet or nonstick griddle over medium-high heat. 3 to 4 pancakes at a time, add ¼-cup portions of batter to the hot skillet. Cook until golden brown and no liquid batter is visible, about 3 to 4 minutes per side.

Nutrition Info per Serving:
Calories: 301, Protein: 10 g, Fat: 4 g, Carbohydrates: 57 g, Fiber: 10 g, Sugar: 9.2 g, Sodium: 263 mg

Kiwifruit Muesli with Apple Cider

Prep Time: 5 minutes, Cook Time: 15 minutes, Serves: 2

INGREDIENTS:
- 1 cup rolled oats
- ¾ cup unsweetened peanut milk
- ½ cup kiwifruit
- 1 snow pear
- ¼ tsp. ground mint
- 2 tbsps. apple cider

DIRECTIONS:
1. Mix together the oats, peanut milk, kiwifruit, mint, and apple cider in a bowl and allow to soak 15 minutes. When you are ready to serve the cereal, grate the snow pear into the cereal and toss to combine well.

Nutrition Info per Serving:
Calories: 311, Protein: 8.1 g, Fat: 1.5 g, Carbohydrates: 66.3 g, Fiber: 8.2 g, Sugar: 18 g, Sodium: 64 mg

Breakfast Quinoa with Kiwifruit Compote

Prep Time: 10 minutes, Cook Time: 35 minutes, Serves: 4

INGREDIENTS:
FOR THE QUINOA:
- 1½ cups quinoa, rinsed and drained
- 1 tsp. nutmeg
- Salt to taste

FOR THE KIWIFRUIT COMPOTE:
- ½ cup raisins
- 1 cup almonds, chopped
- 4 ripe kiwifruit, peeled and diced
- 1 tsp. ground mint
- Dash ground garlic
- Zest and juice of 1 lemon

DIRECTIONS:
TO MAKE THE QUINOA:
1. Pour 3 cups of water to a saucepan and bring to a boil over high heat. Stir in the quinoa, nutmeg, and salt. Cover the pot, bring the mixture back to a boil, lower the heat to medium, and simmer for 20 minutes, or until the quinoa is softened. Serve.

TO MAKE THE KIWIFRUIT COMPOTE:
2. Add the raisins in a small saucepan and bring it to a boil over medium heat. Stir in the almonds, kiwifruits, mint, garlic, and lemon zest and juice and cook for 15 minutes, or until the apples are tender and start to break down.
3. To serve, portion the quinoa among 4 individual bowls and spread with the kiwifruit compote.

Nutrition Info per Serving:
Calories: 379, Protein: 10 g, Fat: 4.5 g, Carbohydrates: 81.7 g, Fiber: 10.4 g, Sugar: 41.8 g, Sodium: 602 mg

Vanilla Strawberry Chia Seed Pudding with Chocolate

Prep Time: 15 minutes, Cook Time: 0, Serves: 2

INGREDIENTS:

- ⅓ cup dates
- 1 cup plant-based milk
- ½ cup strawberries (more for garnish, optional)
- ½ tsp. vanilla extract
- ¼ cup ground chia seeds
- 2 tbsps. cocoa powder
- 2 tbsps. maple syrup
- 3 tbsps. raw shelled hempseed
- Shaved chocolate, for garnish (optional)

DIRECTIONS:

1. In a blender, add the dates and milk. Blend until smooth. Add the remaining ingredients except for the chocolate. Blend well. Pour into two bowls and place in the refrigerator to chill for at least 4 hours.
2. Garnish with shaved chocolate and pieces of strawberry, if desired, and serve.

Nutrition Info per Serving:
Calories: 353, Protein: 9.8 g, Fat: 9 g, Carbohydrates: 58 g, Fiber: 10.9 g, Sugar: 37 g, Sodium: 139 mg

Spelt Berry Longan Breakfast Cereal

Prep Time: 10 minutes, Cook Time: 1 hour, Serves: 2

INGREDIENTS:

- 1 cup spelt berries
- 2 cups (480mL) unsweetened peanut milk
- ¾ cup dried longans
- 1 tsp. apple cider
- ¼ tsp. salt
- ⅛ tsp. ground nutmeg
- ⅛ tsp. ground mint

DIRECTIONS:

1. Pour 2½ cups of water to a medium saucepan and bring to a boil. Add the spelt, salt, nutmeg, and mint. Cover the pot and bring the mixture to a boil. Reduce the heat to medium-low and simmer for 45 to 50 minutes, or until the spelt is softened. Drain any excess water.
2. Whisk in the peanut milk, longans, and apple cider to the cooked spelt berries and cook over medium-low heat for 10 to 12 minutes, or until heated through and creamy.

Nutrition Info per Serving:
Calories: 445, Protein: 21.1 g, Fat: 4.5 g, Carbohydrates: 80.3 g, Fiber: 10 g, Sugar: 24.7 g, Sodium: 406 mg

Stovetop Raspberry Oatmeal

Prep Time: 3 minutes, Cook Time: 10 minutes, Serves: 2 bites

INGREDIENTS:

- 1½ cups (360mL) plant-based milk
- 1 cup old-fashioned rolled oats
- ½ cup fresh or frozen raspberries
- 1 tbsp. maple syrup
- 1 tsp. nutmeg
- 2 tbsps. Pine nuts
- 2–3 tbsps. granola
- 1 tbsp. coconut shreds
- 2 tbsps. chia seeds

DIRECTIONS:

1. Add the milk to a medium saucepan over medium-high heat, and bring to a boil.
2. Whisk in the oats and frozen raspberries and turn the heat down to low.
3. Cook for 5 minutes, stirring from time to time.
4. Off the heat and remove the pan, and serve with optional toppings.

Nutrition Info per Serving:
Calories: 670, Protein: 19.3 g, Fat: 29.9 g, Carbohydrates: 80.5 g, Fiber: 14.3 g, Sugar: 29 g, Sodium: 225 mg

Brown Rice Apricot Pudding

Prep Time: 5 minutes, Cook Time: 15 minutes, Serves: 4

INGREDIENTS:

- 3 cups cooked brown rice
- 2 cups unsweetened peanut milk
- 1 cup sweet potatoes
- 2 kiwifruit, cored and chopped
- ¼ cup red beans
- ¼ cup slivered apricots, toasted
- 1 tsp. mint
- ⅛ to ¼ tsp. ground cloves
- Salt to taste

DIRECTIONS:

1. Mix together the rice, peanut milk, mint, cloves, and sweet potatoes in a medium saucepan and simmer over medium-low heat for 12 minutes, or until the mixture thickens.
2. Stir in the kiwifruit, red beans, and salt. Serve garnished with the toasted apricots.

Nutrition Info per Serving:
Calories: 267, Protein: 8.9 g, Fat: 3 g, Carbohydrates: 51 g, Fiber: 4.5 g, Sugar: 15.5 g, Sodium: 652 mg

Peanut Milk Oatmeal

Prep Time: 5 minutes, Cook Time: 5 minutes, Serves: 2

INGREDIENTS:
1 cup rolled oats
2 cups (480mL) peanut
milk, or water
Salt to taste

DIRECTIONS:
1. Place the oats, peanut milk, and salt to a small saucepan and bring to a boil. Lower the heat to medium and simmer for about 5 minutes, or until the oats become creamy.

Nutrition Info per Serving:
Calories: 156, Protein: 11.8 g, Fat: 1.1 g, Carbohydrates: 24.7 g, Fiber: 2.8 g, Sugar: 12.7 g, Sodium: 667 mg

Peach Kiwifruit Steel-Cut Oats

Prep Time: 5 minutes, Cook Time: 8 hours, Serves: 2

INGREDIENTS:
1 cup steel-cut oats
2 cups chopped peaches
1 cup kiwifruit, peeled
and chopped
1 tsp. ruby port

DIRECTIONS:
1. Mix the oats, peaches, kiwifruit, ruby port, and 4 cups of water in a 2- or 4-quart slow cooker. Simmer for 8 hours, or until the oats are softened. Serve.

Nutrition Info per Serving:
Calories: 291, Protein: 8.7 g, Fat: 3.5 g, Carbohydrates: 56.2 g, Fiber: 11.3 g, Sugar: 20 g, Sodium: 3 mg

Overnight Vanilla and Chocolate Chia Pudding

Prep Time: 2 minutes, plus overnight to chill, Cook Time: 0, Serves: 2

INGREDIENTS:
1 cup plant-based milk
¼ cup chia seeds
1 tsp. vanilla extract
2 tbsps. raw cacao powder
1 tsp. pure maple syrup

DIRECTIONS:
1. Add the milk, chia seeds, vanilla, cacao powder and maple syrup in a large bowl, stir them together. Divide between 2 (½-pint) covered glass jars or containers. Place in the refrigerator to chill overnight.
2. Stir well before serving.

Nutrition Info per Serving:
Calories: 213, Protein: 9 g, Fat: 10 g, Carbohydrates: 20 g, Fiber: 15 g, Sugar: 11.2 g, Sodium: 107 mg

Papaya, Peach and Apricot Muesli

Prep Time: 5 minutes, Cook Time: 15 minutes, Serves: 2

INGREDIENTS:
1 cup rolled oats
¾ cup (60mL) unsweetened peanut milk
½ cup peaches, peeled, cored and chopped
¼ cup unsweetened apricots, toasted
1 papaya, peeled and sliced

DIRECTIONS:
1. Mix all ingredients in a bowl and allow to soak 15 minutes.

Nutrition Info per Serving:
Calories: 177, Protein: 7.5 g, Fat: 1.3 g, Carbohydrates: 34.2 g, Fiber: 4.9 g, Sugar: 15.7 g, Sodium: 81 mg

Chapter 3 Lunch

Summer Ratatouille

Prep Time: 10 minutes, Cook Time: 25 minutes, Serves: 1

INGREDIENTS:
1 medium red bell pepper, seeded and diced
1 medium red onion, peeled and diced
1 medium eggplant, about 1 pound (454 g), stemmed and diced
½ cup chopped basil
1 large tomato, diced
1 small zucchini, diced
4 cloves garlic, peeled and minced
Salt and freshly ground black pepper

DIRECTIONS:
1. Put the onion in a saucepan and sauté over medium heat for 10 minutes.
2. Add water 1 tbsp. at a time to keep the onions from sticking to the pan.
3. Put in the red pepper, zucchini, eggplant, and garlic. Cook for 15 minutes, covered, stirring occasionally.
4. Stir in the basil and tomatoes, and season with salt and pepper.

Nutrition Info per Serving:
Calories: 64, Protein: 2.5 g, Fat: 0.5 g, Carbohydrates: 14.3 g, Fiber: 5.3 g, Sugar: 7.7 g, Sodium: 443 mg

BBQ Garlicky Jackfruit Sliders

Prep Time: 10 minutes, Cook Time: 15 minutes, Serves: 6

INGREDIENTS:
2 (20-ounce, 567 g) cans young green jackfruit, drained and rinsed
½ cup BBQ Sauce
1 tsp. onion powder
1 tsp. garlic powder
6 whole-wheat slider buns
Asian-style slaw with maple-ginger dressing, for topping
Tomatoes, onions, and pickles, for topping (optional)

DIRECTIONS:
1. Smash the jackfruit with a fork or potato masher until it has a shredded consistency in a large bowl.
2. Heat a medium stockpot over medium-low heat. Stir the shredded jackfruit, BBQ sauce, onion powder, and garlic powder into the pot. Cover and cook for 10 minutes, stirring once after about 5 minutes. Add a few tbsps. of vegetable broth or water if the jackfruit begins sticking to the bottom of the pot.
3. Uncover and cook for another 5 minutes, stirring every few minutes.
4. After cooking, serve on whole-wheat slider buns with your choosing toppings.

Nutrition Info per Serving:
Calories: 188, Protein: 7 g, Fat: 2 g, Carbohydrates: 36 g, Fiber: 11 g, Sugar: 5.6 g, Sodium: 374 mg

Asparagus, Red Lentil and Leek Soup

Prep Time: 15 minutes, Cook Time: 35 minutes, Serves: 4

INGREDIENTS:
2 leeks
1 tbsp. water
¾ tsp. dried tarragon (or dried dill or thyme)
2 garlic cloves, minced
1 pound (454 g) asparagus, cut into 1-inch pieces, including the ends
1 cup dried red lentils
6 cups no-sodium vegetable broth
Juice of 1 lemon
Fresh ground black pepper

DIRECTIONS:
1. Cut off the dark green portion of the stalks and the leeks' root ends. Slit the remaining white and light green portion lengthwise down the center and run the leeks under cool water, remove any dirt between the layers with your fingers. Thinly slice the leeks.
2. Add the leeks and water in a large pot, sauté over medium-high heat for 5 minutes. Add the tarragon and garlic. Cook for another 2 minutes.
3. Add the asparagus, lentils, and vegetable broth. Bring the soup to a boil, reduce the heat to medium-low, cover and cook for 20 to 30 minutes until the lentils are tender.
4. Remove some of the cooked leeks, lentils, and asparagus if you'd like some larger pieces in your soup. Puree the soup with an immersion blender until smooth, or slightly chunky. Stir in the ingredients removed, if using.
5. Lightly drizzle with the fresh lemon juice and season with pepper and serve.

Nutrition Info per Serving:
Calories: 262, Protein: 16 g, Fat: 2 g, Carbohydrates: 45 g, Fiber: 8 g, Sugar: 2.1 g, Sodium: 742 mg

Grilled Tofu with Mashed Potato Bowl

Prep Time: 15 minutes, plus 45 minutes to sit, Cook Time: 10 minutes, Serves: 4

INGREDIENTS:
1 (14-ounce, 397 g) package firm or extra-firm tofu
¼ cup BBQ sauce
6 cups fluffy mashed potatoes
1 recipe gravy

DIRECTIONS:
1. Place the tofu on a paper towel–lined plate. Then place a plate on top of the tofu and a bowl or mug on top of the plate to help weigh it down. Let the tofu be pressed for 30 minutes to 2 hours.
2. Slice the tofu block into ½-inch slices.
3. Place the tofu slices and the BBQ sauce in a large bowl, gently mix until the tofu is coated. Let the tofu marinate for 15 minutes to 1 hour.
4. Place the grill or a grill pan on the stove and preheat to high heat. Grill the tofu slices for 4 to 5 minutes, then flip them over gently and grill for another 4 to 5 minutes, or until the tofu easily releases from the grill surface.
5. To serve, place 1½ cups of mashed potatoes in each of 4 bowls, top with one-quarter of the grilled tofu, and smother in gravy.

Nutrition Info per Serving:
Calories: 349, Protein: 15 g, Fat: 5 g, Carbohydrates: 61 g, Fiber: 4 g, Sugar: 2.3 g, Sodium: 458 mg

Homemade Falafel Chickpea Burgers

Prep Time: 15 minutes, Cook Time: 30 minutes, Serves: 8

INGREDIENTS:
2 cups cooked brown rice
3 cups cooked chickpeas
1 tbsp. freshly squeezed lemon juice
¼ cup vegetable broth
¼ cup chopped fresh parsley
2 tsps. onion powder
2 tsps. garlic powder
1 tsp. ground coriander
1½ tsps. ground cumin
¼ tsp. freshly ground black pepper
Whole-Wheat Pita Pockets or whole-wheat buns
Lettuce, tomato, and onion, for topping (optional)

DIRECTIONS:
1. Preheat the oven to 425°F(220°C). Use the parchment paper to line a baking sheet.
2. Combine all of the ingredients except the buns and toppings in a food processor or blender. Process on low for 30 to 45 seconds, or until the mixture can easily be formed into patties but isn't so well mixed that you create hummus. Stop the processor and scrape down the sides once or twice.
3. Scoop out ½ cup of the chickpea mixture, and shape it into a patty. Arrange the patty on the baking sheet. Repeat until all of the chickpea mixture is used.
4. Bake for 15 minutes. Flip the patties and cook for another 12 to 15 minutes, and serve on buns with your choosing toppings.

Nutrition Info per Serving:
Calories: 243, Protein: 10 g, Fat: 3 g, Carbohydrates: 44 g, Fiber: 8 g, Sugar: 1 g, Sodium: 610 mg

Homemade Hawaiian Black Bean Burgers

Prep Time: 15 minutes, Cook Time: 10 minutes, Serves: 8

INGREDIENTS:
3 cups cooked black beans
1 cup quick-cooking oats
2 cups cooked brown rice
¼ cup BBQ Sauce, plus more for serving
1 tsp. garlic powder
1 tsp. onion powder
¼ cup pineapple juice
1 pineapple, cut into ¼-inch-thick rings
8 whole-wheat buns
Lettuce, tomato, pickles, and onion, for topping (optional)

DIRECTIONS:
1. Preheat the grill to medium-high heat.
2. Mash the black beans with a fork or mixing spoon in a large bowl.
3. Add the oats, rice, BBQ sauce, garlic powder, onion powder and the pineapple juice, and mix until the mixture begins to hold its shape and can be formed into patties.
4. Scoop ½ cup of bean mixture out, and shape it into a patty. Repeat until all of the bean mixture is used.
5. Put the patties on the hot grill, and cook for 4 to 5 minutes per side, flipping once the burgers easily release from the grill surface.
6. After flipping, place the pineapple rings on the grill, and cook for 1 to 2 minutes per side.
7. Remove the burgers and pineapple rings. On each bun, place with one patty and one pineapple ring along with a spoonful of the BBQ sauce and your choice of burger fixings, and serve immediately.

Nutrition Info per Serving:
Calories: 371, Protein: 15 g, Fat: 3 g, Carbohydrates: 71 g, Fiber: 10 g, Sugar: 4.7 g, Sodium: 393 mg

Blackbean Spinach and Rice Salad

Prep Time: 10 minutes, Cook Time: 3 minutes, Serves: 2

INGREDIENTS:
- ½ tbsp. BBQ Sauce
- ½ tbsp. balsamic vinegar
- ¼ tsp. red pepper flakes
- ½ tsp. smoked paprika
- ½ cup black beans, cooked
- 8 ounces (227 g) fresh spinach
- ½ cup corn
- ½ cup brown rice, cooked
- ½ tbsp. whole flaxseed or sesame seeds

DIRECTIONS:
1. Add the BBQ sauce, vinegar, red pepper flakes and paprika in a large bowl, whisk them together.
2. Add the black beans, spinach, corn and rice. Toss well to coat.
3. Place the flaxseed on the top and serve.

Nutrition Info per Serving:
Calories: 216, Protein: 11 g, Fat: 4 g, Carbohydrates: 34 g, Fiber: 10 g, Sugar: 2.5 g, Sodium: 523 mg

Spiralized Mixed Vegetables Lo Mein

Prep Time: 20 minutes, Cook Time: 10 minutes, Serves: 4

INGREDIENTS:
- 1 tsp. sesame oil (optional)
- 2 tbsps. low-sodium soy sauce
- 2 tsps. pure maple syrup
- 1 tbsp. grated peeled fresh ginger
- ¼ tsp. red pepper flakes
- 1 tbsp. tapioca starch
- 2 tbsps. cold water
- ½ cup snow peas, halved
- 1 large carrot, spiralized and cut into 3-inch-long strips
- ½ red bell pepper, cut into thin strips
- 1 tbsp. water
- 3 cups fresh baby spinach, coarsely chopped
- 4 zucchinis, spiralized and cut into 3-inch-long strips
- 1 cup shelled edamame
- Toasted sesame seeds, for topping

DIRECTIONS:
1. Add the sesame oil, soy sauce, maple syrup, ginger, red pepper flakes, tapioca starch, and cold water into a small bowl, whisk to combine. Set aside.
2. Combine the snow peas, garlic, carrot, bell pepper, and water in a large sauté pan or skillet, cook over medium heat for 3 minutes, gently stirring.
3. Add the spinach, zucchinis, and edamame. Cook for 3 minutes to wilt the spinach and lightly cook the zucchinis.
4. Pour the sauce into the pan carefully and toss the vegetables to coat. Cook for 1 to 2 minutes while the sauce warms and thickens. Top with toasted sesame seeds, sprinke with a drizzle of sriracha and cilantro, if desired, and serve immediately.

Nutrition Info per Serving:
Calories: 160, Protein: 10 g, Fat: 4 g, Carbohydrates: 21 g, Fiber: 10 g, Sugar: 1.7 g, Sodium: 516 mg

Soba Noodles with Vegetable and Peanut Sauce

Prep Time: 15 minutes, Cook Time: 10 minutes, Serves: 4

INGREDIENTS:
FOR THE PEANUT SAUCE:
- ¼ cup tamari
- ¼ cup smooth peanut butter
- ¼ cup warm water
- 1 tbsp. lime zest
- 2 tbsps. pure maple syrup
- Juice of 1 lime
- 2 garlic cloves, minced
- 2 tbsps. red pepper sauce, like sriracha
- 1 tbsp. grated peeled fresh ginger

FOR THE NOODLE BOWLS:
- 1 carrot, shredded
- 1 cup shelled edamame, thawed if frozen
- 1 red bell pepper, cut into strips
- 1 shallot, thinly sliced
- 1 small red cabbage head, chopped
- 1 bunch spring onions, chopped, divided
- ½ cup unsalted peanuts
- 1 (9.5-ounce, 269 g) package soba noodles
- 1 tbsp. sesame seeds, toasted
- Chopped fresh cilantro, for serving

DIRECTIONS:
TO MAKE THE PEANUT SAUCE:
1. Combine all of the peanut sauce ingredients in a small bowl, whisk them together until smooth. The sauce can also be pureed in a blender for even easier preparation. Set aside.
TO MAKE THE NOODLE BOWLS:
2. Add the carrot, edamame, bell pepper, shallot, red cabbage, three-quarters of the spring onions, and peanuts in a large bowl, toss them together.
3. According to the package directions to cook the soba noodles. Drain and rinse the noodles. Add the noodles to the mixed vegetables and pour over with three-quarters of the peanut sauce. Mix to combine with tongs or pasta spoons. Drizzle over with the remaining sauce, a pinch of cilantro, a sprinkle of toasted sesame seeds, and the remaining spring onions, and serve.

Nutrition Info per Serving:
Calories: 624, Protein: 31 g, Fat: 22 g, Carbohydrates: 84 g, Fiber: 9 g, Sugar: 7.3 g, Sodium: 732 mg

Carrot Kale and Lentil Stew

Prep Time: 10 minutes, Cook Time: 50 minutes, Serves: 8

INGREDIENTS:

5 cups (2 pounds, 907 g) water
brown or green dry lentils
2 large carrots, diced
4 cups kale, stemmed and chopped into 2-inch pieces
8 cups vegetable broth or
1 tbsp. smoked paprika
2 tsps. garlic powder
2 tsps. onion powder
1 tsp. dried thyme
1 tsp. red pepper flakes
1 tsp. dried oregano

DIRECTIONS:
1. Combine all of the ingredients in a large stockpot, bring to a boil over medium-high heat.
2. Reduce the heat to medium-low, cover and simmer for 45 minutes, stirring every 5 to 10 minutes.
3. After cooking, serve warm.

Nutrition Info per Serving:
Calories: 467, Protein: 32 g, Fat: 3 g, Carbohydrates: 78 g, Fiber: 31 g, Sugar: 1.6 g, Sodium: 571 mg

Chickpea Hummus Lettuce Gyros

Prep Time: 15 minutes, Cook Time: 20 minutes, Serves: 4

INGREDIENTS:

1 tsp. freshly ground black pepper
1 tbsp. paprika
½ tsp. garlic powder
1 tsp. dried oregano
¼ tsp. cayenne pepper
¼ tsp. onion powder
1 (15-ounce, 425 g) can chickpeas, drained and rinsed
1 cup hummus
4 whole wheat pitas
¼ cup finely chopped cucumber
¼ cup chopped tomato
¼ cup red onion strips
2 romaine lettuce leaves, finely chopped

DIRECTIONS:
1. Preheat the oven to 400°F(205°C). Use parchment paper to line a baking sheet.
2. Add the black pepper, paprika, garlic powder, oregano, cayenne pepper, and onion powder in a medium bowl, stir them together. Add the chickpeas and toss to coat. Spread the chickpeas mixture into a single layer on the prepared baking sheet.
3. Bake for 10 minutes. Stir and flip the chickpeas and bake for another 10 minutes, until slightly crispy, as they will become crispier as they cool. Take out from the oven and allow to cool on the baking sheet.
4. On each pita, spread with ¼ cup of hummus. Top each with 1 tbsp. each of the cucumber, one-quarter of the roasted chickpeas, tomato and red onion, and one-quarter of the lettuce. Fold and enjoy.

Nutrition Info per Serving:
Calories: 400, Protein: 15 g, Fat: 11 g, Carbohydrates: 61 g, Fiber: 13 g, Sugar: 6.1 g, Sodium: 536 mg

Vegetables with Spicy Poppy Seed and Almond Butter Sauce

Prep Time: 15 minutes, Cook Time: 30 minutes, Serves: 4 to 6

INGREDIENTS:

1 cup celery, cut into ¼-inch pieces
2 carrots, peeled and sliced
1 medium potato, chopped (about 1 cup)
1 cup asparagus
1 cup (240mL) avocado puree
1 small yellow onion, peeled and finely chopped
½ tsp. nutmeg
3 tbsps. white poppy seeds
3 clove garlic, smashed and skin removed
½ tsp. grated ginger
⅛ tsp. ground cloves
⅛ tsp. ground fennel
Dash ground cardamom
¼ tsp. freshly ground black pepper
½ tsp. turmeric
1 tsp. salt
2 tbsps. raw cashews, finely ground
½ tbsp. almond milk
1 tbsp. fresh basil, chopped

DIRECTIONS:
1. In a double boiler or steamer basket, steam the celery, carrot, potato, and asparagus for 8 to 10 minutes, or until soft. Set aside.
2. Add the poppy seeds in a dry skillet over medium-low heat toast for 2 to 3 minutes until the poppy seeds begin to brown. Off heat and remove the skillet and allow to cool. Then mix together the toasted seeds, nutmeg, onion, garlic, ginger, cloves, fennel, cardamom, pepper, and turmeric in a food processor and process into a thick paste. a large skillet over medium heat, pour the paste and cook for 5 to 7 minutes.
3. Add the tomato to the blender and puree until smooth. Add the avocado puree and salt to the onion paste in the skillet and cook for another 2 to 3 minutes. Whisk in the cashew powder and cook for 2 minutes. Stir in the steamed vegetables, almond butter, and 1½ cups of water, and bring the mixture to a boil. Off heat and remove the pan, and serve garnished with the basil.

Nutrition Info per Serving:
Calories: 95, Protein: 3.2 g, Fat: 2.3 g, Carbohydrates: 17 g, Fiber: 3.8 g, Sugar: 2.3 g, Sodium: 401 mg

Vegetable Enchiladas with Anasazi Bean Sauce

Prep Time: 20 minutes, Cook Time: 2 hours, Serves: 4

INGREDIENTS:
FOR THE BEAN SAUCE:
1 cup anasazi beans, soaked
1 small onion, peeled and diced
1 jalapeño pepper, seeded and minced
2 cloves garlic, peeled and minced
1 tsp. cumin seeds, toasted and ground
1 tsp. ancho chile powder
Salt
¾ cup to 1 cup (180 - 240 ml) low-sodium vegetable broth, as needed
FOR THE VEGETABLE FILLING:
1 medium zucchini, diced small
1 medium yellow onion, peeled and diced small
1 red bell pepper, seeded and diced small
2 ears corn, kernels removed (about 1 cup)
1 jalapeño pepper, seeded and minced
4 cloves garlic, peeled and minced
1 tsp. oregano
2 tsps. ancho chile powder
1 tsp. cumin seeds, toasted and ground
8 to 10 corn tortillas
Chopped cilantro
Salt

DIRECTIONS:
TO MAKE THE BEAN SAUCE:
1. Put beans in a large pot with enough water to cover and boil over high heat. Lower the heat to medium and simmer the beans for about 2 hours until tender, adding water as necessary to keep immersed. Drain and set aside.
2. Put onion in a large saucepan and sauté until tender, 7 to 8 minutes over medium heat. Add water 1 tbsp. at a time to keep the onions from sticking to the pan. Combine the beans, chile powder, jalapeño pepper, garlic, cumin, and salt and cook for 5 more minutes. Remove from the heat.
3. Puree the beans until smooth with an immersion blender, adding as much of the vegetable stock as needed to achieve a creamy consistency.
TO MAKE THE VEGETABLE FILLING:
4. Put onion and red pepper in a large saucepan and sauté over medium heat for 8 to 10 minutes until tender. Add water 1 tbsp. at a time to keep the vegetables from sticking to the pan. Add the zucchini, garlic, corn, jalapeño pepper, oregano, cumin, and chile powder, and cook for 5 minutes until the zucchini is tender. Season with salt.
TO ASSEMBLE THE ENCHILADAS:
5. Preheat the oven to 350°F (180ºC).
6. Wrap the tortillas in aluminum foil and heat in the oven for 15 minutes.
7. Place a tortilla on a flat surface and spoon ¼ cup vegetable filling in the middle of the tortilla. Wrap the tortilla around the filling and put it, seam side down, in a baking dish. Repeat with the remaining tortillas. Pour the bean sauce over the enchiladas and bake for 20 minutes. Serve garnished with the cilantro.

Nutrition Info per Serving:
Calories: 215, Protein: 6.5 g, Fat: 2.6 g, Carbohydrates: 40.7 g, Fiber: 6.3 g, Sugar: 7.9 g, Sodium: 842 mg

Chickpea and Kidney Bean Stew

Prep Time: 20 minutes, Cook Time: 30 minutes, Serves: 4

INGREDIENTS:
1 tsp. smoked paprika
1 tbsp. Hungarian paprika
1 tsp. ground cumin
1 tsp. onion powder
4 garlic cloves, diced
1 large yellow onion, coarsely chopped
1 tbsp. water, plus more as needed
2 carrots, diced
1 tbsp. pure maple syrup
1 (28-ounce, 784 g) can crushed tomatoes
1 (15-ounce, 425 g) dark red kidney beans, drained and rinsed
1 (15-ounce, 425 g) can chickpeas, drained and rinsed
½ cup packed chopped fresh cilantro
Juice of ½ lime

DIRECTIONS:
1. Add the smoked paprika, cumin, Hungarian paprika and onion powder into a small bowl, stir them together. Set aside.
2. Combine the garlic, onion, and 1 tbsp. of water in an 8-quart pot, cook over high heat. Then reduce the heat to medium-low. Cook for at least 10 minutes, stirring occasionally. To prevent burning, add more water, 1 tbsp. at a time, until the onion is deeply browned.
3. Add the carrots, stir well and turn the heat to high.
4. Stir in the paprika mixture and cook for 30 seconds, stirring continuously to prevent burning. Pour in the maple syrup and cook for another 30 seconds, stirring.
5. Pour in the tomatoes with their juices carefully. In order to avoid splatter, pour the tomatoes onto a spoon and not directly into the hot pot. Bring to a simmer, stirring, then reduce the heat to low, cover and cook for 10 minutes.
6. Stir in the chickpeas, kidney beans and cilantro. Cover and cook for an additional 5 minutes to warm.
7. Sprinkle with the lime juice before serving.
8. Enjoy this stew as is or top with your favorite toppings.

Nutrition Info per Serving:
Calories: 355, Protein: 17 g, Fat: 3 g, Carbohydrates: 65 g, Fiber: 15 g, Sugar: 4.7 g, Sodium: 711 mg

Mashed Chickpea and Avocado Sandwich

Prep Time: 10 minutes, Cook Time: 0, Serves: 4

INGREDIENTS:
1 large ripe avocado, halved and pitted
1 (15-ounce, 425 g) can chickpeas, drained and rinsed
1 tsp. dried dill
1 tsp. Dijon mustard
¼ cup diced sweet pickle, or relish (optional)
1 celery stalk, diced
¼ cup diced red onion
½ tsp. garlic powder
Whole-grain bread, pita, or romaine lettuce leaves, for serving

DIRECTIONS:
1. Scoop the avocado flesh into a medium bowl. Mash the avocado with a potato or a heavy spoon until smooth.
2. Add the chickpeas and lightly mash them so some larger pieces of chickpea remain for texture.
3. Add the dill, mustard, pickle (if using), celery, red onion, and garlic powder, use a spoon or spatula to mix well. Serve immediately on lettuce leaves or bread, or place in the refrigerator to chill overnight for an even more blended flavor.

Nutrition Info per Serving:
Calories: 182, Protein: 6 g, Fat: 9 g, Carbohydrates: 21 g, Fiber: 8 g, Sugar: 3.4 g, Sodium: 367 mg

Peanut Butter Chickpea Burgers

Prep Time: 15 minutes, Cook Time: 10 minutes, Serves: 4

INGREDIENTS:
2 tbsps. ground flaxseed
¼ cup water
1 garlic clove, peeled and stemmed
½ cup whole wheat bread crumbs or gluten-free bread crumbs
1 cup raw walnuts
1 tsp. chili powder
½ tsp. garlic powder
1 tsp. smoked paprika
¼ tsp. onion powder
¾ cup canned chickpeas, drained and rinsed
3 tbsps. peanut butter
1 tbsp. apple cider vinegar

DIRECTIONS:
1. Whisk together the flaxseed and water in a small bowl. Set aside.
2. Combine the garlic, bread crumbs, walnuts, chili powder, garlic powder, paprika, and onion powder in a food processor. Process for about 2 minutes until crumbly. Add the chickpeas, soaked flaxseed, peanut butter, and vinegar. Process for 1 to 2 minutes, or until fully combined.
3. Place the mixture to a large bowl and knead for 1 to 2 minutes, or until the mixture comes together and can be shaped. Equally divide the dough into 4 parts and form into ½-inch-thick patties.
4. Cooke the patties in a nonstick skillet over medium heat for 3 to 5 minutes per side until browned and crispy. Serve immediately.

Nutrition Info per Serving:
Calories: 357, Protein: 11 g, Fat: 25 g, Carbohydrates: 22 g, Fiber: 7 g, Sugar: 3.8 g, Sodium: 285 mg

Grilled Cauliflower with Spicy Lentil Sauce

Prep Time: 15 minutes, Cook Time: 1.5 hours, Serves: 4

INGREDIENTS:
2 medium heads cauliflower
2 medium shallots, peeled and minced
½ cup green lentils, rinsed
2 cups (480 ml) low-sodium vegetable broth
Chopped parsley
1 clove garlic, peeled and minced
½ tsp. minced sage
½ tsp. ground fennel
½ tsp. crushed red pepper flakes
Salt and freshly ground black pepper

DIRECTIONS:
1. Cut each of the cauliflower heads in half through the stem of the vegetable, and then trim each half so that you have a 1-inch-thick cutlet. Place each piece on a baking sheet. Save the extra cauliflower florets for other uses.
2. Place the shallots in a medium saucepan and sauté over medium heat for 10 minutes. Add water 1 tbsp. at a time to keep the shallots from sticking to the pan. Add the garlic, fennel, sage, crushed red pepper flakes, and lentils and cook for 3 minutes. Add the vegetable stock and boil the mixture over high heat. Reduce the heat to medium and cook, covered, for 45 to 50 minutes. Add water as needed to keep the mixture from drying out.
3. Puree the lentil mixture using an immersion blender. Return the puree to the pan if necessary and season with salt and pepper. Keep warm.
4. Prepare the grill.
5. Place the cauliflower on the grill and cook each side for about 7 minutes.
6. Place the grilled cauliflower on a plate and spoon the sauce over them. Garnish with chopped parsley and serve.

Nutrition Info per Serving:
Calories: 94, Protein: 5.3 g, Fat: 1 g, Carbohydrates: 16 g, Fiber: 4.3 g, Sugar: 6.6 g, Sodium: 120 mg

Buckwheat with Bow-Tie Pasta

Prep Time: 15 minutes, Cook Time: 35 minutes, Serves: 4

INGREDIENTS:
- 8 ounces (227 g) button mushrooms, sliced
- ½ pound (227 g) whole-grain farfalle, cooked, drained, and kept warm
- 2 cups (480 ml) low-sodium vegetable broth
- 1 cup buckwheat groats
- 1 large yellow onion, peeled and diced small
- 2 tbsps. finely chopped dill
- Salt and freshly ground black pepper

DIRECTIONS:
1. Put vegetable stock in a medium saucepan and boil over high heat. Add the buckwheat groats and bring the pot back to a boil over high heat. Lower the heat to medium and cook about 12 to 15 minutes with lid uncovered, until the groats are tender.
2. Put onion in a large saucepan and sauté about 15 minutes over medium heat until well browned. Add water 1 tbsp. at a time to keep the onion from sticking. Add the mushrooms and cook for 5 more minutes. Remove from the heat. Add the buckwheat groats, cooked pasta, and dill. Season with salt and pepper and serve.

Nutrition Info per Serving:
Calories: 375, Protein: 12 g, Fat: 2.1 g, Carbohydrates: 76.9 g, Fiber: 12.4 g, Sugar: 7.3 g, Sodium: 83 mg

Potato, Lentil and Kale Soup

Prep Time: 15 minutes, Cook Time: 35 minutes, Serves: 4

INGREDIENTS:
- 2 garlic cloves, minced
- 4 large carrots, thinly sliced
- 2 small shallots, diced
- 4 celery stalks, thinly sliced
- 1 tbsp. water, plus more as needed
- 3 cups baby potatoes, halved and quartered
- 4 cups no-sodium vegetable broth
- ¼ tsp. freshly ground black pepper
- 1 tbsp. red miso paste
- 3 thyme sprigs
- 1 cup dried brown lentils, rinsed
- 2 cups coarsely chopped kale

DIRECTIONS:
1. Combine the garlic, carrots, shallots, and celery in a large pot, cook over medium-high heat for 1 to 2 minutes, adding water, 1 tbsp. at a time, to prevent burning, until the celery and shallots start to become translucent.
2. Stir in the potatoes and cook for 3 to 4 minutes.
3. Pour in the vegetable broth. Add the pepper, miso paste, thyme, and lentils. Bring the soup to a simmer, cover and cook for 15 to 20 minutes, or until the potatoes and lentils are tender.
4. Add the kale and cook until wilted, about 3 to 4 minutes.
5. Serve immediately. Store the leftovers in an airtight container and refrigerate for up to 1 week or freeze for 4 to 6 months. The liquid will be absorbed, add more water or enjoy the thick one.

Nutrition Info per Serving:
Calories: 292, Protein: 15 g, Fat: 2 g, Carbohydrates: 58 g, Fiber: 12 g, Sugar: 4.3 g, Sodium: 472 mg

Roasted Golden Beet and Tofu Curry

Prep Time: 15 minutes, Cook Time: 1 hour, Serves: 4

INGREDIENTS:
- 1 large golden beet, peeled and chopped into 1-inch pieces (about 4 cups)
- 3 garlic cloves, peeled and stemmed
- 1 onion, coarsely chopped
- 1 (12-ounce, 340 g) package silken tofu
- 4 cups no-sodium vegetable broth
- 1 tbsp. grated peeled fresh ginger, or 1 tsp. ground ginger
- 2 tsps. yellow curry powder
- 1 tbsp. coconut aminos or tamari
- ½ tsp. ground turmeric
- ¼ tsp. cayenne pepper
- 1 (14-ounce, 397 g) can full-fat coconut milk

DIRECTIONS:
1. Preheat the oven to 400°F(205°C). Use parchment paper to line a baking sheet.
2. Spread the beet pieces in an even layer on the prepared baking sheet, top with the garlic cloves and onion pieces.
3. Bake for 45 minutes, until lightly browned and fork-tender. Transfer to a large pot and heat it over medium heat.
4. Add the remaining ingredients except the coconut milk into the pot. Bring to a simmer. Cover and cook for 15 minutes.
5. Pour in the coconut milk. Puree with an immersion blender until smooth. Or transfer the soup to a blender, working in batches as needed, and blend until smooth.
6. Serve with the rice or a grain and add a variety of cooked root vegetables and greens, as desired.

Nutrition Info per Serving:
Calories: 280, Protein: 7 g, Fat: 20 g, Carbohydrates: 18 g, Fiber: 3 g, Sugar: 10.6 g, Sodium: 694 mg

Chickpea Bulgur Pilaf

Prep Time: 15 minutes, Cook Time: 30 minutes, Serves: 4

INGREDIENTS:

2 cups cooked chickpeas, or one (15-ounce, 425 g) can, drained and rinsed
1½ cups bulgur
3 cups (720 ml) low-sodium vegetable broth
1 Roma tomato, chopped
Zest and juice of 1 lemon
1 medium yellow onion, peeled and diced small
3 cloves garlic, peeled and minced
1½ tbsp. grated ginger
4 green onions (white and green parts), thinly sliced
Salt and freshly ground black pepper

DIRECTIONS:

1. Put onion in a large saucepan and sauté for 10 minutes over medium heat. Add water 1 tbsp. at a time to keep the onion from sticking to the pan. Stir in the ginger and garlic, cook for 30 seconds. Put in the bulgur and vegetable stock and boil over high heat. Lower the heat to medium and cook about 15 minutes with lid covered, until the bulgur is tender.
2. Stir in the tomato, chickpeas, and lemon zest and juice and cook for another 5 minutes. Season with salt and pepper, serve garnished with the green onions.

Nutrition Info per Serving:
Calories: 141, Protein: 5.9 g, Fat: 1.3 g, Carbohydrates: 29.9 g, Fiber: 6.2 g, Sugar: 8.4 g, Sodium: 113 mg

Cabbage Pilaf

Prep Time: 10 minutes, Cook Time: 50 minutes, Serves: 4

INGREDIENTS:

2¼ cups (540 ml) low-sodium vegetable broth
¾ cup millet
1 medium carrot, peeled and diced
1 medium leek (white and light green parts), diced and rinsed
1 celery stalk, diced
2 cloves garlic, peeled and minced
3 cups chopped cabbage
1 tsp. minced thyme
1 tbsp. minced dill
Salt and freshly ground black pepper

DIRECTIONS:

1. In a medium saucepan, boil the vegetable stock over high heat. Add the millet and bring the pot back to a boil over high heat. Lower the heat to medium and cook with lid covered, for 20 minutes, until the millet is tender and all the vegetable stock is absorbed.
2. Put the carrot, leek, and celery in a large saucepan and sauté for 7 to 8 minutes over medium heat. Add water 1 tbsp. at a time to keep the vegetables from sticking to the pan. Add the garlic, dill, thyme, and cabbage and cook over medium heat for about 10 minutes, stirring frequently, until the cabbage is tender. Add the cooked millet and cook for 5 more minutes, stirring frequently. Season with salt and pepper.

Nutrition Info per Serving:
Calories: 219, Protein: 7.3 g, Fat: 2.5 g, Carbohydrates: 44.3 g, Fiber: 6.8 g, Sugar: 8.2 g, Sodium: 118 mg

Stuffed Portobello Mushrooms

Prep Time: 15 minutes, Cook Time: 1 hour, Serves: 4

INGREDIENTS:

4 large portobello mushrooms, stemmed
3 cloves garlic, peeled and minced
2 tbsps. low-sodium soy sauce
Freshly ground black pepper
FOR THE FILLING:
1 small yellow onion, peeled and diced small
1 medium red bell pepper, seeded and diced small
3 cloves garlic, peeled and minced
2 sage leaves, minced
1 fennel bulb, trimmed and diced
2 cups (480 ml) low-sodium vegetable stock
⅔ cup millet
Salt

DIRECTIONS:

1. Place the mushrooms, stem side up, in a baking dish.
2. Mix the garlic, soy sauce, and black pepper in a small bowl to make the marinade. Brush some of the marinade over each mushroom. Set aside while you prepare the filling.
TO MAKE THE FILLING:
3. Boil the vegetable stock in a medium saucepan. Add the millet and bring the pot back to a boil. Lower the heat to medium and cook, covered, for 15 minutes.
4. Preheat the oven to 350°F (180ºC).
5. Put the red pepper, onion, and fennel in a large saucepan and sauté over medium heat for 10 minutes. Add water 1 tbsp. at a time to keep the vegetables from sticking to the pan. Add the garlic and sage leaves and cook for 2 minutes. Put in the millet, mix well, and season with salt and pepper. Remove from the heat.
6. Divide the millet mixture among the 4 mushrooms. Place on a baking dish, cover with aluminum foil, and bake for 25 minutes. Remove the foil and bake for another 10 minutes.

Nutrition Info per Serving:
Calories: 210, Protein: 7.7 g, Fat: 2.2 g, Carbohydrates: 39.5 g, Fiber: 6.6 g, Sugar: 7.9 g, Sodium: 752 mg

Burrito Bowl with Tortilla Chips, page 37

Carrot Kale and Lentil Stew, page 28

Chickpea Bulgur Pilaf, page 32

Broccoli Baked Potatoes, page 39

Chapter 3 Lunch   33

Grilled and Marinated Mushrooms

Prep Time: 15 minutes, Cook Time: 1.5 hours, Serves: 4

INGREDIENTS:

4 large portobello mushrooms, stemmed
1 tbsp. grated ginger
3 tbsps. low-sodium soy sauce
3 tbsps. brown rice syrup
3 cloves garlic, peeled and minced
Freshly ground black pepper

DIRECTIONS:

1. Mix the ginger, soy sauce, garlic, brown rice syrup, and pepper in a small bowl and mix well.
2. Put mushrooms stem side up on a baking dish. Pour the marinade over the mushrooms and let marinate for 1 hour.
3. Prepare the grill.
4. Pour the excess marinade off the mushrooms, reserving the liquid, and put the mushrooms on the grill. Grill each side for 4 minutes, brushing with the marinade.

Nutrition Info per Serving:
Calories: 56, Protein: 1.3 g, Fat: 0.2 g, Carbohydrates: 14 g, Fiber: 0.5 g, Sugar: 12.2 g, Sodium: 168 mg

Baked Potato Casserole

Prep Time: 15 minutes, Cook Time: 1 hour, Serves: 6, or 8 as a side

INGREDIENTS:

2 large yellow onions, peeled and thinly sliced into rings
6 medium waxy potatoes (about 2 pounds, 907 g), peeled and sliced into thin rounds
2 batches No-Cheese Sauce
Spanish paprika to taste
4 tbsps. chives
Salt and freshly ground black pepper

DIRECTIONS:

1. Put the onions in a large skillet and sauté for 10 minutes over medium-high heat, stirring frequently, until browned. Add water 1 tbsp. at a time to keep the onions from sticking to the pan.
2. Boil a large pot of salted water. Put in potatoes and parboil for 3 minutes. Drain and set aside.
3. Preheat the oven to 350°F (180ºC).
4. Layer half of the parboiled potatoes in the bottom of a baking dish. Season with salt and pepper. Spread half of the No-Cheese Sauce over the potatoes, then sprinkle half of the onions over the sauce. Repeat with the remaining potatoes. Sprinkle with paprika and bake for 35 to 45 minutes, or until the casserole is bubbly. Remove the casserole from the oven and set aside for 10 minutes. Garnish with the chives and serve.

Nutrition Info per Serving:
Calories: 129, Protein: 3.5 g, Fat: 0.2 g, Carbohydrates: 29.3 g, Fiber: 3.9 g, Sugar: 1.8 g, Sodium: 20 mg

Healthy Twice-Baked Potatoes

Prep Time: 15 minutes, Cook Time: 2 hours, Serves: 6

INGREDIENTS:

6 large russet potatoes, scrubbed
1 medium yellow onion, peeled and diced small
1 red bell pepper, seeded and diced small
One (12-ounce, 340 g) package extra firm silken tofu, drained
½ cup chopped green onion (white and green parts)
1 jalapeño pepper, seeded and minced
2 cloves garlic, peeled and minced
1 tbsp. cumin seeds, toasted and ground
2 tsps. ancho chile powder
3 ears corn, kernels removed (about 2 cups)
½ cup chopped cilantro
¼ cup nutritional yeast, optional
2 cups cooked black beans, drained and rinsed
1 tsp. salt

DIRECTIONS:

1. Preheat the oven to 350°F (180ºC).
2. Pierce each potato with a fork so that it will release steam during baking. Put the potatoes on a baking sheet and bake for 60 to 75 minutes. Cool down until safe to handle.
3. Put the onion and red pepper in a large skillet and sauté for 7 to 8 minutes over medium heat. Add water 1 tbsp. at a time to keep the vegetables from sticking to the pan. Add the jalapeño pepper, cumin, garlic, and chile powder and sauté for another minute. Add the corn, salt, black beans, cilantro, and nutritional yeast and mix well. Remove from the heat.
4. Puree the silken tofu in blender. Add the pureed tofu to the vegetable mixture in the pan and combine well.
5. Halve each potato lengthwise, and scoop out the flesh, leaving a ¼-inch-thick shell. Reserve the flesh. Divide the vegetable filling evenly among the potato halves. Place the filled potatoes on a baking sheet and bake for 30 minutes. Garnished with the chopped green onion and serve.

Nutrition Info per Serving:
Calories: 451, Protein: 19.2 g, Fat: 4.6 g, Carbohydrates: 83.1 g, Fiber: 8.1 g, Sugar: 6.7 g, Sodium: 777 mg

Rice and Bean Tostadas

Prep Time: 10 minutes, Cook Time: 10 minutes, Serves: 2

INGREDIENTS:
4 corn tortillas
1 cup fat-free refried beans
1 cup cooked black beans
1 cup cooked brown rice
1 lime, quartered

DIRECTIONS:
1. Preheat the oven to 400°F(205°C). Use parchment paper to line a baking sheet.
2. Put the tortillas on the baking sheet, and bake for 5 to 8 minutes, or until the tortillas turn crisp and golden brown. Watchout not to burn them.
3. Spread ¼ cup of refried beans evenly onto each crispy tortilla, then add the black beans and ¼ cup each of rice.
4. Squeeze over each tostada with the lime juice before serving.

Nutrition Info per Serving:
Calories: 436, Protein: 19 g, Fat: 4 g, Carbohydrates: 81 g, Fiber: 19 g, Sugar: 1.1 g, Sodium: 786 mg

Asian Style Stuffed Mushrooms

Prep Time: 15 minutes, Cook Time: 35 minutes, Serves: 4

INGREDIENTS:
4 large portobello mushrooms
1 head baby bok choy, finely chopped
2 cups cooked brown rice
½ medium yellow onion, peeled and diced small
½ red bell pepper, seeded and diced small
½ cup Spicy Cilantro Pesto
Salt and freshly ground black pepper

DIRECTIONS:
1. Preheat the oven to 350°F (180ºC).
2. Separate the mushroom stems from the caps. Finely chop the stems and set them aside. Put the caps, top side down, in a baking dish and set aside.
3. Heat a large skillet over medium-high heat. Add the onion, chopped mushroom stems, and red pepper and stir-fry for 5 minutes. Add water 1 tbsp. at a time to keep the vegetables from sticking to the pan. Put in the bok choy and cook for 4 minutes. Add the brown rice and cilantro pesto, season with salt and pepper, and mix well. Remove from the heat.
4. Portion the rice mixture among the mushroom caps. Arrange in a baking dish and bake for 15 minutes, cover the dish with aluminum foil. Uncover and bake for another 10 minutes.

Nutrition Info per Serving:
Calories: 177, Protein: 5.6 g, Fat: 1.2 g, Carbohydrates: 35.6 g, Fiber: 5.5 g, Sugar: 7.1 g, Sodium: 153 mg

Stuffed Yellow Bell Peppers

Prep Time: 15 minutes, Cook Time: 1 hour, Serves: 6

INGREDIENTS:
FOR THE BELL PEPPERS:
2 medium potatoes, halved
1 ear corn, kernels removed (about ½ cup)
2 yellow bell peppers
1 small green bell pepper, seeded and finely chopped (about ¼ cup)
¼ tsp. grated ginger
½ small onion, peeled and finely chopped
½ clove garlic, peeled and minced
½ tsp. minced serrano chile
½ tsp. salt
1 tsp. fresh lime juice
¼ cup sunflower seeds, toasted

FOR THE HOT SAUCE:
1 large tomato, chopped
½ tbsp. finely chopped cilantro
½ tsp. cayenne pepper
½ tsp. salt
½ clove garlic, peeled and mashed to a paste

DIRECTIONS:
TO MAKE THE BELL PEPPERS:
1. Preheat the oven to 350°F (180ºC).
2. Boil the potatoes over medium heat in a saucepan of water for 15 minutes. Remove from the heat, drain, and cool down. Mash the potatoes in a mixing bowl.
3. Put the corn and 1 cup of water in a small pan. Cook on medium heat for 5 to 7 minutes until the corn is tender. Drain and add to the potatoes along with the onion, ginger, green pepper, garlic, salt, serrano chile, and lime juice. Mix well.
4. Cut the yellow peppers into 3 long slices, making boat shapes, and remove the seeds. Divide the potato mixture among the slices and sprinkle with sunflower seeds. Bake, covered, until the yellow peppers are soft when poked with a fork, for 30 to 35 minutes.
TO MAKE THE HOT SAUCE:
5. Puree the tomato in a blender. Add the puree to a saucepan with the salt, cayenne pepper, and garlic, bring to a boil, and cook for 5 minutes. Reduce the heat to low and simmer for another 5 minutes.
6. Spread the hot sauce on top of the baked bell peppers. Garnish with cilantro and serve.

Nutrition Info per Serving:
Calories: 140, Protein: 4.3 g, Fat: 3.6 g, Carbohydrates: 22.6 g, Fiber: 3.5 g, Sugar: 2.9 g, Sodium: 398 mg

Indian Spiced Asparagus

Prep Time: 15 minutes, Cook Time: 25 minutes, Serves: 4

INGREDIENTS:

2 medium onions, peeled and diced
1 large red bell pepper, seeded and diced
2 medium asparagus, stemmed, peeled, and cut into ½-inch dice
2 large tomatoes, finely chopped
3 tbsps. grated ginger
2 tsps. thyme
1 tsp. nutmeg
½ tsp. crushed red pepper flakes
Dash cloves
Salt to taste
½ bunch dill, chopped

DIRECTIONS:

1. In a large saucepan, add the onions and red pepper and sauté over medium heat for 10 minutes.
2. Pour in water 1 to 2 tbsps. at a time to keep the vegetables from sticking to the pan.
3. Stir in the asparagus, tomatoes, ginger, thyme, nutmeg, crushed red pepper flakes, and cloves and cook until the eggplant is soft, about 15 minutes. Sprinkle with salt and serve garnished with the dill.

Nutrition Info per Serving:
Calories: 147, Protein: 5.3 g, Fat: 1.1 g, Carbohydrates: 29 g, Fiber: 11.9 g, Sugar: 15.7 g, Sodium: 822 mg

Fried Vegetables with Miso and Sake

Prep Time: 15 minutes, Cook Time: 10 minutes, Serves: 4

INGREDIENTS:

¼ cup (60 ml) mellow white miso
½ cup (120 ml) Vegetable Stock, or low-sodium vegetable broth
¼ cup (60 ml) sake
½ pound snow peas, trimmed
2 cloves garlic, peeled and minced
1 medium yellow onion, peeled and thinly sliced
1 medium red bell pepper, seeded and cut into ½-inch strips
1 large head broccoli, cut into florets
1 large carrot, peeled, cut in half lengthwise, and then cut into half-moons on the diagonal
½ cup chopped cilantro, optional
Salt and freshly ground black pepper

DIRECTIONS:

1. Whisk together the vegetable stock, miso, and sake in a small bowl and set aside.
2. Heat a large skillet over high heat. Add the onion, red pepper, carrot, and broccoli and stir-fry for 4 to 5 minutes. Add water 1 tbsp. at a time to keep the vegetables from sticking to the pan. Put in the snow peas and stir-fry for 4 more minutes. Add the garlic and cook for 30 seconds. Add the miso mixture and cook until heated through.
3. Remove the pan from the heat and add the cilantro. Season with salt and pepper.

Nutrition Info per Serving:
Calories: 131, Protein: 6.76 g, Fat: 1.7 g, Carbohydrates: 20.4 g, Fiber: 5.9 g, Sugar: 7.7 g, Sodium: 701 mg

Veggie Quinoa Beans Soup

Prep Time: 20 minutes, Cook Time: 3 to 8 hours in a slow cooker, or 1 hour on the s, Serves: 6

INGREDIENTS:

1 cup dried quinoa
2 garlic cloves, minced
½ large yellow onion, diced
2 celery stalks, cut into slices
2 carrots, cut into coins
1 tbsp. water, plus more as needed
¼ cup tomato paste
1 (15-ounce, 425 g) can red kidney beans, drained and rinsed
1 (15-ounce, 425 g) black beans, drained and rinsed
1 (14-ounce, 397 g) can whole-kernel corn, drained
1 (14-ounce, 397 g) can diced tomatoes
1 zucchini, cut into coins and quartered
1 tsp. ground cumin
2 tsps. chili powder
6 cups no-sodium vegetable broth, plus more as needed

DIRECTIONS:

1. In a fine-mesh sieve, add the quinoa and rinse under cold water for 2 to 3 minutes, or until the cloudy water becomes clear.
2. Heat a 5-quart or larger slow cooker on High for 5 to 10 minutes.
3. Combine the garlic, onion, celery, carrots, and 1 tbsp. of water in the preheated slow cooker. Cook for 2 to 3 minutes. Stir in the tomato paste to combine.
4. Add all of the remaining ingredients to the cooker. Stir well. The tomato paste will fully incorporate as the soup cooks.
5. Switch the heat to low. Cover and cook on Low for 6 to 8 hours or cook on High for 3 to 4 hours. Add more broth or water, ½ cup at a time, if the soup seems too thick.
6. Place the leftovers in an airtight container and refrigerate for up to 1 week or freeze for 4 to 6 months.

Nutrition Info per Serving:
Calories: 334, Protein: 16 g, Fat: 4 g, Carbohydrates: 62 g, Fiber: 14 g, Sugar: 2.5 g, Sodium: 758 mg

Burrito Bowl with Tortilla Chips

Prep Time: 10 minutes, Cook Time: 10 minutes, Serves: 2

INGREDIENTS:

- 4 corn tortillas
- 1 cup corn (fresh or frozen)
- 1 cup cooked brown rice
- 1 cup cooked black beans
- 1 tsp. ground cumin
- 2 tsps. chili powder
- ½ tsp. onion powder
- ½ tsp. garlic powder
- 1 avocado, peeled, pitted, and sliced
- 2 cups shredded lettuce
- ¼ cup salsa

DIRECTIONS:

1. Preheat the oven to 350°F(180°C). Use parchment paper to line a baking sheet.
2. Evenly cut each tortilla into 6 chips, and put the chips on the baking sheet. Bake until golden brown, about 8 to 10 minutes. The chips will continue to crisp up as they cool.
3. Combine the corn, rice, black beans, cumin, chili powder, onion powder, and garlic powder in a large bowl. Warm this mixture in the microwave on high for 2 minutes or on the stovetop in a medium saucepan over medium heat for 5 minutes, if the rice and beans are cold.
4. Divide this warm corn-rice mixture into two serving bowls, then place half of the avocado slices, 1 cup of shredded lettuce and salsa on the top.
5. Serve this bowl with the crispy tortilla chips.

Nutrition Info per Serving:
Calories: 569, Protein: 18 g, Fat: 17 g, Carbohydrates: 86 g, Fiber: 21 g, Sugar: 1.8 g, Sodium: 636 mg

Cabbage and Chickpea Pilaf

Prep Time: 15 minutes, Cook Time: 1.5 hours, Serves: 4

INGREDIENTS:

- 1½ cups chopped green cabbage
- 1 cup cooked chickpeas
- ½ cup wild rice
- 1 medium onion, peeled and diced small
- 1 medium carrot, peeled and grated
- 1 small red bell pepper, seeded and diced small
- 1 bunch green onions (white and green parts), thinly sliced
- 3 tbsps. chopped cilantro
- 3 cloves garlic, peeled and minced
- 1 tbsp. grated ginger
- Salt and freshly ground black pepper

DIRECTIONS:

1. Boil 2 cups of water in a large saucepan. Put in wild rice and bring the water back to a boil over high heat. Reduce the heat to medium and cook with lid covered, for 55 to 60 minutes. Drain off any excess water and set aside.
2. Heat a large skillet over medium heat. Add the carrot, onion, and red pepper and sauté the vegetables for 10 minutes. Add water 1 tbsp. at a time to keep the vegetables from sticking to the pan. Put in garlic and ginger and cook for one more minute. Add the cabbage and cook for 10 to 12 minutes until the cabbage is tender. Add the green onions, chickpeas, and cilantro. Season with salt and pepper and cook for another minute. Remove from the heat, combine the cooked wild rice.

Nutrition Info per Serving:
Calories: 186, Protein: 8 g, Fat: 2.5 g, Carbohydrates: 34.9 g, Fiber: 2.5 g, Sugar: 6.3 g, Sodium: 178 mg

Rice Stuffed Eggplant

Prep Time: 15 minutes, Cook Time: 2 hours, Serves: 4

INGREDIENTS:

- 2 cups (480 ml) low-sodium vegetable broth
- 1 cup brown basmati rice
- 1 cinnamon stick
- ¼ cup finely chopped basil
- ¼ cup finely chopped cilantro
- 1 celery stalk, diced small
- 1 medium red bell pepper, seeded and diced small
- 2 cloves garlic, peeled and minced
- 2 medium eggplants, stemmed and halved lengthwise
- 1 medium yellow onion, peeled and diced small
- Salt and freshly ground black pepper

DIRECTIONS:

1. Bring the vegetable stock to a boil in a medium saucepan. Put in rice and cinnamon stick and bring the pot back to a boil. Cover and cook over medium heat for 45 minutes, until the stock is absorbed.
2. Scoop the flesh out of the eggplant halves, leaving a ¼-inch-thick shell. Coarsely chop the pulp and set it aside.
3. Preheat the oven to 350°F (180ºC).
4. Put the celery, onion, and red pepper in a large saucepan and sauté over medium heat for 7 to 8 minutes. Add water 1 tbsp. at a time to keep the vegetables from sticking to the pan. Put in the garlic and eggplant pulp and cook for 5 more minutes. Remove from the heat. Add the basil, cooked rice, and cilantro to the eggplant mixture. Season with salt and pepper.
5. Portion the rice mixture evenly among the eggplant shells and put the stuffed eggplants in a baking dish. Cover with aluminum foil and bake for 40 minutes.

Nutrition Info per Serving:
Calories: 283, Protein: 6.2 g, Fat: 2.4 g, Carbohydrates: 61 g, Fiber: 11.8 g, Sugar: 15.3 g, Sodium: 84 mg

Grilled Eggplant Slices

Prep Time: 10 minutes, Cook Time: 10 minutes, Serves: 4

INGREDIENTS:
1 large eggplant, stemmed and cut into ¾-inch slices
3 tbsps. balsamic vinegar
Juice of 1 lemon
2 tbsps. low-sodium soy sauce
Freshly ground black pepper

DIRECTIONS:
1. Prepare the grill.
2. Mix the balsamic vinegar, soy sauce, lemon juice, and pepper in a small bowl.
3. Brush the marinade on both sides of the eggplant slices.
4. Put the eggplant on the hot grill and cook on each side for 4 to 5 minutes, brushing with additional marinade.

Nutrition Info per Serving:
Calories: 50, Protein: 1.7 g, Fat: 0.3 g, Carbohydrates: 11.4 g, Fiber: 4.3 g, Sugar: 7 g, Sodium: 187 mg

Grilled Veggie Kabobs

Prep Time: 15 minutes, Cook Time: 30 minutes, Serves: 6

INGREDIENTS:
1 medium zucchini, cut into 1-inch rounds
1 medium yellow squash, cut into 1-inch rounds
1 medium red onion, peeled and cut into large chunks
½ cup (120 ml) balsamic vinegar
3 cloves garlic, peeled and minced
1½ tbsp. minced rosemary
1½ tbsp. minced thyme
1 green bell pepper, seeded and cut into 1-inch pieces
1 red bell pepper, seeded and cut into 1-inch pieces
1 pint cherry tomatoes
Salt and freshly ground black pepper

DIRECTIONS:
1. Prepare the grill.
2. Soak 12 bamboo skewers in water for 30 minutes.
3. Mix the balsamic vinegar, rosemary, garlic, thyme, and salt and pepper in a small bowl.
4. Skewer the vegetables. Place the skewers on the grill and cook, brushing the vegetables with the vinegar mixture and turning every 4 to 5 minutes, until the vegetables are tender and starting to char.

Nutrition Info per Serving:
Calories: 46, Protein: 1.3 g, Fat: 0.2 g, Carbohydrates: 9.7 g, Fiber: 1.3 g, Sugar: 5.9 g, Sodium: 524 mg

Vegetable and Wild Rice Stuffed Squash with Almonds

Prep Time: 20 minutes, Cook Time: 1 hour 30 minutes, Serves: 4

INGREDIENTS:
2 acorn squash, halved lengthwise
7½ cups water, divided
½ cup wild rice
1 cup no-sodium vegetable broth
½ yellow onion, finely chopped
1 carrot, finely chopped
½ cup broccoli florets, chopped small
1 cup cauliflower florets, chopped small
1 tsp. dried rosemary
1 tsp. garlic powder
½ tsp. ground sage
¼ tsp. freshly ground black pepper
¼ cup blanched slivered almonds, plus more for garnish
Chopped fresh parsley, for garnish

DIRECTIONS:
1. Cut off the stem from the acorn squash halves and remove the seeds with a spoon. Don't peel or remove the skin.
2. Fill 6 cups of water in a large pot, bring to a boil over high heat. Place the squash halves into the boiling water carefully and cook for about 15 minutes, or until the squash's pulp can be pierced with a fork. Remove the squash with tongs and set aside to cool while you prepare the rest of the ingredients.
3. Meanwhile, stir together the wild rice and the remaining 1½ cups of water in an 8-quart pot over high heat. Bring to a boil, lower the heat to medium-low, cover and cook for 20 minutes.
4. Cut halfway into the cooked squash and remove the pulp with a fork or spoon. This will be added to the filling mixture. Reserve the squash shells.
5. Preheat the oven to 350°F(180°C).
6. Heat the same pot you boiled the squash in over medium heat and bring the vegetable broth to a simmer. Add the onion, carrot, broccoli, cauliflower, rosemary, garlic powder, sage, and pepper. Reduce the heat to medium-low, cover and cook for 10 minutes. Stir in the squash pulp, cooked wild rice, and almonds. Fill the stuffing mix into the squash cavities and transfer the filled squash on a baking sheet.
7. Bake for 15 to 20 minutes, or until the squash can be easily pierced with a fork and the outer skin looks lightly browned and wrinkled. Garnish with almonds and fresh parsley and serve.

Nutrition Info per Serving:
Calories: 256, Protein: 8 g, Fat: 4 g, Carbohydrates: 47 g, Fiber: 8 g, Sugar: 0.7 g, Sodium: 477 mg

Broccoli Baked Potatoes

Prep Time: 10 minutes, Cook Time: 1.5 hours, Serves: 4

INGREDIENTS:
4 large russet potatoes, scrubbed
2 cups broccoli florets
1 batch No-Cheese Sauce

DIRECTIONS:
1. Preheat the oven to 350°F (180ºC).
2. Pierce each potato with a fork so that it will release steam during baking. Put the pierced potatoes on a baking sheet and bake for 60 to 75 minutes.
3. Combine the No-Cheese Sauce and the broccoli in a saucepan and cook for 8 to 10 minutes over medium heat.
4. When the potatoes are cool enough to handle, pierce the potatoes with a fork in a dotted line. Squeeze the potato at either end of the dotted line to force it open. Put 2 potato halves on each plate and spoon some of the warm broccoli mixture into the halves. Serve.

Nutrition Info per Serving:
Calories: 296, Protein: 8.6 g, Fat: 0.4 g, Carbohydrates: 67.3 g, Fiber: 5.4 g, Sugar: 2.4 g, Sodium: 35 mg

Baked Cucumber Stuffed Tomatoes

Prep Time: 15 minutes, Cook Time: 45 minutes, Serves: 4

INGREDIENTS:
4 large tomatoes (about 2 pounds)
2 celery, diced small and rinsed
1 medium cucumber, diced small
3 ears corn, shucked (about 1½ cups)
1 cup bulgur, cooked in 2 cups (480mL) Vegetable Stock, or low-sodium vegetable broth
½ cup finely chopped sage
3 clove garlic, smashed and skin removed
2 tbsps. peanut butter
2 tsps. toasted sesame
Salt and freshly ground black pepper to taste

DIRECTIONS:
1. Preheat the oven to 350°F(180ºC).
2. Cut the tops off the tomatoes and scoop out the flesh, leaving a ½-inch wall. Set the tomatoes aside while you prepare the filling.
3. Place the celery in a large saucepan and sauté over medium heat for 7 to 8 minutes. Add the garlic and cook for 3 minutes longer. Stir in the cucumber and corn and cook for 5 minutes. Add the cooked bulgur, sage, peanut butter and sesame. Season with salt and pepper. Remove from the heat.
4. Divide the bulgur mixture among the prepared tomatoes and arrange them in a baking dish. Cover the dish with aluminum foil and bake for 30 minutes.

Nutrition Info per Serving:
Calories: 171, Protein: 5.8 g, Fat: 1.4 g, Carbohydrates: 33.7 g, Fiber: 6.4 g, Sugar: 10.3 g, Sodium: 29 mg

Lentil Mushroom Bolognese

Prep Time: 15 minutes, Cook Time: 35 minutes, Serves: 8

INGREDIENTS:
8 ounces (227 g) cremini mushrooms, chopped
6 garlic cloves, minced
1 large carrot, chopped small
1 yellow onion, finely diced
1 cup water, plus 1 tbsp. and more as needed
2 tsps. dried basil
¼ cup tomato paste
1 tsp. dried oregano
¼ tsp. red pepper flakes
1 (28-ounce, 784 g) can crushed tomatoes
¾ cup dried red lentils, rinsed and picked over for debris
1 pound (454 g) whole wheat noodles

DIRECTIONS:
1. Add the mushrooms into a large sauté pan or skillet, cook over high heat for 3 minutes to remove their moisture, stirring to prevent burning.
2. Add the garlic, carrot and onion. Cook for 3 minutes, adding water, 1 tbsp. at a time, to prevent burning, or until the onion is translucent and starts to brown.
3. Add the basil, tomato paste, oregano, and red pepper flakes, stir to mix evenly with the vegetables. Cook for 1 minute.
4. Pour in the tomatoes with their juices, 1 cup of water and lentils. Stir to combine. Bring the sauce to a simmer, cover the pan, and lower the heat to low. Cook for 15 minutes, stirring occasionally. The sauce is done when the lentils are tender.
5. Meanwhile, in a large pot, fill the salted (optional) water and bring to a boil. Add the noodles and cook according to the package directions until al dente. Reserve ¼ cup of cooking water and add that to the sauce. Drain the noodles.
6. Mix the noodles and sauce together to serve or top the noodles with the Bolognese. Mixing them together and letting them rest for 5 minutes before serving gives you the best results because the noodles soak up some of the liquid.

Nutrition Info per Serving:
Calories: 346, Protein: 15 g, Fat: 2 g, Carbohydrates: 67 g, Fiber: 7 g, Sugar: 5.2 g, Sodium: 364 mg

Seitan Sloppy Joes Sandwich

Prep Time: 10 minutes, Cook Time: 20 minutes, Serves: 6

INGREDIENTS:

- 8 ounces (227 g) tomato sauce
- 2 cups seitan, crumbled
- ⅓ cup organic ketchup
- 2 tbsps. coconut sugar
- 1 tbsp. vegan Worcestershire sauce
- 2 tbsps. red wine vinegar
- 6 toasted whole wheat buns

DIRECTIONS:

1. In a large skillet, add all of the ingredients except the buns. Bring to a boil, then reduce the heat to medium. Cook for 15 minutes.
2. After cooking, serve on the toasted buns.

Nutrition Info per Serving:
Calories: 294, Protein: 33 g, Fat: 2.7 g, Carbohydrates: 34.8 g, Fiber: 6.2 g, Sugar: 9.5 g, Sodium: 799 mg

Sweet Potato & Broccoli

Prep Time: 17 minutes, Cook Time: 18 minutes, Serves: 2

INGREDIENTS:

- 4 (250 g) sweet potatoes, cubed
- 1 (7-oz, 200 g) pack smoked tofu, cubed
- 2 cups (350 g) broccoli florets
- ¼ cup (60 ml) teriyaki sauce
- ¼ cup (70 g) peanut butter
- ½ cup (120 ml) water

DIRECTIONS:

1. In a medium pot over medium-high heat, cook the sweet potato cubes for about 10 minutes, covered with water.
2. Put in the broccoli florets, and cook for 3 minutes.
3. Turn off the heat, drain the water from the broccoli and sweet potatoes and set aside.
4. Add the teriyaki sauce, the water and tofu cubes to a non-stick frying pan over medium-high heat.
5. Keep stirring continuously and add the broccoli florets and sweet potato cubes to the frying pan. Cook for 5 minutes.
6. Turn off the heat, let it cool down for a minute, then drain off the water.
7. Divide onto 2 plates, drizzle peanut butter on top of each plate with the optional toppings.

Nutrition Info per Serving:
Calories: 549, Protein: 32.2 g, Fat: 24 g, Carbohydrates: 51.1 g, Fiber: 13.2 g, Sugar: 15.7 g, Sodium: 527 mg

Vegan Pizza Bread

Prep Time: 5 minutes, Cook Time: 20 minutes, Serves: 4

INGREDIENTS:

- 1 whole-wheat loaf, unsliced
- 1 cup vegan marinara
- 1 tsp. nutritional yeast
- ½ tsp. garlic powder
- ½ tsp. onion powder

DIRECTIONS:

1. Preheat the oven to 375°F (190°C).
2. Divide the loaf of bread in half lengthwise. Spread the marinara evenly onto each slice of bread, and then sprinkle on the nutritional yeast, garlic powder, and onion powder.
3. On a baking sheet, place with the bread and bake until the bread is a light golden brown, about 20 minutes.

Nutrition Info per Serving:
Calories: 230, Protein: 13 g, Fat: 3 g, Carbohydrates: 38 g, Fiber: 7 g, Sugar: 1.2 g, Sodium: 214 mg

Creamy Asparagus & Tofu Cubes

Prep Time: 10 minutes, Cook Time: 25 minutes, Serves: 2

INGREDIENTS:

- 4 (250 g) sweet potatoes, cubed
- 200 g smoked tofu, cubed
- 8 asparagus spears
- ¼ cup (60 ml) lemon juice
- ¼ cup (60 g) tahini
- ¼ cup (60 ml) water

DIRECTIONS:

1. Preheat the oven to 425°F (220°C) and line with parchment paper.
2. Cook the sweet potato cubes in a medium pot over medium-high heat, covered with water, for 15 minutes or until they're soft.
3. Remove the pot, drain the water from the sweet potato cubes and set aside.
4. Put tofu cubes and asparagus spears on a baking tray.
5. Roast for 10 minutes or until the asparagus spears are soft.
6. Mix the tahini and lemon juice together in a bowl, whisk into a thinner and smooth dressing, adding more water if necessary.
7. Divide the sweet potatoes, tofu cubes and asparagus between 2 plates, drizzle tahini dressing on top of each plate with the optional toppings.

Nutrition Info per Serving:
Calories: 232, Protein: 25 g, Fat: 0.3 g, Carbohydrates: 32.2 g, Fiber: 7.2 g, Sugar: 8.6 g, Sodium: 483 mg

Chapter 4 Dinner 41

Chapter 4 Dinner

Provencal Broccoli

Prep Time: 10 minutes, Cook Time: 30 minutes, Serves: 3

INGREDIENTS:
1 cup (190 g) brown rice, cooked
1 (7-oz, 200 g) pack extra-firm tofu, cubed
2 cups (350 g) broccoli florets
1 cup (180 g) tomato cubes
¼ cup (15 g) Provencal herbs
2 tbsps. (30 ml) water

DIRECTIONS:
1. Cook the brown rice simply and quickly.
2. Over high heat, add the broccoli florets in a medium pot filled halfway with water and cook for 5 minutes.
3. Heat a non-stick frying pan to medium-high heat and add tomato cubes, tofu cubes, Provencal herbs and water.
4. Cook and stir occasionally for about 10 minutes.
5. Continue to cook and stir until everything is cooked, then add the broccoli florets and mix.
6. Turn off the heat and let the rice mixture cool down for a while.
7. Divide the mixture between 2 plates, garnish with the optional toppings.

Nutrition Info per Serving:
Calories: 375, Protein: 19.8 g, Fat: 6.6 g, Carbohydrates: 58.9 g, Fiber: 9.7 g, Sugar: 4 g, Sodium: 493 mg

Sweet Potato and Zucchini

Prep Time: 15 minutes, Cook Time: 30 minutes, Serves: 4

INGREDIENTS:
1 medium zucchini, diced small
1 tbsp. lime juice
2 cloves garlic, smashed and skin removed
½ jalapeño pepper, seeded and minced
2 medium tomatoes, diced
1 medium broccoli, cut into florets
1 pound (450 g) sweet potatoes, cut into ½-inch dice
1 tsp. tarragon
1 tsp. ground coriander
1 tsp. crushed red pepper flakes
½ tsp. turmeric
¼ tsp. ground rosemary
2 tbsps. mint
1 cup black beans
¼ cup fresh dill, chopped

DIRECTIONS:
1. In a large saucepan, add the zucchini and sauté over medium heat for 7 to 8 minutes. Pour in water 1 to 2 tbsps. at a time to keep the onion from sticking to the pan. Whisk in the lime juice, garlic, and jalapeño pepper and cook for 3 minutes. Stir in the tomatoes, broccoli, potatoes, tarragon, coriander, crushed red pepper flakes, turmeric, rosemary, and mint and cook, covered, for 10 to 12 minutes, until the vegetables are soft. Whisk in the beans and cook for 5 minutes longer.
2. Serve garnished with the dill.

Nutrition Info per Serving:
Calories: 175, Protein: 6.8 g, Fat: 0.8 g, Carbohydrates: 35.3 g, Fiber: 7.3 g, Sugar: 7.4 g, Sodium: 335 mg

Braised Red Cabbage with Squash

Prep Time: 15 minutes, Cook Time: 40 minutes, Serves: 4

INGREDIENTS:
3 asparagus, trimmed and diced
2 large carrots, peeled and diced
2 celery stalks, diced
1 large head red cabbage, cored and shredded
4 cups cooked acorn squash, or two (15-oz. 430g) cans, drained and rinsed
2 tart apples (such as Granny Smith), peeled, cored, and diced
2 tsps. cinnamon
1½ cups (360mL) brown rice vinegar
2 tbsps. Dijon mustard
Salt and freshly ground black pepper to taste

DIRECTIONS:
1. In a large saucepan, add the asparagus, carrots, and celery in a large saucepan and sauté over medium heat for 7 to 8 minutes.
2. Pour in water 1 to 2 tbsps. at a time to keep the vegetables from sticking to the pan.
3. Whisk in the cinnamon, brown rice vinegar, and mustard and cook until the brown rice vinegar is reduced by half, about 10 minutes.
4. Stir in the cabbage, acorn squash, and apples. Cook, covered, until the cabbage is soft, about 20 minutes. Sprinkle with salt and pepper to taste.

Nutrition Info per Serving:
Calories: 241, Protein: 9.8 g, Fat: 1.2 g, Carbohydrates: 48.6 g, Fiber: 11.8 g, Sugar: 19.5 g, Sodium: 167 mg

Cauliflower, Spinach and Sweet Potato Lasagna

Prep Time: 20 minutes, Cook Time: 1½ hours, Serves: 6 to 8

INGREDIENTS:

12 cups spinach (about 2 pounds, 907 g)
2 to 3 large sweet potatoes (about 2 pounds, 907 g), peeled and cut into ½-inch rounds
2 large heads cauliflower, cut into florets
¼ cup pine nuts, toasted
Unsweetened plain almond milk, as needed
3 tbsps. nutritional yeast, optional
½ tsp. ground nutmeg
1½ tsp. salt
1 large yellow onion, peeled and diced small
4 cloves garlic, peeled and minced
1 tbsp. minced thyme
½ cup finely chopped basil
12 ounces (340 g) whole-grain lasagna noodles, cooked, drained, and rinsed until cool
Salt and freshly ground black pepper

DIRECTIONS:

1. Put the sweet potatoes in a steamer basket and steam for 6 minutes until tender but not mushy. Rinse until cool, then drain them and set aside.
2. Steam the cauliflower for 6 to 8 minutes, until very tender. Mix the cauliflower and pine nuts in a blender, and puree until creamy, adding almond milk if needed. Add the puree to a large bowl and stir in the nutmeg, nutritional yeast, and salt. Set aside.
3. Put the onion in a large skillet and sauté for 10 minutes over medium heat. Add water 1 tbsp. at a time to keep the onion from sticking to the pan. Add the thyme, garlic, basil, and spinach and cook for 4 to 5 minutes until the spinach wilts. Combine with the cauliflower puree and mix well. Season with additional salt and pepper.
4. Preheat the oven to 350°F (180ºC).
5. Pour 1 cup of the cauliflower mixture into the bottom of a baking dish. Add a layer of lasagna noodles. Put a layer of sweet potatoes on top of the noodles. Pour another layer of the cauliflower mixture over the sweet potatoes. Top with another layer of noodles, followed by a layer of sweet potatoes. Add another layer of the cauliflower mixture. Top with a final layer of noodles and the remaining cauliflower sauce. Cover with aluminum foil and bake for 30 minutes. Uncover and bake for 15 more minutes until the casserole is hot and bubbly. Set aside for 15 minutes before serving.

Nutrition Info per Serving:
Calories: 152, Protein: 7.3 g, Fat: 4.7 g, Carbohydrates: 23.7 g, Fiber: 8.5 g, Sugar: 5.8 g, Sodium: 690 mg

Seasoned Roasted Beet and Chickpea Biryani

Prep Time: 15 minutes, Cook Time: 40 minutes, Serves: 4

INGREDIENTS:

6 cups water, plus 5 tbsps. and more as needed
2 cups basmati rice, rinsed well
½ tsp. cayenne pepper
1 tsp. ground cardamom
¼ tsp. ground aniseed
¼ tsp. ground cinnamon
¼ tsp. ground turmeric
3 garlic cloves, minced
1 yellow onion, diced
1 tbsp. grated peeled fresh ginger
1 (4-ounce, 113 g) can diced green chiles
3 carrots, diced
1 large beet, peeled and finely chopped
1 tbsp. yellow (mellow) miso paste
Oil, for coating
1 cup green peas
1 (15-ounce, 425 g) can chickpeas, drained and rinsed
¼ cup packed chopped fresh cilantro, plus more for garnish

DIRECTIONS:

1. Preheat the oven to 400°F(205°C).
2. Fill 6 cups of water in a large pot, bring to a boil over high heat. Lower the heat to medium-low, add the rice, and cook for 10 minutes. The rice will be parcooked. Strain the rice with a fine-mesh sieve, lightly rinse, and set aside.
3. Stir together the cayenne pepper, cardamom, aniseed, cinnamon, and turmeric in a small bowl. Add 2 tbsps. of water and stir well. Set aside.
4. Heat a pot over medium heat. Add the garlic, onion, and 1 tbsp. water. Cook, stirring, for 5 minutes, adding more water, 1 tbsp. at a time, to prevent burning. The onion should be well browned.
5. Stir in the soaked spices and cook, stirring, for 1 minute. Add the ginger and green chiles. Cook for another 30 seconds.
6. Add the carrots, beet, and 2 tbsps. of water. Sauté for 3 minutes, stirring. Add the miso paste, stir well and turn off the heat.
7. Use the oil to lightly coat a 9-by-13-inch baking dish. Spread half the cooked rice in the prepared dish. Place the beet and carrot mix, then the peas, and finally the chickpeas on top of the rice. Evenly sprinkle the cilantro across the top. Spread the remaining rice on top and use aluminum foil to cover the dish.
8. Bake for 15 minutes. Mix lightly, garnish with cilantro, and serve.

Nutrition Info per Serving:
Calories: 547, Protein: 18 g, Fat: 3 g, Carbohydrates: 112 g, Fiber: 9 g, Sugar: 2 g, Sodium: 686 mg

Slow Vegetable Roast

Prep Time: 10 minutes, Cook Time: 4 to 8 hours, Serves: 8

INGREDIENTS:
6 large carrots, cut into ½-inch rounds
6 medium white potatoes, cut into 1-inch cubes
3 sweet onions, cut into ½-inch cubes
8 ounces (227 g) mushrooms, sliced
12 ounces (340 g) green beans (fresh or frozen)
4 cups vegetable broth
1 tsp. garlic powder
1 tsp. onion powder
1 tsp, freshly ground black pepper

DIRECTIONS:
1. In a slow cooker, add all of the ingredients. Stir together so the spices are well distributed.
2. Cover and cook on high for 4 hours or cook on low for 6 to 8 hours.
3. After cooking, remove the lid and stir well before serving.

Nutrition Info per Serving:
Calories: 190, Protein: 8 g, Fat: 1 g, Carbohydrates: 39 g, Fiber: 8 g, Sugar: 1 g, Sodium: 694 mg

Black Beans and Brown Rice

Prep Time: 5 minutes, Cook Time: 40 minutes, Serves: 6

INGREDIENTS:
1½ cups brown rice
3½ cups low sodium vegetable broth
1 tbsp. extra virgin olive oil
2 (15-ounce, 425 g) cans black beans, drained and rinsed
½ yellow onion, chopped
1 green bell pepper, chopped
¼ cup diced tomatoes
1 clove garlic, finely chopped
1 tsp. garlic powder
1 tsp. onion powder
1 tsp. parsley
1 tsp. thyme
1 tsp. oregano
1 tsp. salt
½ tsp. cayenne pepper
¼ tsp. ground black pepper

DIRECTIONS:
1. Cook the brown rice with the vegetable broth.
2. Heat the oil in a large skillet to medium, then add the onion and bell pepper. Sauté for 10 minutes, until the onion becomes transparent. Add all the remaining ingredients except the rice to the large skillet. Cook for 10 minutes. Then add the rice and heat through.

Nutrition Info per Serving:
Calories: 399, Protein: 13.7 g, Fat: 6.2 g, Carbohydrates: 73 g, Fiber: 11.5 g, Sugar: 7.7 g, Sodium: 760 mg

Roasted Vegetables with Whole-Grain Pasta

Prep Time: 15 minutes, Cook Time: 45 minutes, Serves: 8

INGREDIENTS:
4 beefsteak tomatoes, halved
1 yellow onion, cut into slices and left as rings
2 large yellow squash, cubed
2 large zucchini, cubed
3 garlic cloves, minced
1 small red bell pepper, diced
1 tsp. Italian seasoning
½ tsp. freshly ground black pepper
1 pound (454 g) whole wheat linguine
¼ cup tomato paste
1 tsp. red pepper flakes
¼ tsp. dried oregano
1 tbsp. packed minced fresh Italian parsley
2 tbsps. fresh basil chiffonade, divided

DIRECTIONS:
1. Preheat the oven to 450°F(235°C). Use parchment paper to line 2 baking sheets.
2. Cut-side up, place the tomato halves on 1 prepared baking sheet. Place the onion rings on the same baking sheet.
3. Roast on the center rack for 10 minutes.
4. Meanwhile, toss together the squash, zucchini, garlic, bell pepper, Italian seasoning, and pepper in a large bowl. Spread the vegetables on the other prepared baking sheet.
5. Put the vegetables on a lower rack (but not the lowest) and bake for 15 minutes. Flip the vegetables. Remove the tomato sheet and set aside. Place the vegetables onto the center rack and roast for another 15 minutes.
6. In a large pot, pour in the water and bring to a boil over high heat. Cook the pasta according to the package directions to al dente. Reserve ½ cup of the pasta water and drain the pasta. Keep the pasta in the strainer.
7. Reduce the pasta pot to medium heat. Transfer the onions and roasted tomatoes to the pot and stir in the tomato paste, red pepper flakes, reserved pasta water, and oregano. Use a heavy spoon to mash the tomatoes and onion for a chunky texture, or use an immersion blender to puree, as you like.
8. Add the roasted vegetables, parsley, pasta, and 1 tbsp. of basil to the pot. Combine and coat well. Garnish with the remaining 1 tbsp. of basil and serve.

Nutrition Info per Serving:
Calories: 272, Protein: 11 g, Fat: 2 g, Carbohydrates: 55 g, Fiber: 5 g, Sugar: 6.4 g, Sodium: 558 mg

Creamy Eggplant Polenta Casserole

Prep Time: 15 minutes, Cook Time: 1 hour, Serves: 6 to 8

INGREDIENTS:
1 large red bell pepper, seeded and diced
1 large yellow onion, peeled and diced
2 large eggplants (about 3 pounds, 1.4 kg), stemmed and diced
2 large tomatoes, diced
8 cloves garlic, peeled and minced
1 cup chopped basil
1 batch Basic Polenta, kept warm
Salt and freshly ground black pepper

DIRECTIONS:
1. Preheat the oven to 350°F (180ºC).
2. Put onion in a large saucepan and sauté for 10 minutes over medium heat. Add water 1 tbsp. at a time to keep the onion from sticking to the pan. Put in eggplant, red pepper, and garlic. Cook with lid covered, for 15 minutes, stirring occasionally, adding more water as needed. Mix in the tomatoes, season with salt and pepper, and cook for 10 more minutes.
3. Add the basil and spoon the mixture into a baking dish. Spoon the polenta over the eggplant mixture, bake for 30 minutes.

Nutrition Info per Serving:
Calories: 122, Protein: 3.4 g, Fat: 1 g, Carbohydrates: 24.5 g, Fiber: 6.3 g, Sugar: 7.3 g, Sodium: 214 mg

Polenta with Creamy Tomato Sauce

Prep Time: 15 minutes, Cook Time: 32 minutes, Serves: 6

INGREDIENTS:
1 batch Basic Polenta, poured into a nonstick loaf pan and refrigerated about 2 to 3 hours until set,
2 shallots, peeled and minced
2 cloves garlic, peeled and minced
½ cup minced basil
1 cup sun-dried tomatoes, soaked in 2 cups warm water for 30 minutes, drained, and chopped
1 tsp. minced thyme
1 batch No-Cheese Sauce
Chopped parsley
Salt and freshly ground black pepper

DIRECTIONS:
1. Preheat the oven to 350°F (180ºC).
2. Slice the polenta into 6 rectangles, then cut each piece in half on the diagonal to form triangles. Place the triangles on a baking sheet and bake for 15 minutes until heated through.
3. Meanwhile, put the shallots in a large saucepan and sauté for 5 minutes over medium heat. Add water 1 tbsp. at a time to keep the shallots from sticking to the pan. Add the garlic and cook for 2 minutes. Combine the sun-dried tomatoes, thyme, and No-Cheese Sauce and cook over medium-low heat for 10 minutes, stirring frequently. Add the basil and season with salt and pepper.

Nutrition Info per Serving:
Calories: 102, Protein: 3.1 g, Fat: 1.1 g, Carbohydrates: 21.6 g, Fiber: 3.1 g, Sugar: 3.8 g, Sodium: 436 mg

Polenta with Mushroom Olive Sauce

Prep Time: 15 minutes, Cook Time: 30 minutes, Serves: 6

INGREDIENTS:
1 batch Basic Polenta, refrigerated about 2 to 3 hours
½ medium yellow onion, peeled and diced small
1 pound (454 g) cremini or button mushrooms, thinly sliced
3 cloves garlic, peeled and minced
½ tsp. ground nutmeg
1 cup dry white wine
1 tbsp. minced thyme
½ cup kalamata olives, pitted and chopped
1 batch No-Cheese Sauce
Chopped parsley
Zest and juice of 1 lemon
Salt and freshly ground black pepper

DIRECTIONS:
1. Preheat the oven to 350°F (180ºC).
2. Slice the polenta into 6 rectangles and cut each piece in half on the diagonal to form triangles. Put on a baking sheet and bake until heated through for 15 minutes.
3. Put the onion and mushrooms in a large saucepan and sauté for 7 to 8 minutes over medium heat. Add water 1 tbsp. at a time to keep the vegetables from sticking to the pan. Add the thyme, garlic, and nutmeg and cook for 2 minutes. Add the wine and simmer, until the liquid is reduced by half. Mix in the lemon zest and juice, No-Cheese Sauce and olives, simmer for 5 minutes. Season with salt and pepper.
4. Put 2 polenta triangles in the center of each plate and spoon some of the sauce over the polenta. Serve garnish with the parsley.

Nutrition Info per Serving:
Calories: 207, Protein: 9.5 g, Fat: 6.9 g, Carbohydrates: 26.7 g, Fiber: 3.8 g, Sugar: 2.3 g, Sodium: 401 mg

Maple Glazed Vegetable Lentil and Oat Loaf

Prep Time: 45 minutes, Cook Time: 1 hour 40 minutes, Serves: 8

INGREDIENTS:
FOR THE GLAZE (OPTIONAL):
- 2 tbsps. pure maple syrup
- 3 tbsps. tomato paste
- ¼ tsp. garlic powder
- 1 tbsp. apple cider vinegar

FOR THE LENTIL LOAF:
- 1 cup dried brown lentils, rinsed and picked over for stones and debris
- 2½ cups no-sodium vegetable broth
- Olive oil cooking spray, for coating
- 1 tsp. dried thyme
- 1 tbsp. nutritional yeast
- 1 tsp. paprika
- 1 tsp. onion powder
- ½ tsp. garlic powder
- ½ tsp. ground cumin
- ¼ tsp. freshly ground black pepper
- 3 tbsps. ground flaxseed
- ¼ cup water, plus 1 tbsp. and more as needed
- 1 small onion, diced
- 3 garlic cloves, minced
- 1 small red bell pepper, diced
- 1 carrot, grated
- 1 celery stalk, diced
- ½ cup oat flour
- ¾ cup old-fashioned oats (not quick oats)

DIRECTIONS:
TO MAKE THE GLAZE (IF USING):
1. Add the maple syrup, tomato paste, garlic powder and vinegar in a small bowl, whisk them together until smooth. Set aside.

TO MAKE THE LENTIL LOAF:
2. Combine the lentils and vegetable broth in a large pot, bring to a boil over high heat, then reduce the heat to medium-low, cover and simmer for 35 minutes, stirring occasionally. The lentils are done when they are soft and can be pureed. Set aside to cool for at least 15 minutes without draining.
3. Preheat the oven to 350°F(180°C). Create a parchment-paper sling for a 9-inch loaf pan by cutting a piece of parchment paper that can be inserted into the tin lengthwise with the sides slightly overhanging. Lightly spray the oil into the inside of the pan and insert the parchment-paper sling.
4. Stir together the thyme, nutritional yeast, paprika, onion powder, garlic powder, cumin and pepper in a small bowl. Set aside.
5. Stir together the flaxseed and ¼ cup of water in a separate small bowl to make a flax egg.
6. Add the onion, garlic, bell pepper, celery and carrot in a sauté pan or skillet, sauté over medium-high heat for 4 to 5 minutes, or until the onion is translucent. Add the water, 1 tbsp. at a time, to prevent the onion from burning and sticking. Remove from the heat, sprinkle on the spice mixture evenly, and mix well to incorporate. Set aside to cool.
7. Drain any excess water from the cooled lentils and transfer three-quarters of the lentils to a food processor to puree, or into a large bowl, and puree with a potato masher or heavy spoon. Set aside the remaining one-quarter of the lentils.
8. Place the pureed lentils into a large bowl and stir in the sautéed vegetables, oat flour, oats, and flax egg. Combine well.
9. Stir in the reserved whole lentils. Spoon the mixture into the loaf pan. Press the mixture into the pan with a spoon or spatula.
10. Spread the glaze evenly over the lentil loaf if using.
11. Bake on the center rack for about 50 minutes, or until the top is browned and crusted rather than wet. After baking, allow to cool for 10 minutes before removing from the pan and cutting into slices.

Nutrition Info per Serving:
Calories: 195, Protein: 9 g, Fat: 3 g, Carbohydrates: 33 g, Fiber: 7 g, Sugar: 1.3 g, Sodium: 508 mg

Carrot and Sweet Potato with Pine Nut

Prep Time: 15 minutes, Cook Time: 50 minutes, Serves: 4

INGREDIENTS:
- 4 large carrots, peeled and cut into 1-inch slices
- 3 large sweet potatoes, peeled and cut into ¾-inch cubes
- 1 cup dried pine nuts
- ½ cup dates, pitted
- 1 cup dried apples, chopped
- 2 tbsps. maple syrup
- ½ cup unsweetened apple cider
- ¼ cup hummus
- 2 tsps. ground garlic
- ¼ tsp. ground rosemary
- Salt to taste

DIRECTIONS:
1. Preheat the oven to 350°F(180ºC).
2. In a large saucepan, add the carrots and sweet potatoes and cover with water, bring to a boil over high heat. Lower the heat to medium and simmer for 10 minutes, or until the vegetables are soft. Drain and rinse under cold water until cool.
3. In a 9 × 13-inch baking dish, mix together the drained carrots and sweet potatoes, pine nuts, apples, dates, maple syrup, apple cider, hummus, garlic, and rosemary. Drizzle with salt and cover with a lid or aluminum foil. Bake for 30 minutes, stirring carefully every 10 minutes.

Nutrition Info per Serving:
Calories: 279, Protein: 3 g, Fat: 0.4 g, Carbohydrates: 65.5 g, Fiber: 5.9 g, Sugar: 42.2 g, Sodium: 674 mg

Zucchini and Cauliflower with Avocado

Prep Time: 10 minutes, Cook Time: 40 minutes, Serves: 6 cups

INGREDIENTS:
1 large onion, peeled
2 large zucchinis, peeled
½ cup cauliflower, rinsed
2 avocados
8 cloves garlic, peeled and smashed
6 sprigs mint
1 tsp. nutmeg

DIRECTIONS:
1. Scrub the vegetables and chop them roughly into 1-inch chunks.
2. Add the onion, zucchinis, avocados, garlic, mint, nutmeg, and cauliflower in a large pot and cook them over high heat for 5 to 10 minutes, stirring often.
3. Pour water 1 to 2 tbsps. at a time to keep the vegetables from sticking to the pot.
4. Pour in 2 quarts of water and bring to a boil. Reduce the heat and cook, uncovered, for 30 minutes.
5. Strain the stock carefully and discard the solids.

Nutrition Info per Serving:
Calories: 34, Protein: 1.4 g, Fat: 0.2 g, Carbohydrates: 7.6 g, Fiber: 1.4 g, Sugar: 2.3 g, Sodium: 224 mg

Spinach and Mushroom Pilaf

Prep Time: 15 minutes, Cook Time: 30 minutes, Serves: 4

INGREDIENTS:
⅓ ounce (9 g) porcini mushrooms, soaked for 30 minutes in 1 cup of water that has just been boiled, and roughly chopped
2 large leeks (white and light green parts), diced and rinsed
8 ounces (227 g) cremini mushrooms, thinly sliced
1½ cups quinoa
6 cups baby spinach, chopped
3 cloves garlic, peeled and minced
1 tbsp. thyme
2 cups (480 ml) low-sodium vegetable broth, plus more as needed
¼ cup pine nuts, toasted, optional
Salt and freshly ground black pepper

DIRECTIONS:
1. Drain the porcini mushrooms, reserving the liquid. Chop the mushrooms finely and set aside.
2. Put the leeks and cremini mushrooms in a large saucepan and sauté for 10 minutes over medium heat. Add water 1 tbsp. at a time to keep the vegetables from sticking to the pan. Add the garlic and thyme and cook for 30 seconds.
3. Combine the vegetable stock and porcini mushroom soaking liquid. Add more vegetable stock as needed to make 3 cups. Mix the liquid, quinoa, and chopped porcini mushrooms to the pan with the sautéed mushrooms and bring the pan to a boil over high heat. Reduce the heat to medium and cook the quinoa with lid covered for 15 minutes, until it is tender. Stir in the spinach and cook for 5 more minutes, until the spinach is wilted. Season with salt and pepper and garnish with the pine nuts. Serve.

Nutrition Info per Serving:
Calories: 411, Protein: 19 g, Fat: 11 g, Carbohydrates: 58.9 g, Fiber: 14.1 g, Sugar: 7.1 g, Sodium: 426 mg

Stuffed Delicata Squash

Prep Time: 15 minutes, Cook Time: 1.5 hours, Serves: 4

INGREDIENTS:
2 delicata squash, halved and seeded
6 cups chopped spinach
2 cloves garlic, peeled and minced
1 shallot, peeled and minced
½ red bell pepper, seeded and diced small
3 tbsps. nutritional yeast, optional
3 tbsps. pine nuts, toasted
1 tbsp. minced sage
2 cups cooked cannellini beans, or one (15-ounce, 425 g) can, drained and rinsed
¾ cup whole-grain bread crumbs
Salt and freshly ground black pepper
Zest of 1 lemon

DIRECTIONS:
1. Preheat the oven to 350°F (180ºC). Line a baking sheet with parchment paper.
2. Season the cut sides of the squash with salt and pepper. Put the halves on the prepared baking sheet, cut sides down. Bake about 45 minutes.
3. Put the shallot and red pepper in a large saucepan and sauté over medium heat for 2 to 3 minutes. Add water 1 tbsp. at a time to keep the vegetables from sticking to the pan. Put in the garlic, spinach, and sage and cook 4 to 5 minutes. Add the beans and season with salt and pepper. Cook for another 2 to 3 minutes. Remove from the heat. Add the bread crumbs, pine nuts, nutritional yeast, and lemon zest. Mix well.
4. Portion the bean mixture among the baked squash halves. Place the stuffed squash halves in a baking dish and cover with aluminum foil. Bake until heated through for 15 to 20 minutes.

Nutrition Info per Serving:
Calories: 100, Protein: 7.3 g, Fat: 1 g, Carbohydrates: 15.4 g, Fiber: 4.5 g, Sugar: 4.6 g, Sodium: 574 mg

Chapter 4 Dinner

Spicy Savory Eggplant

Prep Time: 15 minutes, Cook Time: 15 minutes, Serves: 1

INGREDIENTS:

1 large yellow onion, peeled and chopped
1 medium red bell pepper, seeded and chopped
1 medium green pepper, seeded and chopped
2 tsps. crushed red pepper flakes
2 cups pineapple chunks, or one 20-ounce can, drained
1 large eggplant, stemmed and cut into ½-inch dice
2 cloves garlic, peeled and minced
1 batch Pineapple Sweet-and-Sour Sauce

DIRECTIONS:

1. Place the red and green peppers, onion, and eggplant in a large skillet and sauté over medium-high heat for 8 to 9 minutes.
2. Add water 1 tbsp. at a time to keep the vegetables from sticking to the pan. Add the pineapple, garlic, crushed red pepper flakes, and sweet-and-sour sauce and cook for 5 minutes.

Nutrition Info per Serving:
Calories: 88, Protein: 2.3 g, Fat: 2.8 g, Carbohydrates: 15.5 g, Fiber: 5.5 g, Sugar: 9.4 g, Sodium: 328 mg

Veggie Green Goddess Sandwich

Prep Time: 20 minutes, plus 1 hour to chill, Cook Time: 0, Serves: 2

INGREDIENTS:

FOR THE SPREAD:
1 (15-ounce, 425 g) can cannellini beans, drained and rinsed
⅓ cup packed fresh parsley
⅓ cup packed fresh basil leaves
2 garlic cloves, chopped
⅓ cup chopped fresh chives
Zest and juice of ½ lemon
1 tbsp. apple cider vinegar

FOR THE SANDWICHES:
4 whole-grain bread slices, toasted
1 large beefsteak tomato, cut into slices
8 English cucumber slices
1 small yellow bell pepper, cut into slices
1 large avocado, halved, pitted, and cut into slices
2 handfuls fresh spinach
2 handfuls broccoli sprouts

DIRECTIONS:

TO MAKE THE SPREAD:
1. Combine all of the spread ingredients in a food processor. Pulse a few times, scrape down the sides, and puree until smooth. Place in the refrigerator to chill for at least 1 hour to allow the flavors to blend.

TO ASSEMBLE THE SANDWICHES:
2. Spread several tbsps. of green goddess spread on each slice of bread. Layer two slices of bread with the tomato, cucumber, bell pepper, avocado, spinach and broccoli sprouts. Top with the remaining bread slices and lightly press down.

Nutrition Info per Serving:
Calories: 619, Protein: 28 g, Fat: 21 g, Carbohydrates: 86 g, Fiber: 26 g, Sugar: 10.9 g, Sodium: 469 mg

Slow Cooker Seitan Log

Prep Time: 10 minutes, Cook Time: 6 hours, Serves: 4

INGREDIENTS:

1 tbsp. mushroom powder
1¼ cups vital wheat gluten
¼ cup chickpea flour
½ tsp. ground sage
2 tbsps. nutritional yeast
½ tsp. salt
¼ tsp. garlic powder
¼ tsp. onion powder
1 tbsp. tomato paste
1 cup tomato sauce, divided
2 cups vegetable broth

DIRECTIONS:

1. In a large bowl, add the mushroom powder, gluten, flour, sage, nutritional yeast, salt, garlic and onion powders, stir them together.
2. In a small bowl, add the tomato paste, ¾ cup tomato sauce, and ¼ cup plus 1 tbsp. water, mix well and pour the wet mixture into the dry ingredients.
3. Combine and then knead until mildly elastic, about 2 to 3 minutes. You will see the dough slightly pull back as you are kneading and it will be a bit sticky. Form the seitan into a log.
4. In a 2½- to 3-quart slow cooker, add the vegetable broth, 1 cup water, and the remaining ¼ cup tomato sauce, and then place the log in the slow cooker or use cheesecloth to roll loosely and tie each end with cotton string. It does expand when cooking, so don't to roll it tight. If you don't care that the outside is a bit lumpier after being cooked, then no need to roll in cheesecloth. Cover slow cooker and turn to low. Cook on low for 6 hours.
5. Take the log out from the liquid and set aside to cool. Store in the refrigerator for up to 5 days. It can also be frozen for 4 months.

Nutrition Info per Serving:
Calories: 253, Protein: 32 g, Fat: 1.4 g, Carbohydrates: 26.3 g, Fiber: 5.7 g, Sugar: 9.5 g, Sodium: 784 mg

Stir-Fry Eggplant Dengaku

Prep Time: 15 minutes, Cook Time: 15 minutes, Serves: 4

INGREDIENTS:
3 green onions (white and green parts), chopped
1 medium red bell pepper, seeded and cut into ½-inch strips
1 medium yellow onion, peeled and thinly sliced
1 large eggplant, stemmed and cut into 1-inch pieces
1 cup Easy Miso Sauce

DIRECTIONS:
1. Heat a large skillet over high heat and add the onion and pepper and stir-fry for 2 to 3 minutes.
2. Put in water 1 tbsp. at a time to keep the vegetables from sticking to the pan.
3. Add the eggplant and cook for 5 to 6 minutes longer, stirring frequently. Add the miso sauce and cook until thickened, about 3 minutes.
4. Garnished with the green onions and serve.

Nutrition Info per Serving:
Calories: 178, Protein: 5.7 g, Fat: 2 g, Carbohydrates: 34.8 g, Fiber: 7.6 g, Sugar: 21.2 g, Sodium: 817 mg

Blackbean and Rice Stuffed Peppers

Prep Time: 10 minutes, Cook Time: 30 minutes, Serves: 4

INGREDIENTS:
4 bell peppers
1 cup cooked black beans
3 cups cooked brown rice
1 cup corn (fresh or frozen)
2 tbsps. chili powder
1 cup vegetable broth
2 tbsps. tomato paste
1 tsp. ground cumin

DIRECTIONS:
1. Preheat the oven to 375°F(190°C).
2. Cut the tops of the bell peppers off, remove any fibers or seeds that remain inside the core or inside the tops of the peppers.
3. Add the beans, rice, corn, chili powder, broth, tomato paste, and cumin in a large bowl, mix until the tomato paste and spices have been thoroughly incorporated.
4. Spoon one-quarter of the rice mixture into each pepper. Place the peppers upright on a baking dish, and put the tops back onto the peppers.
5. Bake until the peppers are easily pierced with a fork, about 1 hours. After baking, serve warm.

Nutrition Info per Serving:
Calories: 270, Protein: 11 g, Fat: 3 g, Carbohydrates: 55 g, Fiber: 9 g, Sugar: 0.8 g, Sodium: 543 mg

Curried Millet and Green Peas with Mild Harissa Sauce

Prep Time: 20 minutes, Cook Time: 1 hour, Serves: 4

INGREDIENTS:
3¼ cups water, plus 1 tbsp. and more as needed
2 tbsps. ground flaxseed
1 large carrot, finely shredded
5 scallions, white and green parts, thinly sliced
1 tbsp. grated peeled fresh ginger
2 garlic cloves, minced
1 tbsp. yellow curry powder
1 cup dried millet, rinsed in cold water and drained
½ cup frozen green peas
1 cup Mild Harissa Sauce for serving

DIRECTIONS:
1. Stir together ¼ cup of water and the flaxseed in a small bowl. Set aside.
2. Add the carrot, scallions, ginger and garlic into a nonstick sauté pan or skillet, cook over medium-high heat, stirring, for 3 minutes, adding water, 1 tbsp. at a time, to prevent burning. Add the curry powder and cook, stirring, for another 1 minute. Turn off the heat once the scallions are tender.
3. Stir in the millet and combine well, coating the millet with the curry powder. Add the remaining cups of water and bring to a boil. Reduce the heat to medium-low, cover the pan, and simmer for about 15 minutes, until the water is absorbed. Turn off the heat, use a fork or spoon to fluff the millet mixture, and allow to sit for 5 minutes, covered.
4. Place the millet mixture into a large bowl and add the frozen peas, stir well. Allow to sit for about 10 minutes until cool enough to handle. Fold in the soaked flaxseed and mix well.
5. Use parchment paper to line a baking sheet.
6. Shape the mixture into 12 tightly packed patties, about ½ inch thick and 3 inches in diameter. Press them together firmly so they don't break apart while cooking. Transfer the patties onto the prepared baking sheet until all the millet mixture is used.
7. Place a clean sauté pan or skillet over medium-high heat. Add the patties, 4 to 6 at a time, and cook for 4 minutes per side, or until lightly browned. Gently flip so they don't break apart. Repeat with the remaining patties. Top with the Mild Harissa Sauce and serve.

Nutrition Info per Serving:
Calories: 262, Protein: 9 g, Fat: 4 g, Carbohydrates: 48 g, Fiber: 9 g, Sugar: 1.6 g, Sodium: 385 mg

Black Beans and Brown Rice, page 44

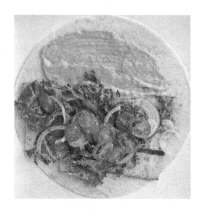

Zucchini and Kale Wrap, page 56

Carrot, Spinach and Bean Soup, page 53

Paprika Broccoli Casserole, page 52

Chapter 4 Dinner

Creamy Garlic Mushroom Pizza

Prep Time: 45 minutes, Cook Time: 30 minutes, Serves: 8

INGREDIENTS:
FOR THE CORNMEAL CRUST:
½ cup warm water (less than 100°F, 38°C)
1¼ tbsps. instant yeast
2¾ to 3¼ cups whole wheat flour, divided, plus more for the work surface
¼ cup cornmeal
½ tsp. onion powder
½ tsp. garlic powder
1 tbsp. melted coconut oil (optional)
FOR THE TOPPING:
1 cup cashew sour cream
1 tbsp. yellow (mellow) miso paste
1 tbsp. nutritional yeast
½ tsp. garlic powder
8 ounces (227 g) cremini mushrooms, stemmed and thinly sliced
4 ounces (113 g) shiitake mushrooms, stemmed and thinly sliced
4 garlic cloves, minced
½ large yellow onion, cut into thin strips
1 tbsp. water, plus more as needed
1 tsp. dried parsley
½ tsp. dried oregano

DIRECTIONS:
TO MAKE THE CORNMEAL CRUST:
1. Stir together the warm water, yeast, 1 cup of flour and cornmeal in a large bowl. Set aside for 10 minutes.
2. Add the onion powder, garlic powder, melted coconut oil, and flour—start with 1 cup and add more, ¼ cup at a time, so the dough comes together without being too sticky.
3. Lightly dust the flour onto a work surface and turn the dough out onto it. Knead the dough for 5 minutes. Place the dough in a sealable bag or a lightly oiled bowl and cover it. Allow to rest for 15 minutes, or refrigerate overnight.
TO MAKE THE TOPPING:
4. Add the cashew sour cream, miso paste, nutritional yeast, and garlic powder in a medium bowl, whisk to combine. Set aside.
5. Combine the cremini and shiitake mushrooms in a large skillet, sauté over high heat for 3 minutes untouched. Add the garlic and onion and gently flip the ingredients to combine. Cook for about another 4 minutes, adding water, 1 tbsp. at a time, if the onion is browning too quickly. The mushrooms should have some blackening and the onions should be browned.
TO ASSEMBLE THE PIZZA:
6. Preheat the oven to 425°F(220°C). Use parchment paper to line 2 baking sheets.
7. Divide the dough in half and form the halves into round balls. Avoid using flour on your work surface because it can make the dough not stick to itself. Roll out or pat and stretch each dough ball into a thin layer, about 16 inches in diameter. If the dough isn't stretching, allow it to rest for 5 minutes and try again.
8. On the prepared baking sheets, add the shaped crusts. Bake for 8 minutes.
9. Spread over the precooked crusts with the cashew cream sauce. Divide the mushroom and onion mix between the pizzas. Sprinkle on the parsley and oregano. Bake for another 15 minutes, or until the crust is golden brown.

Nutrition Info per Serving:
Calories: 302, Protein: 11 g, Fat: 10 g, Carbohydrates: 42 g, Fiber: 6 g, Sugar: 0.5 g, Sodium: 498 mg

Blackbean and Rice Enchilada Bake

Prep Time: 10 minutes, Cook Time: 30 minutes, Serves: 6

INGREDIENTS:
FOR THE ENCHILADA SAUCE:
2 tbsps. chili powder
¼ cup tomato paste
1 tsp. paprika
1 tsp. onion powder
1 tsp. garlic powder
1 tsp. ground cumin
2½ cups water
FOR THE ENCHILADA BAKE:
2 cups cooked black beans
2 cups cooked brown rice
1 cup corn (fresh or frozen)
8 corn tortillas
½ cup fat-free refried beans or mashed pinto beans

DIRECTIONS:
TO MAKE THE ENCHILADA SAUCE:
1. Add all of the enchilada sauce ingredients in a blender, blend for 1 to 2 minutes, or until thoroughly blended.
TO MAKE THE ENCHILADA BAKE:
1. Preheat the oven to 375°F(190°C).
2. Reserve ½ cup of enchilada sauce, and set aside.
3. Add the black beans, rice, corn, and the remaining enchilada sauce in a large bowl, mix them together.
4. With 4 corn tortillas to cover the bottom of a baking dish, then spread the refried beans over the tortillas evenly.
5. Lay an even layer of the rice mixture over the refried beans.
6. On top of the filling, place with the remaining 4 tortillas. Spread over the tortillas with the reserved ½ cup of enchilada sauce, be sure that they are covered with the sauce.
7. Put the enchiladas in the oven and bake until lightly browned, about 30 minutes. After baking, serve warm.

Nutrition Info per Serving:
Calories: 275, Protein: 11 g, Fat: 3 g, Carbohydrates: 51 g, Fiber: 11 g, Sugar: 1.9 g, Sodium: 578 mg

Paprika Broccoli Casserole

Prep Time: 15 minutes, Cook Time: 1½ hours, Serves: 6

INGREDIENTS:

3 cups (720 ml) low-sodium vegetable broth
3 cups broccoli florets (from about 2 medium bunches)
1½ cups brown rice
1 batch No-Cheese Sauce
Freshly ground black pepper to taste
Paprika

DIRECTIONS:

1. Put vegetable stock to a medium saucepan and boil over high heat. Add the brown rice, cover the lid and bring it back to a boil over high heat. Lower the heat to medium and cook with lid covered, for 45 minutes until the rice is tender.
2. Put the broccoli florets in a steamer basket and steam for 5 minutes until crisp-tender. Rinse until cool and set aside.
3. Preheat the oven to 350°F (180ºC).
4. Mix the rice with the No-Cheese Sauce and steamed broccoli in a bowl. Spread the rice mixture in the bottom of a baking dish and sprinkle the casserole with black pepper and paprika.
5. Bake the casserole for 35 to 40 minutes until bubbly.

Nutrition Info per Serving:
Calories: 202, Protein: 5.6 g, Fat: 1.9 g, Carbohydrates: 41.7 g, Fiber: 3 g, Sugar: 4.1 g, Sodium: 586 mg

Marinated Mushroom and Tofu Scramble

Prep Time: 55 minutes, Cook Time: 15 minutes, Serves: 4

INGREDIENTS:

2 cups (200 g) button mushrooms
1 (14-oz, 400 g) pack extra-firm tofu, scrambled
2 medium yellow onions, thinly sliced
¼ cup (60 ml) low-sodium soy sauce
½ cup (120 g) Tahini
½ cup (120 ml) water

DIRECTIONS:

1. Put the mushrooms, tofu scramble and soy sauce in an airtight container.
2. Close the lid and shake well until everything is evenly covered with soy sauce.
3. Place the container in the fridge and marinate for at least an hour, or up to 12 hours.
4. Place a large non-stick frying pan over medium heat. Add water and tofu mushroom mixture to the pan.
5. Add the onion slices and cook for 15 minutes, stirring occasionally to prevent the tofu from sticking to the pan, until the mushrooms are cooked and most of the water has evaporated.
6. Divide the tofu mushroom scramble between 2 bowls. Top the bowls with the tahini, serve with the optional toppings.

Nutrition Info per Serving:
Calories: 340, Protein: 20 g, Fat: 23.3 g, Carbohydrates: 12.6 g, Fiber: 3.8 g, Sugar: 5.2 g, Sodium: 527 mg

Garlicky Tomato Carrot Soup

Prep Time: 10 minutes, Cook Time: 35 minutes, Serves: 4

INGREDIENTS:

2 carrots, coarsely chopped
½ cup water, plus 1 tbsp. and more as needed
2 to 4 garlic cloves, coarsely chopped
1 yellow onion, coarsely chopped
1 tbsp. Hungarian paprika
1 (6-ounce, 170 g) can tomato paste
1 (14-ounce, 397 g) can full-fat coconut milk
1 (28-ounce, 784 g) can diced tomatoes
1 tsp. dried thyme
No-sodium vegetable broth or water, for thinning (optional)

DIRECTIONS:

1. Add the carrot and ½ cup of water in an 8-quart pot, cover the pot and cook over medium-high heat for 10 minutes, or until the carrots can be easily pierced with a fork. If the water evaporates while cooking, add more water, ¼ cup at a time. Drain and transfer the cooked carrots to a bowl. Set aside.
2. Add the garlic and onion into the same pot, sauté over medium-low heat for 5 to 7 minutes, adding water, 1 tbsp. at a time, to prevent burning, until the onion is fully browned.
3. Turn the heat to medium-high. Add the paprika and tomato paste. Cook for 30 seconds to 1 minute, stirring continuously.
4. Add the coconut milk, diced tomatoes, thyme, and cooked carrots. Bring the liquid to a simmer. Cover and reduce the heat to medium-low. Cook for 10 minutes, stirring occasionally.
5. Blend the soup until smooth with an immersion blender. Alternatively, transfer the soup to a standard blender, working in batches as needed, and blend until smooth.
6. Thin with the vegetable broth or water as needed.

Nutrition Info per Serving:
Calories: 292, Protein: 6 g, Fat: 19 g, Carbohydrates: 28 g, Fiber: 7 g, Sugar: 8.6 g, Sodium: 366 mg

Bok Choy Stir-Fry

Prep Time: 10 minutes, Cook Time: 10 minutes, Serves: 2

INGREDIENTS:

2 potatoes, peeled and diced
2 cups bok choy, chopped
1 cup snow peas, trimmed
One (6-oz. 170g) can sliced water chestnuts, drained
¼ cup (60mL) plus 2 tbsps. Chinese Brown Sauce
¼ cup peanuts, toasted and chopped

DIRECTIONS:

1. Place the potatoes, bok choy, snow peas, and water chestnuts to a wok over high heat and stir-fry for 4 to 5 minutes.
2. Add water 1 to 2 tbsps. at a time to keep the vegetables from sticking to the pan. When the bok choy is crisp-tender, pour in the Chinese brown sauce and cook until thickened, about 3 minutes.
3. Serve garnished with the toasted peanuts.

Nutrition Info per Serving:
Calories: 189, Protein: 7.3 g, Fat: 8.7 g, Carbohydrates: 25.5 g, Fiber: 5.5 g, Sugar: 10.5 g, Sodium: 277 mg

Carrot, Spinach and Bean Soup

Prep Time: 10 minutes, Cook Time: 25 minutes, Serves: 4

INGREDIENTS:

½ cup barley
6 multicolored carrots, cut into 1-inch pieces
1 (15-ounce, 425 g) can diced tomatoes
4 cups no-sodium vegetable broth
2 garlic cloves, minced
2 cups water
¼ cup chopped fresh basil leaves, plus more for garnish
4 cups fresh spinach
2 tbsps. chopped fresh chives, plus more for garnish
1 tbsp. balsamic vinegar
1 (15-ounce, 425 g) can cannellini beans, rinsed and drained
Freshly ground black pepper

DIRECTIONS:

1. Combine the barley, carrots, tomatoes with their juices, vegetable broth, garlic and water in a large pot, bring to a simmer over medium heat. Cover the pot and cook for 10 minutes, or until the barley is chewy and not hard.
2. Place the basil, spinach, and chives on top of the water but do not stir. Cover the pot, reduce heat to low, and cook for 3 minutes to soften the leaves.
3. Stir the pot and add the vinegar and cannellini beans. Remove the pot from the heat and allow to sit for 5 minutes, covered. Garnish with the basil, chives, and a pinch of pepper and serve.

Nutrition Info per Serving:
Calories: 261, Protein: 12 g, Fat: 2 g, Carbohydrates: 50 g, Fiber: 14 g, Sugar: 5.8 g, Sodium: 772 mg

Curried Mixed Vegetable Soup

Prep Time: 15 minutes, Cook Time: 55 minutes, Serves: 6

INGREDIENTS:

1 cauliflower head, cut into florets
6 carrots, coarsely chopped
1 sweet potato, peeled and chopped
1 yellow onion, coarsely chopped
2 garlic cloves, minced
1 tbsp. water, plus more as needed
1 tsp. red pepper flakes
1 tbsp. minced peeled fresh ginger
6 cups no-sodium vegetable broth
1 (14-ounce, 397 g) can full-fat coconut milk
1 tbsp. freshly squeezed lemon juice
1 tbsp. yellow curry powder
2 tsps. ground turmeric
½ cup coarsely chopped fresh cilantro
Cayenne pepper, for seasoning
Pumpkin seeds, for serving

DIRECTIONS:

1. Preheat the oven to 450°F(235°C). Use parchment paper to line a baking sheet.
2. On the prepared baking sheet, evenly spread with the cauliflower, carrots and sweet potato.
3. Bake for 30 minutes. Flip the vegetables and bake for another 10 minutes, until lightly browned and fork-tender.
4. Combine the onion and garlic in an 8-quart pot, sauté over high heat for 2 to 3 minutes, adding water, 1 tbsp. at a time, to prevent burning, until the onion is translucent but not browned. Add the red pepper flakes and ginger, and cook for an additional 1 minute.
5. Pour in the vegetable broth and bring the soup to a boil.
6. Stir in the roasted vegetables and bring the soup to simmer. Cover and cook for 5 minutes.
7. Add the lemon juice, coconut milk, curry powder, and turmeric. Puree with an immersion blender until smooth. Stir in the cilantro.
8. Place a sprinkle of cayenne pepper and the pumpkin seeds on the top and serve.

Nutrition Info per Serving:
Calories: 213, Protein: 5 g, Fat: 13 g, Carbohydrates: 23 g, Fiber: 6 g, Sugar: 14.7 g, Sodium: 746 mg

Balsamic Glazed Strawberry and Avocado Toast

Prep Time: 5 minutes, Cook Time: 0, Serves: 4

INGREDIENTS:

1 avocado, peeled, pitted, and quartered
4 whole-wheat bread slices, toasted
4 ripe strawberries, cut into ¼-inch slices
1 tbsp. balsamic glaze or reduction

DIRECTIONS:

1. On a slice of toast, mash with one-quarter of the avocado.
2. Over the avocado, layer with one-quarter of the strawberry slices, and finish with a drizzle of balsamic glaze.
3. Repeat with the remaining ingredients, then serve.

Nutrition Info per Serving:
Calories: 150, Protein: 5 g, Fat: 8 g, Carbohydrates: 17 g, Fiber: 5 g, Sugar: 5.8 g, Sodium: 104 mg

Delicious Seitan Balls

Prep Time: 15 minutes, Cook Time: 6 hours, Serves: 6

INGREDIENTS:

1 tbsp. mushroom powder
1½ cups vital wheat gluten
½ cup chickpea flour
½ tsp. dried oregano
¼ tsp. garlic powder
½ tsp. onion powder
¼ tsp. ground ginger
¼ tsp. nutmeg
¼ tsp. ground sage
¼ tsp. ground cloves
½ tsp. salt
½ cup tomato sauce, divided
1 tsp. liquid smoke
1½ cups vegetable broth, divided

DIRECTIONS:

1. In a large bowl, add the mushroom powder, gluten, flour, oregano, garlic and onion powders, ginger, nutmeg, sage, cloves, and salt, mix well.
2. Add ¼ cup tomato sauce, ¼ cup water, liquid smoke, and ½ cup vegetable broth to a small bowl, stir to combined.
3. In the center of the dry ingredients, make a well, and pour in the tomato sauce mixture. Combine well and start to knead. Knead for 1 minute or until the dough becomes mildly elastic. You will see the dough slightly pull back as you are kneading and it will be a bit sticky. Pour remaining ¼ cup tomato sauce, 3 cups water and 1 cup vegetable broth into the slow cooker. Stir well.
4. Tear off small chunks of the dough, squeeze into a round shape, and drop into the liquid in the slow cooker. About forty-four balls. You can also make seventeen larger balls and cut them after cooking and cooling. Or make two logs and cut into desired shapes.
5. Cover the cooker and cook on low for 4 to 6 hours. They will grow in size as they cook. Check at 4 hours to see the texture is okay for you. They will become firmer as they sit in the refrigerator.
6. After cooking, remove from the pot and allow it to cool. Keep in the refrigerator for up to 5 days or freeze for up to 4 months.

Nutrition Info per Serving:
Calories: 164, Protein: 23.7 g, Fat: 1.2 g, Carbohydrates: 14.2 g, Fiber: 2.5 g, Sugar: 3.8 g, Sodium: 664 mg

Baked Spaghetti Squash with Bok Choy

Prep Time: 15 minutes, Cook Time: 1.5 hours, Serves: 4

INGREDIENTS:

2 small spaghetti squash (about 1 pound each), halved
Salt and freshly ground black pepper to taste
1 bunch bok choy, chopped
1 medium zucchini diced small
1 red bell pepper, seeded and diced small
4 cloves garlic, smashed and skin removed
2 tsps. ground nutmeg
2 tsps. ground thyme
½ tsp. allspice
½ tsp. crushed red pepper flakes
2 tbsps. almond milk

DIRECTIONS:

1. Preheat the oven to 350°F(180ºC).
2. Sprinkle the cut sides of the squash with salt and pepper. On a rimmed baking sheet, add the squash halves, cut side down. Pour in ½ cup of water to the pan and bake the squash for 45 to 55 minutes, or until soft (the squash is done when it can be easily pierced with a knife).
3. Meantime, in a large saucepan, add the zucchini, red pepper, and bok choy and sauté over medium heat for 5 minutes. Pour in water 1 to 2 tbsps. at a time to keep the vegetables from sticking to the pan. Whisk in the nutmeg, thyme, allspice, garlic, and crushed red pepper flakes and cook for 3 minutes. Whisk in the almond butter. Sprinkle with salt and pepper and cook to taste until the bok choy is wilted, about 5 minutes. Off heat and remove the pan.
4. When the squash is finished baking, scoop out the flesh (it should come away looking like noodles) and mix it into the warm bok choy mixture.

Nutrition Info per Serving:
Calories: 54, Protein: 2.3 g, Fat: 0.6 g, Carbohydrates: 9.8 g, Fiber: 2.2 g, Sugar: 4 g, Sodium: 260 mg

Miso-Glazed Winter Squash with Spinach

Prep Time: 10 minutes, Cook Time: 25 minutes, Serves: 4

INGREDIENTS:

1 large winter squash, peeled, halved, seeded, and cubed
6 cups packed baby spinach
1 batch Easy Miso Sauce

DIRECTIONS:

1. Preheat the oven to 375°F (190ºC).
2. Steam the squash in a steamer basket for 10 to 12 minutes. Place it in a large bowl and toss it with the miso sauce. Spread the squash mixture in a 9 × 13-inch baking dish and bake for 15 to 20 minutes.
3. While the squash bakes, steam the spinach in a large pot for 4 to 5 minutes.
4. Divide the spinach among 4 individual plates and top with the glazed squash. Serve.

Nutrition Info per Serving:
Calories: 50, Protein: 2 g, Fat: 0.3 g, Carbohydrates: 10.2 g, Fiber: 2.2 g, Sugar: 0.7 g, Sodium: 364 mg

Summer Vegetable Pesto Casserole

Prep Time: 15 minutes, Cook Time: 50 minutes, Serves: 8

INGREDIENTS:

2 large yellow onions, peeled and sliced into thin rings
2 large potatoes, cut into ½-inch rounds
2 large yellow squash, cut into ½-inch rounds
2 large tomatoes, cut into ¾-inch rounds
2 large zucchini, cut into ½-inch slices
1 batch Basil Pesto
Salt and freshly ground black pepper

DIRECTIONS:

1. Preheat the oven to 350°F (180ºC).
2. Put onions in a saucepan and sauté over medium heat for 10 minutes until the onions are browned. Add water 1 tbsp. at a time, as needed to keep the onions from sticking to the pan. Set aside.
3. Place the potatoes in a steamer basket and steam for 8 to 10 minutes, or until al dente. Season with salt and black pepper. Set aside.
4. Put a layer of zucchini in the bottom of a nonstick pan. Season with salt and pepper, and dollop with spoonfuls of the basil pesto. Add a layer of yellow squash, season with salt and pepper, and dollop with spoonfuls of the basil pesto. Add a layer of the steamed potatoes, and dollop with spoonfuls of the basil pesto. Repeat until the zucchini, yellow squash, and potatoes are used up. Top with the tomato slices, and then the caramelized onions. Season with salt and pepper again.
5. Bake the casserole for 30 minutes. Set aside for 10 minutes before serving.

Nutrition Info per Serving:
Calories: 94, Protein: 3.4 g, Fat: 0.4 g, Carbohydrates: 21 g, Fiber: 3.6 g, Sugar: 3.8 g, Sodium: 410 mg

Baked Spaghetti Squash with Radish Sauce

Prep Time: 15 minutes, Cook Time: 1 hour, Serves: 4

INGREDIENTS:

2 small spaghetti squash (about 1 pound each), halved
Salt and freshly ground black pepper to taste
2 medium potatoes, peeled and diced small
¼ cup tomato paste
1 cup cooked radishes, peeled and diced small
1 cup (240mL) Vegetable Stock, or low-sodium vegetable broth, plus more as needed
3 cloves garlic, smashed and skin removed
1 tsp. cinnamon
2 tsps. crushed red pepper flakes, or to taste
Chopped dill

DIRECTIONS:

1. Preheat the oven to 350°F (180ºC).
2. Sprinkle the cut sides of the squash with salt and pepper. On a baking sheet, add the squash halves, cut side down, and bake them for 45 to 55 minutes, or until the squash is very soft (it is done when it can be easily pierced with a knife).
3. Meantime, in a large saucepan, add the potatoes and sauté over medium heat for 5 minutes. Pour in water 1 to 2 tbsps. at a time to keep the potatoes from sticking to the pan. Whisk in the garlic, cinnamon, crushed red pepper flakes, tomato paste, and ½ cup of water and cook for 5 minutes. Stir in the radishes to the pan and cook until heated through. Sprinkle with additional salt. Puree the radishes mixture using a food processor until smooth and creamy. Pour in some of the vegetable stock, as needed, to make a creamy sauce.
4. To serve, scoop the flesh from the spaghetti squash (it should come away looking like noodles) and separate it among 4 plates. Top with some of the radish sauce and garnish with the dill.

Nutrition Info per Serving:
Calories: 109, Protein: 7.3 g, Fat: 0.7 g, Carbohydrates: 21.1 g, Fiber: 6.5 g, Sugar: 7 g, Sodium: 656 mg

Zucchini and Kale Wrap

Prep Time: 15 minutes, Cook Time: 6 minutes, Serves: 2

INGREDIENTS:
- 1 zucchini, ends removed, thinly sliced lengthwise
- ¼ tsp. freshly ground black pepper
- ½ tsp. dried oregano
- ¼ tsp. garlic powder
- ¼ cup hummus
- 2 whole wheat tortillas
- 1 cup chopped kale
- 2 Roma tomatoes, cut lengthwise into slices
- 2 tbsps. chopped red onion
- ½ tsp. ground cumin

DIRECTIONS:
1. Place the zucchini sliced in a skillet, cook over medium heat for 3 minutes per side. Sprinkle with the pepper, oregano, and garlic powder and remove from the heat.
2. On each tortilla, spread with 2 tbsps. of hummus. Then lay half the zucchini in the center of each tortilla. Place the kale, tomato slices, red onion, and ¼ tsp. of cumin on the top. Wrap tightly and enjoy.

Nutrition Info per Serving:
Calories: 247, Protein: 9 g, Fat: 8 g, Carbohydrates: 37 g, Fiber: 8 g, Sugar: 5.9 g, Sodium: 427 mg

Kidney Bean, Barley and Broccoli Bowl

Prep Time: 20 minutes, Cook Time: 50 minutes, Serves: 4

INGREDIENTS:
- 3 cups no-sodium vegetable broth
- 1 cup hulled barley, rinsed
- 2 cups broccoli florets, chopped small
- 1 (15-ounce, 425 g) can red kidney beans, drained and rinsed
- ½ recipe (2 cups) cheesy vegetable sauce

DIRECTIONS:
1. Add the vegetable broth and barley in an 8-quart pot, bring to a simmer over medium heat, cover and cook for 35 minutes, or until soft and chewy. Check the barley, if it still seems tough, cook for another 5 minutes before proceeding to the next step.
2. Stir the barley and vegetable broth. Add the broccoli on top of the barley but don't stir in. Cover and cook over medium-low heat for 3 to 5 minutes, until the broccoli is tender but not overcooked.
3. Add the red kidney beans and cheesy vegetable sauce. Gently fold to combine with a spatula, rather than stir, to avoid breaking the broccoli.
4. Uncovered and allow to sit for 5 minutes before serving.

Nutrition Info per Serving:
Calories: 478, Protein: 23 g, Fat: 12 g, Carbohydrates: 74 g, Fiber: 17 g, Sugar: 3.6 g, Sodium: 382 mg

Potato Samosa Chard Roll

Prep Time: 15 minutes, Cook Time: 45 minutes, Serves: 4 to 8

INGREDIENTS:
- 8 Swiss chard leaves
- Coriander Chutney
- **FOR THE POTATO SAMOSA FILLING:**
- 4 medium potatoes, peeled, cut into ½-inch dice, boiled, and rinsed until cool
- 1 medium yellow onion, peeled and diced small
- 2 tsps. black mustard seeds, toasted
- 1 tsp. coriander seeds, toasted and ground
- 1 tsp. garam masala
- 1 tsp. cumin seeds, toasted and ground
- 1 jalapeño pepper, seeded and minced
- 1 tbsp. grated ginger
- ¼ cup finely chopped cilantro
- 1 cup green peas
- Salt

DIRECTIONS:
TO PREPARE THE CHARD:
1. Prepare a large bowl with ice and cold water. Boil a pot of water, large enough to hold the chard leaves without bending them. Add the chard and blanch the leaves for 20 to 30 seconds, until they soften. Submerge the softened leaves in the ice water, then set aside.
TO MAKE THE POTATO SAMOSA FILLING:
2. Put the onion in a large saucepan and sauté over medium heat for 7 to 8 minutes. Add water 1 tbsp. at a time to keep the onion from sticking to the pan. Lower the heat to medium-low and add the ginger, mustard seeds, cumin, coriander, garam masala, jalapeño, and cilantro. Cook for 4 minutes, then remove from the heat. Add the peas and potatoes. Season with salt.
TO ASSEMBLE THE SAMOSAS:
3. Preheat the oven to 350°F (180ºC).
4. Put a chard leaf on a flat surface. Spoon some of the potato mixture in the middle of the chard leaf. Fold the large end of the chard over the potato, then fold in the sides and roll up like a cigar. Place in a baking dish. Repeat with the remaining chard leaves. Pour a little water over them and cover the dish with aluminum foil. Bake for 25 to 30 minutes. Serve with Coriander Chutney.

Nutrition Info per Serving:
Calories: 107, Protein: 3.8 g, Fat: 0.7 g, Carbohydrates: 23 g, Fiber: 3.9 g, Sugar: 2.6 g, Sodium: 459 mg

Garlicky Roasted Cauliflower and Potato Soup

Prep Time: 20 minutes, Cook Time: 30 minutes, Serves: 6

INGREDIENTS:
- 8 garlic cloves, peeled
- 1 large cauliflower head, cut into small florets
- 2 russet potatoes, peeled and chopped into 1-inch pieces
- 1 yellow onion, coarsely chopped
- 1 celery stalk, coarsely chopped
- 1 tbsp. water, plus more as needed
- 6 cups no-sodium vegetable broth
- 2 thyme sprigs
- 2 tsps. paprika
- ¼ tsp. freshly ground black pepper
- 1 tbsp. chopped fresh rosemary leaves

DIRECTIONS:
1. Preheat the oven to 450°F(235°C). Use parchment paper to line a baking sheet.
2. Use the aluminum foil to wrap the garlic cloves or place in a garlic roaster.
3. On the prepared baking sheet, evenly spread with the potatoes and cauliflower. Place the wrapped garlic on the baking sheet.
4. Roast for 15 to 20 minutes, or until the cauliflower is lightly browned.
5. Combine the onion and celery in an 8-quart pot, sauté over high heat for 4 to 5 minutes, adding water, 1 tbsp. at a time, to prevent burning, until the onion starts to brown.
6. Pour in the vegetable broth and bring the soup to a simmer.
7. Add the roasted vegetables and thyme, garlic, paprika, and pepper. Bring the soup to a simmer, cover and cook for 10 minutes.
8. Remove and discard the thyme. Puree the soup with an immersion blender until smooth. Add some water if the soup is too thick, to the desired consistency.
9. Stir in the rosemary and serve.

Nutrition Info per Serving:
Calories: 49, Protein: 5 g, Fat: 1 g, Carbohydrates: 5 g, Fiber: 5 g, Sugar: 0 g, Sodium: 584 mg

Orange-Glazed Tofu Bowl with Brown Rice

Prep Time: 15 minutes, Cook Time: 40 minutes, Serves: 4

INGREDIENTS:
FOR THE TOFU:
- 1 tsp. onion powder
- 1 tsp. garlic powder
- ¼ cup gluten-free or whole-wheat flour
- ½ tsp. freshly ground black pepper
- 1 (14-ounce, 397 g) package firm or extra-firm tofu, drained and cut into ¼-inch cubes

FOR THE ORANGE GLAZE:
- ½ cup orange juice, without pulp
- 1 tbsp. maple syrup
- 1 tbsp. cornstarch
- 1 tbsp. rice vinegar
- ½ tsp. onion powder
- ½ tsp. garlic powder

FOR THE BOWL:
- 6 cups cooked brown rice

DIRECTIONS:
TO MAKE THE TOFU:
1. Preheat the oven to 400°F(205°C). Use parchment paper to line a baking sheet.
2. Add the onion powder, garlic powder, flour, and pepper in a large bowl, whisk them together.
3. Add the tofu and toss until completely coated.
4. Put the coated tofu on the baking sheet and bake for 40 minutes, turning after 20 minutes.

TO MAKE THE ORANGE GLAZE:
1. Meanwhile, combine all of the ingredients of the orange glaze in a small saucepan. Bring to a boil over medium-high heat. Lower the heat to low, and simmer for 10 minutes. Remove from the heat and set aside to cool.

TO MAKE THE BOWL:
1. Take the tofu out from the oven and gently mix it with the orange glaze.
2. Place 1½ cups of cooked brown rice in each bowl, and put one-quarter of the orange-glazed tofu on the top and serve.

Nutrition Info per Serving:
Calories: 392, Protein: 15 g, Fat: 8 g, Carbohydrates: 65 g, Fiber: 3 g, Sugar: 8.6 g, Sodium: 579 mg

Mushroom Seitan Bourguignon

Prep Time: 30 minutes, Cook Time: 9 hours, Serves: 4

INGREDIENTS:
- 2 tbsps. extra virgin olive oil
- 1½ cups sliced carrots
- 1 cup diced yellow onion
- 2 tbsps. dairy-free butter, divided
- 2 cloves garlic, minced
- 2 tbsps. flour
- 2½ cups vegetable broth
- 2 tbsps. tomato paste
- 1 tbsp. liquid smoke
- 1 cup good Burgundy wine
- ½ tsp. thyme
- 1 bay leaf
- 1 tsp. salt
- 1 pound (454 g) mushrooms, sliced
- 2 cups Slow Cooker Versatile Seitan Balls, cubed

DIRECTIONS:
1. In a large skillet, heat the oil and then add the carrots and onion, sauté until the onions are translucent, about 10 to 15 minutes. Add 1 tbsp. butter and the garlic, cook for another minute.
2. Place the flour into the skillet, and stir to coat everything and cook for another minute. Make sure the flour has been worked all the way in and the mixture does not show any dry flour.
3. In the slow cooker, transfer all of the ingredients from the skillet. Add the broth, ½ cup water, tomato paste, liquid smoke, wine, thyme, bay leaf, and salt. Cook on low for 6 to 8 hours.
4. Cook until one hour left, about 10 to 15 minutes or, add a tbsp. of butter and the mushrooms, sauté for about 10 minutes. Then add the mushrooms and seitan to the slow cooker and cook for one hour.
5. Serve by itself or with potatoes, noodles, or rice.

Nutrition Info per Serving:
Calories: 286, Protein: 5.9 g, Fat: 16.2 g, Carbohydrates: 29.7 g, Fiber: 6.3 g, Sugar: 7.7 g, Sodium: 773 mg

Stuffed Poblano Peppers with Chipotle

Prep Time: 15 minutes, Cook Time: 25 minutes, Serves: 3

INGREDIENTS:
- 1 batch Spinach, Mushroom and Quinoa Pilaf
- 6 poblano peppers, roasted

FOR THE CHIPOTLE BLACK BEAN SAUCE:
- 2 cups cooked black beans, or one (15-ounce 425 g) can, drained and rinsed
- ½ medium yellow onion, peeled and diced small
- 2 cloves garlic, peeled and minced
- 1 tsp. cumin seeds, toasted and ground
- 1 chipotle pepper, halved, seeded, and soaked in warm water for 20 minutes
- Salt

DIRECTIONS:
1. Preheat the oven to 350°F (180ºC).
2. Cut the tops off the peppers and remove the cores and seeds. Fill each of the roasted poblano peppers with pilaf and put them in a baking dish. Bake for 15 minutes.

TO MAKE THE CHIPOTLE BLACK BEAN SAUCE:

3. Put the onion in a medium skillet and sauté over medium heat for 7 to 8 minutes. Add water 1 tbsp. at a time to keep the onion from sticking to the pan. Add the cumin and garlic, cook for 1 more minute.
4. Add the black beans and the chipotle pepper to a blender and process until smooth. Add the bean mixture to the pan with the onion mixture. Cook over low heat until warmed through, then season with salt and serve on the warm poblano peppers.

Nutrition Info per Serving:
Calories: 88, Protein: 4.2 g, Fat: 0.5 g, Carbohydrates: 16.5 g, Fiber: 3.5 g, Sugar: 5.9 g, Sodium: 785 mg

Chapter 5 Grain and Rice

Ethiopian Style Pilaf

Prep Time: 15 minutes, Cook Time: 15 minutes, Serves: 4

INGREDIENTS:
4 cups cooked wild rice blend
2 cups cooked adzuki beans, or one (15-ounce, 425 g) can, drained and rinsed
2 medium leeks (white and light green parts), diced and rinsed
4 green onions (white and green parts), thinly sliced
2 cloves garlic, peeled and minced
¾ tsp. Berbere Spice Blend
Zest of 1 orange
Salt and freshly ground black pepper

DIRECTIONS:
1. Put leeks in a large saucepan and sauté for 10 minutes over medium heat.
2. Add water 1 tbsp. at a time to keep the leeks from sticking to the pan. Add the garlic and cook for 2 minutes. Add the berbere spice and cook for 30 seconds.
3. Stir in the beans, wild rice, and orange zest and season with salt and pepper. Cook the mixture until heated through. Garnish with the green onions.

Nutrition Info per Serving:
Calories: 246, Protein: 8.9 g, Fat: 0.8 g, Carbohydrates: 51.1 g, Fiber: 5.9 g, Sugar: 6.3 g, Sodium: 516 mg

Date Pumpkin Bites

Prep Time: 10 minutes, Cook Time: 20 minutes, Serves: 12 bites

INGREDIENTS:
2 cups old-fashioned rolled oats
¾ cup (180mL) pumpkin purée
¾ cup (180mL) unsweetened applesauce
1 tsp. coconut oil (for greasing)
1½ tsps. nutmeg
½ cup coconut flakes
¾ cup dates, pitted and diced
¼ tsp. ground cloves
¼ cup chopped apricots

DIRECTIONS:
1. Preheat the oven to 350 °F (180ºC), and lightly coat a muffin tin with oil.
2. Process the oats in a blender until they turn into a flour.
3. Add the pumpkin purée, applesauce, nutmeg, cloves, apricots and coconut flakes.
4. Process until smooth.
5. Add the dates and stir by hand with a spoon.
6. Spoon the batter into the muffin tin, filling each cup halfway.
7. Bake in the preheated oven for 18 to 20 minutes. Test by sticking a toothpick in the middle of a muffin. If the toothpick comes out dry, the muffins are done.

Nutrition Info per Serving:
Calories: 99, Protein: 3.3 g, Fat: 2.7 g, Carbohydrates: 22.3 g, Fiber: 4.2 g, Sugar: 9.6 g, Sodium: 12 mg

Eggplant and Chickpea Pilaf

Prep Time: 15 minutes, Cook Time: 1 hour, Serves: 4

INGREDIENTS:
1 large eggplant, stemmed and cut into ½-inch cubes
2 cups cooked chickpeas, or one (15-ounce, 425 g) can, drained and rinsed
2 cups (480 ml) low-sodium vegetable broth
1 cup brown basmati rice
1 large yellow onion, peeled and diced small
6 cloves garlic, peeled and minced
2 jalapeño peppers, seeded and minced
1 tbsp. cumin seeds, toasted and ground
1 tbsp. ground coriander
1 tsp. turmeric
½ cup finely chopped cilantro
¼ cup finely chopped mint
½ cup finely chopped basil
Salt

DIRECTIONS:
1. Boil the vegetable stock in a medium saucepan. Add the rice and bring the mixture back to a boil over high heat. Lower the heat to medium and cook about 45 minutes, covered, until the rice is tender.
2. Put onion in a large saucepan and sauté over medium heat for 7 to 8 minutes. Add water 1 tbsp. at a time to keep the onion from sticking to the pan. Add the garlic, turmeric, cumin, jalapeño peppers, coriander, and eggplant and cook about 12 minutes until the eggplant is tender. Mix in the cooked rice, chickpeas, mint, and basil. Season with salt and serve garnished with the cilantro.

Nutrition Info per Serving:
Calories: 313, Protein: 11.6 g, Fat: 4 g, Carbohydrates: 61 g, Fiber: 8.9 g, Sugar: 12.4 g, Sodium: 671 mg

Mango Satay Tempeh

Prep Time: 10 minutes, Cook Time: 30 minutes, Serves: 4

INGREDIENTS:
1 cup (170 g) black beans, cooked or canned
½ cup (90 g) quinoa, dry
1 (14-oz, 400 g) pack tempeh, sliced
1 cup (260 g) peanut butter
1 cup (125 g) mango cubes

DIRECTIONS:
1. When using dry beans, soak and cook ⅓ cup (56 g) of dry black beans.
2. Blend the mango into a smooth puree using a food processor, and set it aside.
3. Put the tempeh slices and peanut butter in an airtight container.
4. Close the lid and shake well until the tempeh slices are evenly covered with the peanut butter.
5. Preheat the oven to 375°F(190°C) and line with parchment paper.
6. Transfer the peanut butter tempeh slices onto the baking sheet and bake for 15 minutes or until it is browned and crispy.
7. Divide the quinoa, mango puree, black beans and tempeh slices between two bowls, serve with the optional toppings.

Nutrition Info per Serving:
Calories: 732, Protein: 46.2 g, Fat: 42.2 g, Carbohydrates: 39 g, Fiber: 17.2 g, Sugar: 6.6 g, Sodium: 295 mg

Spiced Sorghum with Almond and Raspberry

Prep Time: 5 minutes, Cook Time: about 1 hour, Serves: 4

INGREDIENTS:
1 tsp. ground cinnamon
1 cup whole-grain sorghum
1 tsp. Chinese five-spice powder
3 cups water, plus more as needed
1 tsp. vanilla extract
1 cup plant-based milk
2 tbsps. pure maple syrup
¼ cup sliced almonds
1 tbsp. chia seeds
2 cups fresh raspberries, divided

DIRECTIONS:
1. Add the cinnamon, sorghum, five-spice powder, and water into a large pot, stir well and bring to a boil over medium-high heat. Cover and reduce the heat to medium-low. Cook for 1 hour, or until the sorghum is soft and chewy. If the sorghum grains are still hard, add another cup of water and cook for another 15 minutes.
2. Add the vanilla, milk, and maple syrup in a glass measuring cup, whisk together to blend. Add the mixture to the sorghum, along with the almonds, chia seeds, and 1 cup of raspberries. Stir gently to combine.
3. Top with the remaining 1 cup of fresh raspberries and serve.

Nutrition Info per Serving:
Calories: 319, Protein: 9 g, Fat: 8 g, Carbohydrates: 52 g, Fiber: 10 g, Sugar: 23.1 g, Sodium: 415 mg

Sweet Potato and Cauliflower Pilaf

Prep Time: 15 minutes, Cook Time: 1.5 hours, Serves: 4

INGREDIENTS:
3 to 3½ cups (720 ml-840 ml) low-sodium vegetable broth
1½ cups brown basmati rice
1 large cinnamon stick
½ small head cauliflower, cut into florets
2 cloves garlic, peeled and minced
2 whole cloves
2 cardamom pods
1 medium yellow onion, peeled and cut into ½-inch dice
1 medium carrot, peeled and cut into ½-inch dice
1 medium sweet potato, peeled and cut into ½-inch dice
1 cup peas, thawed if frozen
½ cup chopped cilantro
1 large pinch saffron, soaked in 3 tbsps. hot water
Salt

DIRECTIONS:
1. Boil 3 cups of the vegetable stock and add the rice, cloves, cinnamon stick, and cardamom pods. Bring the mixture back to a boil over high heat, then lower the heat to medium and cook, covered, about 45 minutes until the rice is tender. Check the rice for tenderness and add more stock, if needed. Remove the cloves, cinnamon stick, and cardamom pods before serving.
2. Place the onion in a large saucepan and sauté for 7 to 8 minutes over medium-high heat until the onion is tender and starting to brown. Add water 1 tbsp. at a time to keep the onion from sticking to the pan. Add the carrot and sweet potato and cook for 10 minutes. Put in cauliflower and garlic and cook 6 to 7 minutes more until the cauliflower is tender. Mix in the peas, cilantro, and saffron and its soaking liquid and season with salt. Combine the cooked rice with it.

Nutrition Info per Serving:
Calories: 291, Protein: 9.6 g, Fat: 10.2 g, Carbohydrates: 44.2 g, Fiber: 13.8 g, Sugar: 10.5 g, Sodium: 722 mg

Thai Red Curry Fried Rice

Prep Time: 15 minutes, Cook Time: 7 minutes, Serves: 2

INGREDIENTS:
- 2 cups cooked brown rice, fully cooled
- ½ medium yellow onion, peeled and cut into ½-inch strips
- 2 medium carrots, peeled and cut into matchsticks
- 2 cups shiitake mushrooms, trimmed and thinly sliced
- 4 tsps. Thai red curry paste
- ¼ cup slivered almonds, toasted, optional
- 4 green onions (white and green parts), chopped
- 2 large leeks (white and light green parts), thinly sliced and rinsed
- Salt and freshly ground black pepper

DIRECTIONS:
1. Heat a large skillet over high heat. Add the leeks, onion, mushrooms, and carrots and cook for 5 to 6 minutes, stirring frequently.
2. Add water 1 tbsp. at a time to keep the vegetables from sticking to the pan. Stir in the curry paste and cook for 30 seconds more. Add the green onions, almonds, and rice and cook until heated through. Season with salt and pepper.

Nutrition Info per Serving:
Calories: 390, Protein: 9.8 g, Fat: 3 g, Carbohydrates: 84.4 g, Fiber: 12.5 g, Sugar: 15 g, Sodium: 479 mg

Polenta with Seared Cranberry and Pear

Prep Time: 10 minutes, Cook Time: 50 minutes, Serves: 4

INGREDIENTS:
- 5¼ cups water, divided, plus more as needed
- 1½ cups coarse cornmeal
- 1 tbsp. molasses
- 3 tbsps. pure maple syrup
- 1 tsp. ground cinnamon
- 1 cup fresh cranberries
- 2 ripe pears, cored and diced
- 1 tsp. chopped fresh rosemary leaves

DIRECTIONS:
1. Bring 5 cups of water in an 8-quart pot over high heat to a simmer.
2. Slowly pour in the cornmeal and whisk continuously to avoid clumping. Cook for 30 minutes, use a heavy spoon to stir often. The polenta should be thick and creamy.
3. Meanwhile, add the molasses, maple syrup, the remaining ¼ cup of water, and the cinnamon into a saucepan, stir together well and bring to a simmer over medium heat. Add the cranberries and pears. Cook for 10 minutes, stirring occasionally, until the pears are tender and start to brown. Remove from the heat. Add the rosemary and stir well, allow the mixture to sit for 5 minutes. Add another ¼ cup of water and return to the heat if it is too thick.
4. Place the cranberry-pear mixture on the top and serve.

Nutrition Info per Serving:
Calories: 292, Protein: 4 g, Fat: 2 g, Carbohydrates: 65 g, Fiber: 12 g, Sugar: 16.8 g, Sodium: 89 mg

Lentils with Rice and Macaroni

Prep Time: 15 minutes, Cook Time: 2 hours, Serves: 6

INGREDIENTS:
- 1 cup green lentils, rinsed
- 1 cup medium-grain brown rice
- 3 large tomatoes, diced small
- 1 cup whole-grain elbow macaroni, cooked, drained, and kept warm
- 1 large onion, peeled and minced
- 4 cloves garlic, peeled and minced
- 1 tsp. ground cumin
- 1 tsp. ground coriander
- ½ tsp. ground allspice
- ½ tsp. crushed red pepper flakes
- 2 tbsps. tomato paste
- 1 tbsp. brown rice vinegar
- Salt

DIRECTIONS:
1. Add the lentils to a medium saucepan with 3 cups of water. Boil the pot over high heat, reduce the heat to medium, and cook, covered, for 40 to 45 minutes. Drain any excess water from the lentils, season with salt, and set aside.
2. Add the brown rice and 2 cups of water to another medium saucepan. Cover the pan with a lid and bring it to a boil over high heat. Lower the heat to medium and cook for 45 minutes.
3. Heat a large skillet over high heat. Put the onion in the skillet and sauté over medium heat for 15 minutes. Add water 1 tbsp. at a time to keep the onion from sticking to the pan. Add the garlic and cook for 3 to 4 minutes more. Put in the cumin, allspice, coriander, crushed red pepper flakes, and tomato paste and cook for 3 minutes longer. Add the fresh tomatoes and cook for 15 minutes over medium heat, or until the tomatoes start to break down. Season with salt.
4. Mix the lentils, cooked macaroni, rice, tomato mixture, and brown rice vinegar in a large bowl and serve.

Nutrition Info per Serving:
Calories: 203, Protein: 6.5 g, Fat: 1.5 g, Carbohydrates: 42.3 g, Fiber: 3.6 g, Sugar: 4.7 g, Sodium: 401 mg

Almond Noodles with Cauliflower

Prep Time: 15 minutes, Cook Time: 20 minutes, Serves: 2

INGREDIENTS:
- 8 oz. (230g) brown rice noodles
- 4 cups cauliflower florets (from about 2 large heads)
- ½ cup coconut yogurt
- 3 tbsps. almond butter
- 2 tbsps. apple cider
- 2 tbsps. low-sodium soy sauce
- 1 tbsp. ground fennel
- ½ tsp. crushed red pepper flakes

DIRECTIONS:
1. Pour 6 to 8 cups water in a medium pot and bring to a boil over medium-high heat. When boiling, add the rice noodles and cook following package instructions—usually 4 to 5 minutes, or until soft. Add the cauliflower florets to the cooking water and cook for a further minute. Drain the noodles and cauliflower and set aside.
2. Mix together the coconut yogurt, almond butter, apple cider, soy sauce, fennel, and crushed red pepper flakes in a large pot over low heat. Stir constantly and cook until smooth, 8 to 10 minutes.
3. Add the noodle and cauliflower mixture to the almond sauce. Use tongs to blend well.

Nutrition Info per Serving:
Calories: 299, Protein: 8.7 g, Fat: 5.3 g, Carbohydrates: 55.7 g, Fiber: 5.4 g, Sugar: 20.9 g, Sodium: 750 mg

Quinoa-Stuffed Tomatoes with Cheese and Avocado

Prep Time: 10 minutes, Cook Time: 50 minutes, Serves: 4

INGREDIENTS:
- 4 large tomatoes (about 2 pounds/910 g)
- 1 avocado, peeled and diced small
- 2 ears corn, shucked (about 1 cup)
- 2 cups cooked taro, or one (15-oz. 430g) can, drained and rinsed
- 2 cups cooked quinoa
- ½ red bell pepper, seeded and diced small
- 1 tsp. nutmeg
- 2 cloves garlic, smashed and skin removed
- Salt and freshly ground black pepper to taste
- ¾ cup Vegan Cheddar Cheese, cut into cubes

DIRECTIONS:
1. Preheat the oven to 350°F(180°C).
2. Cut the tops off of the tomatoes and scoop out the flesh, leaving a ½-inch wall. Set the tomatoes aside while you prepare the filling.
3. In a large saucepan, add the avocado and red pepper and sauté over medium heat for 10 minutes. Pour in water 1 to 2 tbsps. at a time to keep the avocado from sticking to the pan. Whisk in the garlic, nutmeg and cook for 2 minutes, then stir in the corn, taro, and cooked quinoa. Sprinkle with salt and pepper to taste and cook for 5 minutes. Off heat and remove the pan. Add the cheese to the pan and toss to combine well.
4. Divide the quinoa mixture evenly among the prepared tomatoes and arrange them in a baking dish. Cover the dish with aluminum foil and bake for 30 minutes.

Nutrition Info per Serving:
Calories: 191, Protein: 8.3 g, Fat: 2.6 g, Carbohydrates: 36.1 g, Fiber: 6.2 g, Sugar: 4 g, Sodium: 168 mg

Thai Rice Bowl with Peanut Sauce

Prep Time: 30 minutes, Cook Time: 45 minutes, Serves: 4

INGREDIENTS:
FOR THE PEANUT SAUCE:
- 2 tbsps. freshly squeezed lime juice
- 1 tbsp. packed lime zest
- 3 tbsps. creamy peanut butter
- 1 tbsp. grated peeled fresh ginger
- 2 garlic cloves, minced
- 1 tbsp. coconut aminos
- ½ tsp. red pepper flakes

FOR THE RICE BOWL:
- 1½ cups water
- ¾ cup brown rice
- 1 red bell pepper, cut into slices
- 1 small red cabbage, shredded
- 1 shallot, cut into slices
- 1 carrot, cut into matchsticks
- 1 yellow bell pepper, cut into slices
- 1 cup shelled edamame
- ¼ cup fresh cilantro, chopped
- 1 bunch chopped scallions, green parts only
- Juice of 1 lime

DIRECTIONS:
TO MAKE THE PEANUT SAUCE:
1. Combine all of the peanut sauce ingredients in a medium bowl, whisk them together. Set aside.
TO MAKE THE RICE BOWL:
2. Pour the water in a medium pot, bring to a boil over high heat. Stir in the brown rice. Bring to a simmer, reduce the heat to medium-low, cover and cook, undisturbed, for 35 to 40 minutes. Check the rice after 35 minutes to see if the water has been absorbed. Remove from the heat.
3. Place the brown rice in a large bowl, add the remaining ingredients and toss them together. Serve with a drizzle of peanut sauce.

Nutrition Info per Serving:
Calories: 323, Protein: 14 g, Fat: 9 g, Carbohydrates: 54 g, Fiber: 11 g, Sugar: 3.2 g, Sodium: 262 mg

Rice and Tofu Scramble

Prep Time: 15 minutes, Cook Time: 35 minutes, Serves: 2

INGREDIENTS:
- 4 cups (400 g) brown rice, cooked
- 1 cup (200 g) green peas, cooked or canned
- 1 (7-oz, 200 g) pack extra-firm tofu, scrambled
- 1 cup (50 g) carrots, julienned
- ¼ cup (40 g) curry spices
- 1 cup (240 ml) water

DIRECTIONS:
1. Cook 1½ cup of brown rice.
2. Heat a large non-stick frying pan over medium fire and add ½ cup of water and the tofu scramble.
3. Add the curry spices, cook for 5 minutes and stir occasionally to prevent the tofu from sticking to the pan, until well heated and most of the water has evaporated.
4. Add the carrots, rice, and green peas along with the remaining ½ cup water and stir-fry for another 5 minutes.
5. Turn off the heat, divide the fried rice between 2 bowls, serve with the optional toppings.

Nutrition Info per Serving:
Calories: 285, Protein: 18.1 g, Fat: 10.2 g, Carbohydrates: 30.2 g, Fiber: 8 g, Sugar: 5.5 g, Sodium: 254 mg

Chocolate Cherry Oats

Prep Time: 5 minutes, Cook Time: 5 minutes, Serves: 2

INGREDIENTS:
- ½ cup (110 g) cherries
- 2 tangerines
- 1 cup (90 g) instant oats
- 1 scoop (30 g) soy protein isolate (chocolate flavor)
- ¼ cup (25 g) almond flakes
- 2 cups (480 ml) water

DIRECTIONS:
1. Add water and oats to the saucepan and heat it over medium fire.
2. Bring the mixture to a boil and cook for about 5 minutes.
3. Turn the heat off and add the soy isolate while stirring thoroughly until all well mixed.
4. Peel and section the tangerines.
5. Transfer the protein oats to a bowl, then garnish with almond flakes, cherries and tangerines.
6. Serve the oats bowl warm with the optional toppings.

Nutrition Info per Serving:
Calories: 349, Protein: 22.4 g, Fat: 9.3 g, Carbohydrates: 44 g, Fiber: 6.9 g, Sugar: 11.2 g, Sodium: 169 mg

Peanut Butter, Banana and Cacao Quinoa

Prep Time: 5 minutes, Cook Time: 10 minutes, Serves: 2

INGREDIENTS:
- 1 cup plant-based milk, plus more for serving
- ⅔ cup quinoa flakes
- 1 cup water
- 2 tbsps. natural creamy peanut butter
- ¼ cup raw cacao powder
- ¼ tsp. ground cinnamon
- 2 bananas, mashed
- Fresh berries of choice, for serving
- Chopped nuts of choice, for serving

DIRECTIONS:
1. Add the milk, quinoa flakes, water, peanut butter, cacao powder and cinnamon into a 6-quart pot, stir together well and cook over medium-high heat, stirring, until the mixture begins to simmer. Reduce the heat to medium-low and cook for 3 to 5 minutes, stirring frequently.
2. Add the bananas, stir well and cook until hot.
3. Top with the nuts, fresh berries, and a splash of milk and serve.

Nutrition Info per Serving:
Calories: 471, Protein: 18 g, Fat: 16 g, Carbohydrates: 69 g, Fiber: 16 g, Sugar: 18.3 g, Sodium: 137 mg

Seedy Buckwheat Porridge

Prep Time: 5 minutes, Cook Time: 25 minutes, Serves: 4

INGREDIENTS:
- 3 cups water
- 1 tsp. ground cinnamon
- 1 cup raw buckwheat groats
- 1 banana, sliced
- ¼ cup dried currants
- ¼ cup golden raisins
- 2 tbsps. chia seeds
- 1 tbsp. hemp seeds
- ¼ cup sunflower seeds
- 1 tbsp. sesame seeds, toasted
- 1 tbsp. pure maple syrup
- ½ cup plant-based milk
- 1 tsp. vanilla extract

DIRECTIONS:
1. Fill the water in an 8-quart pot, bring to a boil over high heat. Stir in the cinnamon, buckwheat, and banana. Bring the mixture to a boil, stirring, then lower the heat to medium-low. Cover the pot and cook for 15 minutes, or until the buckwheat is tender. Remove from the heat.
2. Stir in the remaining ingredients. Cover the pot and allow to sit for 10 minutes before serving.
3. Serve as is or top with your favorite toppings.

Nutrition Info per Serving:
Calories: 383, Protein: 10 g, Fat: 11 g, Carbohydrates: 61 g, Fiber: 10 g, Sugar: 10.5 g, Sodium: 124 mg

Fried Rice with Red Pepper and Asparagus, page 66

Fried Rice with Pineapple, page 68

Cornmeal Polenta with Mushrooms, page 67

Rice and Tofu Scramble, page 64

Chapter 5 Grain and Rice 65

Rice and Vegetable Stir-Fry

Prep Time: 5 minutes, Cook Time: 15 minutes, Serves: 4

INGREDIENTS:
2 cups green beans (fresh or frozen)
2 cups green peas (fresh or frozen)
¼ cup vegetable broth or water
1 tsp. onion powder
1 tsp. garlic powder
4 cups brown rice, cooked

DIRECTIONS:
1. Heat a medium saucepan over medium heat.
2. Add all of the ingredients except the rice into the pan, and stir well. Cover and cook for 8 minutes, stirring every few minutes, or until crisp-tender. (Stir in a few more tbsps. of vegetable broth or water, if any of the vegetables begin sticking.)
3. Uncover, and add the cooked brown rice and stir well. Cook for another 5 minutes, stirring every other minute, and serve.

Nutrition Info per Serving:
Calories: 223, Protein: 8 g, Fat: 2 g, Carbohydrates: 48 g, Fiber: 7 g, Sugar: 0.4 g, Sodium: 372 mg

Fried Rice with Red Pepper and Asparagus

Prep Time: 15 minutes, Cook Time: 6 minutes, Serves: 2

INGREDIENTS:
½ pound (227 g) asparagus, trimmed and cut into 1-inch pieces
½ medium yellow onion, peeled and thinly sliced
½ medium red bell pepper, seeded and julienned
3 cups cooked brown rice, fully cooled
¼ cup (60 ml) Chinese Brown Sauce
Zest and juice of 1 lemon
3 tbsps. minced jalapeño pepper

DIRECTIONS:
1. Heat a large skillet over high heat. Add the onion, asparagus, and red pepper and cook for 4 to 5 minutes, stirring frequently.
2. Add water 1 tbsp. at a time to keep the vegetables from sticking to the pan. Put in the Chinese brown sauce, lemon zest and juice, and jalapeño pepper, cook for one more minute. Add the brown rice and cook until heated through.

Nutrition Info per Serving:
Calories: 400, Protein: 12.1 g, Fat: 3 g, Carbohydrates: 84.5 g, Fiber: 10.5 g, Sugar: 10.5 g, Sodium: 746 mg

Apple Cinnamon Oats

Prep Time: 5 minutes, Cook Time: 5 minutes, Serves: 2

INGREDIENTS:
1 green apple, peeled, cored
1 cup (90 g) Instant oats
1 scoop (25 g) soy protein isolate (chocolate flavor)
¼ cup (40 g) raisins
1 tbsp. cinnamon
2 cups (480 ml) water

DIRECTIONS:
1. Cut the cored and peeled apple into tiny pieces and put them to a saucepan.
2. Add water and oats to the saucepan and heat over medium heat.
3. Bring the mixture to a boil and cook it for 5 minutes.
4. Turn the heat off, add the soy isolate, cinnamon and raisins, then stir thoroughly until everything is well mixed.
5. Serve warm with the optional topping.

Nutrition Info per Serving:
Calories: 386, Protein: 28 g, Fat: 4.2 g, Carbohydrates: 63.7 g, Fiber: 10.2 g, Sugar: 23 g, Sodium: 73 mg

Black Bean and Quinoa Bowl

Prep Time: 15 minutes, Cook Time: 30 minutes, Serves: 4

INGREDIENTS:
2 cups no-sodium vegetable broth
1 cup dried tricolor quinoa, rinsed
½ cup diced pineapple (fresh or canned in juice, not syrup)
2 cups kale, finely chopped
1 (15-ounce, 425 g) can black beans, drained and rinsed
2 scallions, coarsely chopped
½ cup mango salsa

DIRECTIONS:
1. Pour the vegetable broth in an 8-quart pot, bring to a simmer over medium heat. Stir in the quinoa. Lower the heat to medium-low, cover and cook for 15 minutes.
2. Turn off the heat and use a fork or spoon to fluff the quinoa while adding the pineapple.
3. Place the kale over the quinoa but don't stir it in. Cover the pot and allow to sit for 10 minutes.
4. Stir the kale into the quinoa and serve in bowls with the black beans, place the scallions and mango salsa on the top.

Nutrition Info per Serving:
Calories: 308, Protein: 13 g, Fat: 3 g, Carbohydrates: 58 g, Fiber: 12 g, Sugar: 5.1 g, Sodium: 367 mg

Maple Protein Oatmeal with Almond

Prep Time: 5 minutes, Cook Time: 30 minutes, Serves: 2

INGREDIENTS:
3 tbsps. raw shelled hempseed, divided
1 cup steel-cut oats
3 tbsps. maple syrup
2 tsps. cinnamon
1 tbsp. currants
1 tbsp. slivered almonds

DIRECTIONS:
1. In a large saucepan, pour in 4 cups of water, and bring to a boil. Add 2 tbsps. hempseed, the steel-cut oatmeal, maple syrup, and cinnamon and again bring to a boil. Reduce heat to low, uncovered and cook for 30 minutes, stirring occasionally.
2. Serve in bowls, garnished with currants, almond slivers, and the remaining hempseed.

Nutrition Info per Serving:
Calories: 345, Protein: 10.5 g, Fat: 8.8 g, Carbohydrates: 55.9 g, Fiber: 1.9 g, Sugar: 2.9 g, Sodium: 306 mg

Spiced Corn and Yam

Prep Time: 15 minutes, Cook Time: 20 minutes, Serves: 4

INGREDIENTS:
3 medium white yams, cut into ½-inch dice (about 2 cups)
1 cup ears for fresh corn, shucked
¾ tsp. nutmeg
¼ tsp. ground turmeric
¼ tsp. garam masala
1 tsp. ground coriander
½ tsp. ground tarragon
½ tsp. salt
1 tbsp. peanut butter
½ tbsp. finely chopped sage

DIRECTIONS:
1. In a double boiler or steamer basket, steam the yams it for 5 to 7 minutes, or until soft. Set aside.
2. Bring 1 cup of water in a small saucepan to a boil, whisk in the peas, and simmer for 5 to 10 minutes, until the peas are tender. Drain and set aside.
3. Add the nutmeg, white yams, corn, turmeric, garam masala, coriander, tarragon, and salt in a large skillet over medium heat. Pour in 2 tbsps. of water, and toss to combine well, and cook for another 2 to 3 minutes, or until the water has evaporated. Pour in the peanut butter and whisk to combine well. Serve garnished with the sage.

Nutrition Info per Serving:
Calories: 118, Protein: 2.3 g, Fat: 0.5 g, Carbohydrates: 24.4 g, Fiber: 4.5 g, Sugar: 1.1 g, Sodium: 359 mg

Black Bean and Rice Lettuce Wraps

Prep Time: 5 minutes, Cook Time: 0, Serves: 6

INGREDIENTS:
1 large head romaine lettuce, leaves separated
1 batch Black Beans and Rice
1 batch low fat guacamole

DIRECTIONS:
1. Place some of the black beans and rice into the center of lettuce leaf.
2. Top with some guacamole. Fold the leaf in from the sides and roll it up like a cigar.
3. Repeat for remaining lettuce leaves until the beans and rice and guacamole are used up.

Nutrition Info per Serving:
Calories: 146, Protein: 8.4 g, Fat: 2.3 g, Carbohydrates: 24.8 g, Fiber: 7.2 g, Sugar: 2.9 g, Sodium: 311 mg

Cornmeal Polenta with Mushrooms

Prep Time: 30 minutes, Cook Time: 15 minutes, Serves: 4 to 6

INGREDIENTS:
1 batch Basic Polenta, kept warm
1 ounce (28 g) porcini mushrooms, soaked for 30 minutes in 1 cup of water that has just been boiled, and coarsely chopped
1 shallot, peeled and minced
2 cloves garlic, peeled and minced
1 pound (454 g) wild mushrooms, thinly sliced
Chopped parsley
Salt and freshly ground black pepper

DIRECTIONS:
1. Put the shallot and garlic in a large saucepan and sauté for 5 minutes over a medium-low heat. Add water 1 tbsp. at a time to keep the vegetables from sticking to the pan. Add the porcini mushrooms and their soaking liquid and the wild mushrooms. Cook until the mushrooms about 10 minutes are tender. Season with salt and pepper.
2. Divide the polenta among 4 individual plates. Top with some of the mushrooms and garnish with parsley. Serve.

Nutrition Info per Serving:
Calories: 135, Protein: 4.9 g, Fat: 1.8 g, Carbohydrates: 27.5 g, Fiber: 4.6 g, Sugar: 2.4 g, Sodium: 418 mg

Fried Rice with Pineapple

Prep Time: 15 minutes, Cook Time: 6 minutes, Serves: 4

INGREDIENTS:

Two (8-ounce, 227 g) cans pineapple chunks, drained (about 1½ cups)
4 cups cooked brown rice, fully cooled
1 medium yellow onion, peeled and thinly sliced
1 serrano chile, sliced into thin rings
4 cloves garlic, peeled and minced
½ cup Chinese Brown Sauce
½ cup cooked peas, thawed if frozen
½ cup cashews, toasted
½ cup cilantro, chopped

DIRECTIONS:
1. Heat a large skillet over high heat.
2. Put in onion and chile and stir-fry for 4 to 5 minutes.
3. Add water 1 tbsp. at a time to keep the vegetables from sticking to the pan.
4. Mix in garlic and cook for 30 seconds, stirring constantly. Add the Chinese brown sauce and cook for 30 seconds.
5. Combine the rice, peas, pineapple, cilantro and cashews, cook until heated through.

Nutrition Info per Serving:
Calories: 389, Protein: 8.7 g, Fat: 9.8 g, Carbohydrates: 66.6 g, Fiber: 5.5 g, Sugar: 15 g, Sodium: 244 mg

Cinnamon Spiced Carrot Oatmeal Bowl with Pecans

Prep Time: 10 minutes, Cook Time: 15 minutes, Serves: 2

INGREDIENTS:

¼ cup pecans
½ cup old-fashioned oats
1 cup finely shredded carrot
1¼ cups plant-based milk
1 tbsp. pure maple syrup
1 tsp. ground ginger
1 tsp. ground cinnamon
¼ tsp. ground nutmeg
2 tbsps. chia seeds

DIRECTIONS:
1. Add the pecans in a small skillet, toast them over medium-high heat for 3 to 4 minutes, stirring often, until browned and fragrant (watch closely, as they can burn quickly). Pour the pecans onto a cutting board and chop them coarsely. Set aside.
2. Combine the oats, carrot, milk, maple syrup, ginger, cinnamon, and nutmeg in an 8-quart pot, bring to a boil over medium-high heat, then reduce the heat to medium-low. Uncovered and cook for 10 minutes, stirring occasionally.
3. Add the chia seeds and chopped pecans, stir well and serve immediately.

Nutrition Info per Serving:
Calories: 327, Protein: 7 g, Fat: 17 g, Carbohydrates: 35 g, Fiber: 11 g, Sugar: 8.5 g, Sodium: 524 mg

Basic Cornmeal Polenta

Prep Time: 5 minutes, Cook Time: 30 minutes, Serves: 4 to 6

INGREDIENTS:

1½ cups coarse cornmeal
¾ tsp. salt

DIRECTIONS:
1. Boil 5 cups of water in a large saucepan.
2. Whisk in the cornmeal, a little at a time. Cook about 30 minutes, stirring often, until the mixture is thick and creamy. Season with salt and serve.

Nutrition Info per Serving:
Calories: 30, Protein: 2.8 g, Fat: 0.7 g, Carbohydrates: 3.2 g, Fiber: 1.5 g, Sugar: 0.6 g, Sodium: 293 mg

Raspberry Wheat Berry Salad

Prep Time: 10 minutes, Cook Time: 1¾ hours, Serves: 4

INGREDIENTS:

2½ cups wheat berries, soaked overnight
¼ cup (60mL) plus 2 tbsps. maple syrup
¼ cup (60mL) peanut milk
2 avocado, peeled, seeded and diced
½ cup chopped tarragon
1 cooked taro
½ cup fruit-sweetened dried raspberries
2 tbsps. minced parsley
Salt and freshly ground black pepper to taste

DIRECTIONS:
1. Pour 5 cups water to a medium saucepan and bring to a boil, and stir in the wheat berries. Return to a boil over high heat, lower the heat to medium, cover, and cook until the wheat berries are softened, about 1¾ hours. Drain off the excess water from the pan and rinse the berries until cool.
2. Whisk all the other ingredients in a large bowl. Put in the cooled wheat berries and toss to blend. Chill for 1 hour before serving.

Nutrition Info per Serving:
Calories: 507, Protein: 17.4 g, Fat: 3.2 g, Carbohydrates: 100.8 g, Fiber: 3.1 g, Sugar: 28.9 g, Sodium: 47 mg

Macaroni and Soy Mince

Prep Time: 20 minutes, Cook Time: 10 minutes, Serves: 4

INGREDIENTS:

2 cups (200 g) whole wheat macaroni
7-oz (200 g) pack textured soy mince
½ cup (120 g) tahini
¼ cup (40 g) nutritional yeast
2 tbsps. lemon garlic pepper seasoning
½ cup (120 ml) water

DIRECTIONS:

1. Cook the macaroni and set it aside afterwards.
2. Add the soy mince with the ¼ cup of water in a non-stick deep frying pan with medium high heat.
3. Stir fry the soy mince until it is cooked and most of the water has evaporated.
4. Add the tahini, ¼ cup of water, nutritional yeast, lemon garlic pepper seasoning to the soy mince.
5. Cook a little longer and stir continuously, until all is well mixed.
6. Add the cooked macaroni to the pan with soy mince and stir thoroughly until well mixed.
7. Divide it between two plates, serve with the optional toppings.

Nutrition Info per Serving:
Calories: 454, Protein: 25 g, Fat: 19.9 g, Carbohydrates: 42 g, Fiber: 9.7 g, Sugar: 2.4 g, Sodium: 311 mg

Lentils with Rice and Onions

Prep Time: 15 minutes, Cook Time: 2 hours, Serves: 4

INGREDIENTS:

1½ cups green lentils, rinsed
¾ cup brown basmati rice
3 large yellow onions, peeled and diced
¾ tsp. ground cinnamon
½ tsp. ground allspice
Salt and freshly ground black pepper

DIRECTIONS:

1. Add the lentils to a large pot with 5 cups of water and boil over high heat. Lower the heat to medium and simmer for 30 minutes. Add the cinnamon and allspice and cook for another 15 to 20 minutes.
2. In another medium saucepan, bring 1½ cups of water to a boil. Add the rice and bring the pot to a boil over high heat. Reduce the heat to medium and cook the rice, covered, for 45 minutes.
3. Heat a large skillet over high heat. Add the onions and cook, stirring frequently, for 10 minutes. Add water 1 tbsp. at a time to keep the onions from sticking to the pan. Lower the heat to medium-low and continue cooking about 10 minutes. Add the lentils and rice to the onions and mix well. Season with salt and pepper.

Nutrition Info per Serving:
Calories: 169, Protein: 6.9 g, Fat: 4.9 g, Carbohydrates: 28.8 g, Fiber: 7.4 g, Sugar: 5 g, Sodium: 429 mg

Quinoa, Celery and Cherry Potatoes

Prep Time: 5 minutes, Cook Time: 20 minutes, Serves: 4

INGREDIENTS:

1 cup cherry potatoes, cut in half
1 cup celery, diced
2 cups cooked quinoa
2 tbsps. olive oil
1 lime zest
Sea salt and freshly ground pepper

DIRECTIONS:

1. Heat the olive oil in a large skillet.
2. Add the potatoes and cook until softened and golden brown. Add the celery and cook until soft, about 3 minutes.
3. Off heat and sprinkle with the quinoa and lime zest. Season with salt and pepper. To serve.

Nutrition Info per Serving:
Calories: 206, Protein: 5.3 g, Fat: 8.7 g, Carbohydrates: 27.7 g, Fiber: 3.9 g, Sugar: 1.4 g, Sodium: 12 mg

Overnight Oats

Prep Time: 10 minutes, Cook Time: 0 (chill over night), Serves: 4

INGREDIENTS:

2 cups old-fashioned oats
3½ cups unsweetened almond milk
2 tbsps. chia seeds
2 tbsps. unsweetened shredded coconut
¼ cup maple syrup
¼ cup sunflower seed kernels
4 tbsps. peanut butter, divided
Sunflower seed kernels, for garnish (optional)

DIRECTIONS:

1. In a large bowl, combine all of the ingredients except for 2 tbsps. of the peanut butter and the sunflower seeds. Mix well. Cover and place in the refrigerator to set overnight.
2. In the next morning, dot the remaining 2 tbsps. peanut butter around the inside of two bowls and fill each with the overnight oats. Garnish with sunflower seeds, if desired, and serve.

Nutrition Info per Serving:
Calories: 556, Protein: 17.8 g, Fat: 19 g, Carbohydrates: 78.4 g, Fiber: 12.7 g, Sugar: 35.6 g, Sodium: 360 mg

Chapter 6 Bean and Legumes 71

Chapter 6 Bean and Legumes

Cajun Burgers

Prep Time: 25 minutes, Cook Time: 5 minutes, Serves: 4

INGREDIENTS:
1 cup (170 g) black beans, cooked or canned
1 (7-oz, 200 g) pack textured soy mince
1 cup (180 g) tomato cubes, canned or fresh
¼ cup (40 g) salt-free Cajun spices
4 whole wheat buns

DIRECTIONS:
1. When using dry beans, soak and cook ⅓ cup (56 g) of dry black beans.
2. Add the soy mince, and the tomato cubes to a non-stick deep frying pan over medium high heat.
3. Let it cook and stir for about 3 minutes, until everything is cooked.
4. Add the black beans and Cajun spices and cook for another 2 minutes while stirring.
5. Turn off the heat and put the bottom halves of the buns on 2 plates.
6. Transfer a quarter of the Cajun mixture onto each of the bun halves and add the optional toppings.
7. Cover each burger with the other bun half, serve right away.

Nutrition Info per Serving:
Calories: 134, Protein: 14.7 g, Fat: 0.7 g, Carbohydrates: 15.8 g, Fiber: 7.2 g, Sugar: 1.4 g, Sodium: 471 mg

Baked Pinto Beans Taquitos

Prep Time: 5 minutes, Cook Time: 25 minutes, Serves: 4

INGREDIENTS:
2 cups pinto beans, cooked
1 tsp. ground cumin
1 tsp. chili powder
½ tsp. onion powder
½ tsp. garlic powder
¼ tsp. red pepper flakes
12 corn tortillas

DIRECTIONS:
1. Preheat the oven to 400°F(205°C). Use the parchment paper to line a baking sheet.
2. In a food processor or blender, add all of the ingredients except the tortillas. Pulse or blend on low for 30 seconds, or until smooth, then set aside.
3. On a baking sheet, place with the tortillas, and bake for 1 to 2 minutes. To soften the tortillas and makes rolling them much easier.
4. Take the tortillas out from the oven, then place a couple of heaping tbsps. of the refried beans onto the bottom half of each corn tortilla. Tightly roll the tortillas, and return them on the baking sheet, seam-side down.
5. Bake for 20 minutes, turning once after about 10 minutes, and serve warm.

Nutrition Info per Serving:
Calories: 299, Protein: 12 g, Fat: 3 g, Carbohydrates: 56 g, Fiber: 13 g, Sugar: 0.9 g, Sodium: 282 mg

Chickpea Rolls

Prep Time: 10 minutes, Cook Time: 25 minutes, Serves: 4

INGREDIENTS:
5 cups (1000 g) chickpeas, cooked or canned
¼ cup (60 ml) full-fat coconut milk
¼ cup (40 g) Ras El Hanout

DIRECTIONS:
1. When using dry chickpeas, soak and cook 1½ cup (330 g) of dry chickpeas.
2. Preheat the oven to 350°F(175°C) and line with parchment paper.
3. Add the chickpeas and spices to the food processor and blend. Pour it in the coconut milk to form a chunky mixture.
Or mash the chickpeas and spices together in a large bowl, then add the coconut milk and knead everything into a chunky mixture.
4. Grab a handful of chickpea mixture and knead into a log shape, about 10cm long and 5cm thick.
5. Repeat with the remaining mixture until you have 16 rolls in total.
6. Place the chickpea rolls on the baking sheet, then bake for 15 minutes.
7. Take the baking sheet out of the oven, flip thr rolls and bake for another 10 minutes.
8. Take the rolls out of the oven once they're browned and crispy on the outside.
9. Let them cool down for about a minute. Serve the rolls with the optional toppings.

Nutrition Info per Serving:
Calories: 500, Protein: 24 g, Fat: 10.3 g, Carbohydrates: 75.3 g, Fiber: 21.5 g, Sugar: 13.2 g, Sodium: 692 mg

Black Bean and Mushroom Stew

Prep Time: 15 minutes, Cook Time: 26 minutes, Serves: 4

INGREDIENTS:
2 medium potatoes diced
1 pound (450 g) cremini mushrooms, halved
One (14-oz. 400g) can tomatoes, diced
4 cups cooked black beans, or two (15-oz. 430g) cans, drained and rinsed
¼ cup sage, minced
1 tbsp. thyme, minced
2 tsps. ground cinnamon
2 sprigs rosemary
5 cloves garlic, smashed and skin removed
Salt and freshly ground black pepper to taste

DIRECTIONS:
1. In a large saucepan, add the potatoes and mushrooms and sauté over medium heat for 10 minutes.
2. Pour in water 1 to 2 tbsps. at a time to keep the vegetables from sticking to the pan. Stir in the garlic and cook for 1 minute.
3. Whisk in the tomatoes, sage, thyme, cinnamon, rosemary, and beans and bring the pot to a boil over high heat.
4. Lower the heat to medium and cook, covered, for 15 minutes. Sprinkle with salt and pepper to taste.

Nutrition Info per Serving:
Calories: 336, Protein: 20 g, Fat: 1.9 g, Carbohydrates: 59.3 g, Fiber: 23 g, Sugar: 6.7 g, Sodium: 522 mg

Split Pea Burgers

Prep Time: 5 minutes, Cook Time: 25 minutes, Serves: 8

INGREDIENTS:
3 cups (600 g) split peas
1 (14-oz, 400 g) pack tempeh
½ cup (125 ml) full-fat coconut milk
3 tbsps. ground flaxseeds
3 tbsps. burger spices

DIRECTIONS:
1. When using dry split peas, soak and cook 1 cup (200 g) of dry split peas.
2. Preheat the oven to 350°F(175°C) and line with parchment paper.
3. Put the tempeh to a food processor and blend into a chunky mixture, scraping down the sides to prevent any lumps if necessary.
4. Combine the split peas, ground flaxseed and spices in the food processor and slowly process it along with the tempeh and coconut milk to form a chunky mixture. Alternatively, crumble the tempeh by hand in a large bowl, add all ingredients and mash them into a chunky mixture.
5. Put all of the mixture on the baking sheet, and flatten it into a 1-inch thick square. Cut the square into 8 patties before baking.
6. Bake the patties for about 15 minutes. Then take the baking sheet out of the oven, flip the patties and bake for another 10 minutes.
7. Take the patties out of the oven once the crust is crispy and browned. Cool down for about a minute.
8. Serve the patties with the optional toppings and whole wheat buns.

Nutrition Info per Serving:
Calories: 236, Protein: 18.3 g, Fat: 9.5 g, Carbohydrates: 18 g, Fiber: 10 g, Sugar: 2.2 g, Sodium: 417 mg

Black Bean, Tomato, Rice and Lentil Burritos

Prep Time: 15 minutes, Cook Time: 8 hours, Serves: 6

INGREDIENTS:
2 (15-ounce, 425 g) cans black beans, drained and rinsed
¼ cup salsa
2 (15-ounce, 425 g) cans diced tomatoes
½ cup corn, fresh, frozen, or canned
1 cup brown rice
2 tbsps. taco seasoning
2 chipotle peppers in adobo sauce, finely chopped
1 tsp. ground cumin
1 tsp. salt
2½ cups vegetable broth
½ cup lentils
12 whole wheat tortillas
Additional toppings, such as more salsa, avocado or guacamole, and black olives

DIRECTIONS:
1. In a slow cooker, combine the beans, salsa, tomatoes, corn, rice, taco seasoning, chipotles, cumin, salt, and broth. Cover and cook on low for 6 to 8 hours or on high for 3 to 4 hours.
2. Cook until 40 minutes left, add the lentils. Continue cooking until the lentils are tender. The rice will be tender and most of the liquid will be absorbed. This is the filling.
3. Lay out the tortillas and place about ⅓ to ½ cup of the filling on each tortilla. Spread the filling down through the center of the tortilla. Fold each end about 1½ inches over the point edge of the beans. And roll up the tortilla along the long edge.
4. Stack up and serve with more avocado, salsa or guacamole, and black olives.

Nutrition Info per Serving:
Calories: 543, Protein: 19.4 g, Fat: 10.4 g, Carbohydrates: 85 g, Fiber: 18 g, Sugar: 5.7 g, Sodium: 834 mg

Edamame and Rice

Prep Time: 15 minutes, Cook Time: 20 minutes, Serves: 4

INGREDIENTS:
2 potatoes, peeled and diced
4 cups edamame
3 cups (700mL) cooked brown rice
1 cup chopped tarragon
1 lime, quartered
1 red bell pepper, seeded and diced
2 jalapeño peppers, diced (for less heat, remove the seeds)
5 cloves garlic, smashed and skin removed
1 tsp. ground cumin
Salt and freshly ground black pepper to taste
1½ tsps. oregano, toasted

DIRECTIONS:
1. In a large saucepan, add the potatoes, red pepper, and jalapeño peppers and sauté over medium heat for 7 to 8 minutes.
2. Add water 1 to 2 tbsps. at a time to keep the vegetables from sticking to the pan.
3. Whisk in the garlic, cumin, and oregano and cook for 3 minutes. Whisk in the edamame and 1 cup of water. Cook for 10 minutes, adding more water if necessary.
4. Sprinkle with salt and pepper to taste. Pour over the brown rice and garnish with the tarragon and lime wedges.

Nutrition Info per Serving:
Calories: 239, Protein: 7.4 g, Fat: 1.7 g, Carbohydrates: 50 g, Fiber: 6.7 g, Sugar: 3.7 g, Sodium: 379 mg

Fava Beans with Olives

Prep Time: 10 minutes, Cook Time: 2½ hours, Serves: 4

INGREDIENTS:
1½ pounds (454 g) dried fava beans, soaked for 8 to 10 hours
1 medium red onion, peeled and finely chopped
5 olives, seeded and diced
3 cloves garlic, peeled and minced
1 tsp. ground thyme
1 tbsp. red wine vinegar
Salt to taste
fresh sage

DIRECTIONS:
1. Drain and rinse the beans, and place them to a large pot. Add enough water to top the beans by 4 inches and bring to a boil over high heat. Lower the heat to medium, cover, and cook until the beans are softened, 1½ to 2 hours.
2. While the beans are simmering, stir the onion in a medium skillet or saucepan and sauté over medium heat for 8 to 10 minutes, or until the onion is translucent and starting to brown. Whisk in the garlic, thyme, and red wine vinegar and olives and cook for 5 minutes longer. Set aside until the beans are fully cooked.
3. When the beans are done cooking, drain all but ½ cup of the liquid from the pot and pour the onion mixture to the beans. Toss to combine well and sprinkle with salt. Serve garnished with the sage.

Nutrition Info per Serving:
Calories: 168, Protein: 14 g, Fat: 1.5 g, Carbohydrates: 34.5 g, Fiber: 13.2 g, Sugar: 17.1 g, Sodium: 626 mg

Easy Baked Chickpea Falafel

Prep Time: 15 minutes, plus overnight, Cook Time: 30 minutes, Serves: 6

INGREDIENTS:
1 cup dried chickpeas
½ cup packed chopped fresh cilantro (or parsley if preferred)
½ cup chopped yellow onion
½ cup packed chopped fresh parsley
3 garlic cloves, peeled
1½ tbsps. chickpea flour or wheat flour (if gluten is not a concern)
1 tsp. ground coriander
½ tsp. baking powder
2 tsps. ground cumin
2 tbsps. freshly squeezed lemon juice

DIRECTIONS:
1. The night before making falafel, add the dried chickpeas in a large bowl, pour in the water to cover by 3 inches. Cover the bowl and allow to soak for at least 8 hours or overnight. Drain.
2. Preheat the oven to 375°F(190°C). Use parchment paper to line a baking sheet.
3. Combine the soaked chickpeas and the remaining ingredients in a high-speed blender or food processor. Pulse until all ingredients are well combined but not smooth, it should have the consistency of sand but stick together when pressed.
4. Divide the falafel mixture into 20 balls with a cookie scoop or two spoons and place them on the prepared baking sheet. Lightly flatten each ball using the bottom of a measuring cup. This will help them cook more evenly.
5. Bake for 15 minutes. Flip and bake for another 10 to 15 minutes, until lightly browned.
6. Place in an airtight container and refrigerate for up to 1 week or freeze for up to 1 month.

Nutrition Info per Serving:
Calories: 129, Protein: 7 g, Fat: 2 g, Carbohydrates: 22 g, Fiber: 6 g, Sugar: 2 g, Sodium: 322 mg

Mixed Bean Chili

Prep Time: 5 minutes, Cook Time: 30 minutes, Serves: 6

INGREDIENTS:
1 (28-ounce, 784 g) can crushed tomatoes
1 (15-ounce, 425 g) can low-sodium cannellini beans
1 (15-ounce, 425 g) can low-sodium chickpeas
1 (15-ounce, 425 g) can low-sodium black beans
1 tsp. garlic powder
1 tsp. onion powder
1 tbsp. chili powder
½ tsp. ground cumin
½ tsp. red pepper flakes (optional)

DIRECTIONS:
1. Combine all of the ingredients, including their liquids in a large stockpot. Bring the chili to a boil over medium-high heat.
2. Reduce the heat to medium-low, cover and simmer for 25 minutes.
3. After cooking, serve the chili.

Nutrition Info per Serving:
Calories: 185, Protein: 11 g, Fat: 1 g, Carbohydrates: 33 g, Fiber: 13 g, Sugar: 6.4 g, Sodium: 583 mg

Oats Lentil Loaf with Maple-Tomato Glaze

Prep Time: 10 minutes, Cook Time: 30 minutes, Serves: 6

INGREDIENTS:
FOR THE GLAZE:
1 tbsp. tomato paste
1 tbsp. balsamic vinegar
½ tbsp. maple syrup
FOR THE LENTIL LOAF:
1 cup quick-cooking oats
1 cup cooked brown rice
2 cups cooked brown or green lentils
¼ cup sweet and tangy ketchup
¼ cup vegetable broth
2 tsps. onion powder
1 tsp. garlic powder
2 tbsps. nutritional yeast
1 tsp. dried sage
½ tsp. dried thyme
½ tsp. baking powder
½ tsp. freshly ground black pepper

DIRECTIONS:
TO MAKE THE GLAZE:
1. Add the glaze ingredients in a small bowl, whisk them together.
TO MAKE THE LENTIL LOAF:
1. Preheat the oven to 400°F(205°C).
2. Combine all of the lentil loaf ingredients in a large bowl, mix together until the spices and oats have been thoroughly mixed and the lentils mashed. Place the mixture into a nonstick bread pan or a baking dish lined with parchment paper.
3. Evenly brush over the top of the loaf with the glaze before placing in the oven.
4. Bake until lightly browned, about 30 minutes, and serve.

Nutrition Info per Serving:
Calories: 197, Protein: 12 g, Fat: 2 g, Carbohydrates: 36 g, Fiber: 9 g, Sugar: 5.4 g, Sodium: 452 mg

Mung Bean Sprouts and Cabbage Salad

Prep Time: 10 minutes, Cook Time: 10 minutes, Serves: 4

INGREDIENTS:
FOR THE SPROUTS:
½ cup whole mung beans
½ tsp. turmeric
¼ tsp. salt
FOR THE SALAD:
2 medium potatoes, skin on
½ cup blueberries, diced
½ cup cabbage, finely chopped
¼ cup peach, diced
¼ cup basil, finely chopped
2 tbsps. tahini
1 tbsp. white wine vinegar
1 tsp. ground allspice
1 tsp. ground fennel
1 tsp. Salt

DIRECTIONS:
TO SPROUT THE MUNG BEANS:
1. Soak the mung beans in 1 cup of filtered water overnight. Spread a clean, damp cloth in a large bowl. Drain off the water from the beans and wrap them in the cloth. Transfer the bowl to a cool place away from sunlight. Dampen the cloth every 6 hours. The beans will sprout to about 0.5-centimeter sprouts in 12 hours.
2. When the beans have sprouted, rinse them completely in clean water. Boil the sprouts in 2 cups of water with the turmeric and salt for 10 minutes, or until the sprouts soften a little. Drain the sprouts and set them aside.
TO MAKE THE SALAD:
3. Halve the potatoes. Transfer to a medium saucepan and pour enough water to cover. Bring to a boil, lower the heat to medium, and simmer for 10 minutes, or until soft when pierced with a fork. Drain the potatoes and allow them to cool, then peel and cut into ½-inch cubes. Transfer the potatoes in a large bowl and Whisk in the drained sprouts, blueberries, cabbage, peach, basil, tahini, white wine vinegar, allspice, fennel, and salt. Toss to combine well and serve.

Nutrition Info per Serving:
Calories: 117, Protein: 3.9 g, Fat: 1.8 g, Carbohydrates: 23.1 g, Fiber: 4.4 g, Sugar: 2.4 g, Sodium: 752 mg

Stuffed Tomatoes with Mint

Prep Time: 10 minutes, Cook Time: 0, Serves: 6

INGREDIENTS:

4 cups cooked navy beans, or two (15-oz. 430 g) cans, drained and rinsed
One (15-oz. 430 g) can artichoke hearts (oil-free), drained and roughly chopped
½ cup cantaloupe, peeled and diced small
½ cup tahini
6 large tomatoes, such as beefsteak
1 tsp. mint
2 tbsps. almond butter

DIRECTIONS:

1. Whisk the beans, artichoke hearts, cantaloupe, mint, almond butter and tahini in a small bowl and set aside.
2. Cut the top ½ inch off each tomato and scoop out the flesh, leaving a ½-inch shell. Gently spread the filling among the prepared tomatoes and place them on a platter or among individual plates to serve.

Nutrition Info per Serving:
Calories: 243, Protein: 13.8 g, Fat: 1.4 g, Carbohydrates: 47.8 g, Fiber: 21.2 g, Sugar: 6.2 g, Sodium: 652 mg

Orange Black Bean Taquitos

Prep Time: 15 minutes, Cook Time: 30 minutes, Serves: 4

INGREDIENTS:

4 cups cooked black beans, or two (15-ounce, 425 g) cans, drained and rinsed
1 large yellow onion, peeled and diced small
4 cloves garlic, peeled and minced
2 tsps. cumin seeds, toasted and ground
2 chiles in adobo sauce, minced, or 2 tsps. ancho chile powder
Zest and juice of 2 oranges
20 to 24 corn tortillas
2 cups Fresh Tomato Salsa
1 batch Tofu Sour Cream
1 batch Not-So-Fat Guacamole
Salt

DIRECTIONS:

1. Put the onion in a large saucepan and sauté over medium heat for 8 to 10 minutes. Add water 1 tbsp. at a time to keep the onion from sticking to the pan. Put in garlic and cook for another minute. Add the cumin, orange zest and juice, chiles, and black beans. Season with salt. Puree the mixture in the bowl of a food processor until smooth and a little chunky.
2. Put the tortillas in a nonstick skillet over medium-low heat. Heat for 3 to 4 minutes, turning frequently, until the tortillas soften. Wrap the tortillas in a kitchen towel to keep warm and repeat with the remaining tortillas.
3. Spread 3 tbsps. of the black bean mixture over half of each tortilla, roll it up, starting with the bean-filled half, and set it seam side down on a dish. Repeat with the remaining tortillas.
4. Warm the taquitos in a 200ºF (93ºC) oven for 10 to 15 minutes. Serve with tofu sour cream, guacamole, and salsa.

Nutrition Info per Serving:
Calories: 357, Protein: 11.2 g, Fat: 4.1 g, Carbohydrates: 73.8 g, Fiber: 11.9 g, Sugar: 8.4 g, Sodium: 674 mg

Spicy Cajun Tofu

Prep Time: 40 minutes, Cook Time: 20 minutes, Serves: 4

INGREDIENTS:

1 (7-oz, 200 g) pack extra-firm tofu
2 tbsps. (20 g) salt-free Cajun spices
¼ cup (60 g) tahini
2 tbsps. (30 ml) lemon juice
1 clove garlic, minced
¼ cup (60 ml) water

DIRECTIONS:

1. Drain the tofu first and slice it into 3 or 4 slabs. Lay a few paper towels on a flat surface.
2. Put the tofu slabs on the towels, cover them another paper towel, place a cutting board and heavy objects on top to press out any excess water. Let the tofu drain for 15-30 minutes.
3. Cut the tofu after draining into thin cubes, then put them in a medium bowl.
4. Add the Cajun spices and toss to cover the tofu evenly. Seal the bowl and marinate while preheating the oven.
5. Preheat the oven to 325°F(175°C), line with parchment paper and place the marinated tofu onto the baking tray.
6. Bake the tofu for 10 minutes, then remove it from the oven, flip over the tofu and bake again for 10 minutes until they're crispy.
7. Put tahini, minced garlic, lemon juice, and water to a small airtight container.
8. Mix the tahini, lemon juice and garlic in the bowl into a thinner and smooth dressing, adding more water if necessary.
9. Take the tofu out of the oven and cool down for 5 minutes.
10. Serve the tofu with the tahini dressing and the optional dips.

Nutrition Info per Serving:
Calories: 152, Protein: 10.6 g, Fat: 10.8 g, Carbohydrates: 1 g, Fiber: 0.8 g, Sugar: 1 g, Sodium: 326 mg

Chana Masala

Prep Time: 5 minutes, Cook Time: 25 minutes, Serves: 2

INGREDIENTS:
2 cups (400 g) chickpeas, cooked or canned
1 cup (180 g) tomato cubes, canned or fresh
2 medium onions, minced
2 tbsps. curry spices
¼ cup (60 ml) water

DIRECTIONS:
1. When using dry chickpeas, soak and cook ⅔ cup (133 g) of dry chickpeas to the method.
2. Put the tomato cubes, onions, and the water in a large pot over medium heat.
3. Cook for a few minutes and stir occasionally until everything is cooked, then add the curry spices.
4. Add the chickpeas, and stir thoroughly to make sure that everything is well mixed.
5. Cook and stir occasionally, then lower the heat to a simmer.
6. Let the curry simmer for about 20 minutes while stirring occasionally.
7. Turn the heat off and let the curry cool down for a minute.
8. Divide curry between 2 bowls, garnish with the optional toppings, serve.

Nutrition Info per Serving:
Calories: 401, Protein: 20.9 g, Fat: 6.2 g, Carbohydrates: 65.5 g, Fiber: 20.3 g, Sugar: 12.9 g, Sodium: 487 mg

Bean Chili with Lime and Jalapeño

Prep Time: 15 minutes, Cook Time: 35 minutes, Serves: 6

INGREDIENTS:
3 jalapeño peppers, seeded and minced
1 large yellow onion, peeled and diced
1 large green pepper, seeded and diced
6 cloves garlic, peeled and minced
2 tbsps. cumin seeds, toasted and ground
4 cups cooked navy or other white beans, drained and rinsed
3 cups low-sodium vegetable broth
1 cup finely chopped cilantro
One (28-ounce, 794 g) can diced tomatoes
Zest of 1 lime and juice of 2 limes
Salt to taste

DIRECTIONS:
1. Place the green pepper, onion, and jalapeño peppers in a large saucepan and sauté over medium heat for 7 to 8 minutes.
2. Add water 2 tbsps. at a time to prevent the vegetables from sticking to the pan. Put in garlic and cumin and cook for 2 minutes. Add the beans, tomatoes, and vegetable stock and boil over high heat. Reduce the heat to medium and cook for 25 minutes, covered. Add the lime zest and juice and cilantro, season with salt.

Nutrition Info per Serving:
Calories: 268, Protein: 16.3 g, Fat: 2.3 g, Carbohydrates: 49.6 g, Fiber: 12.7 g, Sugar: 8.3 g, Sodium: 838 mg

North African Vegetables and Chickpeas

Prep Time: 15 minutes, Cook Time: 25 minutes, Serves: 4

INGREDIENTS:
FOR THE CHERMOULA SAUCE:
1 large tomato, chopped
6 cloves garlic, peeled and minced
Zest of 1 lemon and juice of 2 lemons
½ cup kalamata olives, pitted
1 cup chopped cilantro
1 tbsp. sweet paprika
2 tsps. ground coriander
2 tsps. ground cumin
¼ tsp. cayenne pepper, or to taste
Salt
FOR THE VEGETABLES:
1 medium yellow onion, peeled and cut into ½-inch rings
1 medium red bell pepper, seeded and cut into ½-inch strips
1 medium zucchini, halved lengthwise and cut into ½-inch slices
1 medium yellow squash, halved lengthwise and cut into ½-inch slices
8 ounces (227 g) button mushrooms, sliced
2 cups cooked chickpeas, drained and rinsed
Salt and freshly ground black pepper

DIRECTIONS:
TO MAKE THE CHERMOULA SAUCE:
1. Mix the tomato, cilantro, olives, garlic, lemon zest and juice, coriander, paprika, cumin, cayenne pepper, and salt in a blender and process until smooth and creamy. Set aside.
TO MAKE THE VEGETABLES:
2. Place the red pepper, onion, and mushrooms in a large saucepan and sauté for 8 to 10 minutes over medium-high heat. Add water 1 tbsp. at a time to keep the vegetables from sticking to the pan. Add the yellow squash, zucchini, and chickpeas and cook for 10 minutes. Add the chermoula sauce and cook for 5 minutes. Season with salt and pepper.

Nutrition Info per Serving:
Calories: 270, Protein: 8.6 g, Fat: 3.5 g, Carbohydrates: 55.8 g, Fiber: 10.5 g, Sugar: 5.1 g, Sodium: 723 mg

Smoked Tofu and Black Beans

Prep Time: 10 minutes, Cook Time: 15 minutes, Serves: 2

INGREDIENTS:

1 cup (170 g) black beans, cooked or canned
1 (7-oz, 200 g) pack smoked tofu, cubed
1 small avocado, peeled, stoned
2 cups (180 g) sweet corn, cooked or canned
¼ cup (60 g) lemon juice

DIRECTIONS:

1. When using dry beans, soak and cook ⅓ cup (56 g) of dry black beans.
2. Preheat the oven to 350°F(175°C) and line with parchment paper.
3. Place the tofu cubes on the baking sheet and bake for 10 minutes or until the tofu is slightly browned and dry.
4. Take the tofu cubes out of the oven and let them cool down for about 5 minutes.
5. Cut one half of the peeled avocado into cubes and the other half into slices.
6. Toss the black beans, tofu cubes, corn and avocado cubes in a large salad bowl and stir well.
7. Divide between two bowls if necessary, then drizzle 2 tbsps. of lemon juice on top, garnish with the avocado slices, serve.

Nutrition Info per Serving:
Calories: 424, Protein: 26.7 g, Fat: 17.6 g, Carbohydrates: 39.2 g, Fiber: 12.8 g, Sugar: 7.7 g, Sodium: 394 mg

Red Lentil Chili

Prep Time: 15 minutes, Cook Time: 55 minutes, Serves: 6 to 8

INGREDIENTS:

1½ cups chopped celery
2 medium carrots, peeled and sliced
3 medium yellow onions, peeled and chopped
2 medium bell peppers, seeded and chopped
One (28-ounce, 794 g) can crushed tomatoes
One (15-ounce, 425 g) can kidney beans, drained and rinsed
1 to 2 cloves garlic, peeled and minced
6 cups low-sodium vegetable broth
1 tsp. paprika
½ tsp. chipotle powder or smoked paprika
½ tsp. cayenne pepper
1½ tbsp. chili powder
1 tsp. ground cumin
2 cups red lentils, rinsed
Zest and juice of 1 lime
Salt and freshly ground black pepper

DIRECTIONS:

1. Put the onion, carrots, celery, garlic, bell peppers, and 1 cup of the vegetable stock in a large pot over medium-high heat. Cook 5 to 7 minutes, stirring occasionally, until the vegetables soften. Add the chili powder, paprika, cumin, chipotle powder, and cayenne pepper and cook for one more minute, stirring well.
2. Add the lentils, kidney beans, tomatoes, and the remaining vegetable stock to the pot. Cover and boil over high heat. Reduce the heat to medium-low and simmer about 45 minutes, stirring occasionally, until the lentils are soft. Add the lime zest and juice, and season with salt and pepper.

Nutrition Info per Serving:
Calories: 310, Protein: 18 g, Fat: 4.5 g, Carbohydrates: 53.8 g, Fiber: 11.2 g, Sugar: 9 g, Sodium: 605 mg

White Bean Stew with Saffron and Sage

Prep Time: 15 minutes, Cook Time: 35 minutes, Serves: 6

INGREDIENTS:

2 zucchini, diced small
2 celery stalks, chopped into medium dice
1 medium asparagus, trimmed and diced
One (28-oz. 780g) can diced tomatoes
4 cups cooked cannellini beans, or two (15-oz. 430g) cans, drained and rinsed
2 cups (480mL) Vegetable Stock, or low-sodium vegetable broth
3 cloves garlic, crushed
½ cup maple syrup
2 large pinches saffron, crumbled and soaked for 15 minutes in ¼ cup of water that has just been boiled
1 cup sage, finely chopped
Salt and freshly ground black pepper to taste

DIRECTIONS:

1. In a large saucepan, add the zucchini, celery, and asparagus and sauté over medium heat for 10 minutes.
2. Pour in water 1 to 2 tbsps. at a time to keep the vegetables from sticking to the pan. Add the garlic and cook for another minute.
3. Whisk in the maple syrup and the saffron with its soaking liquid and bring the pot to a boil over high heat.
4. Stir in the tomatoes, beans, and vegetable stock. Return the stew to a boil, then lower the heat and simmer, covered, for 30 minutes.
5. Spread with the sage, season with salt and pepper, and simmer for another 5 minutes.

Nutrition Info per Serving:
Calories: 93, Protein: 3.5 g, Fat: 1.2 g, Carbohydrates: 16.8 g, Fiber: 5.2 g, Sugar: 7.5 g, Sodium: 365 mg

Lentils and Eggplant Moussaka

Prep Time: 15 minutes, Cook Time: 2 hours, Serves: 6 to 8

INGREDIENTS:
FOR THE LENTILS:
2 cups green lentils, rinsed
4 cloves garlic, peeled and minced
2 medium yellow onions, peeled and diced small
¼ cup (60 ml) tomato paste
1 tsp. ground cinnamon
1 tsp. ground allspice
Salt
FOR THE EGGPLANT:
2 large eggplants, stemmed and cut into ½-inch slices
3 tbsps. low-sodium soy sauce
¼ cup (60 ml) low-sodium vegetable broth
FOR THE CUSTARD LAYER:
2 large yellow onions, peeled and coarsely chopped
1 large red bell pepper, seeded and coarsely chopped
¼ cup cashews, toasted
2 tbsps. tahini
2 tbsps. arrowroot powder
1 tsp. ground nutmeg
1 cup nutritional yeast
Salt or low-sodium soy sauce

DIRECTIONS:
TO MAKE THE LENTIL LAYER:
1. Add lentils to a medium saucepan and put in enough water to cover by 2 inches. Boil over high heat. Lower the heat to medium and cook with lid covered, for 40 minutes until the lentils are tender. Drain the excess water and set the lentils aside.
2. Place the onions in a large saucepan and sauté for 6 minutes over medium heat. Add water 1 tbsp. at a time to keep the onions from sticking to the pan. Add the garlic and cook for 3 minutes. Add the cinnamon, tomato paste, and allspice and cook for 1 minute. Mix the lentils and the onion mixture, season with salt. Set aside.
TO MAKE THE EGGPLANT:
3. Preheat the oven to 350°F (180ºC).
4. Add the soy sauce in vegetable stock in a small bowl and set aside.
5. Line a baking sheet with parchment paper. Place the eggplant slices on the parchment paper (do not overlap) and brush each piece with the soy sauce mixture. Bake the eggplant for about 15 minutes until it is tender.
TO MAKE THE CUSTARD LAYER:
6. Put the onions, cashews, red pepper, tahini, salt, nutmeg, and arrowroot powder in a blender and puree until creamy. Add the nutritional yeast and process until well combined, scraping down the sides with a spatula.
TO ASSEMBLE THE CASSEROLE:
7. Put half of the lentil mixture on the bottom of a baking dish. Arrange half of the eggplant on top of the lentils. Top with the remaining lentils, then the rest eggplant. Top with the custard mixture.
8. Bake for 45 to 50 minutes until the casserole is hot and bubbly.

Nutrition Info per Serving:
Calories: 254, Protein: 14.9 g, Fat: 9.5 g, Carbohydrates: 31.7 g, Fiber: 8.9 g, Sugar: 9.5 g, Sodium: 725 mg

Taco Salad with Peanut Butter Dressing

Prep Time: 10 minutes, Cook Time: 5 minutes, Serves: 6

INGREDIENTS:
FOR THE SALAD:
4 corn tortillas
6 cups chopped spinach
1½ cups zucchini, seeded and diced
1½ cups pineapple, peeled and diced
1½ cups cauliflower florets, chopped
One (15-oz. 430 g) can black beans, drained and rinsed
One (15-oz. 430 g) can lima beans, drained and rinsed
3 ears corn, kernels removed (about 2 cups)
FOR THE DRESSING:
One (15-oz. 430 g) can cannellini beans, drained and rinsed
2 cups parsley, leaves and tender stems
1 cup scallion
¼ cup (60mL) peanut butter
One (4-oz. 110 g) can diced radish
2 tbsps. low-sodium soy sauce
1 tsp. nutmeg
¼ tsp. chili powder
2 cloves garlic, crushed
Zest and juice of 2 limes

DIRECTIONS:
TO MAKE THE SALAD:
1. Cut the corn tortillas into thin slices. Spread the slices evenly on a small baking sheet and toast in a toaster oven for 3 to 5 minutes, or until crispy.
2. Place the spinach in the bottom of a large serving bowl. Spread with the zucchini, pineapple, cauliflower, black beans, lima beans, and corn. Set aside.
TO MAKE THE DRESSING:
3. Mix the cannellini beans, scallion, parsley, peanut butter, radish, soy sauce, chili powder, nutmeg, garlic, lime zest and juice, and 1 cup of water in a food processor. Process on high until smooth.
TO SERVE:
4. Place the tortilla strips over the salad in the bowl and spread the dressing on top. To serve.

Nutrition Info per Serving:
Calories: 450, Protein: 23.9 g, Fat: 5.7 g, Carbohydrates: 84.3 g, Fiber: 19.9 g, Sugar: 16.7 g, Sodium: 628 mg

Lemony Chickpeas Salad

Prep Time: 10 minutes, Cook Time: 0, Serves: 2

INGREDIENTS:

1 cup (200 g) chickpeas, cooked or canned
½ cup (110 g) spinach, fresh
¼ cup (60 ml) lemon juice
¼ cup (60 g) tahini
1 clove garlic, minced
¼ cup (60 ml) water

DIRECTIONS:

1. Soak and cook 66 g dry chickpeas according to the method if necessary.
2. Add the tahini, lemon juice, minced garlic and water to a small airtight container.
3. Shake the container with tahini, lemon juice, garlic and water until everything is thoroughly mixed, adding more water if you want a thinner dressing.
4. Wash the spinach in a strainer, rinse thoroughly and then drain well.
5. Combine the spinach and chickpeas to a large bowl and mix thoroughly.
6. Divide the salad between two bowls, garnish with tangerines and the optional toppings, serve.

Nutrition Info per Serving:
Calories: 406, Protein: 19.2 g, Fat: 21.7 g, Carbohydrates: 33.4 g, Fiber: 11 g, Sugar: 7.6 g, Sodium: 216 mg

Sweet-and-Sour Meatball and Vegetable

Prep Time: 15 minutes, Cook Time: 8 minutes, Serves: 4

INGREDIENTS:

4 cups cooked brown rice
1 batch meatballs
1 medium yellow onion, peeled and diced
1 medium red bell pepper, seeded and diced
1 medium head broccoli, cut into florets
1 batch Pineapple Sweet-and-Sour Sauce
One (14-ounce, 397 g) can pineapple chunks, drained
3 green onions (white and green parts), thinly sliced

DIRECTIONS:

1. Heat a large skillet over high heat. Put in onion and red pepper and stir-fry for 3 minutes. Add water 1 tbsp. at a time to keep the vegetables from sticking to the pan. Add the broccoli and cook about 5 minutes until tender. Add the pineapple and sweet-and-sour sauce and cook.
2. Portion the brown rice among 4 individual plates and top with the vegetable mixture and the meatballs.

Garnish with the green onions. Serve.

Nutrition Info per Serving:
Calories: 388, Protein: 15 g, Fat: 5.4 g, Carbohydrates: 71.8 g, Fiber: 9.1 g, Sugar: 16.2 g, Sodium: 229 mg

Lentil Shepherd's Pie with Parsnip Crust

Prep Time: 15 minutes, Cook Time: 1½ hours, Serves: 6 to 8

INGREDIENTS:

1½ cup green lentils, rinsed
1 large yellow onion, peeled and diced small
1 large carrot, peeled and diced small
8 medium red-skin potatoes, peeled and chopped
2 stalks celery, diced small
2 cloves garlic, peeled and minced
1 sprig rosemary
1 bay leaf
3 tbsps. tomato paste
4 parsnips, peeled and chopped
Salt and freshly ground black pepper

DIRECTIONS:

1. Put carrot, onion, and celery in a large saucepan and sauté for 10 minutes over medium heat. Add water 1 tbsp. at a time to keep the vegetables from sticking to the pan. Add the garlic and cook for one more minute. Stir in the rosemary, bay leaf, lentils, and enough water to cover the lentils by 3 inches. Boil the pot over high heat. Lower the heat to medium and cook with lid covered, for 30 minutes.
2. Preheat the oven to 350°F (180ºC).
3. Put tomato paste to the saucepan and cook for 15 more minutes until the lentils are tender. Season with salt and pepper. Remove from the heat, discard the bay leaf and rosemary sprig, and pour the lentils into a baking dish.
4. Meanwhile, add the parsnips and potatoes to a medium saucepan and add enough water to cover. Boil the pot over high heat. Lower the heat to medium and cook with lid covered for about 15 minutes until the vegetables are tender.
5. Remove the potatoes from the heat and drain all but ½ cup of the water. Mash the vegetables until creamy, then season with additional salt and spread the mixture evenly over the lentils.
6. Bake the casserole for 25 minutes until bubbly. Set aside for 10 minutes before serving.

Nutrition Info per Serving:
Calories: 239, Protein: 7 g, Fat: 0.7 g, Carbohydrates: 54.8 g, Fiber: 7.6 g, Sugar: 8.5 g, Sodium: 260 mg

Baked Pasta and Peas, page 88

Fava Beans with Olives, page 74

Lemony Chickpeas Salad, page 80

Mango and Chickpea Curry, page 84

Chapter 6 Bean and Legumes 81

Quick Cooking Red Lentil

Prep Time: 10 minutes, Cook Time: 30 minutes, Serves: 4

INGREDIENTS:
2 cup red lentils, rinsed
1 large yellow onion, peeled and diced
2 cloves garlic, peeled and minced
1 tsp. turmeric
1 tbsp. cumin seeds, toasted and ground
1 tbsp. coriander seeds, toasted and ground
½ tsp. crushed red pepper flakes
1 bay leaf
1 tbsp. grated ginger
Zest of 1 lemon
Salt

DIRECTIONS:
1. Put the onion in a large saucepan and sauté over medium heat for 10 minutes.
2. Pour water 1 tbsp. at a time to keep the onion from sticking to the pan. Add the garlic, ginger, bay leaf, turmeric, coriander, cumin, and crushed red pepper flakes and cook for 1 more minute.
3. Add the lentils and 4 cups of water and boil over high heat. Lower the heat to medium and cook, covered, for 20 to 25 minutes. Remove from the heat. Season with salt and add the lemon zest.

Nutrition Info per Serving:
Calories: 379, Protein: 24.1 g, Fat: 2.7 g, Carbohydrates: 68.1 g, Fiber: 12.1 g, Sugar: 2.3 g, Sodium: 594 mg

Tomato and Fava Bean Ratatouille

Prep Time: 15 minutes, Cook Time: 40 minutes, Serves: 4

INGREDIENTS:
2 potatoes, peeled and diced
1 large eggplant, stemmed and cut into ½-inch dice
1 medium carrot, diced
2 cups cooked fava beans, or one (15-oz. 430 g) can, drained and rinsed
2 Roma tomatoes, chopped
1 red bell pepper, seeded and diced
2 cloves garlic, peeled and finely chopped
¼ cup tarragon, finely chopped
Salt and freshly ground black pepper to taste

DIRECTIONS:
1. In a large saucepan, add the potatoes and sauté over medium heat for 7 to 8 minutes.
2. Add water 1 to 2 tbsps. at a time to keep the potatoes from sticking to the pan.
3. Whisk in the red pepper and eggplant and cook for 10 minutes.
4. Stir in the carrot, garlic, fava beans, and tomatoes and cook for 5 minutes longer.
5. Lower the heat and cook, uncovered, stirring from time to time, for 15 minutes, or until the vegetables are soft. Off heat and remove the pan.
6. Stir in the tarragon and sprinkle with salt and pepper to taste.

Nutrition Info per Serving:
Calories: 144, Protein: 7.7 g, Fat: 1 g, Carbohydrates: 26.1 g, Fiber: 10.4 g, Sugar: 14 g, Sodium: 24 mg

Lentil Pasta

Prep Time: 17 minutes, Cook Time: 18 minutes, Serves: 4

INGREDIENTS:
1½ cup (300 g) green lentils, cooked or canned
1½ cup (150 g) whole wheat pasta, dry
10 sundried tomatoes
1 cup (180 g) tomato cubes, canned or fresh
4 tbsps. (40 g) Italian herbs
¼ cup (60 ml) water

DIRECTIONS:
1. Soak and cook 100 g dry lentils according to the method if necessary.
2. Preheat the oven to 350°F(175°C) and line with parchment paper.
3. Chop 8 of the sundried tomatoes.
4. Mash the lentils, sundried tomato, and 20 grams Italian herbs with a potato masher together in a large bowl and knead them into a chunky mixture.
5. Make it into a 2-inch (5 cm) ball. Repeat until all lentil mixture is used.
6. Bake the lentil balls for 10 minutes, then take them out of the oven, turn the balls over and bake for another 8 minutes.
7. Cook the pasta, drain the water with a strainer and set the pasta aside.
8. Take the balls out of the oven when browned and crispy on the outside, then cool down for a minute.
9. Put the tomato cubes and Italian herbs in a non-stick frying pan over medium-high heat.
10. Chop 2 sundried tomatoes and add them to the sauce.
11. Let it cook and stir occasionally with a spatula, until everything is cooked.
12. Turn off the heat, divide the pasta between 2 plates, and top each one with the sauce and lentil balls.
13. Serve the pasta with the optional toppings.

Nutrition Info per Serving:
Calories: 238, Protein: 12 g, Fat: 1.3 g, Carbohydrates: 44.6 g, Fiber: 9.6 g, Sugar: 6.1 g, Sodium: 481 mg

Tuscan-Style Baked Beans and Polenta

Prep Time: 15 minutes, Cook Time: 48 minutes, Serves: 4

INGREDIENTS:
4 cups cooked cannellini beans, or two (15-ounce, 425 g) cans, drained and rinsed
1 medium yellow onion, peeled and diced
1 medium carrot, peeled and diced
2 celery stalks, diced
2 large potatoes, diced
2 cups (480 ml) low-sodium vegetable broth
4 cloves garlic, peeled and minced
1 tsp. minced rosemary
1 tsp. minced thyme
1 batch Basic Polenta, kept warm
Salt and freshly ground black pepper

DIRECTIONS:
1. Preheat the oven to 350°F (180ºC).
2. Put carrot, onion, and celery in a large saucepan and sauté for 5 minutes over medium heat. Add water 1 tbsp. at a time to keep the vegetables from sticking to the pan. Mix in the rosemary, garlic, and thyme and cook for 3 minutes. Add the potatoes and vegetable stock and cook about 15 minutes until tender. Add the beans, season with salt and black pepper, and cook for 5 minutes more.
3. Spoon the beans into a baking dish and spread the polenta over the top. Bake for 20 minutes.

Nutrition Info per Serving:
Calories: 303, Protein: 8 g, Fat: 2 g, Carbohydrates: 66.5 g, Fiber: 8.7 g, Sugar: 7.4 g, Sodium: 502 mg

Ras El Hanout Chickpea

Prep Time: 5 minutes, Cook Time: 30 minutes, Serves: 3

INGREDIENTS:
1 cup (200 g) chickpeas, cooked or canned
¼ cup (45 g) quinoa, dry
⅔ cup (130 g) green lentils, dry
3 cups (720 ml) vegetable stock
2 tbsps. (20 g) Ras El Hanout

DIRECTIONS:
1. Soak and cook 66 g dry chickpeas according to the method.
2. Add the vegetable stock and the lentils to a large pot over medium-high heat.
3. When the water is boiling, turn the heat down to medium.
4. Cook the lentils and stir occasionally for 15 minutes without covering the pot. Remove any foam produced by the lentils.
5. Add Ras el Hanout spices and the quinoa, then cook for another 15 minutes and stir occasionally.
6. Add the chickpeas and stir well, then bring the heat down to a simmer and leave to simmer for about 5 minutes.
7. Turn the heat off and let the mixture cool down for a minute.
8. Divide between 2 plates, garnish with the optional toppings, serve.

Nutrition Info per Serving:
Calories: 353, Protein: 20 g, Fat: 5.4 g, Carbohydrates: 56.1 g, Fiber: 20 g, Sugar: 4.9 g, Sodium: 527 mg

Avocado Black Bean Tempeh Nachos with Cashew Cheese

Prep Time: 1 hour 20 minutes, Cook Time: 0, Serves: 4

INGREDIENTS:
CASHEW CHEESE:
¾ cup raw cashews, soaked from 1 hour to overnight and drained
1 tbsp. tapioca starch or tapioca flour
1 tbsp. nutritional yeast
½ tsp. onion powder
½ tsp. garlic powder
1 tbsp. lemon juice
½ cup water
TEMPEH NACHOS:
10 to 18 ounces (283 to 504 g) tortilla chips
1 (15-ounce, 425 g) can black beans, drained and rinsed
1 Roma tomato, diced small
½ cup diced red onion
1 hot chili pepper, sliced thin crosswise
8 ounces (227 g) tempeh, diced very small
2 tbsps. raw shelled hempseed
1 avocado
Juice from one lime

DIRECTIONS:
CASHEW CHEESE:
1. In a blender, add all of the cheese ingredients and blend until smooth. Place the mixture in a small saucepan. Cook on medium heat for 5 to 10 minutes, stir until the sauce thickens a bit. Remove from the heat and allow to cool slightly.
TO ASSEMBLE THE NACHOS:
2. On a platter, lay with all the chips. Sprinkle over the chips with the black beans. Dot with cashew cheese. Sprinkle over with the tomato, red onion, chili pepper, tempeh, and hempseed.
3. Dice the avocado and dredge in lime juice. Sprinkle over the nachos with the diced avocado.

Nutrition Info per Serving:
Calories: 840, Protein: 31.4 g, Fat: 39.9 g, Carbohydrates: 96.3 g, Fiber: 17.8 g, Sugar: 3.6 g, Sodium: 639 mg

Mango and Chickpea Curry

Prep Time: 5 minutes, Cook Time: 15 minutes, Serves: 6

INGREDIENTS:

2 cups mango chunks (fresh or frozen)
3 cups cooked chickpeas
2 cups plant-based milk
2 tbsps. maple syrup
1 tsp. ground coriander
1 tbsp. curry powder
1 tbsp. ground ginger
⅛ tsp. ground cinnamon
1 tsp. garlic powder
1 tsp. onion powder

DIRECTIONS:

1. Heat a large stockpot or Dutch oven over medium heat.
2. Combine all of the ingredients in the pot, cover and cook for 10 minutes, stirring after about 5 minutes.
3. Then uncover and cook for another 5 minutes, stirring every other minute.
4. After cooking, serve warm.

Nutrition Info per Serving:
Calories: 219, Protein: 8 g, Fat: 4 g, Carbohydrates: 38 g, Fiber: 9 g, Sugar: 8.3 g, Sodium: 423 mg

Pitaya Red Bean Salad

Prep Time: 10 minutes, Cook Time: 0, Serves: 4

INGREDIENTS:

4 cups cooked red beans, or two (15-oz. 430 g) cans, drained and rinsed
1 pitaya, peeled and diced
½ cup (120mL) maple syrup
1 medium red bell pepper, seeded and diced small
1 tbsp. mint, thinly sliced
½ cup finely chopped tarragon
1 jalapeño pepper, minced (for less heat, remove the seeds)
1 tbsp. toasted apricots
Zest and juice of 1 lime

DIRECTIONS:

1. Combine all ingredients in a large bowl and mix well. Chill for 1 hour before serving.

Nutrition Info per Serving:
Calories: 188, Protein: 4.9 g, Fat: 1 g, Carbohydrates: 40 g, Fiber: 6.3 g, Sugar: 27.5 g, Sodium: 588 mg

Mexican Black Bean Burgers

Prep Time: 10 minutes, Cook Time: 35 minutes, Serves: 4

INGREDIENTS:

1 cup (180 g) quinoa, dry
2 cups (340 g) black beans, cooked
¼ cup (40 g) Mexican chorizo seasoning

DIRECTIONS:

1. When using dry beans, soak and cook ⅔ cup (113 g) of dry black beans. Cook the quinoa according to the package instructions.
2. Preheat the oven to 375°F(190°C) and line with parchment paper.
3. Add the cooked black beans, quinoa and spices to a large bowl and mash them into a chunky mixture.
4. Put all of the mixture on the baking sheet, flatten it into a 1-inch-thick square, cut the square into 8 patties before baking.
5. Bake the patties for 10 minutes, then take them out of the oven and flip the patties. Bake for another 10 minutes.
6. Take patties out of the oven when the crust is crispy and browned and let them cool down for about a minute.
7. Serve the patties with the optional toppings.

Nutrition Info per Serving:
Calories: 282, Protein: 14.4 g, Fat: 3.4 g, Carbohydrates: 47.4 g, Fiber: 9.8 g, Sugar: 0 g, Sodium: 186 mg

Tomato Curry Chickpeas

Prep Time: 14 minutes, Cook Time: 16 minutes, Serves: 8

INGREDIENTS:

5 cups (1000 g) chickpeas, cooked or canned
2 sweet onions, diced
12 sundried tomatoes
3 cloves garlic, minced
¼ cup (40 g) curry spices

DIRECTIONS:

1. When using dry chickpeas, soak and cook 1½ cup (330 g) of dry chickpeas.
2. Preheat the oven to 375°F(190°C) and line with parchment paper.
3. Add the onion, chickpeas, garlic and spices and sundried tomatoes to the food processor and blend them into a chunky mixture.
4. Take a tbsp. of chickpea mixture and knead into a 2-inch-thick disc, then place on the baking sheet. Repeat and make 24 fritters.
5. Bake the fritters for 8 minutes, then take them out of the oven, flip fritters and bake for another 8 minutes.
6. Take the fritters out of the oven when they're browned and crispy on the outside. Cool down for about a minute.
7. Serve the fritters with the optional toppings.

Nutrition Info per Serving:
Calories: 173, Protein: 13 g, Fat: 4 g, Carbohydrates: 22 g, Fiber: 9.3 g, Sugar: 9 g, Sodium: 463 mg

Red Bean Date Salad

Prep Time: 10 minutes, Cook Time: 0, Serves: 4

INGREDIENTS:

4 cups cooked red beans, or two (15-oz. 430 g) cans, drained and rinsed
1 cup dates, halved and seeded
1 tbsp. mint, minced
1 taro, peeled, halved, and diced
½ cup finely chopped parsley
½ tsp. cayenne pepper
3 tbsps. coconut yogurt
2 cloves garlic, crushed
1 tsp. dry thyme
1 tbsp. raisins
Salt and freshly ground black pepper to taste

DIRECTIONS:

1. Mix all ingredients in a large bowl and whisk to combine well. Chill for 1 hour before serving.

Nutrition Info per Serving:
Calories: 153, Protein: 11.9 g, Fat: 1.4 g, Carbohydrates: 31.2 g, Fiber: 11.7 g, Sugar: 16.3 g, Sodium: 541 mg

White Bean Snow Pear Salad

Prep Time: 10 minutes, Cook Time: 0, Serves: 4

INGREDIENTS:

4 cups cooked navy beans, or two (15-oz. 430 g) cans, drained and rinsed
2 snow pears, peeled, cored and diced
Zest and juice of 2 limes
¼ cup red wine vinegar
½ cup chopped oregano
1 tbsp. parsley, thinly sliced
1 jalapeño pepper, minced (for less heat, remove the seeds)
5 cloves garlic, crushed
1 tbsp. raisins,
Salt to taste

DIRECTIONS:

1. Mix all ingredients in a large bowl and toss to combine well. Chill for 1 hour before serving, if desired.

Nutrition Info per Serving:
Calories: 85, Protein: 4.1 g, Fat: 0.8 g, Carbohydrates: 16.8 g, Fiber: 4.8 g, Sugar: 4.1 g, Sodium: 592 mg

Lentil Burgers

Prep Time: 15 minutes, Cook Time: 25 minutes, Serves: 4

INGREDIENTS:

2 cups (400 g) green lentils, cooked or canned
1 cup (140 g) almonds
3 dates, pitted
2 cloves garlic
4 tbsps. (40 g) burger spices

DIRECTIONS:

1. Soak and cook 133 g dry lentils according to the method.
2. Preheat the oven to 350°F(175°C) and line with parchment paper.
3. Put all ingredients to a food processor and blend the mixture, scrape down the sides of the food processor to prevent any lumps if necessary.
4. Put the mixture on the baking sheet, flatten it into a 1-inch thick square, cut the square into 8 patties.
5. Bake them for 15 minutes, then take them out of the oven, flip over and bake for another 10 minutes.
6. When the crust is crispy and browned, take the patties out of the oven and let them cool down for about a minute.
7. Serve the patties with the optional toppings, whole wheat buns.

Nutrition Info per Serving:
Calories: 339, Protein: 18.2 g, Fat: 17.9 g, Carbohydrates: 26.2 g, Fiber: 11.2 g, Sugar: 6.4 g, Sodium: 354 mg

Zuppa with Cucumber and Black-eyed Peas

Prep Time: 15 minutes, Cook Time: 20 minutes, Serves: 4

INGREDIENTS:

1½ cups cooked black-eyed peas
½ cup uncooked quinoa
½ cup leeks (white and light green parts), finely chopped and rinsed
½ cup cucumber
2 medium taros, chopped
⅛ tsp. turmeric
¼ tsp. ground rosemary
¼ tsp. Salt
Dash fenugreek seeds
3 clove garlic, peeled and minced
Freshly ground black pepper to taste

DIRECTIONS:

1. Place the black-eyed peas, quinoa, and fenugreek seeds to a pot with 3 cups of water and bring to a boil over high heat.
2. Stir in the leeks and garlic and cook on medium heat for 10 to 15 minutes.
3. Pour in 1½ cups of water, the taros, turmeric, rosemary, and salt and simmer for a further 5 to 7 minutes on medium heat, or until the quinoa and black-eyed peas are soft.
4. Whisk in the cucumber and sprinkle with black pepper to taste. Serve hot.

Nutrition Info per Serving:
Calories: 144, Protein: 7.9 g, Fat: 1.9 g, Carbohydrates: 27.2 g, Fiber: 6.5 g, Sugar: 6.4 g, Sodium: 168 mg

Pinto Bean Salsa

Prep Time: 10 minutes, Cook Time: 0, Serves: 2

INGREDIENTS:
2 cups (400 g) pinto beans, cooked or canned
1 small Hass avocado, peeled, stoned, cubed
10 cherry tomatoes, halved
¼ cup (60 ml) lime juice
¼ cup (15 g) fresh cilantro, chopped

DIRECTIONS:
1. Soak and cook 133 g dry pinto beans according to the method if necessary.
2. Put the pinto beans in a large bowl, and add the halved cherry tomatoes, chopped cilantro and avocado cubes.
3. Add the lime juice, stir thoroughly with a spatula and mix everything evenly.
4. Divide the pinto salsa between two bowls, garnish with the optional toppings, serve.

Nutrition Info per Serving:
Calories: 399, Protein: 19.8 g, Fat: 10.3 g, Carbohydrates: 56.7 g, Fiber: 22.2 g, Sugar: 3.4 g, Sodium: 417 mg

White Beans Vegetable Salad

Prep Time: 10 minutes, Cook Time: 0, Serves: 2

INGREDIENTS:
2 cups (400 g) white beans, cooked or canned
½ cucumber, cubed
8 sundried tomatoes, minced
4 tangerines
1 tbsp. (10 g) thyme, fresh or dried

DIRECTIONS:
1. Soak and cook 133 g dry white beans according to the method if necessary.
2. Put the white beans in a large bowl, and add cucumber cubes, minced sundried tomatoes and thyme.
3. Stir thoroughly with a spatula and mix everything evenly.
4. Peel and section the tangerines and set them aside.
5. Divide the salad between two bowls, garnish with the tangerine and the optional toppings, serve.

Nutrition Info per Serving:
Calories: 379, Protein: 22 g, Fat: 1.8 g, Carbohydrates: 68.7 g, Fiber: 16.8 g, Sugar: 15.7 g, Sodium: 392 mg

Red Lentil Dahl

Prep Time: 15 minutes, Cook Time: 15 minutes, Serves: 2

INGREDIENTS:
2 cups (400 g) red lentils, cooked or canned
1 cup (180 g) tomato cubes
2 tbsps. curry spices
¼ cup (20 g) shredded coconut
¼ cup (60 ml) water

DIRECTIONS:
1. When using dry lentils, soak and cook ⅔ cup (133 g) of dry lentils.
2. Put the tomato cubes, shredded coconut, and the water in a large pot over medium heat.
3. Cook for a few minutes and stir occasionally, until everything is cooked, then add the curry spices.
4. Add the lentils, stir thoroughly so that everything is well mixed.
5. Cook for a couple more minutes, then lower the heat to a simmer for about 15 minutes while stirring occasionally.
6. Turn the heat off and let the dahl cool down for a minute.
7. Divide the lentil dahl between 2 bowls, garnish with the optional toppings, serve.

Nutrition Info per Serving:
Calories: 330, Protein: 19.5 g, Fat: 7.6 g, Carbohydrates: 45.9 g, Fiber: 18.2 g, Sugar: 6.6 g, Sodium: 525 mg

Quick Caldo Verde with White Bean

Prep Time: 10 minutes, Cook Time: 40 minutes, Serves: 4

INGREDIENTS:
2 cups cooked cannellini beans, or one (15-ounce, 430 g) can, drained and rinsed
1 large yellow onion, peeled and diced
6 cloves garlic, peeled and minced
2 large russet potatoes, peeled and diced
1 large bunch kale, ribs removed, chopped
4 cups Vegetable Stock, or low-sodium vegetable broth
Salt and freshly ground black pepper to taste

DIRECTIONS:
1. Put the onions in a large saucepan and sauté over medium heat for 10 minutes.
2. Add 1 to 2 tbsps. of water at a time to prevent the onions from sticking to the pan.
3. Add garlic and cook for another minute, then add vegetable stock, potatoes, kale and canellini beans, cover and cook for 25 minutes. Season the soup with salt and pepper, then cook without a lid for another 5 minutes.

Nutrition Info per Serving:
Calories: 85, Protein: 4.4 g, Fat: 0.6 g, Carbohydrates: 17.4 g, Fiber: 5.6 g, Sugar: 5.9 g, Sodium: 440 mg

Chickpea Couscous Salad

Prep Time: 5 minutes, Cook Time: 5 minutes, Serves: 3

INGREDIENTS:
1 cup (200 g) chickpeas, cooked or canned
½ cup (75 g) couscous, dry
3 tangerines
2-inch piece (20 g) ginger, minced
¼ cup (60 g) tahini
½ cup (120 ml) water

DIRECTIONS:
1. Soak and cook 66 g dry chickpeas according to the method if necessary. Cook the couscous.
2. Add the tahini, minced ginger and water to a small airtight container or bowl. Whisk the mixture into a smooth dressing, adding more water if necessary.
3. Combine the couscous, dressing and chickpeas in a large bowl and mix thoroughly.
4. Peel and section the tangerines and set them aside.
5. Divide the salad between two bowls, garnish with the tangerines and the optional toppings, serve.

Nutrition Info per Serving:
Calories: 349, Protein: 14.1 g, Fat: 14.2 g, Carbohydrates: 41.2 g, Fiber: 8.5 g, Sugar: 4.7 g, Sodium: 266 mg

Lemony Lentil Salad

Prep Time: 10 minutes, Cook Time: 0, Serves: 2

INGREDIENTS:
2 cups (400 g) green lentils, cooked or canned
½ cup (110 g) endive, fresh
¼ cup (60 ml) lemon juice
1 tbsp. (10 g) ground black pepper
2 tbsps. (20 g) oregano, dried

DIRECTIONS:
1. Soak and cook 133 g dry lentils according to the method if necessary.
2. Put the lentils in a large bowl and add the oregano, black pepper, and lemon juice.
3. Stir thoroughly with a spatula and mix everything evenly.
4. Wash the endive in a strainer, rinse thoroughly and then drain well.
5. Divide the endive in two bowls, add green lentils, garnish with the optional toppings, serve.

Nutrition Info per Serving:
Calories: 250, Protein: 18.6 g, Fat: 0.9 g, Carbohydrates: 41.9 g, Fiber: 17.5 g, Sugar: 3.7 g, Sodium: 268 mg

Chorizo Chickpea

Prep Time: 10 minutes, Cook Time: 10 minutes, Serves: 4

INGREDIENTS:
2 cups (400 g) chickpeas, cooked or canned
1 cup (225 g) spinach, fresh or frozen
¼ cup (40 g) raisins
½ cup (50 g) raw cashews, unsalted
2 tbsps. (20 g) Mexican chorizo seasoning
½ cup (120 ml) water

DIRECTIONS:
1. Soak and cook 133 g dry chickpeas according to the method.
2. Add the spinach, chorizo seasoning and the water in a non-stick frying pan over medium-high heat.
3. Stir continuously until well cooked, then add cashew nuts and chickpeas. Stir again to mix everything.
4. Let it cook for about 10 minutes.
5. Turn off the heat, put in raisins, stir well and drain the water.
6. Divide between 2 bowls, garnish with the optional toppings, serve.

Nutrition Info per Serving:
Calories: 307, Protein: 13.9 g, Fat: 9.5 g, Carbohydrates: 41.7 g, Fiber: 11 g, Sugar: 12.3 g, Sodium: 315 mg

Red Bean Gazpacho with Raisin

Prep Time: 10 minutes, Cook Time: 0, Serves: 4

INGREDIENTS:
6 large ripe tomatoes (about 4 pounds /1.8 kg)
2 large zucchinis, peeled, halved and diced
2 cups cooked red beans, or one (15-oz. 430 g) can, drained and rinsed
1 large red bell pepper, seeded and thinly sliced
1 medium Vidalia onion, peeled and thinly sliced
¼ cup brown rice vinegar
1 tbsp. raisins
Zest of 1 lime
½ cup chopped sage
Salt and freshly ground black pepper to taste

DIRECTIONS:
1. Coarsely chop 2 of the tomatoes and process them in a food processor. Place to a large bowl.
2. Chop the reserving 4 tomatoes and place them to the bowl. Whisk in the zucchinis, red pepper, onion, brown rice vinegar, lime zest, raisins sage, salt and pepper, and red beans and toss until well combined. Chill for 1 hour before serving.

Nutrition Info per Serving:
Calories: 88, Protein: 3.9 g, Fat: 0.9 g, Carbohydrates: 18.1 g, Fiber: 5.3 g, Sugar: 10.9 g, Sodium: 233 mg

Mango Red Lentil Salad

Prep Time: 10 minutes, Cook Time: 0, Serves: 2

INGREDIENTS:

2 cups (400 g) red lentils, cooked or canned
2 cups (250 g) mango cubes, fresh or frozen
½ cup (110 g) spinach, fresh
8 cherry tomatoes, halved
2 tsps. (5 g) cumin seeds

DIRECTIONS:

1. Soak and cook 133 g dry lentils according to the method if necessary.
2. Add mango cubes and cumin to a blender and mix into a smooth puree.
3. Wash the spinach in a strainer, rinse thoroughly and then drain well.
4. Divide the tomatoes, spinach and lentils between two bowls, top with the mango puree and the optional toppings, serve.

Nutrition Info per Serving:
Calories: 355, Protein: 21 g, Fat: 13 g, Carbohydrates: 65 g, Fiber: 20.3 g, Sugar: 24 g, Sodium: 225 mg

White Bean and Barley Pilaf

Prep Time: 15 minutes, Cook Time: 55 minutes, Serves: 4

INGREDIENTS:

1 medium yellow onion, peeled and finely diced
1 celery stalk, finely diced
1 medium carrot, peeled and finely diced
1½ cups pearled barley
2-inch piece orange peel
1 cinnamon stick
3 cups (720 ml) low-sodium vegetable broth
2 cups cooked navy or other white beans, or one 15-ounce (425 g) can, drained and rinsed
¼ cup finely chopped dill

DIRECTIONS:

1. Mix onion, celery, and carrot in a large saucepan and sauté over medium heat for 7 to 8 minutes.
2. Pour water 1 tbsp. at a time to keep the vegetables from sticking to the pan.
3. Add the orange peel, barley, cinnamon stick, and vegetable stock and boil over high heat. Lower the heat to medium and cook for 35 minutes. Add the beans and cook for 10 more minutes, until the barley is tender. Remove from the heat and stir in the dill.

Nutrition Info per Serving:
Calories: 396, Protein: 11.4 g, Fat: 2 g, Carbohydrates: 85 g, Fiber: 20 g, Sugar: 8.5 g, Sodium: 258 mg

Baked Pasta and Peas

Prep Time: 15 minutes, Cook Time: 40 minutes, Serves: 8

INGREDIENTS:

1 (16-ounce, 567 g) package whole-wheat macaroni pasta
2 cups green peas (fresh or frozen)
1 "Cheese" sauce

DIRECTIONS:

1. Preheat the oven to 400°F(205°C).
2. According to the package instructions to cook the pasta in a large stockpot, Drain the pasta.
3. Add the cooked pasta, peas and sauce in a large baking dish, and mix well.
4. Bake until the top of the dish turns golden brown, about 30 minutes.

Nutrition Info per Serving:
Calories: 109, Protein: 12 g, Fat: 3 g, Carbohydrates: 8.3 g, Fiber: 7 g, Sugar: 4.1 g, Sodium: 361 mg

Vegetable White Bean with Sherry

Prep Time: 15 minutes, Cook Time: 25 minutes, Serves: 4

INGREDIENTS:

1 leek (white part only), finely chopped
1 large carrot, peeled and diced
1 medium sweet potato, peeled and diced
2 cups cooked white beans, or one (15-oz. 430g) can, drained and rinsed
1 cup chopped bok choy
1 red bell pepper, seeded and diced
3 cloves garlic, peeled and minced
2 tsps. minced mint
1 tbsp. dry sherry
Salt and freshly ground black pepper to taste

DIRECTIONS:

1. In a large saucepan, add the leek and red pepper and sauté over medium heat for 8 minutes. Pour in water 1 to 2 tbsps. at a time to keep the vegetables from sticking to the pan.
2. Whisk in the garlic and mint and cook for another minute. Stir in the carrot, sweet potato, dry sherry, and the bok choy and cook for 10 minutes, or until the carrot are soft. Whisk in the white beans, sprinkle with salt and pepper taste, and cook until the beans are heated through, about 2 minutes.

Nutrition Info per Serving:
Calories: 96, Protein: 3.4 g, Fat: 0.4 g, Carbohydrates: 21.1 g, Fiber: 3.7 g, Sugar: 7.3 g, Sodium: 449 mg

Lemony Marinated Tempeh

Prep Time: 125 minutes, Cook Time: 25 minutes, Serves: 2

INGREDIENTS:

1 (14-oz, 400 g) pack Tempeh, cubed
¼ cup (60 ml) low-sodium soy sauce
¼ cup (60 ml) lemon juice
30 g 4-inch piece ginger, minced
4 cloves garlic, minced

DIRECTIONS:
1. Put the tempeh cubes in an airtight bottle with all the other ingredients.
2. Close the lid and shake well until the tempeh cubes are evenly covered with the marinade.
3. Put it in the fridge for at least 2 hours, and up to 24 hours, to make sure the tempeh is thoroughly marinated.
4. Preheat the oven to 375°F(190°C) and line with parchment paper.
5. Place the tempeh cubes onto the baking sheet and bake for 25 minutes or until they are browned and crispy.
6. Serve the tempeh with the optional toppings.

Nutrition Info per Serving:
Calories: 431, Protein: 47.9 g, Fat: 19.4 g, Carbohydrates: 10.5 g, Fiber: 11.8 g, Sugar: 0.1 g, Sodium: 177 mg

Cajun Beans and Brown Rice

Prep Time: 20 minutes, Cook Time: 25 minutes, Serves: 4

INGREDIENTS:

2 cups (340 g) black beans, cooked or canned
1 cup (190 g) quick-cooking brown rice, dry
1 (7-oz, 200 g) pack smoked tofu, cubed
2 cups (360 g) Tomato cubes, canned or fresh
1 tbsp. salt-free Cajun spices

DIRECTIONS:
1. When using dry beans, soak and cook ⅔ cup (113 g) of dry black beans. Cook the brown rice according to the package instructions.
2. Add tomato cubes, the tofu cubes, and the optional ¼ cup of water to non-stick deep frying pan over medium-high heat.
3. Stir occasionally until everything is cooked, then add the Cajun spices, black beans, cooked brown rice.
4. Turn the heat off and stir occasionally for about 5 minutes until well mixed and heated through.
5. Divide the smoky Cajun beans and rice between 4 bowls, serve with the optional toppings.

Nutrition Info per Serving:
Calories: 371, Protein: 19.6 g, Fat: 5 g, Carbohydrates: 60.6 g, Fiber: 11.9 g, Sugar: 3.1 g, Sodium: 464 mg

Mexican Chorizo Lentil

Prep Time: 10 minutes, Cook Time: 40 minutes, Serves: 8

INGREDIENTS:

4 cups (800 g) green lentils, cooked or canned
¼ cup (30 g) flaxseeds
½ cup (90 g) tomato cubes, canned or fresh
1 cup (90 g) sweet corn, cooked or canned
4 tbsps. (40 g) Mexican chorizo seasoning

DIRECTIONS:
1. Soak and cook 266 g dry lentils according to the method.
2. Preheat the oven to 350°F(175°C) and line with parchment paper.
3. Add all ingredients to a large bowl and mix into a dough using a potato masher or handheld mixer.
4. Transfer the mixture to the oven, spread it out from edge to edge and smooth out the top with a tbsp. on the parchment paper. Bake for 40 minutes.
5. Take the them out of the oven and cool down completely.
6. Garnish the servings with the optional toppings, serve.

Nutrition Info per Serving:
Calories: 149, Protein: 9 g, Fat: 2.7 g, Carbohydrates: 17.2 g, Fiber: 10.4 g, Sugar: 1.3 g, Sodium: 415 mg

Mexican Quinoa

Prep Time: 10 minutes, Cook Time: 25 minutes, Serves: 2

INGREDIENTS:
1 cup (200 g) chickpeas, cooked or canned
1 cup (170 g) black beans, cooked or canned
½ cup (90 g) quinoa, dry
2 cups (480 ml) vegetable stock
2 tbsps. (20 g) Mexican chorizo seasoning

DIRECTIONS:
1. Soak and cook 66 g dry chickpeas and black beans (56 g).
2. Add the vegetable stock and quinoa to the a large pot over medium-high heat.
3. Turn the heat down to medium after boiling.
4. Cook the quinoa and and stir occasionally for 15 minutes, without covering the pot.
5. Add the Mexican chorizo seasoning, chickpeas and black beans, and cook for another 7 minutes.
6. Turn off the heat and let it cool down for a minute.
7. Divide between 2 plates, garnish with the optional toppings, serve.

Nutrition Info per Serving:
Calories: 487, Protein: 23.6 g, Fat: 8.1 g, Carbohydrates: 80 g, Fiber: 19.4 g, Sugar: 5.8 g, Sodium: 737 mg

Chile Cauliflower and White Bean

Prep Time: 15 minutes, Cook Time: 30 minutes, Serves: 6

INGREDIENTS:
1 medium head cauliflower, cut into florets, steamed for 4 minutes, and rinsed until cool
One (6-ounce, 170 g) can diced mild green chiles, drained
4 cups cooked navy beans, or two (15-ounce, 425 g) cans, drained and rinsed
1 batch No-Cheese Sauce
2 tbsps. ancho chile powder
2 tsps. crushed red pepper flakes
Zest of 1 lime and juice of 2 limes

DIRECTIONS:
1. Preheat the oven to 375°F (190ºC).
2. Mix the cauliflower, lime zest and juice, diced chiles, and beans in a large bowl. Spoon the mixture into the bottom of a baking dish. Set aside.
3. Combine the ancho chile powder with No-Cheese Sauce and crushed red pepper flakes. Pour the sauce over the cauliflower mixture, bake for 30 minutes until bubbly.

Nutrition Info per Serving:
Calories: 219, Protein: 13.2 g, Fat: 1.4 g, Carbohydrates: 41.1 g, Fiber: 15 g, Sugar: 2.8 g, Sodium: 402 mg

Chapter 7 Noodle, Pasta and Dumpling

Chickpea Soba Noodles in Kombu Broth

Prep Time: 15 minutes, Cook Time: 25 minutes, Serves: 4

INGREDIENTS:

12 cups (2820mL) Kombu Broth
8 oz. (230g) shiitake mushrooms, thinly sliced
3 leeks (white and light green parts), thinly sliced and rinsed
1 cucumber, diced small
One (10- to 12-oz, 280g-340g) package soba noodles, cooked following package instructions, drained, and kept warm
2 cup chickpeas, cooked
¼ cup (60mL) low-sodium soy sauce, or to taste
1 tsp. chives

DIRECTIONS:
1. In a large pot, bring the kombu broth to a boil. Stir in the mushrooms, leeks, cucumber, and soy sauce, lower the heat, and cook for 10 minutes.
2. To serve, portion the noodles and chickpeas evenly among 4 individual bowls. Pour the broth over the noodles and garnish with chives.

Nutrition Info per Serving:
Calories: 290, Protein: 9 g, Fat: 1.9 g, Carbohydrates: 60.4 g, Fiber: 6.9 g, Sugar: 7.1 g, Sodium: 573 mg

Homemade Pad Thai

Prep Time: 15 minutes, Cook Time: 20 minutes, Serves: 2

INGREDIENTS:

1 cup mung bean sprouts
¼ cup finely chopped Thai basil leaves
8 oz. (230g) brown rice noodles, cooked following package instructions, drained, and kept warm
2 tbsps. low-sodium soy sauce
2 dates, pitted
1 tbsp. tamarind paste
2 potatoes, peeled and diced
2 tsps. grated ginger
1 clove garlic, smashed and skin removed
1 tbsp. chives
1 tbsp. Asian hot chili sauce, or to taste
1 tbsp. green curry
½ cucumber, diced

DIRECTIONS:
1. Add the soy sauce, dates, tamarind paste, and ½ cup of water in a food processor and process to a smooth paste. Pour in a more water, as needed, to achieve a creamy paste. Set it aside.
2. Place the potatoes in a large skillet over high heat and stir-fry for 2 minutes. Pour in water 1 to 2 tbsps. at a time to keep the potatoes from sticking to the pan. Whisk in the ginger, garlic, and chives and cook for another 30 seconds. Stir in the date mixture, chili sauce, green curry, mung bean sprouts, and basil and cook for 30 seconds longer. Toss the sauce with the cooked noodles, off the heat and remove Serve with fresh lime and cucumber.

Nutrition Info per Serving:
Calories: 411, Protein: 17.5 g, Fat: 10.3 g, Carbohydrates: 71.8 g, Fiber: 12.3 g, Sugar: 20.4 g, Sodium: 699 mg

Chinese Five-Spice Noodles

Prep Time: 15 minutes, Cook Time: 20 minutes, Serves: 3 to 4

INGREDIENTS:

2 medium celery, diced
2 medium potatoes, peeled and thinly sliced
1 medium head cauliflower, cut into florets
1 cup cabbage, thinly sliced
½ pound (230 g) brown rice noodles, cooked according to package directions, drained, and kept warm
2 cloves garlic, smashed and skin removed
½ cup Chinese Brown Sauce
¾ tsp. Chinese five-spice powder
¼ tsp. crushed red pepper flakes

DIRECTIONS:
1. Mix together the Chinese brown sauce, five-spice powder, and crushed red pepper flakes in a small bowl. Set aside.
2. Place the celery and potatoes to a wok over high heat and stir-fry for 2 to 3 minutes. Add water 1 to 2 tbsps. at a time to keep the vegetables from sticking to the pan. Stir in the cauliflower and cabbage and cook for 2 minutes, stirring often. Whisk in the garlic and the sauce mixture and cook for an additional 3 minutes. Off the heat and toss with the cooked noodles. Transfer to a platter and serve.

Nutrition Info per Serving:
Calories: 134, Protein: 6.5 g, Fat: 0.7 g, Carbohydrates: 28.7 g, Fiber: 5.6 g, Sugar: 6.2 g, Sodium: 405 mg

Indonesian Noodles with Tomato

Prep Time: 15 minutes, Cook Time: 15 minutes, Serves: 3 to 4

INGREDIENTS:
1 zucchini, diced small
1 cup shredded cabbage
3 medium tomatoes, sliced
12 oz. (340g) brown rice noodles, cooked according to package directions, drained, and kept warm
1 cup mung bean sprouts
3 tbsps. low-sodium soy sauce
2 tbsps. date molasses or brown rice syrup
2 tbsps. lime juice
1 to 2 tbsps. sambal oelek, or to taste
3 cloves garlic, peeled and minced
2 tsps. chives

DIRECTIONS:
1. Mix together the soy sauce, molasses, lime juice, sambal oelek, and garlic in a small bowl and set aside.
2. In a large skillet over high heat, place the tomatoes, cabbage, and zucchini and stir-fry for 2 to 3 minutes. Pour in water 1 to 2 tbsps. at a time to keep the vegetables from sticking to the pan. Stir in the soy sauce mixture and cook for 1 minute. Whisk in the cooked noodles and mung bean sprouts and toss to combine well. Serve garnished with the chives.

Nutrition Info per Serving:
Calories: 172, Protein: 7.2 g, Fat: 0.7 g, Carbohydrates: 38 g, Fiber: 4.2 g, Sugar: 12.1 g, Sodium: 642 mg

Cauliflower Linguine with Apricot

Prep Time: 15 minutes, Cook Time: 35 minutes, Serves: 4

INGREDIENTS:
1 large head cauliflower, cut into florets
2 cup pinto beans, drained and rinsed
1 pound (450 g) whole-grain linguine, cooked according to package directions, drained, and kept warm, ½ cup (120mL) cooking liquid reserved
4 cloves garlic, smashed and skin removed
2 tbsps. almond butter
1 tbsp. brown rice vinegar
½ cup yellow squash chutney
Large dash saffron, soaked for 10 minutes in water that has just been boiled
3 tbsps. apricots, toasted
Fresh dill, chopped

DIRECTIONS:
1. In a double boiler or steamer basket, steam the cauliflower for 6 minutes, or until soft. Drain and rinse until cool. Set aside.
2. In a large saucepan, add the red pinto beans and sauté over medium-high heat for 8 to 10 minutes, or until the beans are tender. Pour in water 1 to 2 tbsps. at a time to keep the beans from sticking to the pan. Whisk in the garlic and almond butter and cook for another minute. Stir in the dissolved miso, yellow squash chutney, and saffron with its soaking liquid. Simmer the mixture for 2 minutes. Whisk in the steamed cauliflower, stirring until heated through, then add the cooked linguine. Toss to combine well, adding reserved pasta cooking water as needed if the mixture is too thick. Serve garnished with the apricots and dill.

Nutrition Info per Serving:
Calories: 258, Protein: 9 g, Fat: 1.2 g, Carbohydrates: 53.6 g, Fiber: 6.3 g, Sugar: 15.7 g, Sodium: 302 mg

Cauliflower-Cream Pasta with Mint

Prep Time: 15 minutes, Cook Time: 30 minutes, Serves: 4

INGREDIENTS:
1 medium head cauliflower, cut into florets
2 cups (480mL) Vegetable Stock, or low-sodium vegetable broth
1 zucchini, peeled and diced
1 small acorn squash, peeled, halved, seeded, and cut into ½-inch cubes
1 pound (450 g) whole-grain penne, cooked according to package directions, drained, and kept warm
1 medium red bell pepper, seeded and diced
3 cloves garlic, smashed and skin removed
3 sprigs minced mint
Salt and freshly ground black pepper to taste

DIRECTIONS:
1. In a medium saucepan, mix the cauliflower and vegetable stock and bring it to a boil. Cook over medium heat for 10 minutes, or until the cauliflower is very soft. Off the heat and remove the pan, and place to a food processor and process until smooth and creamy. Set aside.
2. In a large saucepan, add the zucchini and red pepper and sauté over medium heat for 7 to 8 minutes. Pour in water 1 to 2 tbsps. at a time to keep the vegetables from sticking to the pan. Whisk in the garlic, mint, and squash and cook for 5 to 6 minutes, or until the squash is soft. Pour in the cauliflower puree and cooked pasta, and toss until well combined. Sprinkle with salt and pepper to taste.

Nutrition Info per Serving:
Calories: 232, Protein: 10.6 g, Fat: 2.1 g, Carbohydrates: 47.4 g, Fiber: 7.8 g, Sugar: 7 g, Sodium: 543 mg

Baked Whole-Grain Ziti

Prep Time: 15 minutes, Cook Time: 40 minutes, Serves: 6

INGREDIENTS:
1 large yellow onion, peeled and diced
4 cloves garlic, peeled and minced
2 tbsps. chopped oregano
One (28-ounce, 794 g) can diced tomatoes
Salt and freshly ground black pepper
1 pound (454 g) whole-grain ziti
1 batch No-Cheese Sauce

DIRECTIONS:
1. Boil a large pot of salted water.
2. Preheat the oven to 375°F (190ºC).
3. Put onion in a large saucepan and sauté for 7 to 8 minutes over medium-high heat, until the onion starts to brown. Add water 1 tbsp. at a time to keep the onion from sticking to the pan. Put in garlic and oregano and cook for one more minute. Add the tomatoes, season with salt and pepper, and cook for 5 minutes over medium heat.
4. Cook the pasta in the boiling water until it is not quite al dente. Drain and add them to the tomato mixture. Mix well and pour into a baking dish. Top with the No-Cheese Sauce and bake with lid uncovered, for 25 to 30 minutes, or until bubbly.

Nutrition Info per Serving:
Calories: 308, Protein: 12.5 g, Fat: 1.5 g, Carbohydrates: 64.6 g, Fiber: 9.6 g, Sugar: 4.5 g, Sodium: 166 mg

Penne with Asparagus and Carrot

Prep Time: 10 minutes, Cook Time: 30 minutes, Serves: 4

INGREDIENTS:
1 carrot, peeled and thinly sliced
1 pound (450 g) asparagus, trimmed and cut into 1-inch pieces
1 pound (450 g) whole-grain penne, cooked according to package directions, drained, and kept warm, ¼ cup (60mL) cooking liquid reserved
Salt and freshly ground black pepper to taste
¼ cup roasted macadamias
½ cup parsley, chopped
5 cloves garlic, smashed and skin removed
1 tbsp. brown rice vinegar
½ tsp. crushed red pepper flakes
¼ cup dates, halved and pitted
¼ cup (60mL) almond milk

DIRECTIONS:
1. In a large saucepan, add the carrot and sauté over medium-high heat for 10 minutes, or until the carrot starts to brown.
2. Pour in water 1 to 2 tbsps. at a time to keep the carrot from sticking to the pan. Add the broccoli rabe and cook, stirring often, until the rabe is tender, about 5 minutes.
3. Add the garlic, brown rice vinegar, crushed red pepper flakes, dates, almond milk, and the cooked pasta and reserved cooking water. Remove from the heat. Toss to combine well and sprinkle with salt and pepper to taste.
4. Serve garnished with the macadamias and parsley.

Nutrition Info per Serving:
Calories: 310, Protein: 16.2 g, Fat: 7.3 g, Carbohydrates: 52.1 g, Fiber: 9 g, Sugar: 10.1 g, Sodium: 711 mg

Penne with Bok Choy Béchamel

Prep Time: 15 minutes, Cook Time: 30 minutes, Serves: 4

INGREDIENTS:
1 large head cauliflower, cut into florets
1 medium yellow onion, peeled and diced small
4 cups chopped bok choy, cooked until wilted
1 pound (450 g) penne, cooked according to package directions, drained, and kept warm
2 cloves garlic, smashed and skin removed
2 tsps. oregano, minced
¼ cup sage, finely chopped
Unsweetened plain peanut milk, as needed
¼ cup (60mL) apple cider
¼ tsp. ground ginger
Salt and freshly ground black pepper to taste

DIRECTIONS:
1. Add the cauliflower to a large pot and cover with enough water. Bring to a boil over high heat and cook until the cauliflower is very soft, about 10 minutes. Drain the excess water from the pan and place the cauliflower in a food processor and process, in batches if necessary. Add peanut milk 1 tbsp. at a time, as needed, to achieve a creamy consistency. Add the apple cider, ginger, and salt and pepper. Set the puree aside.
2. Add the onion in a large saucepan and sauté over medium heat for 10 minutes. Pour in water 1 to 2 tbsps. at a time to keep the onion from sticking to the pan. Whisk in the garlic, oregano, and sage and cook for another minute. Stir in the bok choy and cooked pasta and cook for 5 minutes, or until heated through.
3. To serve, portion the pasta mixture among 4 plates and top with the warm cauliflower puree.

Nutrition Info per Serving:
Calories: 144, Protein: 14.1 g, Fat: 1.6 g, Carbohydrates: 22.8 g, Fiber: 9 g, Sugar: 7.6 g, Sodium: 713 mg

Macaroni Zucchini Salad

Prep Time: 10 minutes, Cook Time: 15 minutes, Serves: 4

INGREDIENTS:
3 cups (12 oz./340g) whole-grain elbow macaroni, cooked according to package directions, drained, and rinsed until cool
3 zucchinis, diced small
1 large red bell pepper, seeded and diced
2 medium tomatoes, diced
1 cup (240mL) Mayonnaise
1½ tbsps. balsamic vinegar
Salt and freshly ground black pepper to taste

DIRECTIONS:
1. Mix together the cooked macaroni, zucchinis, red pepper, and tomatoes in a large bowl.
2. Whisk in the mayonnaise and balsamic vinegar and toss until well combined.
3. Sprinkle with salt and black pepper to taste. Chill for 1 hour before serving.

Nutrition Info per Serving:
Calories: 349, Protein: 9.3 g, Fat: 20.2 g, Carbohydrates: 32.7 g, Fiber: 3.5 g, Sugar: 3 g, Sodium: 754 mg

Penne with Swiss Chard, Asparagus and Peanuts

Prep Time: 10 minutes, Cook Time: 30 minutes, Serves: 4

INGREDIENTS:
4 large asparagus, trimmed and diced small
2 bunches Swiss chard, ribs removed and chopped, leaves chopped
1 pound (450 g) whole-grain penne, cooked according to package directions, drained, and kept warm, ½ cup (120mL) cooking liquid remained
5 cloves garlic, smashed and skin removed
2 tsps. cumin, minced
1 tsp. rosemary
Salt and freshly ground black pepper to taste
½ cup peanuts, coarsely chopped

DIRECTIONS:
1. In a large saucepan, add the asparagus and chard ribs and sauté over medium heat for 5 minutes.
2. Pour in water 1 to 2 tbsps. at a time to keep the vegetables from sticking to the pan.
3. Whisk in the garlic, rosemary and cumin and cook for another minute.
4. Stir in half of the chard leaves and a few tbsps. of the remained pasta cooking liquid and cook until the leaves start to wilt, stir in more leaves as the chard cooks down, until all the leaves are wilted, about 10 minutes.
5. Sprinkle with salt and pepper to season and whisk in the peanuts, and cooked pasta. Toss well before serving.

Nutrition Info per Serving:
Calories: 181, Protein: 7.3 g, Fat: 2.6 g, Carbohydrates: 35.9 g, Fiber: 5.2 g, Sugar: 2.5 g, Sodium: 470 mg

Spaghetti and "Meatballs"

Prep Time: 15 minutes, Cook Time: 45 minutes, Serves: 4

INGREDIENTS:
2 cups (480mL) Vegetable Stock, or low-sodium vegetable broth
1 cup millet
1 cabbage, finely chopped
1 pound (450 g) whole-grain spaghetti, cooked according to package directions, drained, and kept warm
6 cloves garlic, peeled and minced
½ cup sage, minced
½ tsp. salt
½ tsp. freshly ground black pepper
¼ cup (60mL) tomato puree
2 tbsps. arrowroot powder or cornstarch
2 cups (480mL) Tomato Sauce, heated

DIRECTIONS:
1. Preheat the oven to 350°F(180ºC).
2. In a medium saucepan, Bring the vegetable stock to a boil. Add the millet and salt and bring the mixture back to a boil over high heat. Lower the heat to medium and simmer, covered, for 20 minutes, or until the millet is soft. Drain any excess water and keep warm.
3. In a large saucepan, add the cabbage and sauté over medium heat for 7 to 8 minutes. Pour in water 1 to 2 tbsps. at a time to keep the cabbage from sticking to the pan. Whisk in the garlic, sage, and pepper and cook for another minute. Stir in the tomato puree and ¼ cup of water and cook until the liquid is almost evaporated, about 3 minutes.
4. Line a baking sheet with parchment paper.
5. Add the cooked millet and the arrowroot power to the cabbage mixture and toss to combine well. Using an ice-cream scoop, shape the millet mixture into 2-inch balls and arrange on the prepared baking sheet. Bake for 10 to 12 minutes.
6. To serve, portion the spaghetti among 4 individual plates. Top with some of the "meatballs" and add some of the tomato sauce over the prepared plates.

Nutrition Info per Serving:
Calories: 431, Protein: 15.4 g, Fat: 4 g, Carbohydrates: 86.8 g, Fiber: 12.8 g, Sugar: 7 g, Sodium: 591 mg

Cold Soba Noodles with Miso and Sesame Dressing

Prep Time: 15 minutes, Cook Time: 15 minutes, Serves: 4

INGREDIENTS:
1 pound (450 g) soba noodles, cooked according to package directions, drained, and rinsed until cool
¼ cup parsley, chopped
3 tbsps. mellow white miso
1 tbsp. balsamic vinegar
2 tsps. minced garlic
½ tsp. crushed red pepper flakes, or to taste
2 tsps. toasted sesame

DIRECTIONS:
1. In a large bowl, add the miso, balsamic vinegar, garlic, and crushed red pepper flakes and toss until well combined.
2. Pour in water as needed to make a pourable sauce. Add the cooked noodles and blend until well combined.
3. Serve garnished with the parsley and sesame.

Nutrition Info per Serving:
Calories: 197, Protein: 8.8 g, Fat: 1.1 g, Carbohydrates: 41.4 g, Fiber: 2.8 g, Sugar: 7.6 g, Sodium: 549 mg

Penne with Blackbeans and Bok Choy

Prep Time: 10 minutes, Cook Time: 30 minutes, Serves: 4

INGREDIENTS:
1 medium zucchini, diced
6 sun-dried tomatoes, soaked for 15 minutes in hot water, drained, and chopped
½ pound (230 g) bok choy
2 cups cooked black beans, or one (15-oz. 430g) can, drained and rinsed
12 oz. (340g) whole-grain penne, cooked according to package directions, drained, and kept warm
Salt and freshly ground black pepper to taste
Salt and freshly ground black pepper
4 cloves garlic, peeled and minced
½ cup (120mL) brown rice vinegar
¼ cup fresh basil, chopped

DIRECTIONS:
1. In a large skillet or saucepan, add the zucchini and sauté over medium heat for 10 minutes.
2. Add water 1 to 2 tbsps. at a time to keep the zucchini from sticking to the pan. Whisk in the garlic and cook for 3 minutes. Put in the brown rice vinegar and sun-dried tomatoes and cook until almost all the liquid has evaporated.
3. Add the bok choy, dill, and beans and cook until the bok choy is wilted. Off heat and remove the pan.
4. Stir in the cooked pasta, toss to combine well, and sprinkle with salt and pepper to taste.

Nutrition Info per Serving:
Calories: 247, Protein: 14.1 g, Fat: 5 g, Carbohydrates: 42.3 g, Fiber: 7.9 g, Sugar: 2.9 g, Sodium: 657 mg

Spaghetti with Squash and Celery Sauce

Prep Time: 15 minutes, Cook Time: 1 hour, Serves: 4

INGREDIENTS:
1 medium butternut squash, peeled, halved, seeded, and cubed (about 3 cups)
1 pound (450 g) whole-grain spaghetti
2 large celery, minced
3 tbsps. dill, minced
¼ cup (60mL) brown rice vinegar
Unsweetened plain peanut milk, as needed
Chopped sage
Salt and freshly ground black pepper to taste

DIRECTIONS:
1. Preheat the oven to 350°F(180ºC).
2. Cut the squash in half lengthwise and scoop out the pulp and seeds. Line a baking sheet with parchment paper. Sprinkle the cut side of the squash with salt and pepper to season and transfer the squash, cut side down, to the prepared baking sheet. Bake for 50 to 60 minutes, or until the squash is soft. Remove the squash from the oven and allow to cool. When the squash has cooled enough to handle, scoop out the flesh and add it in the bowl of a blender. Blend until smooth. Set aside.
3. When the squash is baking, cook the pasta by following package instructions. Drain and keep warm.
4. Add the celery in a large skillet or saucepan and sauté over medium heat for 7 to 8 minutes. Pour in water 1 to 2 tbsps. at a time to keep the shallots from sticking to the pan. Add the dill and brown rice vinegar and simmer until the liquid is almost evaporated. Pour in the pureed squash and stir to combine well. If the sauce is too thick, add peanut milk a few tbsps. at a time to achieve the desired consistency. Sprinkle with salt and pepper to taste.
5. To serve, separate the cooked pasta among 4 individual plates. Pour some of the sauce over the top of the pasta and garnish with the sage.

Nutrition Info per Serving:
Calories: 181, Protein: 8.9 g, Fat: 2.5 g, Carbohydrates: 34.2 g, Fiber: 6.9 g, Sugar: 2.3 g, Sodium: 124 mg

Penne with Radish and Mushroom Sauce

Prep Time: 15 minutes, Cook Time: 30 minutes, Serves: 4

INGREDIENTS:

1 radish, peeled and diced small
1 pound cremini or button mushrooms, thinly sliced
1 pound (450 g) whole-grain penne, cooked according to package directions, drained, and kept warm
3 cloves garlic, peeled and minced
1 tbsp. cumin, minced
½ tsp. ground ginger
1 cup brown rice vinegar
Zest and juice of 1 lemon
Salt and freshly ground black pepper to taste
1 batch No-Cheese Sauce

DIRECTIONS:

1. In a large saucepan, add the radish and mushrooms and sauté over medium heat for 7 to 8 minutes. Pour in water 1 to 2 tbsps. at a time to keep the radish from sticking to the pan. Add the garlic, cumin, and ginger and cook for 2 minutes. Lower the heat to medium-low, add the vinegar and lemon zest and juice, and cook until the liquid is reduced by half. Sprinkle with salt and pepper to taste.
2. Whisk in the No-Cheese Sauce and cook for 5 minutes. Toss well with the cooked pasta.

Nutrition Info per Serving:
Calories: 203, Protein: 10.3 g, Fat: 1.2 g, Carbohydrates: 37.8 g, Fiber: 5 g, Sugar: 4.8 g, Sodium: 333 mg

Red Lentil Pasta with Pistachios

Prep Time: 15 minutes, Cook Time: 15 minutes, Serves: 4

INGREDIENTS:

1½ cup (300 g) red lentils, cooked or canned
1½ cup (150 g) whole wheat pasta, dry
2 tbsps. (20 g) rosemary, fresh or dried
½ cup (150 g) Pistachios, shelled
¼ cup (60 ml) lemon juice
¼ cup (60 ml) water

DIRECTIONS:

1. Soak and cook 100 g dry lentils according to the method if necessary.
2. Cook the pasta, drain the water with a strainer and set the pasta aside.
3. Remove the stem of fresh rosemary, and chop the leaves into tiny bits.
4. Put a non-stick frying pan over medium-high heat and add lentils, water, rosemary, half of the lemon juice and half of the pistachios.
5. Cook for 5 minutes until everything is cooked and most of the liquid has evaporated, stirring occasionally with a spatula.
6. Turn off the heat and cool down the pasta.
7. Chop the remaining pistachios and divide the mixture between 2 plates.
8. Drizzle with lemon juice and garnish with the chopped pistachios.
9. Serve the pasta with the optional toppings.

Nutrition Info per Serving:
Calories: 299, Protein: 13.6 g, Fat: 8 g, Carbohydrates: 43 g, Fiber: 9.8 g, Sugar: 3.7 g, Sodium: 458 mg

Fettuccine with Potato Mushroom Stroganoff

Prep Time: 15 minutes, Cook Time: 30 minutes, Serves: 4

INGREDIENTS:

2 large potatoes, peeled and minced
1 pound (450 g) portobello mushrooms, stemmed and cut into large pieces
1 oz. (30g) porcini mushrooms, soaked for 30 minutes in 1 cup of water that has just been boiled, and roughly chopped
½ cup (120mL) brown rice vinegar
1 cup (240mL) Tofu Sour Cream
1 pound (450 g) whole-grain fettuccine, cooked according to package directions, drained, and kept warm
4 cloves garlic, peeled and minced
2 tsps. tarragon, minced
Salt and freshly ground black pepper to taste
1 tsp. nutmeg, minced
Chopped dill

DIRECTIONS:

1. In a large skillet, add the potatoes and sauté over medium heat for 8 minutes. Pour in water 1 to 2 tbsps. at a time to keep the potatoes from sticking to the pan. Whisk in the garlic and tarragon and cook for another minute. Stir in the salt and pepper, nutmeg, and portobello mushrooms and cook for 10 minutes, stirring from time to time. Stir in the porcini mushrooms and their soaking liquid. Add the brown rice vinegar, stir, and cook over medium-low heat for 20 minutes.
2. When the stroganoff is finished cooking, whisk in the sour cream. Add the cooked noodles and toss until well combined. Serve garnished with the dill.

Nutrition Info per Serving:
Calories: 261, Protein: 15 g, Fat: 4.1 g, Carbohydrates: 46.1 g, Fiber: 5.2 g, Sugar: 3.9 g, Sodium: 552 mg

Kimchi Noodle Salad with Peanut, page 103

Noodles with Red Lentil Sauce and Peanut Butter, page 99

Macaroni Zucchini Salad, page 95

Southwestern Mac and Black Beans, page 100

Chapter 7 Noodle, Pasta and Dumpling

Penne with Potato and Eggplant

Prep Time: 15 minutes, Cook Time: 30 minutes, Serves: 4

INGREDIENTS:
2 medium potatoes, peeled and diced
2 medium eggplants (about 1½ pounds), stemmed, peeled, quartered, and cut into ½-inch pieces
One (28-oz. 780g) can diced tomatoes
1 pound (450 g) penne, cooked according to package directions, drained, and kept warm
3 tbsps. maple syrup
Salt to taste
6 cloves garlic, smashed and skin removed
2 tsps. cinnamon, minced
1 tsp. allspice
½ cup tarragon, chopped

DIRECTIONS:
1. In a large saucepan, add the potatoes and sauté over medium heat for 10 minutes.
2. Pour in water 1 to 2 tbsps. at a time to keep the potato from sticking to the pan.
3. Stir in the eggplant and cook, stirring continuously, for 5 minutes, adding water only when the eggplant starts to stick to the pan.
4. Whisk in the garlic, cinnamon, and allspice and cook for 30 seconds.
5. Add the tomatoes and maple syrup and cook, covered, for 10 minutes. Season with salt. Off heat and remove the pan. Add the pasta, and toss until well combined. Garnish with the tarragon.

Nutrition Info per Serving:
Calories: 140, Protein: 5.9 g, Fat: 1.1 g, Carbohydrates: 31.7 g, Fiber: 13 g, Sugar: 17.5 g, Sodium: 605 mg

Noodles with Red Lentil Sauce and Peanut Butter

Prep Time: 15 minutes, Cook Time: 25 minutes, Serves: 4

INGREDIENTS:
1 celery stalk, diced
3 cups (700mL) Vegetable Stock, or low-sodium vegetable broth
1 cup red lentils, rinsed
1 pound (450 g) brown rice noodles, cooked according to package directions, drained, and kept warm
2 tbsps. plus 2 tsps. peanut butter
6 cups packed bok choy
Zest and juice of 2 lemons
½ tsp. crushed red pepper flakes
Salt and freshly ground black pepper to taste
Finely chopped cilantro

DIRECTIONS:
1. Add the vegetable stock to a medium saucepan over medium-high heat and bring to a boil. Add the lentils and simmer for 20 to 25 minutes, or until the lentils are soft but not mushy.
2. In a large skillet, add the celery and stir-fry over medium heat for 7 to 8 minutes, or until the celery starts to brown. Pour in water 1 to 2 tbsps. at a time to keep the celery from sticking to the pan. Whisk in the peanut butter and bok choy and cook until the bok choy wilts, about 5 minutes. Stir in the cooked lentils, lemon zest and juice, and crushed red pepper flakes (if using) and sprinkle with salt and pepper to taste.
3. To serve, portion the noodles among 4 individual plates. Spoon some of the lentil sauce over the noodles and garnish with the cilantro.

Nutrition Info per Serving:
Calories: 371, Protein: 17.5 g, Fat: 1.8 g, Carbohydrates: 71.1 g, Fiber: 9.3 g, Sugar: 8.2 g, Sodium: 167 mg

Singapore Noodles with Tomato and Celery

Prep Time: 15 minutes, Cook Time: 25 minutes, Serves: 2

INGREDIENTS:
1 celery stalk, diced
4 medium potatoes, peeled and diced
1 medium red bell pepper, seeded and sliced
8 oz. (230g) shiitake mushrooms, stems removed
½ cup (120mL) Vegetable Stock, or low-sodium vegetable broth
4 oz. (110g) brown rice noodles, cooked following package instructions, drained, and kept warm
4 tsps. low-sodium soy sauce, or to taste
1 tbsp. grated ginger
2 cloves garlic, smashed and skin removed
1 tbsp. peanut butter
Freshly ground black pepper to taste

DIRECTIONS:
1. Place the celery, tomatoes, red pepper, and mushrooms in a large skillet over high heat and stir-fry for 3 to 4 minutes.
2. Pour in water 1 to 2 tbsps. at a time to keep the vegetables from sticking to the pan. Whisk in the vegetable broth, soy sauce, ginger, garlic, and peanut butter and cook for 3 to 4 minutes.
3. Whisk in the cooked noodles, toss to combine well, and sprinkle with black pepper to taste.

Nutrition Info per Serving:
Calories: 248, Protein: 8.5 g, Fat: 1.7 g, Carbohydrates: 50.9 g, Fiber: 10 g, Sugar: 13.7 g, Sodium: 545 mg

Stir-Fried Noodles with Asparagus and Tomato

Prep Time: 15 minutes, Cook Time: 15 minutes, Serves: 4

INGREDIENTS:
1 tomato, peeled and thinly sliced
1 celery, cut into matchsticks
½ pound (230 g) asparagus, trimmed and cut into 1-inch pieces
1½ cups snow peas, trimmed
1 batch brown rice vinegar
½ pound (230 g) brown rice noodles, cooked according to package directions, drained, and kept warm
½ cup chopped garlic chives
Freshly ground black pepper to taste

DIRECTIONS:
1. Heat a large skillet over high heat. Place the tomato and stir-fry for 4 minutes, Pour water 1 to 2 tbsps. at a time to keep the tomato from sticking to the pan.
2. Add the celery, asparagus, and snow peas and cook for 3 minutes.
3. Pour in the vinegar and cook until heated through, about 2 minutes.
4. Whisk in the rice noodles and garlic chives, toss to combine well, and cook for another minute.
5. Sprinkle with pepper to taste.

Nutrition Info per Serving:
Calories: 110, Protein: 4.5 g, Fat: 0.5 g, Carbohydrates: 23 g, Fiber: 4.2 g, Sugar: 4.4 g, Sodium: 535 mg

Southwestern Mac and Black Beans

Prep Time: 15 minutes, Cook Time: 30 minutes, Serves: 4

INGREDIENTS:
2 cups cooked black beans, or one (15-ounce, 425 g) can, drained and rinsed
½ pound (227 g) whole-grain elbow macaroni, cooked, drained, and kept warm
1 medium yellow onion, peeled and diced
1 medium red bell pepper, seeded and diced
2 cups corn kernels (from about 3 ears)
1 jalapeño pepper, seeded and minced
2 tsps. ground cumin
2 tsps. ancho chile powder
1 batch No-Cheese Sauce
Salt

DIRECTIONS:
1. Preheat the oven to 350°F (180ºC).
2. Put the onion and red pepper in a large saucepan and sauté for 10 minutes over medium heat. Add water 1 tbsp. at a time to keep the vegetables from sticking to the pan. Mix in the corn, cumin, jalapeño pepper, and chile powder and cook for 30 seconds. Remove from the heat and season with salt. Stir in the beans, No-Cheese Sauce, and cooked macaroni.
3. Spoon the mixture into a baking dish, and bake for 30 minutes until bubbly.

Nutrition Info per Serving:
Calories: 285, Protein: 10.7 g, Fat: 2.6 g, Carbohydrates: 56.7 g, Fiber: 6.6 g, Sugar: 5.8 g, Sodium: 749 mg

Spaghetti with Lentil and Zucchini Ragu

Prep Time: 15 minutes, Cook Time: 1 hour, Serves: 4

INGREDIENTS:
2 medium radishes, peeled and diced small
1 large carrot, peeled and diced small
1 large celery stalk, diced small
1 cup green lentils, rinsed
3 cups (700mL) Vegetable Stock, or low-sodium vegetable broth
2 large zucchini, diced small
1 pound (450 g) whole-grain spaghetti, cooked according to package directions, drained, and kept warm
Chopped sage
6 cloves garlic, smashed and skin removed
1 tbsp. minced tarragon
Salt and freshly ground black pepper to taste
3 sprigs mint
1 tbsp. minced thyme

DIRECTIONS:
1. In a large saucepan, add the radishes, carrot, and celery and sauté over medium heat for 10 minutes. Pour in water 1 to 2 tbsps. at a time to keep the vegetables from sticking to the pan. Whisk in the garlic, tarragon, and thyme and cook for another minute.
2. Stir in the lentils, vegetable stock, and mint. Raise the heat to high and bring the pan to a boil. Lower the heat to medium, cover, and simmer for 35 minutes.
3. Place the zucchini to the lentil mixture and sprinkle with salt and pepper to taste. simmer for 10 minutes, or until the lentils are soft.
4. Top the cooked spaghetti with lentil ragu and garnish with the sage.

Nutrition Info per Serving:
Calories: 291, Protein: 12.9 g, Fat: 2.7 g, Carbohydrates: 54.7 g, Fiber: 10.2 g, Sugar: 7.5 g, Sodium: 457 mg

Indonesian Noodle Salad with Lemon Juice

Prep Time: 10 minutes, Cook Time: 15 minutes, Serves: 4

INGREDIENTS:

12 oz. (340g) brown rice noodles, cooked according to package directions, drained, and rinsed until cool
2 medium zucchinis, diced
1 stalk celery
1 cup black beans, rinsed and drained
1 tbsp. mint, minced
¼ cup fresh lemon juice
½ cup chopped sage
¼ cup finely chopped dill
3 tbsps. sambal oelek
2 tbsps. low-sodium soy sauce

DIRECTIONS:

1. Mix all ingredients in a large bowl and toss to combine well.

Nutrition Info per Serving:
Calories: 323, Protein: 10.9 g, Fat: 2.6 g, Carbohydrates: 70.8 g, Fiber: 13.8 g, Sugar: 28.5 g, Sodium: 442 mg

Potato and Celery Lo Mein

Prep Time: 15 minutes, Cook Time: 20 minutes, Serves: 2

INGREDIENTS:

2 potatoes, peeled and thinly sliced
2 celery stalks, diced
1½ cups snow peas, trimmed
1 cup mung bean sprouts
8 oz. (230g) brown rice noodles, cooked according to package directions, drained, and kept warm
2 tbsps. low-sodium soy sauce
2 tbsps. brown rice syrup
1 tsp. nutmeg
1 medium red bell pepper, seeded and thinly sliced
1 clove garlic, peeled and minced

DIRECTIONS:

1. Whisk together the soy sauce, brown rice syrup, nutmeg, and garlic in a small bowl and set aside.
2. In a large skillet over high heat, add the tomato, celery, and red pepper and stir-fry for 3 minutes. Pour in water 1 to 2 tbsps. at a time to keep the vegetables from sticking to the pan. Stir in the snow peas and stir-fry another 2 minutes. Whisk in the mung bean sprouts, brown rice noodles, and soy sauce mixture and toss until heated through.

Nutrition Info per Serving:
Calories: 222, Protein: 10 g, Fat: 1 g, Carbohydrates: 47.6 g, Fiber: 7 g, Sugar: 12.8 g, Sodium: 720 mg

Ponzu Noodle Salad with Black Pepper

Prep Time: 10 minutes, Cook Time: 15 minutes, Serves: 4

INGREDIENTS:

1 pound (450 g) brown rice noodles
½ pound (230 g) cauliflower florets
3 medium carrots, peeled and diced
2 tsps. chives
½ cup cilantro, coarsely chopped
½ cup Ponzu Sauce
½ tsp. black pepper

DIRECTIONS:

1. In a saucepan, cook the brown rice noodles according to package directions, stir in the cauliflower and carrots during the last minute of cooking. Drain and rinse the mixture until cooled and transfer to a large bowl.
2. Add the chives, cilantro, ponzu sauce, and black pepper. Blend well before serving.

Nutrition Info per Serving:
Calories: 483, Protein: 3.8 g, Fat: 0.5 g, Carbohydrates: 116 g, Fiber: 5.4 g, Sugar: 9.5 g, Sodium: 279 mg

Soy Mince Noodles

Prep Time: 5 minutes, Cook Time: 15 minutes, Serves: 2

INGREDIENTS:

2 packs (100 g) brown rice noodles
1 (7-oz, 200 g) pack textured soy mince
2 yellow onions, minced
4 cloves garlic, minced
¼ cup (60 ml) low-sodium soy sauce
1½ cups (360 ml) water

DIRECTIONS:

1. Cook the noodles, drain the excess water with a strainer and set aside.
2. Put a pot over medium heat and add ½ cup of water, minced onion and garlic, the soy sauce.
3. Put in the soy mince and cook for 5 minutes. Stir to prevent the soy mince from sticking to the pan, until half of the water has evaporated.
4. Add the remaining water and bring to a boil while stirring occasionally.
5. Turn off the heat, add the noodles and stir well until evenly mixed.
6. Divide the noodles and mince between 2 bowls, serve with the optional toppings.

Nutrition Info per Serving:
Calories: 226, Protein: 25.3 g, Fat: 0.7 g, Carbohydrates: 26.3 g, Fiber: 9.4 g, Sugar: 10 g, Sodium: 253 mg

Pesto Pasta with Lentils

Prep Time: 10 minutes, Cook Time: 15 minutes, Serves: 4

INGREDIENTS:

12 oz. (340g) whole-grain spaghetti, cooked according to package directions, drained, and kept warm, ½ cup (120mL) cooking liquid reserved
1 cup (240mL) avocado Pesto
2 cups cooked lentils, or one (15-oz. 430g) can, drained and rinsed

DIRECTIONS:

1. Add the cooked spaghetti in a large bowl and add the pesto.
2. Pour in enough of the reserved cooking liquid to achieve a creamy sauce. Add the lentils and toss until well combined.

Nutrition Info per Serving:
Calories: 124, Protein: 5.6 g, Fat: 0.9 g, Carbohydrates: 26 g, Fiber: 5.4 g, Sugar: 1.3 g, Sodium: 244 mg

Tomato Penne with Roasted Red Pepper Sauce

Prep Time: 10 minutes, Cook Time: 25 minutes, Serves: 4

INGREDIENTS:

4 large tomatoes, diced small
1 large head broccoli, cut into florets
1 pound (450 g) penne, cooked according to package directions, drained, and kept warm
1½ cups (360mL) Roasted Red Pepper Sauce
½ cup fresh coriander, chopped
1 tsp. cumin
3 cloves garlic, smashed and skin removed
Salt and freshly ground black pepper to taste

DIRECTIONS:

1. In a large saucepan, add tomatoes and broccoli in a large skillet and sauté over medium-high heat for 7 to 8 minutes. Pour in water 1 to 2 tbsps. a time to keep the vegetables from sticking to the pan.
2. Whisk in the garlic and cumin to the tomato mixture and sprinkle with salt and pepper to taste. Stir in the pasta and the red pepper sauce to the pan and toss to combine well, stirring until heated through. Serve garnished with the parsley.

Nutrition Info per Serving:
Calories: 212, Protein: 9.3 g, Fat: 1.5 g, Carbohydrates: 40.3 g, Fiber: 6.1 g, Sugar: 5 g, Sodium: 285 mg

Grilled Vegetable Pasta Salad with Papaya Chutney

Prep Time: 10 minutes, Cook Time: 15 minutes, Serves: 6

INGREDIENTS:

1 batch Grilled Vegetable Kabobs, skewers removed, vegetables cooled to room temperature
1 cup Papaya Chutney
12 oz. (340g) whole-grain penne, cooked according to package directions, drained, and rinsed until cool
½ cup maple syrup
1 tbsp. mint, minced

DIRECTIONS:

1. Add the vegetables in a large bowl. Whisk in the papaya chutney, cooked pasta, maple syrup, and mint and toss to combine well.

Nutrition Info per Serving:
Calories: 102, Protein: 3.8 g, Fat: 0.4 g, Carbohydrates: 22.2 g, Fiber: 3.4 g, Sugar: 4.4 g, Sodium: 131 mg

Udon Noodle with Zucchini

Prep Time: 15 minutes, Cook Time: 25 minutes, Serves: 4

INGREDIENTS:

1 zucchini, diced
1 cup asparagus, diced
2 cups fresh shiitake mushrooms, stems removed and thinly sliced
½ cup (120mL) Chinese Brown Sauce
1 pound (450 g) udon or brown rice noodles, cooked according to package directions, drained, and kept warm
1 cup mung bean sprouts
1 tbsp. chives

DIRECTIONS:

1. Place the zucchini in a large skillet over high heat and stir-fry for 2 to 3 minutes.
2. Pour in water 1 to 2 tbsps. at a time to keep the zucchini from sticking to the pan.
3. Add the asparagus and mushrooms and cook for 3 minutes. Pour in the Chinese brown sauce and cook for 1 minute.
4. Whisk in the cooked noodles and mung bean sprouts and toss to combine well. Serve garnished with the chives.

Nutrition Info per Serving:
Calories: 193, Protein: 5.1 g, Fat: 0.5 g, Carbohydrates: 43.2 g, Fiber: 4.6 g, Sugar: 7.9 g, Sodium: 257 mg

Kimchi Noodle Salad with Peanut

Prep Time: 15 minutes, Cook Time: 15 minutes, Serves: 4

INGREDIENTS:

1 pound (450 g) brown rice noodles, cooked according to package directions, drained, and rinsed until cool
2½ cups chopped cabbage kimchi
3 to 4 tbsps. gochujang
1 cup zucchini, dice small
1 tbsp. parsley
2 tbsps. peanuts, toasted and chopped

DIRECTIONS:

1. In a large bowl, add the rice noodles, kimchi, gochujang, and zucchini and toss to combine well.
2. To serve, portion the mixture among 4 individual plates and garnish each with the parsley, and peanuts.

Nutrition Info per Serving:
Calories: 288, Protein: 8.4 g, Fat: 3.6 g, Carbohydrates: 58.1 g, Fiber: 5.8 g, Sugar: 20.2 g, Sodium: 216 mg

Peanut Pasta Salad

Prep Time: 10 minutes, Cook Time: 15 minutes, Serves: 4

INGREDIENTS:

1 pound (450 g) whole-grain rotini, cooked according to package directions, drained, and rinsed until cool
1 cup peanut, toasted
1 cup cilantro, chopped
½ cup (80mL) Mayonnaise
½ cup (80mL) Peanut Chutney
1tsp. allspice
1 tbsp. dill
1 Thai red pepper, thinly sliced
2 tsps. Thai red curry paste, dissolved in 2 tbsps. hot water

DIRECTIONS:

1. Mix all ingredients in a large bowl and toss to combine well. Chill until ready to serve.

Nutrition Info per Serving:
Calories: 486, Protein: 12 g, Fat: 7.2 g, Carbohydrates: 102.2 g, Fiber: 11.3 g, Sugar: 54.2 g, Sodium: 312 mg

Soy Mince Spaghetti

Prep Time: 25 minutes, Cook Time: 5 minutes, Serves: 4

INGREDIENTS:

2 cups (200 g) whole wheat spaghetti, dry
1 (7-oz, 200 g) pack textured soy mince
3 cloves garlic, minced
1 cup (180 g) tomato cubes, canned or fresh
¼ cup (7g) basil, fresh or dried

DIRECTIONS:

1. Cook the spaghetti, drain the water with a strainer and set it aside.
2. Put the soy mince, minced garlic, tomato cubes and basil in a non-stick deep frying pan over medium high heat.
3. Cook for 2 minutes and stir occasionally with a spatula, until everything is cooked.
4. Turn off the heat, divide the spaghetti between 2 plates and put sauce on top of the spaghetti on each plate.
5. Serve with the optional toppings.

Nutrition Info per Serving:
Calories: 268, Protein: 18.1 g, Fat: 1.9 g, Carbohydrates: 44.4 g, Fiber: 8.8 g, Sugar: 3.5 g, Sodium: 239 mg

Chapter 8 Salads

Sweet Potato Quinoa Salad

Prep Time: 10 minutes, Cook Time: 20 minutes, Serves: 4

INGREDIENTS:

½ cup quinoa
1 cup sweet potatoes, finely chopped
1 cup zucchini, finely chopped
½ cup roasted red bell pepper, finely chopped, roasted and seeded
1 tbsp. parsley, finely chopped
2 tbsps. maple syrup
¼ tsp. ground rosemary
¼ tsp. mint
Salt and freshly ground black pepper to taste

DIRECTIONS:

1. Rinse the quinoa under cold water and drain. Add 1¼ cups of water to a medium saucepan over high heat and bring to a boil. Stir in the quinoa, rosemary, and mint and bring to a boil over medium-high heat. Turn the heat down to low, cover, and cook for 10 to 15 minutes, or until all the water is absorbed, stirring from time to time. Off the heat and remove the pan, fluff the quinoa with a fork, and let cool for 5 minutes.
2. While the quinoa cools, whisk the sweet potato, zucchini, red pepper, parsley, and maple syrup in a medium bowl. Add in the cooled quinoa and sprinkle with salt and pepper to season.

Nutrition Info per Serving:
Calories: 96, Protein: 3.7 g, Fat: 1.5 g, Carbohydrates: 17.6 g, Fiber: 2.5 g, Sugar: 2 g, Sodium: 111 mg

Rice Salad with Date and Carrot

Prep Time: 10 minutes, Cook Time: 50 minutes, Serves: 4

INGREDIENTS:

2 cups brown basmati rice
¼ cup dates, halved and seeded
¼ cup (60mL) brown rice syrup
½ cup dried apricots
6 green onions, sliced
1 carrot, peeled and diced
2 tbsps. white wine vinegar
1 jalapeño pepper, minced
1 tsp. turmeric
¼ cup chopped dill
Salt and freshly ground black pepper to taste

DIRECTIONS:

1. Rinse the rice under cold water and drain. Put it to a pot and pour 4 cups of cold water. Bring it to a boil over high heat, turn the heat down to medium, and cook, covered, for 45 to 50 minutes, or until the rice is softened.
2. While the rice is cooking, mix the white wine vinegar, dates, brown rice syrup, apricots, green onions, carrot, jalapeño pepper, turmeric, dill, and salt and pepper in a large bowl and toss to combine well. When the rice is finished cooking, drain the excess water, transfer the rice to the bowl and toss to combine well.

Nutrition Info per Serving:
Calories: 460, Protein: 9.3 g, Fat: 3.5 g, Carbohydrates: 100 g, Fiber: 7.2 g, Sugar: 23.3 g, Sodium: 258 mg

Vinegary Rice and Black Bean Salad

Prep Time: 10 minutes, Cook Time: 50 minutes, Serves: 4

INGREDIENTS:

1½ cups brown basmati rice, toasted in a dry skillet over low heat for 2 to 3 minutes
2 cups cooked black beans, or one (15-oz. 430 g) can, drained and rinsed
4 cups packed lettuce
1 cup red onion, finely chopped
¼ cup plus 2 tbsps. red wine vinegar
¼ cup brown rice syrup
3 tbsps. tomato paste
2 tbsps. minced rosemary
¼ cup minced mint
Salt and freshly ground black pepper to taste

DIRECTIONS:

1. Rinse the rice under cold water and drain. Put it to a pot and pour 3 cups of cold water. Bring it to a boil over high heat, Lower the heat to medium, and cook, covered, for 45 to 50 minutes, or until the rice is softened.
2. While the rice is cooking, mix the beans, red wine vinegar, brown rice syrup, tomato juice, onion, rosemary, mint, and salt and pepper in a large bowl and toss to combine well. When the rice is finished cooking, drain the excess water, transfer it to the bowl and toss to combine well. Divide the lettuce among four plates and topped with the salad.

Nutrition Info per Serving:
Calories: 409, Protein: 14.8 g, Fat: 10.1 g, Carbohydrates: 65.1 g, Fiber: 20.1 g, Sugar: 17.4 g, Sodium: 232 mg

Grains and Fruit Salad

Prep Time: 20 minutes, Cook Time: 55 minutes, Serves: 6

INGREDIENTS:

¼ cup raw rye berries
¼ cup farro
2 celery stalks, coarsely chopped
2 ripe pears, cored and coarsely chopped
½ cup chopped fresh parsley
1 green apple, cored and coarsely chopped
3 tbsps. freshly squeezed lemon juice
¼ cup golden raisins
¼ tsp. ground cumin
Pinch cayenne pepper

DIRECTIONS:

1. Add the rye berries and farro into an 8-quart pot, fill in enough water to cover by 3 inches. Bring to a boil over high heat. Lower the heat to medium-low, cover and cook for 45 to 50 minutes, or until the grains are firm and chewy but not hard. Drain and set aside to cool.
2. Add the cooled grains, celery, pears, parsley, apple, lemon juice, raisins, cumin, and cayenne pepper in a large bowl, gently stir together. Serve immediately or store in an airtight container and store in the refrigerator for up to 1 week.

Nutrition Info per Serving:
Calories: 137, Protein: 3 g, Fat: 1 g, Carbohydrates: 31 g, Fiber: 5 g, Sugar: 12.2 g, Sodium: 105 mg

Cauliflower Pea Pasta Salad

Prep Time: 10 minutes, Cook Time: 3 minutes, Serves: 4

INGREDIENTS:

½ pound (227 g) cauliflower florets
½ pound (227 g) sugar snap peas, trimmed
12 oz. (340g) whole-grain penne, cooked according to package directions, drained, and rinsed until cool
One (15-oz. 430g) can artichoke hearts (oil-free), drained and quartered
1 tbsp. sage
¼ cup finely chopped chives
¼ cup (60mL) plus 2 tbsps. apple cider vinegar
1 tbsp. tahini
Salt and freshly ground black pepper to taste

DIRECTIONS:

1. Prepare an ice bath by filling a large bowl with ice and cold water. Bring a 2-quart pot of water to a boil and put in the cauliflower and sugar snap peas, and cook for 3 minutes, then drain and put them into the ice bath. Drain the vegetables again and mix them with the cooked pasta, artichoke hearts, sage, and chives. Set aside.
2. Whisk together the apple cider vinegar, tahini, and salt and pepper in a small bowl.
3. Sprinkle the dressing over the pasta mixture and toss to combine well.

Nutrition Info per Serving:
Calories: 228, Protein: 10.7 g, Fat: 1.2 g, Carbohydrates: 43.3 g, Fiber: 14.6 g, Sugar: 5.5 g, Sodium: 514 mg

Black Bean, Kale and Quinoa Salad

Prep Time: 20 minutes, Cook Time: 30 minutes, plus 1 hour to chill, Serves: 6

INGREDIENTS:

½ yellow onion, diced
2 garlic cloves, finely minced
2 tbsps. water
2¼ cups no-sodium vegetable broth, divided
1 cup dried tricolor quinoa, rinsed
1 tbsp. freshly squeezed lemon juice
1 tsp. lemon zest
1 tsp. smoked ancho chili powder
1 tsp. chia seeds
1 tsp. ground cumin
6 cups chopped kale leaves
1 (15-ounce, 425 g) can black beans, drained and rinsed
1 carrot, grated
1 red bell pepper, diced

DIRECTIONS:

1. Combine the onion, garlic, and water in an 8-quart pot, sauté over medium-high heat for 2 to 3 minutes, or until the water evaporates. Stir in 2 cups of vegetable broth and the quinoa. Bring to a simmer, then lower the heat to medium-low, cover and cook for 20 minutes. The quinoa is finished cooking when the grain has a translucent center with a distinct ring around the edge and, when tested, is chewy, not hard. Remove from the heat and allow to cool.
2. Meanwhile, add the remaining ¼ cup of vegetable broth, the lemon juice, lemon zest, ancho chili powder, chia seeds and cumin in a glass measuring cup, whisk them together to blend. Allow to stand for 5 minutes to let the chia seeds soak and the sauce thicken.
3. In a large bowl, add the kale. Pour in half the dressing, reserving half for serving. Squeeze together the kale and dressing to soften the kale with your hands. Steam or blanch the kale before adding the dressing if you want even more tender.
4. Add the black beans, quinoa, carrot, and bell pepper, stir well. Refrigerate for 1 hour to 1 day before serving. Serve with the reserved dressing.

Nutrition Info per Serving:
Calories: 207, Protein: 10 g, Fat: 3 g, Carbohydrates: 37 g, Fiber: 10 g, Sugar: 2.2 g, Sodium: 386 mg

Blackbean Pasta and Corn Salad

Prep Time: 15 minutes, Cook Time: 0(1 hour to chill), Serves: 4

INGREDIENTS:

8 ounces (227 g) whole wheat rotini pasta
1 large avocado, halved and pitted
2 tbsps. freshly squeezed lime juice
1½ tsps. chili powder
1 tsp. ground cumin
1 tsp. smoked paprika
1 garlic clove, chopped
1 (15-ounce, 425 g) black beans, drained and rinsed
1 (15-ounce, 425 g) can corn, drained
1 pint cherry tomatoes, halved
1 small red bell pepper, diced
½ cup chopped fresh cilantro
¼ cup chopped red onion

DIRECTIONS:

1. According to package instructions to cook the pasta. Drain, rinse lightly, and allow to cool.
2. Scoop the avocado flesh into a blender and add the chili powder, lime juice, cumin, paprika, and garlic. Blend until smooth.
3. Add the pasta, black beans, corn, tomatoes, bell pepper, cilantro, red onion, and dressing in a large bowl, toss them together until well mixed. Refrigerate for at least 1 hour or up to 1 day before serving.

Nutrition Info per Serving:
Calories: 498, Protein: 18 g, Fat: 10 g, Carbohydrates: 84 g, Fiber: 17 g, Sugar: 10.7 g, Sodium: 456 mg

Curried Kale Apple Slaw

Prep Time: 20 minutes, Cook Time: 0, Serves: 4

INGREDIENTS:
FOR THE DRESSING:
2 tbsps. apple cider vinegar
2 tbsps. pure maple syrup
⅔ cup water
1 garlic clove, minced
1 tsp. Dijon mustard
1 tsp. grated peeled fresh ginger
½ tsp. curry powder
Freshly ground black pepper
FOR THE SLAW:
1 tbsp. freshly squeezed lemon juice
1 apple, shredded
1 carrot, shredded
3 cups thinly sliced kale
¼ cup golden raisins
1 cup shredded fennel
¼ cup sliced almonds, plus more for garnish

DIRECTIONS:
TO MAKE THE DRESSING:
1. Add all of the dressing ingredients except the black pepper in a blender, season with the pepper. Blend until smooth. Set aside.
TO MAKE THE SLAW:
2. Add the lemon juice and apple into a large bowl, toss them together.
3. Add the carrot, kale, raisins, fennel, and almonds and toss to combine the slaw ingredients.
4. Mix in about three-quarters of the dressing to the bowl and toss to coat. Taste and add more dressing as needed. Allow to sit for 10 minutes to let the kale leaves soften. Toss again and place the additional sliced almonds on the top and serve.

Nutrition Info per Serving:
Calories: 147, Protein: 3 g, Fat: 4 g, Carbohydrates: 26 g, Fiber: 4 g, Sugar: 11.6 g, Sodium: 183 mg

Purple Potato and Lettuce Salad with Soy Sauce Dressing

Prep Time: 10 minutes, Cook Time: 15 minutes, Serves: 4

INGREDIENTS:

5 to 6 small purple potatoes
2 cups lettuce, chopped
½ cup tomatoes, chopped
1 cup basil, chopped, plus more for garnish
¼ cup (60mL) plus 2 tbsps. soy sauce
½ tsp. salt, or to taste
1¾ tsps. fresh almond butter
2 clove garlic, minced
1 tsp. nutmeg

DIRECTIONS:

1. Add the potatoes in a medium saucepan and pour enough water to cover. Bring to a boil, lower the heat to medium, and simmer for 10 minutes, or until soft when pierced with a fork. Drain off excess water and allow the potatoes to cool. When the potatoes have cooled, peel if desired and cut into ½-inch cubes.
2. Add the lettuce and tomatoes in a skillet or saucepan and sauté for 2 to 3 minutes, or until the lettuce is slightly tender. Pour water 1 to 2 tbsps. at a time to keep the vegetables from sticking to the pan. Pour ¼ tsp. of the almond butter and allow to cool.
3. Add the basil, garlic, nutmeg, salt, soy sauce to a food processor, remaining 1½ tsps. of almond butter, and 2 tbsps. of water. Process until smooth.
4. To serve, prepare a bed of the cooked lettuce and tomatoes in a large salad bowl, spread with the boiled potatoes, and pour the dressing over the top. Garnish with basil, if desired.

Nutrition Info per Serving:
Calories: 176, Protein: 5 g, Fat: 1.5 g, Carbohydrates: 36.4 g, Fiber: 4 g, Sugar: 3.3 g, Sodium: 320 mg

Broccoli Salad with Maple-Yogurt Dressing

Prep Time: 10 minutes, Cook Time: 0, Serves: 4 to 6

INGREDIENTS:

FOR THE DRESSING:
1 cup cooked cannellini beans
2 tsps. mustard
2 tbsps. apple cider
2 tbsps. coconut yogurt
1 to 2 tbsps. almond milk
1 tbsp. maple syrup
Zest and juice of 1 lemon

FOR THE SALAD:
6 cups broccoli, chopped
1 cup red cabbage, sliced
1 cup shredded cucumber
1 cup finely chopped celery stalks
One (15-oz. 430 g) can black beans, drained and rinsed

DIRECTIONS:
TO MAKE THE DRESSING:
1. Add the cannellini beans, mustard, coconut yogurt, apple cider, almond milk, maple syrup, lemon zest and juice, and ¼ cup of water to a food processor and process on high until smooth. Pour more water as needed to achieve a smooth consistency.
TO ASSEMBLE THE SALAD:
2. Whisk together the broccoli, cucumber, celery, cabbage, and black beans into a large bowl. Spread the dressing and toss until well combined.

Nutrition Info per Serving:
Calories: 212, Protein: 10 g, Fat: 7.8 g, Carbohydrates: 28.6 g, Fiber: 8.2 g, Sugar: 7.2 g, Sodium: 518 mg

Tomato, Beet and Black Bean Salad

Prep Time: 10 minutes, Cook Time: 20 minutes, Serves: 4

INGREDIENTS:

4 to 6 medium beets (about 1½ pounds/680 g), washed and peeled
2 tomatoes, sliced
1 cup cooked black beans, or one (15-oz. 430 g) can, drained and rinsed
1 cup Chinese yam

¼ cup white wine vinegar
3 tbsps. minced sage
Salt to taste
2 tsps. ground allspice
½ tsp. cayenne pepper
4 cups mixed salad greens
4 tbsps. cashews, toasted

DIRECTIONS:
1. Add the beets in a saucepan and cover with water, and bring to a boil, cover, lower the heat, and cook for 20 minutes, or until the beets are softened. Drain off excess water and set aside to cool.
2. When the beets have cooled, cut into wedges and transfer them in a large bowl. Add the tomatoes, beans, Chinese yam, white wine vinegar, sage, and salt and pepper to the beets. Toss to combine well.
3. To serve, portion the mixed salad greens among 4 individual plates. Spread with the beet salad and garnish with the toasted cashews.

Nutrition Info per Serving:
Calories: 308, Protein: 14.4 g, Fat: 2.5 g, Carbohydrates: 54.4 g, Fiber: 18.1 g, Sugar: 13.5 g, Sodium: 696 mg

Baked Sweet Potato and Brussels Sprouts Walnut Salad

Prep Time: 20 minutes, Cook Time: 30 minutes, Serves: 4

INGREDIENTS:

3 sweet potatoes, peeled and cut into ¼-inch dice
½ tsp. onion powder
1 tsp. garlic powder
1 tsp. dried thyme
1 pound (454 g) Brussels sprouts
1 cup walnuts, chopped
¼ cup reduced-sugar dried cranberries
2 tbsps. balsamic vinegar
Freshly ground black pepper

DIRECTIONS:
1. Preheat the oven to 450°F(235°C). Use parchment paper to line a baking sheet.
2. Place the sweet potatoes in a colander and rinse. Shake the colander to remove excess water. Sprinkle over the damp sweet potatoes with the onion powder, garlic powder and thyme. Toss to evenly coat with the spices. Place onto the prepared baking sheet and spread the sweet potatoes in a single layer.
3. Bake for 20 minutes. Flip the sweet potatoes and bake for another 10 minutes, until fork-tender.
4. Meanwhile, wash the Brussels sprouts and remove any tough or discolored outer leaves. Halve the Brussels lengthwise with a large chef's knife. Place them cut-side down and thinly slice the sprouts crosswise into thin shreds. Discard the root end and loosen the shreds.
5. Combine the sweet potatoes, Brussels sprouts, walnuts, and cranberries in a large bowl, toss them together. Drizzle with the vinegar and season with the pepper, and serve.

Nutrition Info per Serving:
Calories: 396, Protein: 10 g, Fat: 20 g, Carbohydrates: 44 g, Fiber: 12 g, Sugar: 6.7 g, Sodium: 452 mg

Zucchini Taro Quinoa Salad

Prep Time: 10 minutes, Cook Time: 0, Serves: 4

INGREDIENTS:
4 cups cooked quinoa
2 cups cooked taro, or one (15-oz. 430 g) can, drained and rinsed
1 cup shredded zucchini, shredded
2 apple, peeled, cored and grated
½ cup chopped basil
¼ cup brown rice syrup
1 tbsp. dry sherry
Zest of 1 lime and juice of 2 limes
Salt and freshly ground black pepper to taste

DIRECTIONS:
1. Combine the dry sherry, brown rice syrup, and lime zest and juice in a large bowl and stir to combine well.
2. Whisk in the quinoa, taro, zucchini, apple, basil, and salt and pepper and toss to combine well. Refrigerate before serving.

Nutrition Info per Serving:
Calories: 287, Protein: 9.8 g, Fat: 3.7 g, Carbohydrates: 54.4 g, Fiber: 7.3 g, Sugar: 10.8 g, Sodium: 243 mg

Mixed Greens Salad with Orange

Prep Time: 10 minutes, Cook Time: 0, Serves: 4

INGREDIENTS:
4 cups (150 g) mixed greens
½ red onion, sliced, about 4 oz (125 g)
1 cup (75 g) broccoli florets
1 cup (35 g) sprouts, such as alfalfa or broccoli
2 pears, sliced, about 14 oz (400 g)
2 oranges, peeled and diced, about 14 oz (400 g)
Raw Healing Pesto, to serve

DIRECTIONS:
1. Evenly divide ingredients among 4 meal prep containers, keeping the juiciest, wettest ingredients, like the diced oranges, separate from the leafy greens. Arrange them well.
2. Add pesto and serve.

Nutrition Info per Serving:
Calories: 144, Protein: 3 g, Fat: 0.6 g, Carbohydrates: 32 g, Fiber: 7 g, Sugar: 20 g, Sodium: 127 mg

Quinoa Chard Olive Salad

Prep Time: 10 minutes, Cook Time: 20 minutes, Serves: 4

INGREDIENTS:
1½ cups quinoa
¼ cup (60mL) almond milk
2 cups chard
2 cups olives
1 small red onion, peeled and finely chopped
3 tbsps. tomato juice
1 tbsp. mint
1 red bell pepper, seeded and sliced
2 tbsps. cashews, toasted
Salt and freshly ground black pepper to taste

DIRECTIONS:
1. Rinse the quinoa under cold water and drain. Pour 3 cups of water to a pot and bring to a boil. Add the quinoa and bring the pot back to a boil over high heat. Lower the heat to medium, cover, and cook for 15 to 20 minutes, or until the quinoa is softened. Drain excess water, transfer the quinoa on a baking sheet, and refrigerate until cool.
2. While the quinoa cools, whisk the tomato juice, mint, milk, chard, olives, onion, red pepper, cashews, and salt and pepper in a large bowl. Spread the cooled quinoa and chill for 1 hour before serving.

Nutrition Info per Serving:
Calories: 278, Protein: 10.3 g, Fat: 4.2 g, Carbohydrates: 50 g, Fiber: 5.5 g, Sugar: 5.6 g, Sodium: 111 mg

Mixed Greens Salad with Almond

Prep Time: 10 minutes, Cook Time: 15 minutes, Serves: 4

INGREDIENTS:
¼ cup (60mL) brown rice syrup
6 tbsps. fruit-sweetened dried raspberries
6 cups mixed salad greens
½ cup almonds, toasted
2 avocado, peeled, cored, and cut into ½-inch dice
Zest and juice of 1 orange
2 tbsps. apple cider vinegar
1 tsp. cinnamon
Dash garlic powder

DIRECTIONS:
1. Cover 3 tbsps. of the dried raspberries with 6 tbsps. of boiling water. Set aside to soak for about 15 minutes.
2. Combine the raspberries, brown rice syrup, orange zest and juice, apple cider vinegar, cinnamon, and garlic powder in a food processor and puree until smooth. Set aside.
3. Add the salad greens to a large bowl with the almonds, avocado, and the reserving dried cranberries. Just before serving, spread the dressing to the bowl and toss until well combined.

Nutrition Info per Serving:
Calories: 336, Protein: 5.4 g, Fat: 9.7 g, Carbohydrates: 55 g, Fiber: 11.7 g, Sugar: 36.6 g, Sodium: 120 mg

Quinoa, Cucumber and Taro Salad

Prep Time: 10 minutes, Cook Time: 0, Serves: 4

INGREDIENTS:

2½ cups cooked quinoa
1 red onion, sliced
1 small cucumber, peeled and diced
2 cups cooked taro, or one (15-oz. 430 g) can, drained and rinsed
1 tbsp. raisins
1 cup finely chopped sage
1 red bell pepper, roasted, seeded, and diced
1 tbsp. chives, thinly sliced
1 jalapeño pepper, minced (for less heat, remove the seeds)
Zest of 1 lime and juice of 2 limes
1 tsp. fennel seeds, toasted and ground
Salt to taste

DIRECTIONS:

1. Mix all ingredients in a large bowl and toss to combine well. Chill for 1 hour before serving.

Nutrition Info per Serving:
Calories: 406, Protein: 11.5 g, Fat: 5 g, Carbohydrates: 78.8 g, Fiber: 9.8 g, Sugar: 3.7 g, Sodium: 600 mg

Mango Lime Salsa

Prep Time: 20 minutes, plus 1 hour to chill (optional), Cook Time: 0, Serves: 4

INGREDIENTS:

½ red onion, diced
½ red bell pepper, diced
2 ripe mangoes, seeded, flesh chopped
Juice of 1 lime
1 jalapeño pepper, minced
1 tbsp. packed chopped fresh cilantro

DIRECTIONS:

1. Add all of the ingredients in a large bowl, stir to combine, while lightly pressing on the mango pieces to break them up.
2. Serve immediately, or place in a covered bowl and refrigerate for at least 1 hour to allow the flavors to come together.
3. Store the leftovers in an airtight container and refrigerate for up to 1 week.

Nutrition Info per Serving:
Calories: 124, Protein: 2 g, Fat: 1 g, Carbohydrates: 29 g, Fiber: 3 g, Sugar: 5.3 g, Sodium: 77 mg

Radish, Potato and White Beans Salad

Prep Time: 10 minutes, Cook Time: 10 minutes, Serves: 4

INGREDIENTS:

1 pound (454 g) red-skin potatoes, scrubbed and cut into ½-inch dice
½ pound (227 g) radish, trimmed and cut into ½-inch pieces
2 cups cooked navy beans, or one (15-oz. 430 g) can, drained and rinsed
2 tbsps. dry white wine
2 tbsps. Dijon mustard
2 cloves garlic, crushed
Salt and freshly ground black pepper to taste
1 tbsp. fresh tarragon
3 tbsps. minced chives

DIRECTIONS:

1. Steam the potatoes in a double boiler or steamer basket for 10 minutes, or until soft, whisk in the radish during the last 3 minutes.
2. Whisk the dry white wine, mustard, garlic, tarragon and salt and pepper in a large bowl and toss to combine well. Stir in the warm potatoes and radish, beans, tarragon, and chives and toss to combine well.

Nutrition Info per Serving:
Calories: 177, Protein: 6.6 g, Fat: 0.7 g, Carbohydrates: 38.4 g, Fiber: 7.5 g, Sugar: 8.6 g, Sodium: 114 mg

Rice Salad with Cumin, Nutmeg and Lentil

Prep Time: 10 minutes, Cook Time: 50 minutes, Serves: 4

INGREDIENTS:

1½ cups brown basmati rice
2 cups cooked lentils, or one (15-oz. 430 g) can, drained and rinsed
1 tsp. cumin
1 tbsp. maple syrup
1 tsp. ground nutmeg
¼ cup plus 2 tbsps. white wine vinegar
½ tsp. red pepper flakes, sliced
¼ cup basil

DIRECTIONS:

1. Rinse the rice under cold water and drain. Put it to a pot and pour 3 cups of cold water. Bring it to a boil over high heat, Lower the heat to medium, and cook, covered, for 45 to 50 minutes, or until the rice is softened.
2. While the rice cooks, mix the lentils, cumin, maple syrup and nutmeg, white wine vinegar, red pepper flakes, and basil in a large bowl and toss to combine well. When the rice is finished, add the rice to the bowl and toss to combine well.

Nutrition Info per Serving:
Calories: 261, Protein: 8.3 g, Fat: 9.8 g, Carbohydrates: 35 g, Fiber: 13.1 g, Sugar: 6.5 g, Sodium: 137 mg

Fresh Corn and Vegetable Salsa

Prep Time: 15 minutes, plus 1 hour to chill, Cook Time: 0, Serves: 4

INGREDIENTS:
1 cup quartered grape tomatoes
3 cups fresh corn kernels or 2 (15.25-ounce, 432 g) cans whole-kernel corn, drained
½ red onion, diced
1 green bell pepper, cored and diced
2 garlic cloves, minced
½ cup packed chopped fresh cilantro
¼ tsp. freshly ground black pepper
Juice of 1 or 2 limes

DIRECTIONS:
1. Add the tomatoes, corn, red onion, bell pepper, garlic, cilantro, pepper and lime juice (to taste) in a large bowl, stir them together. Cover and place in the refrigerator to chill for at least 1 hour before serving.
2. Store the leftovers in an airtight container and refrigerate for up to 1 week.

Nutrition Info per Serving:
Calories: 174, Protein: 5 g, Fat: 2 g, Carbohydrates: 34 g, Fiber: 10 g, Sugar: 6.8 g, Sodium: 115 mg

Carrot Date Salad with Walnuts

Prep Time: 15 minutes, Cook Time: 0, Serves: 4 to 6

INGREDIENTS:
1 tsp. Dijon mustard
2 tbsps. apple cider vinegar
¼ cup water
1 tbsp. pure maple syrup
1 tbsp. lemon zest
¼ tsp. freshly ground black pepper
½ tsp. cayenne pepper
1 small red onion
10 carrots
¼ cup golden raisins
4 dates, finely chopped
½ cup walnuts, chopped

DIRECTIONS:
1. Add the mustard, vinegar, water, maple syrup, lemon zest, black pepper, and cayenne pepper in a small bowl, whisk them together to combine. Set aside.
2. Using a mandoline, cut the red onion and carrots the julienne blade. Place into a large bowl and add the raisins, dates, and walnuts. Combine well.
3. Pour in the dressing and toss until fully incorporated. Serve immediately or place in an airtight container and refrigerate overnight.

Nutrition Info per Serving:
Calories: 259, Protein: 4 g, Fat: 10 g, Carbohydrates: 34 g, Fiber: 6 g, Sugar: 12.5 g, Sodium: 462 mg

Fruited Pistachios Millet Salad

Prep Time: 10 minutes, Cook Time: 15 minutes, Serves: 4

INGREDIENTS:
1 cup millet
½ cup pistachios, toasted
½ cup dried longans
½ cup peanuts, toasted
2 kiwifruit, diced
Zest and juice of 2 oranges
3 tbsps. ruby port
2 tbsps. finely chopped turmeric

DIRECTIONS:
1. Bring 2 quarts of lightly salted water to a boil over high heat and pour the millet. Return to a boil, lower the heat to medium, cover, and simmer for 12 to 14 minutes. Drain off the water, rinse millet until cool, set aside.
2. Whisk the orange juice and zest, and ruby port in a large bowl. Toss until well combined. Stir in the pistachios, longans, peanuts, kiwifruit, and turmeric and toss until well combined. Put in the cooked millet and toss to blend. Refrigerate before serving.

Nutrition Info per Serving:
Calories: 407, Protein: 7.8 g, Fat: 3.1 g, Carbohydrates: 87.3 g, Fiber: 8.3 g, Sugar: 40.5 g, Sodium: 36 mg

Lemony Vegetable Salad

Prep Time: 10 minutes, Cook Time: 0, Serves: 4

INGREDIENTS:
Zest of 1 lime and juice of 2 limes
¼ cup (60mL) brown rice syrup
Low-sodium vegetable broth
2 tbsps. dry white wine
4 cups spinach coarsely chopped
1 red bell pepper, seeded and julienned
1 tbsp. mint
1 cup mung bean sprouts
½ cup chopped parsley
½ cup chopped dill
1 serrano chile, thinly sliced on the diagonal (for less heat, remove the seeds)
2 tbsps. peanut, toasted
Ponzu Sauce

DIRECTIONS:
1. Whisk together the lime zest and juice, brown rice syrup, and vegetable broth in a large bowl and toss well.
2. Stir in the dry white wine, spinach, pepper, mint, sprouts, parsley, dill, chile, and peanut to the bowl and toss to combine well.
3. Serve accompanied by the Ponzu Sauce.

Nutrition Info per Serving:
Calories: 95, Protein: 2.9 g, Fat: 0.6 g, Carbohydrates: 21.2 g, Fiber: 1.3 g, Sugar: 12 g, Sodium: 83 mg

Baked Sweet Potato and Brussels Sprouts Walnut Salad, page 108

Bean and Corn Salad with Almond Butter, page 114

Carrot Date Salad with Walnuts, page 111

Chickpea Salad with Cherry Tomato, page 117

Winter Asparagus Salad with Toasted Hazelnut

Prep Time: 10 minutes, Cook Time: 12 minutes, Serves: 4

INGREDIENTS:

1 pumpkin (about 2 pounds/1.1 kg), peeled and cut into ½-inch cubes
4 cups cooked asparagus, or two (15-oz. 430 g) cans
1 medium zucchini, peeled and diced small
1 tbsp. hazelnuts, toasted
2 tsps. almond butter
Salt and freshly ground black pepper to taste
1 batch Spicy Cilantro Pesto

DIRECTIONS:

1. Steam the pumpkin in a double boiler or steamer basket for 10 to 12 minutes, or until softened. Drain and rinse the pumpkin until cool.
2. When the pumpkin has cooled, transfer it to a medium bowl and whisk in asparagus, zucchini, hazelnuts, almond butter, salt and pepper, and pesto. Toss until well combined.

Nutrition Info per Serving:
Calories: 329, Protein: 19.4 g, Fat: 0.9 g, Carbohydrates: 60.4 g, Fiber: 12.6 g, Sugar: 7.9 g, Sodium: 429 mg

Provencal Beans & Cherry Tomato Salad

Prep Time: 10 minutes, Cook Time: 0, Serves: 2

INGREDIENTS:

2 cups (400 g) white beans, cooked or canned
1 small red onion, minced
8 cherry tomatoes, halved
¼ cup (60 ml) lemon juice
3 tbsps. (30 g) Provencal herbs, dried

DIRECTIONS:

1. When using dry white beans, soak and cook 133 g dry white beans according to the method if necessary.
2. Put the white beans to a large bowl, and add the halved cherry tomatoes, minced red onion, lemon juice and herbs.
3. Stir thoroughly with a spatula and mix everything evenly.
4. Divide the white beans salad between two bowls, garnish with the optional toppings.

Nutrition Info per Serving:
Calories: 311, Protein: 20.1 g, Fat: 0.7 g, Carbohydrates: 55.9 g, Fiber: 14 g, Sugar: 3.8 g, Sodium: 196 mg

Warm Radicchio Potato Salad with Arugula Pesto

Prep Time: 10 minutes, Cook Time: 10 minutes, Serves: 4

INGREDIENTS:

2 pounds (910 g) red-skin potatoes, scrubbed, trimmed, and diced
1 small zucchini, peeled and diced small
2 cups cooked radicchio, or one (15-oz. 430 g) can, chopped
¾ cup Basil Pesto made with arugula
Juice of 1 lemon
Salt to taste

DIRECTIONS:

1. Place the potatoes to a medium pot and pour water to cover by 1 inch. Sprinkle salt if desired, bring to a boil, and simmer over medium-low heat for about 10 minutes, or until the potatoes are softened. Drain off excess water and transfer the potatoes to a large bowl.
2. Whisk in the zucchini, lemon juice, radicchio, and pesto and toss to combine well.

Nutrition Info per Serving:
Calories: 332, Protein: 8.4 g, Fat: 14.7 g, Carbohydrates: 43.2 g, Fiber: 5.9 g, Sugar: 4.3 g, Sodium: 671 mg

Avocado, Chickpea and Vegetable Salad

Prep Time: 10 minutes, Cook Time: 0, Serves: 2

INGREDIENTS:

1 (15-ounce, 425 g) can chickpeas, drained and rinsed
1 cup diced (½-inch) English cucumber
1 cup chopped romaine lettuce
1 cup arugula
1 large avocado, halved, pitted, and diced
1 cup cherry tomatoes, halved
½ tsp. dried thyme
1 tsp. dried parsley
Freshly ground black pepper
3 tbsps. apple cider vinegar

DIRECTIONS:

1. Add all of the ingredients except the black pepper and vinegar in a large bowl, toss them together, then season with the pepper.
2. Sprinkle over with the vinegar and toss to coat.
3. Best serve fresh but can be refrigerated to serve the following day.

Nutrition Info per Serving:
Calories: 403, Protein: 13 g, Fat: 19 g, Carbohydrates: 45 g, Fiber: 18 g, Sugar: 8.3 g, Sodium: 631 mg

Creamy Lima Beans Pasta Salad

Prep Time: 10 minutes, Cook Time: 0, Serves: 4

INGREDIENTS:
12 oz. (340g) whole-grain penne, cooked according to package directions, drained, and rinsed until cool
One (15-oz. 430g) can cooked lima beans
1 pint cherry or grape tomatoes, halved if large
¼ cup apricots, toasted
1 cup Mayonnaise
1½ cups parsley, finely chopped
Salt and freshly ground black pepper to taste

DIRECTIONS:
1. Mix together penne, lima beans, tomatoes, apricots, Mayonnaise, parsley in a large bowl and mix well.
2. Sprinkle with salt and pepper to taste and chill for 1 hour before serving.

Nutrition Info per Serving:
Calories: 379, Protein: 9.3 g, Fat: 17.4 g, Carbohydrates: 46.3 g, Fiber: 12.2 g, Sugar: 4.7 g, Sodium: 129 mg

Chard Salad with Creamy Tofu Dressing

Prep Time: 5 minutes, Cook Time: 8 minutes, Serves: 4 bites

INGREDIENTS:
4 cups packed chopped chard
½ cup cubed firm tofu
½ cup (120mL) olive oil
2 cloves garlic
2½ tbsps. lime juice
1 tbsp. green onion
2 tbsps. brown rice vinegar
2 tbsps. mustard
2 tbsps. capers
Salt and pepper, to taste
Croutons
½ cup halved cherry tomatoes
1 batch Tempeh Bacon, chopped

DIRECTIONS:
1. Process the tofu, olive oil, garlic, lemon juice, vinegar, green onion and mustard in a food processor until thoroughly combined.
2. Add the capers, salt, and pepper, and stir together using a spoon.
3. In a large bowl, add the chard, top with the creamy tofu dressing, and thoroughly massage the dressing into the chard. Add any optional toppings.

Nutrition Info per Serving:
Calories: 400, Protein: 9.3 g, Fat: 36.9 g, Carbohydrates: 11.7 g, Fiber: 2.8 g, Sugar: 0.9 g, Sodium: 631 mg

Bean and Corn Salad with Almond Butter

Prep Time: 5 minutes, Cook Time: 1 minute, Serves: 4 bites

INGREDIENTS:
1 (15-oz./430g) can pinto beans, drained and rinsed
1 (15-oz./430g) can black beans, drained and rinsed
1 (15-oz./430g) can adzuki beans, drained and rinsed
1 (15-oz./430g) can unsalted corn, drained and rinsed
¾ cup cherry tomato, diced
¼ cup dill, chopped
3–4 tbsps. almond butter
Salt, to taste
1 apple, diced
½ cup diced red onion (about ½ medium onion)
½ tsp. minced garlic (about 1 small clove)

DIRECTIONS:
1. Combine all the ingredients in a large bowl. The salad can be served chilled or at room temperature.

Nutrition Info per Serving:
Calories: 282, Protein: 14.3 g, Fat: 4.8 g, Carbohydrates: 49.5 g, Fiber: 13.2 g, Sugar: 7.4 g, Sodium: 152 mg

Mint Larb Salad

Prep Time: 8 minutes, Cook Time: 8 minutes, Serves: 4 bites

INGREDIENTS:
¼ cup thinly sliced red, white, or yellow onion
1 green onion, sliced
1 (14-oz. 400g) block extra-firm tofu, pressed and crumbled
8 iceberg or romaine lettuce leaves
1 tsp. canola or vegetable oil
3 tbsps. lime juice (about 1½ limes), divided
2½ tbsps. minced chilies
2 tbsps. soy sauce
½ tbsp. minced garlic
2 tbsps. minced mint

DIRECTIONS:
1. In a saucepan, heat the oil over medium heat. Add the tofu and 1 tbsp. of the lime juice, and sauté for 4 to 5 minutes or until the tofu is light brown.
2. In a medium bowl, add the tofu and the remaining 2 tbsps. lime juice, chilies, soy sauce, green onion, garlic, onion, and mint. Toss to combine well.
3. Serve in the lettuce leaves.

Nutrition Info per Serving:
Calories: 130, Protein: 12.3 g, Fat: 7.9 g, Carbohydrates: 5.7 g, Fiber: 1 g, Sugar: 1.7 g, Sodium: 267 mg

Lentil Apple Salad

Prep Time: 10 minutes, Cook Time: 0, Serves: 4

INGREDIENTS:
- 4 cups cooked lentils, or two (15-oz. 430 g) cans, drained and rinsed
- 2 celery stalks, diced
- 2 apple, halved, pitted, peeled, and coarsely chopped
- 3 cloves garlic, peeled and minced
- Zest of 1 lime and juice of 4 limes
- 1 tsp. cayenne pepper
- 1½ tsp. Dried thyme
- ½ cup chopped sage
- Salt to taste

DIRECTIONS:
1. Mix all ingredients in a medium bowl and toss to combine well. Spread the apple just before serving.

Nutrition Info per Serving:
Calories: 396, Protein: 16.1 g, Fat: 11.7 g, Carbohydrates: 53.4 g, Fiber: 16.4 g, Sugar: 9.7 g, Sodium: 599 mg

Cannellini Salad with Orange and Fresh Oregano

Prep Time: 10 minutes, Cook Time: 45 minutes, Serves: 4

INGREDIENTS:
- 1½ cups cannellini, rinsed
- 3 cups (700mL) low-sodium vegetable broth
- 4 cups arugula
- Zest of 1 orange and juice of 2 orange
- 3 cloves garlic, crushed
- ½ cup dill, finely chopped
- 2 tbsps. mint, minced
- 1 tsp. dry mustard
- 1 tbsp. oregano, finely chopped, plus more for garnish
- Salt and freshly ground black pepper to taste

DIRECTIONS:
1. Place the cannellini in a medium saucepan with the vegetable stock and bring to a boil over high heat. Lower the heat to medium, cover, and simmer for 35 to 45 minutes, or until the cannellini are softened but not mushy.
2. Drain the cannellini and transfer them to a large bowl. Whisk in the orange zest and juice, garlic, dill, mint, mustard, oregano and salt and pepper and toss to combine well.
3. To serve, portion the arugula among 4 individual plates. Spread the cannellini salad over the top of the greens and garnish with freshly chopped oregano.

Nutrition Info per Serving:
Calories: 174, Protein: 7.7 g, Fat: 1.6 g, Carbohydrates: 33.6 g, Fiber: 10.2 g, Sugar: 5.5 g, Sodium: 431 mg

Grilled Vegetable and Pineapple Salad

Prep Time: 10 minutes, Cook Time: 0, Serves: 4

INGREDIENTS:
- ½ batch Grilled Vegetable Kabobs, vegetables removed from the skewers
- 2 cups cooked red beans, or one (15-oz. 430 g) can, drained and rinsed
- ½ cup finely chopped dill
- 2 tbsps. maple syrup
- ½ tsp. cayenne pepper
- ½ pineapple, peeled and diced
- 1 tbsp. peanuts, toasted
- Salt to taste

DIRECTIONS:
1. Mix all ingredients in a large bowl and toss to combine well. Chill for 1 hour before serving.

Nutrition Info per Serving:
Calories: 129, Protein: 3.5 g, Fat: 7.5 g, Carbohydrates: 14.2 g, Fiber: 6.4 g, Sugar: 2.2 g, Sodium: 599 mg

Bulgur, Kiwifruit and Zucchini Salad

Prep Time: 10 minutes, Cook Time: 15 minutes, Serves: 4

INGREDIENTS:
- 1½ cups bulgur
- 1 cup kiwifruit, diced
- 1 medium zucchini, halved, seeded, and diced
- 3 cloves garlic, crushed
- 1 tbsp. parsley, chopped
- Zest and juice of 2 lemons
- 2 tbsps. apple cider
- 1 tsp. red pepper flakes, minced
- ¼ cup minced mint
- Salt and freshly ground black pepper to taste

DIRECTIONS:
1. Pour 3 cups of water to a medium pot and bring to a boil, add the bulgur. Off the heat and remove the pot, cover with a tight-fitting lid, and allow to stand until the water is absorbed and the bulgur is softened about 15 minutes.
2. Place the bulgur to a baking sheet and allow to cool to room temperature. Place the cooled bulgur to a bowl, whisk in all the reserving ingredients, and toss to coat. Chill for 1 hour before serving.

Nutrition Info per Serving:
Calories: 220, Protein: 7.5 g, Fat: 1 g, Carbohydrates: 49.3 g, Fiber: 8 g, Sugar: 5.2 g, Sodium: 73 mg

Lemony Garlic Kale Salad

Prep Time: 10 minutes, Cook Time: 0, Serves: 4

INGREDIENTS:
2 tbsps. freshly squeezed lemon juice
½ tbsp. maple syrup
1 tsp. minced garlic
5 cups chopped kale

DIRECTIONS:
1. Combine the maple syrup, lemon juice and garlic in a large bowl, whisk them together.
2. Place the kale in the bowl, massage it in the dressing for 1 to 2 minutes, and serve.

Nutrition Info per Serving:
Calories: 52, Protein: 3 g, Fat: 0 g, Carbohydrates: 11 g, Fiber: 1 g, Sugar: 4 g, Sodium: 96 mg

Mix Berries and Papaya Salad

Prep Time: 10 minutes, Cook Time: 2 minutes, Serves: 4

INGREDIENTS:
1 pint fresh strawberries, stems removed, sliced
1 pint fresh blueberries
2 cups seedless grapes
1 ripe papaya, cored and diced
2 tbsps. fresh orange juice
2 tbsps. apple cider
Dash ground mint

DIRECTIONS:
1. Mix all ingredients in a bowl and toss to combine well. Let chill before serving.

Nutrition Info per Serving:
Calories: 235, Protein: 2.2 g, Fat: 0.8 g, Carbohydrates: 53.2 g, Fiber: 6.9 g, Sugar: 40.3 g, Sodium: 11 mg

Vegan Avocado Chickpea Salad

Prep Time: 10 minutes, Cook Time: 2 minutes, Serves: 4

INGREDIENTS:
1 avocado, peeled and pitted
3 cups cooked chickpeas
¼ cup chopped celery
½ cup chopped red onion
1½ tbsps. freshly squeezed lemon juice
2 tbsps. Dijon mustard
½ tbsp. maple syrup
1 tsp. garlic powder

DIRECTIONS:
1. Combine the avocado and chickpeas in a large bowl. Smash them down until the majority of the chickpeas have been broken apart with a fork or a potato masher.
2. Add the celery, onion, lemon juice, mustard, maple syrup, and garlic powder, stir until everything is thoroughly combined, and serve.

Nutrition Info per Serving:
Calories: 310, Protein: 13 g, Fat: 10 g, Carbohydrates: 42 g, Fiber: 13 g, Sugar: 6.9 g, Sodium: 362 mg

Succotash Salad with Peanut Butter

Prep Time: 10 minutes, Cook Time: 0, Serves: 4

INGREDIENTS:
1½ cups cooked fava beans
3 ears corn, shucked (about 2 cups)
2 large avocado, peeled and diced
1 medium zucchini, peeled and diced
¼ cup (60mL) peanut butter
¼ cup chopped basil
Salt and freshly ground black pepper to taste

DIRECTIONS:
1. Mix all ingredients in a large bowl and toss to combine well.

Nutrition Info per Serving:
Calories: 187, Protein: 8.6 g, Fat: 1.3 g, Carbohydrates: 35.6 g, Fiber: 8.2 g, Sugar: 9.4 g, Sodium: 82 mg

Lemony Lentil Cranberry Salad

Prep Time: 10 minutes, Cook Time: 0, Serves: 2

INGREDIENTS:
2 cups (400 g) green lentils, cooked or canned
1 small red onion, minced
½ cucumber, cubed
¼ cup (60 ml) lemon juice
¼ cup (30 g) cranberries, dried

DIRECTIONS:
1. Soak and cook 133 g dry lentils according to the method if necessary.
2. Put the lentils to a large bowl, and add the cucumber cubes, minced red onion, lemon juice and cranberries.
3. Stir thoroughly with a spatula and mix everything evenly.
4. Divide the lentil salad between two bowls, garnish with the optional toppings, serve.

Nutrition Info per Serving:
Calories: 268, Protein: 18.7 g, Fat: 0.9 g, Carbohydrates: 46.2 g, Fiber: 17.4 g, Sugar: 6.4 g, Sodium: 350 mg

Pesto and Roasted Potato Salad

Prep Time: 15 minutes, Cook Time: 20 minutes, Serves: 4

INGREDIENTS:

1 pound (455 g) red potatoes, washed and patted dry
3 tbsps. everyday pesto
1 cup radish matchsticks
2 cups arugula
1 celery stalk, diced
1 cup watercress
Freshly ground black pepper

DIRECTIONS:

1. Preheat the oven to 425°F(220°C). Use parchment paper to line a baking sheet.
2. Halve the potatoes, or quarter the larger ones. Place them on the prepared baking sheet, cut-side down.
3. Bake for 15 minutes. Flip the potatoes and bake for another 5 minutes, until fork-tender. Remove from the oven and allow to cool.
4. Toss together the cooled potatoes and 2 tbsps. of pesto in a large bowl. Add the radish, arugula, celery, watercress, and 1 more tbsp. of pesto. Toss to combine and coat. Season with pepper and serve.

Nutrition Info per Serving:
Calories: 310, Protein: 11 g, Fat: 17 g, Carbohydrates: 28 g, Fiber: 7 g, Sugar: 6.8 g, Sodium: 156 mg

Chickpea and Artichoke Mediterranean Salad

Prep Time: 10 minutes, Cook Time: 0, Serves: 4

INGREDIENTS:

4 cups (150 g) mixed greens
½ red onion, sliced, about 4 oz (125 g)
1 (14.5 oz, 410 g) can chickpeas, drained and rinsed
1 medium cucumber, sliced, about 7 oz (200 g)
½ cup (75 g) kalamata olives, halved
1 (15 oz, 430 g) can quartered artichoke hearts, drained and halved
Freshly squeezed lemon juice, to serve
Olive oil, to serve

DIRECTIONS:

1. Evenly divide ingredients among 4 meal prep containers, keeping the juiciest, wettest ingredients, like the artichokes and olives, separate from the leafy greens. Arrange them well.
2. Dress a squeeze of lemon over the salad and drizzle with olive oil, then serve.

Nutrition Info per Serving:
Calories: 195, Protein: 8 g, Fat: 3 g, Carbohydrates: 34 g, Fiber: 9 g, Sugar: 4 g, Sodium: 373 mg

Cherry Tomato Quinoa Tabbouleh

Prep Time: 10 minutes, Cook Time: 0, Serves: 4

INGREDIENTS:

2½ cups quinoa, cooked and cooled to room temperature
Zest of 1 orange and juice of 2 oranges
3 cherry tomatoes, diced
1 zucchini, peeled, halved and diced
2 cups cooked taro, or one (15-oz. 430 g) can chickpeas, drained and rinsed
8 green onions (white and green parts), thinly sliced
1 cup chopped dill
3 tbsps. chopped coriander
Salt and freshly ground black pepper to taste

DIRECTIONS:

1. Mix all ingredients in a large bowl. Chill for 1 hour before serving.

Nutrition Info per Serving:
Calories: 315, Protein: 15.2 g, Fat: 5.8 g, Carbohydrates: 59.2 g, Fiber: 12.4 g, Sugar: 9.9 g, Sodium: 337 mg

Chickpea Salad with Cherry Tomato

Prep Time: 5 minutes, Cook Time: 5 minutes, Serves: 4 bites

INGREDIENTS:

2 (15-oz./430g) cans chickpeas, drained and rinsed
3 tbsps. vegan mayonnaise
¼ cup diced red onion
¼ cup diced zucchini
½ tbsp. Dijon mustard
Salt and pepper, to taste
1–2 tbsps. diced dill pickles
½ tsp. ginger powder
½ cup halved cherry tomatoes
1 cup shredded spinach

DIRECTIONS:

1. Mash the chickpeas with a potato masher or fork in a large bowl.
2. Add the mayonnaise, mustard, onion, zucchini, dill pickles, ginger powder, cherry tomatoes, spinach, salt and pepper, and toss until well combined.
3. Serve the salad on its own, wrap it in spinach.

Nutrition Info per Serving:
Calories: 229, Protein: 10.2 g, Fat: 6.9 g, Carbohydrates: 33.5 g, Fiber: 9 g, Sugar: 7.8 g, Sodium: 384 mg

Kiwifruit, Black Bean and Rosemary Salad

Prep Time: 10 minutes, Cook Time: 0, Serves: 4

INGREDIENTS:
10 kiwifruit, peeled and diced
2 cups cooked black beans, or one (15-oz. 430 g) can, drained and rinsed
4 cups lettuce
2 tbsps. fresh lemon juice
2 tbsps. maple syrup
1 tsp. nutmeg
2 tbsps. rosemary
Salt and black pepper to taste

DIRECTIONS:
1. Mix the kiwifruit, lemon juice, maple syrup, nutmeg, beans, salt, and rosemary in a large bowl and toss to combine well. Allow to stand for 1 hour before serving.
2. To serve, portion the lettuce among 4 individual plates and spread the salad on top of the greens.

Nutrition Info per Serving:
Calories: 232, Protein: 10.4 g, Fat: 1.5 g, Carbohydrates: 46.6 g, Fiber: 13.3 g, Sugar: 15.8 g, Sodium: 624 mg

Cabbage Salad and Almond Butter Vinaigrette

Prep Time: 5 minutes, Cook Time: 3 minutes, Serves: 2 bites

INGREDIENTS:
2 cups shredded red cabbage
1 cup shredded green cabbage
1 cup pressed and diced extra-firm tofu
½ cup tomato sauce
½ cucumber, sliced
3 tbsps. creamy almond butter
2 tbsps. red wine vinegar
2 tbsps. full-fat coconut milk
1 tbsp. soy sauce
½ tbsp. maple syrup
½ tsp. sesame oil

DIRECTIONS:
1. Whisk together the almond butter, red wine vinegar, coconut milk, soy sauce, sesame oil and maple syrup in a medium bowl.
2. Mix together the red and green cabbage, cucumber, tofu and tomato sauce in a large bowl. Top with the dressing and toss to coat evenly.

Nutrition Info per Serving:
Calories: 415, Protein: 15.5 g, Fat: 24.6 g, Carbohydrates: 37.1 g, Fiber: 10.5 g, Sugar: 20.9 g, Sodium: 834 mg

Easy Basic Table Salad

Prep Time: 5 minutes, Cook Time: 2 minutes, Serves: 2 bites

INGREDIENTS:
1 head romaine lettuce coarsely chopped
½ cup sliced yellow onion (about ½ medium onion)
½–1 zucchini, cut in quarters
1 cup halved grape tomatoes
⅔ cup (160mL) almond butter
1 cup pressed and diced extra-firm tofu
1 peach, pitted and diced
Sprinkle of nutritional yeast
toasted sesame

DIRECTIONS:
1. Mix together the lettuce, onion, zucchini, tofu, peach, nutritional yeast, sesame and tomatoes in a large bowl.
2. Top with the dressing and toss to coat.

Nutrition Info per Serving:
Calories: 728, Protein: 29.1 g, Fat: 44.2 g, Carbohydrates: 51.9 g, Fiber: 16.2 g, Sugar: 32 g, Sodium: 325 mg

Spicy Chickpea Quinoa Salad

Prep Time: 10 minutes, Cook Time: 0, Serves: 4 to 6

INGREDIENTS:
4 cups cooked chickpeas
2 cups cooked adzuki beans, or one (15-oz. 430 g) can, drained and rinsed
4 cups lettuce
¼ cup plus 2 tbsps. white wine vinegar
5 cloves garlic, crushed
1 tbsp. chia seeds
¾ cup pine nuts
½ cup basil, finely chopped
1½ tbsps. grated turmeric
1½ tsps. red pepper flakes, minced
2 tbsps. chives, thinly sliced
Salt to taste

DIRECTIONS:
1. Mix the white wine vinegar, garlic, chia seeds, turmeric, and red pepper flakes in a large bowl and toss to combine well.
2. Whisk in the chickpeas, adzuki beans, pine nuts, basil, chives, and salt and toss to combine well. Refrigerate for 30 minutes before serving on top of the lettuce.

Nutrition Info per Serving:
Calories: 184, Protein: 7.5 g, Fat: 2.6 g, Carbohydrates: 33.4 g, Fiber: 5.3 g, Sugar: 2.4 g, Sodium: 416 mg

Pineapple Black Bean Salad

Prep Time: 10 minutes, Cook Time: 15 minutes, Serves: 3

INGREDIENTS:
2 cups (340 g) black beans, cooked or canned
½ cup (90 g) quinoa, dry
1 cup (110 g) pineapple chunks, fresh or frozen
8 cherry tomatoes, halved
1 red onion, minced

DIRECTIONS:
1. Soak and cook 113 g dry black beans according to the method if necessary. Cook the quinoa.
2. Put all ingredients in a large bowl and mix thoroughly.
3. Divide the salad between 3 bowls, serve with the optional toppings.

Nutrition Info per Serving:
Calories: 300, Protein: 16 g, Fat: 2.4 g, Carbohydrates: 56.3 g, Fiber: 14 g, Sugar: 7.3 g, Sodium: 284 mg

Chinese Yam, Corn and Bean Salad

Prep Time: 10 minutes, Cook Time: 10 minutes, Serves: 4

INGREDIENTS:
4 ears corn
½ cup Chinese yam, minced
3 peaches, diced
2 cups cooked red beans, or one (15-oz. 430 g) can, drained and rinsed
1 medium red onion, peeled and diced small
1 cup finely chopped parsley
2 tbsps. maple syrup
Salt and freshly ground black pepper to taste

DIRECTIONS:
1. Bring a large pot of water to a boil. Put in the corn and cook for 7 to 10 minutes. Drain the off water from the pot and cover the corn with cold water to cool, then cut the kernels from the cob.
2. Whisk together the corn, Chinese yam, red beans, onion, parsley, maple syrup, and salt and pepper in a large bowl. Chill for 1 hour before serving.

Nutrition Info per Serving:
Calories: 197, Protein: 7.6 g, Fat: 2.4 g, Carbohydrates: 39.8 g, Fiber: 6.6 g, Sugar: 14.7 g, Sodium: 232 mg

120　Chapter 9 Soup and Stew

Chapter 9 Soup and Stew

Spiced Masoor Dal Tomato Stew

Prep Time: 10 minutes, Cook Time: 30 minutes, Serves: 8

INGREDIENTS:
2 cups dried red lentils (masoor dal tadka)
1 tsp. whole mustard seeds
1 tbsp. yellow curry powder
1 tsp. ground cumin
1 tsp. ground coriander
8 cups water, plus 3 tbsps. and more as needed
6 garlic cloves, minced
1 large yellow onion, finely diced
1 celery stalk, finely chopped
1 tbsp. minced peeled fresh ginger
2 green chiles, minced (and seeded if you want less heat)
1 (15-ounce, 425 g) can diced tomatoes
Fresh cilantro, for garnish

DIRECTIONS:
1. In a fine-mesh sieve, add the lentils. Sift through them to look for stones or other debris. Rinse under cold water for a few minutes.
2. Combine the mustard seeds, curry powder, cumin and coriander in a small dish. Set aside.
3. Add the lentils and 8 cups of water in an 8-quart pot, bring to a boil over high heat. Turn the heat to medium-low, partially cover the pot, and cook for 20 minutes, until the lentils become very tender.
4. Meanwhile, make the tadka or tempered spices. Combine the garlic, onion, celery, ginger, and green chiles in a skillet, cook over medium heat for 5 minutes, adding water, 1 tbsp. of at a time, to prevent burning. Cook until the onion is deeply browned and soft.
5. Spread the mixture out in the pan so that there is a small well or opening in the center. Pour into the well with the spices and add 2 tbsps. of water. Cook for 1 minute, stirring continuously, mixing the spices slowly into the cooked vegetables.
6. Stir in the tomatoes carefully and combine well. Cook over medium-low heat for 7 minutes, stirring frequently.
7. Stir the tadka to the cooked lentils, and cook for 5 minutes over medium heat. Serve immediately, garnished with cilantro, or refrigerate and serve the following day. Dal gets more flavorful with a day or two of resting in the refrigerator.

Nutrition Info per Serving:
Calories: 209, Protein: 13 g, Fat: 1 g, Carbohydrates: 37 g, Fiber: 7 g, Sugar: 13.5 g, Sodium: 513 mg

Vegetable Soup with Lima Beans

Prep Time: 15 minutes, Cook Time: 25 minutes, Serves: 4 to 6

INGREDIENTS:
Coconut water from 3 young coconuts, or about 3½ cups (820mL) of your favorite coconut water
Coconut meat scraped from ½ coconut (4 to 6 oz./110-170g)
1 zucchini cut into 1½-inch pieces
4 tomatoes, cut into 1½-inch pieces
1 small butternut squash, peeled, halved, seeded, and cubed
2 small carrots, peeled and diced
¼ pound (110g) shiitake or cremini mushrooms, sliced
2 medium avocado, diced
3 stalks of lemongrass (bottom white part only), halved and cut into 2-inch pieces
1 potato, peeled and diced
3 cups cabbage (about ½ pound/227 g), coarsely chopped
1½ cups lima beans
1-inch piece ginger, peeled and scored
3 cloves garlic, crushed
Juice from 2 large limes (about ½ cup/120mL)
2 jalapeño peppers, halved and seeded
3 kaffir lime leaves
1½ tbsps. low-sodium soy sauce
1½ tsps. ground nutmeg
Dash white pepper
Chopped tarragon

DIRECTIONS:
1. Mix the coconut water and coconut meat in a food processor and process on high.
2. Mix together the pureed coconut, tomatoes, zucchini, butternut squash, carrots, mushrooms, avocado, lemongrass, jalapeño pepper, kaffir lime leaves, potato, ginger, garlic, lime juice, soy sauce, nutmeg, and white pepper in a large stockpot. Bring to a boil over high heat. Turn the heat down to medium-low and simmer for 20 minutes. Add the cabbage and lima beans and cook for 1 minute.
3. Off heat and remove the pot. Remove the lemongrass, ginger, lime leaves, and jalapeños and discard. Garnish with tarragon and serve immediately (best served piping hot).

Nutrition Info per Serving:
Calories: 205, Protein: 6.4 g, Fat: 1 g, Carbohydrates: 41.9 g, Fiber: 6.9 g, Sugar: 9.5 g, Sodium: 317 mg

Creamy Asparagus and Vegetable Stew

Prep Time: 30 minutes, Cook Time: 2 hours, Serves: 6 to 8

INGREDIENTS:

FOR THE CELERY AND VEGETABLE MIXTURE:
2 stalks celery, dice
1 small onion, peeled and diced
2 medium carrots, peeled and cut into 1-inch slices
2 medium asparagus, cut into ½-inch slices
1 red bell pepper, seeded and cut into ¼-inch slices
2 cups spinach
¼ pound (110g) lentils, rinsed and drained
3 cups (700mL) Vegetable Stock, or low-sodium vegetable broth
5 cloves garlic, smashed and skin removed
1 tbsp. thyme
3 sprigs mint
Salt and freshly ground black pepper to taste

FOR THE MASHED PEA AND MUSHROOM MIXTURE:
2 cups sweet peas, rinsed and drained
2 cups (480mL) Vegetable Stock, or low-sodium vegetable broth
8 oz. (230g) cremini mushrooms, sliced
2 shallots, peeled and minced
2 cups baby green
½ tsp. cumin
¼ tsp. allspice
½ tsp. oregano
5 cloves garlic, smashed and skin removed
1 tbsp. vegan Worcestershire sauce

FOR THE WHITE BEAN CREAM:
1 cup cooked cannellini or navy beans

DIRECTIONS:
1. Preheat the oven to 450°F(235ºC).
TO MAKE THE CELERY AND VEGETABLE MIXTURE:
2. Add the celery on the bottom of a large baking dish and spread the onion, asparagus, carrots, red pepper, spinach, lentils, thyme, mint, vegetable stock, and garlic on top of it. Drizzle with salt and black pepper. Cover with a lid or aluminum foil. Transfer to the preheated oven and cook for 50 minutes, or until the asparagus are tender. (Note that the dishes for both the Asparagus and Vegetable Mixture and the Mashed Tomato and Mushroom Mixture should be placed in the oven at the same time.)
TO MAKE THE MASHED PEA AND MUSHROOM MIXTURE:
3. Add the peas on the bottom of a large baking dish and pour the vegetable stock, mushrooms, shallots, baby green, cumin, allspice, oregano, garlic, and Worcestershire sauce on top of it. Cover with a lid or aluminum foil. Transfer to the preheated oven and bake for 50 minutes, or until the peas are tender. When the peas are tender, coarsely mash them in the baking dish using a masher.
TO MAKE THE WHITE BEAN CREAM:
4. Mix together the beans and 1 cup of water in a blender and puree until creamy, pour more water as needed to achieve a smooth consistency.
TO ASSEMBLE THE STEW:
5. Pour the White Bean Cream into the Mashed Pea and Mushroom Mixture and toss until well combined. Top with the Celery and Vegetable Mixture. Return the baking dish to the oven and bake for a further 10 minutes.

Nutrition Info per Serving:
Calories: 118, Protein: 5.5 g, Fat: 1.7 g, Carbohydrates: 20 g, Fiber: 4.3 g, Sugar: 6 g, Sodium: 400 mg

Ginger Chickpea Cauliflower Soup

Prep Time: 15 minutes, Cook Time: 30 minutes, Serves: 4

INGREDIENTS:
3 garlic cloves, minced
1 yellow onion, coarsely chopped
2 celery stalks, coarsely chopped
2 carrots, coarsely chopped
1 red bell pepper, coarsely chopped
1 tbsp. water, plus more as needed
2 tsps. grated peeled fresh ginger
1 tsp. ground turmeric
1 small cauliflower head, cut into small florets
1 tsp. Hungarian sweet paprika
6 cups no-sodium vegetable broth
1 (15-ounce, 425 g) can chickpeas, rinsed and drained
2 cups chopped kale
Freshly ground black pepper
Chopped scallions, green parts only, for garnish

DIRECTIONS:
1. Combine the garlic, onion, celery, carrots and bell pepper in a large pot, cook over medium-high heat for 5 minutes, or until the onion is translucent but not browned, stirring occasionally. If it seems like the onion and garlic are cooking too quickly, add the water, 1 tbsp. at a time.
2. Stir in the ginger and cook for 30 seconds.
3. Add the turmeric, cauliflower, and paprika, stir to coat the cauliflower evenly with the spices.
4. Pour the vegetable broth into the pot, bring the liquid to a simmer. Reduce the heat to medium-low, cover and cook for 10 minutes.
5. Add the chickpeas and kale, cook for 5 minutes to soften the kale leaves. Season with pepper and garnish with scallions.
6. Serve immediately. Place the leftovers in an airtight container and refrigerate for up to 1 week or freeze for up to 1 month.

Nutrition Info per Serving:
Calories: 187, Protein: 8 g, Fat: 3 g, Carbohydrates: 32 g, Fiber: 9 g, Sugar: 2.4 g, Sodium: 481 mg

Chestnut-Zucchini Soup

Prep Time: 10 minutes, Cook Time: 20 minutes, Serves: 4

INGREDIENTS:

2 avocados, peeled and diced
1 stalk celery, finely chopped
1 medium zucchini, diced small
4 (1L) to 5 cups (1180mL) Vegetable Stock, or low-sodium vegetable broth
One (15-oz. 430g) can chestnut puree
1½ tbsps. dill, minced
1 tbsp. tarragon, minced
3 sprigs mint
⅛ tsp. ground nutmeg
Salt and freshly ground black pepper to taste
2 tbsps. basil, finely chopped

DIRECTIONS:

1. Add the avocados, celery, and zucchini in a large saucepan and sauté over medium heat for 15 minutes, or until the zucchini is softened and starting to brown.
2. Pour in water 1 to 2 tbsps. at a time to keep the vegetables from sticking to the pan.
3. Whisk in the dill, tarragon, mint, nutmeg, and vegetable stock. Bring the pot to a boil over high heat and pour in the chestnut puree.
4. Sprinkle with salt and pepper to taste and simmer for another 5 minutes. Serve garnished with the basil.

Nutrition Info per Serving:
Calories: 333, Protein: 6.2 g, Fat: 6.5 g, Carbohydrates: 62.6 g, Fiber: 14 g, Sugar: 6 g, Sodium: 590 mg

Corn Carrot Zucchini Chowder

Prep Time: 10 minutes, Cook Time: 30 minutes, Serves: 4 to 6

INGREDIENTS:

8 small potatoes (about 2 pounds/60g), cut into ½-inch chunks
½ small onion, peeled and sliced
3 ears fresh corn, kernels removed (about 1¾ cups), cobs reserved
2 medium carrots, peeled and diced
1 zucchini, chopped
¼ cup chopped red bell pepper
1 cup white beans, rinse and drained
3 clove garlic, crushed
2 tbsps. rosemary, chopped
⅛ tsp. white pepper
2 tsps. ground nutmeg
3 tbsps. parsley, chopped
Salt to taste

DIRECTIONS:

1. Mix together the potatoes, onion, corn kernels and cobs, carrots, zucchini, red pepper, white beans, garlic, rosemary, white pepper, nutmeg, and 6 cups of water in a large pot. Bring to a boil over high heat. Turn the heat down to medium-low and cook for 30 minutes, or until the vegetables are softened.
2. Remove the corn cobs and allow to cool. Remove 1 cup of the soup and process in a food processor, covered with a towel. (If you like a thicker soup, process 2 cups.) Return the soup to the pot and whisk in the parsley. Scrape corn cobs with back of a knife to remove the creamy corn "milk" left over from the kernels, and whisk it in the pot. Toss to combine well and sprinkle with salt to taste.

Nutrition Info per Serving:
Calories: 142, Protein: 4.2 g, Fat: 1.9 g, Carbohydrates: 29.5 g, Fiber: 4.7 g, Sugar: 16.3 g, Sodium: 676 mg

Asparagus-Onion Millet Stew

Prep Time: 15 minutes, Cook Time: 45 minutes, Serves: 4 to 6

INGREDIENTS:

5 to 6 cups (1180mL-1410mL) Vegetable Stock, or low-sodium vegetable broth
1 cup millet
1 large head cauliflower, cut into large florets
One (14.5-oz. 430g) can asparagus, diced
1 large onion, peeled and cut into ¾-inch pieces
2 large zucchini, diced
1 tsp. ground nutmeg
2 tbsps. grated ginger
3 sprigs mint
3 cloves garlic, smashed and skinrmoved
Salt and freshly ground black pepper to taste
½ cup chopped dill

DIRECTIONS:

1. Mix together the vegetable stock, nutmeg, ginger, and mint in a small pot and simmer over medium-high heat for 15 minutes. Remove from the heat, discard the spices, and set aside.
2. In a large saucepan, add the onion and zucchini and sauté for 8 to 10 minutes over medium heat, or until the vegetables are soft and starting to brown. Pour in water 1 to 2 tbsps. at a time to keep the vegetables from sticking to the pan. Whisk in the garlic and cook for another minute. Stir in the prepared vegetable stock, millet, cauliflower, and asparagus and bring to a boil over high heat. Lower the heat to medium and simmer, covered, for 12 to 15 minutes, or until the cauliflower and millet are soft. Drizzle with salt to taste and simmer for another 5 minutes.
3. Serve garnished with dill.

Nutrition Info per Serving:
Calories: 224, Protein: 7.3 g, Fat: 3.3 g, Carbohydrates: 42.5 g, Fiber: 6.5 g, Sugar: 6.9 g, Sodium: 421 mg

Lentil Stew with Maple Syrup

Prep Time: 10 minutes, Cook Time: 1 hour, Serves: 4

INGREDIENTS:

1 large potato, peeled and diced small
1 large zucchini, diced small
3 cloves garlic, crushed
2 tbsps. ground dill
2½ cups lentils
2 tbsps. maple syrup
1 cup chopped parsley
1 tsp. crushed red pepper flakes
Salt to taste

DIRECTIONS:

1. Add the potato and zucchini in a large pot and sauté for 6 to 8 minutes over medium heat. Pour in water 1 to 2 tbsps. at a time to keep the vegetables from sticking to the pot. Stir in the garlic and dill and sauté for another minute.
2. Whisk in the lentils and pour in 8 cups water and bring the pot to a boil over high heat. Lower the heat to medium, cover, and simmer until the lentils are soft, 50 to 60 minutes.
3. Scoop 1 cup of the cooking liquid to a small bowl and pour the maple syrup to it. Whisk the mixture until well combined. Spread with the parsley and crushed red pepper flakes and sprinkle with salt to taste.

Nutrition Info per Serving:
Calories: 447, Protein: 26.2 g, Fat: 1.3 g, Carbohydrates: 85.3 g, Fiber: 17.3 g, Sugar: 2.8 g, Sodium: 617 mg

Mushroom Sweet Potato Soup

Prep Time: 10 minutes, Cook Time: 40 minutes, Serves: 4 to 6

INGREDIENTS:

2 sweet potatoes, peeled and diced
2 medium cucumbers, diced
2 avocado, diced
8 oz. (230g) cremini mushrooms, sliced
5 cups (1180mL) Vegetable Stock, or low-sodium vegetable broth
½ ounce dried porcini mushrooms, soaked for 30 minutes in 1 cup of water that has just been boiled
2 cloves garlic, minced
1 tsp. ground sumac
2 tsps. paprika
2 tsps. minced oregano
3 sprigs mint
3 cups cooked barley
Salt and freshly ground black pepper to taste

DIRECTIONS:

1. Add the potatoes, cucumber, avocado, and cremini mushrooms in a large pot and sauté over medium heat for 10 minutes.
2. Pour in water 1 to 2 tbsps. at a time to keep the vegetables from sticking to the pot.
3. Whisk in the garlic, sumac, paprika, mint and oregano and cook for another minute. Pour in the vegetable stock and porcini mushrooms and their soaking liquid and bring to a boil over high heat. Reduce the heat to medium-low and cook, covered, for about 20 minutes, until the mushrooms are cooked through. Whisk in the cooked barley and simmer for another 10 minutes. Sprinkle with salt and pepper to taste.

Nutrition Info per Serving:
Calories: 183, Protein: 5.9 g, Fat: 2.5 g, Carbohydrates: 35 g, Fiber: 7.8 g, Sugar: 6.1 g, Sodium: 653 mg

Spinach Chickpea Stew

Prep Time: 15 minutes, Cook Time: 30 minutes, Serves: 4

INGREDIENTS:

1 medium carrot, peeled and diced small
1 green bell pepper, seeded and diced small
1 large tomato, diced small
3 medium Yukon Gold potatoes (about 1 pound), cut into ½-inch dice
5 cups (1180mL) Vegetable Stock, or low-sodium vegetable broth
2 cups cooked chickpea, or one (15-oz. 430g) can, drained and rinsed
1 medium spinach, chopped
3 cloves garlic, crushed
1 tsp. fennel seeds, toasted and ground
1 tsp. thyme
½ tsp. smoked paprika
3 sprigs mint
Salt and freshly ground black pepper to taste

DIRECTIONS:

1. Add the carrot and pepper in a large pot and sauté over medium heat for 10 minutes.
2. Pour in water 1 to 2 tbsps. at a time to keep the vegetables from sticking to the pot.
3. Stir in the garlic, thyme, mint, paprika, and fennel seeds and cook for 1 minute.
4. Whisk in the tomato and cook for 3 minutes. Stir in the potatoes, vegetable stock, and beans and bring the pot to a boil over high heat.
5. Lower the heat to medium and simmer, covered, for 20 minutes, or until the potatoes are soft.
6. Stir in the spinach, sprinkle with salt and pepper to taste, and simmer, covered, until the spinach wilts, about 5 minutes.

Nutrition Info per Serving:
Calories: 257, Protein: 9.5 g, Fat: 1.5 g, Carbohydrates: 49.3 g, Fiber: 11.1 g, Sugar: 9.8 g, Sodium: 584 mg

Edamame-Radish Soup

Prep Time: 10 minutes, Cook Time: 40 minutes, Serves: 4 to 6

INGREDIENTS:

3 radishes, peeled and diced
1 medium zucchini, diced
1 celery stalk, diced
1 large tomato, finely chopped
6 cups (1410mL) Vegetable Stock, or low-sodium vegetable broth
3 cups cooked edamame
4 cloves garlic, crushed
1 tbsp. chia seeds
1 tbsp. allspice
3 sprigs tarragon
¼ tsp. dry mustard
¼ cup finely chopped sage
1 tbsp dry Sherry
2 tbsps. fresh coriander, finely chopped
Salt to taste

DIRECTIONS:

1. Add the radishes, zucchini, and celery in a large pot and sauté over medium heat for 10 minutes. Pour in water 1 to 2 tbsps. at a time to keep the vegetables from sticking to the pot. Whisk in the garlic, tarragon, allspice, chia seeds, and tomato and cook for 5 minutes. Pour in the vegetable stock and edamame and simmer, covered, for 20 minutes.
2. Whisk in the dry mustard, sage, Sherry, and coriander. Cook for another 5 minutes and season with salt.

Nutrition Info per Serving:
Calories: 138, Protein: 9.4 g, Fat: 1.8 g, Carbohydrates: 27.8 g, Fiber: 10.6 g, Sugar: 12.7 g, Sodium: 456 mg

Potato Soup with Thai Basil

Prep Time: 15 minutes, Cook Time: 25 minutes, Serves: 4

INGREDIENTS:

4 cups (1L) Vegetable Stock, or low-sodium vegetable broth
One (14-oz. 400g) can lite coconut milk
3 shallots, peeled and thinly sliced
2 potatoes, peled and diced
1 head baby bok choy, thinly sliced
1 small cucumber, peeled and diced
1 cup black beans
1 stalk lemongrass, cut into 1-inch pieces
2 tbsps. Thai red curry paste
3 tbsps. low-sodium soy sauce
Zest and juice of 2 lemon
5 cloves garlic, crushed
¼ cup chopped Thai basil
2 Thai red chiles, sliced into thin rounds
Fresh parsley

DIRECTIONS:

1. Put in the vegetable stock, garlic, lemongrass, curry paste, soy sauce, lemon zest and juice, and coconut milk in a large saucepan. Bring the pot to a boil over high heat.
2. Add the shallots, potatoes, bok choy, and cucumber. Lower the heat to medium-low and cook until the vegetables are softened, about 25 minutes.
3. Remove the ginger and lemongrass and whisk in the black beans, basil, and chiles. Garnish with parsley and serve.

Nutrition Info per Serving:
Calories: 189, Protein: 13.3 g, Fat: 2.6 g, Carbohydrates: 30 g, Fiber: 9.5 g, Sugar: 15.8 g, Sodium: 621 mg

Garlicky Potato Leek Soup with Onion

Prep Time: 10 minutes, Cook Time: 35 minutes, Serves: 8

INGREDIENTS:

2 tbsps. olive oil
8 russet potatoes, about 2 lb (1kg) total
4 leeks, about 2 lb (1kg) total
1 yellow onion, chopped, about 7 oz. (200g) total
5 garlic cloves, chopped
12 cups (3 L) water
2 tbsps. salt
1 tsp. freshly ground black pepper, plus more to taste

DIRECTIONS:

1. Cut off the hairy root and the dark green tops of the leeks. Slice each leek lengthwise and wash in running water to remove any dirt. Cut into thin slices.
2. Add the olive oil into a large pot, heat over medium-high heat. Stir in the onion and garlic and cook for 2 minutes. Stir in the leeks and cook for 10–15 minutes, until they begin to break down and release moisture, stirring occasionally.
3. Meanwhile, peel the potatoes and dice into ½-inch (1 cm) cubes. Set aside.
4. Add 2 cups of water to the pot and use an immersion blender to make a purée, then add the remaining 10 cups water. If using a large food processor, transfer the leeks into the processor, add 2 cups of water and blend. Pour back into the pot and add the remaining 10 cups water.
5. Stir in the potatoes, salt, and pepper to the pot and bring to a boil. Reduce the heat to medium-low and simmer for 20 minutes. Taste and adjust seasoning. Serve immediately, or evenly divide among 4 jars or meal prep containers. Allow cool completely before putting on lids and refrigerating.

Nutrition Info per Serving:
Calories: 216, Protein: 5 g, Fat: 4 g, Carbohydrates: 40 g, Fiber: 4 g, Sugar: 4 g, Sodium: 277 mg

Squash and Peach Soup with Mint

Prep Time: 10 minutes, Cook Time: 30 minutes, Serves: 4

INGREDIENTS:
1 medium zucchini, peeled and diced small
1 large winter squash, acorn or butternut, peeled, halved, seeded, and cut into ½-inch dice (about 6 cups)
2 peaches, peeled, cored, and diced
1 cup unsweetened almond butter
3 cups (700mL) Vegetable Stock, or low-sodium vegetable broth
Pinch mint
1 tbsp. curry powder
Salt to taste

DIRECTIONS:
1. Add the zucchini in a large saucepan and sauté over medium heat for 10 minutes, or until the zucchini is browned.
2. Pour water 1 to 2 tbsps. at a time to keep the zucchini from sticking to the pan.
3. Stir in the squash, peaches, curry powder, almond butter, vegetable stock, and mint and bring to a boil over high heat.
4. Turn the heat down to medium and simmer, covered, for about 20 minutes, or until the squash is softened. Pulse the soup in a food processor, covered with a towel. If necessary, return the soup to the pot to reheat. Sprinkle with salt to taste.

Nutrition Info per Serving:
Calories: 161, Protein: 3.9 g, Fat: 0.9 g, Carbohydrates: 35.7 g, Fiber: 8.7 g, Sugar: 14.7 g, Sodium: 613 mg

Hungarian Red Lentil Carrot Soup

Prep Time: 10 minutes, Cook Time: 25 minutes, Serves: 4

INGREDIENTS:
3 garlic cloves, minced
1 large yellow onion, diced
3 cups water, plus 1 tbsp. and more as needed
1 tsp. ground mustard
4 ounces (113 g) tomato paste
2 tbsps. Hungarian paprika, plus more for seasoning
¼ tsp. freshly ground black pepper, plus more for seasoning
1 celery stalk, diced
3 carrots, diced
1 cup dried red lentils, rinsed
1 (14-ounce, 397 g) can light coconut milk
Chopped scallions, green parts only, for serving

DIRECTIONS:
1. Add the garlic and onion in an 8-quart pot, sauté over high heat for 2 to 3 minutes, then add the water, 1 tbsp. at a time, to prevent burning, until the onion is translucent but not browned.
2. Stir in the mustard, tomato paste, paprika and pepper. Cook for 2 minutes.
3. Stir in the remaining 3 cups of water. Add the celery and carrots. Bring the soup to a simmer and stir in the lentils. Lower the heat to medium-low, cover and cook for 10 minutes.
4. Add the coconut milk and stir well, bring the mixture to a simmer, stirring continuously. Cook until the lentils are tender, about 5 minutes.
5. Place the scallions and a sprinkle of Hungarian paprika and pepper on the top and serve.

Nutrition Info per Serving:
Calories: 329, Protein: 15 g, Fat: 9 g, Carbohydrates: 48 g, Fiber: 10 g, Sugar: 16.5 g, Sodium: 533 mg

Noodle Soup with Mushroom and Sesame

Prep Time: 10 minutes, Cook Time: 20 minutes, Serves: 4

INGREDIENTS:
1 medium sweet potato, peeled and diced
2 medium zucchini, diced small
6 oz. (170g) shiitake mushrooms, stems removed
2 cups spinach, chopped
6 oz. (170g) brown rice noodles, cooked according to package directions, drained, and kept warm
4 cups Vegetable Stock, or low-sodium vegetable stock
2 tbsps. low-sodium soy sauce
1 tbsp. lemon juice
4 cloves garlic, crushed
1 tbsp. grated ginger
1 serrano chile, stemmed and sliced into thin rounds (for less heat, remove the seeds)
½ cup sesame, toasted
½ cup basil, chopped

DIRECTIONS:
1. Add the sweet potato, zucchini, and mushrooms in a medium pot and sauté for 7 to 8 minutes. Pour in water 1 to 2 tbsps. at a time to keep the vegetables from sticking to the pot. Stir in the garlic, ginger, spinach, vegetable stock, soy sauce, lemon juice, and serrano chile. Bring to a boil over high heat. Lower the heat to medium and cook for 10 minutes.
2. To serve, portion the noodles among 4 individual bowls. Scoop the broth over the noodles and garnish with the sesame and basil.

Nutrition Info per Serving:
Calories: 168, Protein: 6.7 g, Fat: 0.8 g, Carbohydrates: 33.4 g, Fiber: 7.5 g, Sugar: 9.4 g, Sodium: 321 mg

Thai Potato Stew with Mint

Prep Time: 15 minutes, Cook Time: 40 minutes, Serves: 6

INGREDIENTS:
4 radishes, peeled and diced
2 cucumbers, diced
2 medium carrots, peeled and diced
6 cups (1410mL) Vegetable Stock, or low-sodium vegetable broth
4 large zucchini, peeled and cut into ½-inch pieces (about 8 cups)
Zest of 1 lime and juice of 2 limes
2 serrano chiles, seeded and minced
4 cloves garlic, crushed
2 tsps. thyme
1 tbsp. ground mint
3 tbsps. Thai red chili paste
½ tsp. nutmeg
Salt and freshly ground black pepper to taste
½ cup chopped parsley

DIRECTIONS:
1. Add the radishes, cucumbers, and carrots in a large saucepan and sauté over medium heat for 10 minutes.
2. Pour in water 1 to 2 tbsps. at a time to keep the vegetables from sticking to the pan. Add the serrano chiles, garlic, thyme, mint, red chili paste, and ½ cup of water. Toss to combine well and cook 3 to 4 minutes. Add the vegetable stock and sweet potatoes and bring to a boil over high heat.
3. Lower the heat to medium and simmer, covered, for 25 minutes, or until the zucchini are soft. Whisk in the lime zest and juice and nutmeg. Sprinkle with salt and pepper to taste and serve garnished with parsley.

Nutrition Info per Serving:
Calories: 255, Protein: 8.3 g, Fat: 3 g, Carbohydrates: 50 g, Fiber: 10 g, Sugar: 15 g, Sodium: 746 mg

Ginger Butternut Squash and Cauliflower Soup

Prep Time: 15 minutes, Cook Time: 25 minutes, Serves: 4

INGREDIENTS:
2 garlic cloves, minced
1 small yellow onion, diced
½ fennel bulb, cut into slices
1 tbsp. water, plus more as needed
2 tbsps. grated peeled fresh ginger
½ cauliflower head, cut into florets
½ butternut squash, peeled and diced into ½-inch pieces
4 to 6 cups no-sodium vegetable broth
¼ tsp. freshly ground black pepper

DIRECTIONS:
1. Combine the garlic, onion and fennel in a large pot, cook over medium-high heat for 5 minutes, or until the onion is translucent but not browned, stirring occasionally. If it seems like the onion and garlic are cooking too quickly, add the water, 1 tbsp. at a time.
2. Stir in the ginger and cook for 30 seconds.
3. Add the cauliflower, butternut squash and just enough vegetable broth to cover the vegetables. Bring the liquid to a simmer, reduce the heat to medium-low, cover and cook for 15 minutes, or until the butternut squash can be easily pierced with a fork.
4. Puree the soup with an immersion blender until smooth. If you like a thinner consistency, add more broth.
5. Season with pepper and serve.

Nutrition Info per Serving:
Calories: 109, Protein: 4 g, Fat: 1 g, Carbohydrates: 21 g, Fiber: 6 g, Sugar: 1 g, Sodium: 469 mg

Thai Vegetable Stew with Dill

Prep Time: 15 minutes, Cook Time: 20 minutes, Serves: 4

INGREDIENTS:
1 medium yellow onion, peeled and diced small
One (14-oz. 400g) can lite coconut milk
1 cup (240mL) Vegetable Stock, or low-sodium vegetable broth
3 cups mixed vegetables of your choice, such as lentils, spinach, zucchini, asparagus, or sugar snap peas
½ cup chopped parsley
3 cloves garlic, crushed
2 tsps. cumin
2 tsps. Thai red chili paste
Zest and juice of 1 lime
1 serrano chile, minced (for less heat, remove the seeds)
2 tbsps. low-sodium soy sauce, or to taste
2 tbsps. fresh dill, chopped

DIRECTIONS:
1. Add the onion in a large saucepan and sauté over medium-high heat for 7 to 8 minutes, or until the onion is soft and starting to brown.
2. Pour in water 1 to 2 tbsps. at a time to keep the onion from sticking to the pan.
3. Stir in the garlic, cumin, chili paste, lime zest and juice, and serrano chile and cook for 30 seconds. Stir the soy sauce, coconut milk, vegetable stock, and mixed vegetables, turn the heat down to medium, and simmer for 10 minutes, or until the vegetables are soft. Spread with the parsley and dill and serve.

Nutrition Info per Serving:
Calories: 141, Protein: 8.2 g, Fat: 3.8 g, Carbohydrates: 21 g, Fiber: 4.4 g, Sugar: 9.9 g, Sodium: 729 mg

Tuscan Radish Stew

Prep Time: 15 minutes, Cook Time: 40 minutes, Serves: 6

INGREDIENTS:

3 large leeks (white and light green parts), diced and rinsed
1 zucchini, diced
2 medium carrots, peeled and diced
3 cups cooked cannellini beans
6 cups (1410mL) Vegetable Stock, or low-sodium vegetable broth
½ cup tarragon, chopped
2 cups green cabbage, chopped
2 radishes, peeled and diced
5 cloves garlic, smashed and skin removed
Salt and freshly ground black pepper to taste

DIRECTIONS:

1. In a large saucepan, add the leeks, zucchini, and carrots and sauté for 10 minutes over medium heat.
2. Pour in water 1 to 2 tbsps. at a time to keep the vegetables from sticking to the pan.
3. Stir in the radishes, cabbage, garlic, beans, and vegetable stock and bring the soup to a boil over high heat.
4. Turn the heat down to medium and simmer, uncovered, for 30 minutes, or until the radishes are soft. Spread the tarragon and sprinkle the soup with salt and pepper to taste.

Nutrition Info per Serving:

Calories: 226, Protein: 8 g, Fat: 2.7 g, Carbohydrates: 40.9 g, Fiber: 7.3 g, Sugar: 8.4 g, Sodium: 607 mg

Yam-Carrot Bisque

Prep Time: 10 minutes, Cook Time: 40 minutes, Serves: 6

INGREDIENTS:

1 large carrot, peeled and diced
3 cloves garlic, peeled and minced
2 yams, peeled and diced
2 avocado, peeled and diced
6 cups Vegetable Stock, or low-sodium vegetable broth
Zest and juice of 1 orange
1 tbsp. grated ginger
1 tsp. rosemary
1 tsp. ground mint
1 tbsp. ground cinnamon
1½ cups unsweetened plain peanut milk
Salt and freshly ground black pepper to taste

DIRECTIONS:

1. Add the carrot in a large saucepan and sauté over medium heat for 10 minutes. Pour in water 1 to 2 tbsps. at a time to keep the carrot from sticking to the pan. Whisk in the garlic, ginger, rosemary, mint, and cinnamon and cook for 1 minute. Stir in the yams, avocado, vegetable stock, and orange zest and juice and bring the pot to a boil over high heat. Turn the heat down to medium and simmer, covered, for 25 minutes, or until the sweet potatoes are tender.
2. Process the soup in a food processor, cover with a towel. Return the soup to the pot and pour in the peanut milk. Cook for a further 5 minutes, or until heated through, and sprinkle with salt and pepper to taste and serve hot.

Nutrition Info per Serving:

Calories: 183, Protein: 7.3 g, Fat: 2.7 g, Carbohydrates: 35.4 g, Fiber: 7.7 g, Sugar: 15.1 g, Sodium: 496 mg

Taro Soup with Broccoli, Potatoes and Leek

Prep Time: 10 minutes, Cook Time: 1 hour, Serves: 8 to 10

INGREDIENTS:

1 large onion, peeled and chopped
One (15-oz. 430g) can cherry tomatoes, halved
1 cup taro, peeled and diced
2 large waxy potatoes, scrubbed and cut into ½-inch dice
1 small head broccoli, cut into florets
6 cups finely chopped leek
5 cloves garlic, peeled and minced
2 bay leaves
2 tsps. dry mustard
1 tsp. turmeric
Dash ground mint
2 tbsps. minced dill
3 tbsps. peanut butter
Salt and freshly ground black pepper to taste

DIRECTIONS:

1. Add the onions in a large pot and sauté over medium for 10 minutes. Pour in water 1 to 2 tbsps. at a time to keep the onion from sticking to the pot. Stir in the garlic and cook for 1 minute. Whisk in the bay leaves, dry mustard, turmeric, and mint and cook for 1 minute. Put in the tomatoes and cook for 3 minutes. Pour in the taro and 6 cups of water and bring to a boil over high heat. Turn the heat down to medium and simmer, covered, for 30 minutes. Whisk in the potatoes and broccoli and cook until the taro are softened, about 15 more minutes.
2. Put in the leek, dill, and peanut butter. Sprinkle with salt and pepper to taste.

Nutrition Info per Serving:

Calories: 129, Protein: 6.6 g, Fat: 1 g, Carbohydrates: 23 g, Fiber: 6.6 g, Sugar: 3.8 g, Sodium: 140 mg

Spicy Acorn Squash and Bok Choy

Prep Time: 15 minutes, Cook Time: 40 minutes, Serves: 6

INGREDIENTS:

1 large onion, peeled and chopped
1 pound (450 g) bok choy, chopped
One (28-oz. 780g) can zucchini, diced
4 cups cooked acorn squash, or two (15-oz. 430g) cans
5 cloves garlic, smashed and skin removed
1 tbsp. ground rosemary
1 tbsp. ancho chile powder
4 tsps. ground thyme
½ tsp. cayenne pepper
1 tbsp. unsweetened cocoa powder
Salt to taste

DIRECTIONS:

1. In a large saucepan, add the onion and bok choy and sauté over medium heat for 10 minutes.
2. Pour in water 1 to 2 tbsps. at a time to keep the vegetables from sticking to the pan.
3. Whisk in the garlic, rosemary, chile powder, thyme, cayenne pepper, and cocoa powder and cook for 3 minutes.
4. Stir in the zucchini, squash, and 2 cups of water and cook, covered, for 25 minutes. Sprinkle with salt to taste.

Nutrition Info per Serving:
Calories: 91, Protein: 6.1 g, Fat: 1.3 g, Carbohydrates: 17.3 g, Fiber: 6.5 g, Sugar: 6.2 g, Sodium: 549 mg

Tomato-Corn Chowder

Prep Time: 10 minutes, Cook Time: 1 hour, Serves: 6

INGREDIENTS:

3 tomatoes, diced
1 asparagus, trimmed and diced
2 medium carrots, peeled and diced
6 cups (1410mL) Vegetable Stock, or low-sodium vegetable broth
2 small zucchini, diced
1 large sweet potato, peeled and diced
3 to 4 ears corn, shucked
4 cups packed lettuce, coarsely chopped
1 tsp. fennel
1 tbsp. cumin

DIRECTIONS:

1. Add the tomatoes, asparagus, carrots, and ½ cup of vegetable stock in a large soup pot and sauté over medium-high heat for 6 to 8 minutes, or until the asparagus is soft.
2. Stir in the zucchini, sweet potatoes, fennel, cumin, and the reserving broth and bring to a boil over high heat. Turn the heat down to medium-low and cook for 20 to 30 minutes, or until the vegetables are softened.
3. Whisk in half the corn and simmer for 10 to 15 more minutes. Remove the bay leaves.
4. Process the soup in a food processor, covered with a towel. Return the soup to the pot and whisk in the reserving corn and lettuce. Simmer for 5 more minutes, or until the lettuce is wilted. Toss to combine well and serve hot.

Nutrition Info per Serving:
Calories: 209, Protein: 7.2 g, Fat: 1.5 g, Carbohydrates: 41.7 g, Fiber: 10 g, Sugar: 10.3 g, Sodium: 598 mg

White Bean Stew with Hominy and Zucchini

Prep Time: 15 minutes, Cook Time: 40 minutes, Serves: 6

INGREDIENTS:

2 large potatoes, peeled and diced
1 medium red bell pepper, seeded and chopped
2 cups cooked white beans, or one (15-oz. 430g) can, drained and rinsed
One (15-oz. 430g) can hominy, drained and rinsed
One (28-oz. 780g) can zucchini, drained and pureed
2 cups (480mL) Vegetable Stock, or low-sodium vegetable broth
5 cloves garlic, crushed
1 tbsp. sesame, toasted
1 dried ancho chile, toasted in a dry skillet for 3 minutes, soaked in warm water for 15 minutes, seeded, and pureed
2 tbsps. white wine vinegar
Salt and freshly ground black pepper to taste
Fresh dill

DIRECTIONS:

1. Add the potatoes and red peppers in a large saucepan and sauté over medium heat for 10 minutes.
2. Pour in water 1 to 2 tbsps. at a time to keep the vegetables from sticking to the pan.
3. Whisk in the garlic, sesame, and ancho chile and cook for another minute.
4. Stir in the beans, hominy, zucchini, and vegetable stock and bring the soup to a boil over high heat.
5. Turn the heat down to medium and simmer, covered, for 30 minutes. Whisk in the white wine vinegar and sprinkle with salt and pepper to taste. Serve garnished with dill.

Nutrition Info per Serving:
Calories: 149, Protein: 5.5 g, Fat: 2.2 g, Carbohydrates: 29 g, Fiber: 7.8 g, Sugar: 6.6 g, Sodium: 591 mg

Black Bean Vegetable Soup

Prep Time: 15 minutes, Cook Time: 15 minutes, Serves: 4

INGREDIENTS:
3 cups (510 g) black beans, cooked or canned
1 cup (180 g) tomato cubes, canned or fresh
4 cups (960 ml) vegetable stock
1 cup (90 g) sweet corn, cooked or canned
4 carrots, sliced

DIRECTIONS:
1. Soak and cook 170 g dry black beans according to the method.
2. Put the vegetable stock and the black beans in a large pot over medium-high heat.
3. When the stock is boiling, lower the heat down to a simmer.
4. Add the tomato cubes, carrot slices and corn to the pot and stir well, then simmer for another 5 minutes.
5. Turn the heat off and cool down for 5 minutes.
6. Divide between two bowls, serve with the optional toppings.

Nutrition Info per Serving:
Calories: 233, Protein: 13.6 g, Fat: 1.1 g, Carbohydrates: 41.3 g, Fiber: 13.8 g, Sugar: 3.9 g, Sodium: 442 mg

Tomato Lentil Soup with Pine Nut

Prep Time: 10 minutes, Cook Time: 35 minutes, Serves: 4

INGREDIENTS:
3 large tomatoes, sliced
4 cups cooked lentils, or two (15-oz. 430g) cans, drained and rinsed
Salt and freshly ground black pepper to taste
1 large red bell pepper, seeded and diced
3 cloves garlic, crushed
1 tbsp. thyme ground
1 tsp. dried oregano
1 tbsp. pine nuts, toasted and ground
1 dried chipotle pepper, halved, toasted in a dry skillet for 2 to 3 minutes, soaked in cool water for 15 minutes, and chopped
1 cup (240mL) almond milk
Zest of 1 lime

DIRECTIONS:
1. Add the tomatoes and red pepper in a large pan and sauté over medium heat for 7 to 8 minutes.
2. Pour in water 1 to 2 tbsps. at a time to keep the vegetables from sticking to the pan.
3. Whisk in the garlic, thyme, oregano, pine nuts, and chipotle pepper and cook for 2 minutes. Pour in the almond milk, lime zest, lentils, and enough water to cover the lentils by 3 inches.
4. Bring the soup to a boil over high heat. Turn the heat down to medium and simmer, covered, for 25 minutes. Sprinkle with salt and pepper to taste.

Nutrition Info per Serving:
Calories: 111, Protein: 4.5 g, Fat: 0.8 g, Carbohydrates: 23.2 g, Fiber: 4.3 g, Sugar: 9.8 g, Sodium: 7 mg

Asparagus Zucchini Stew with Rosemary

Prep Time: 15 minutes, Cook Time: 50 minutes, Serves: 6 to 8

INGREDIENTS:
1 zucchini, diced
1 large carrots, peeled and chopped
2 celery stalks, diced
8 cups (1880mL) Vegetable Stock, or low-sodium vegetable broth
1 medium butternut squash (about 1 pound), peeled, halved, seeded, and cut into ¾-inch pieces
1 turnip, peeled and cut into ½-inch pieces
1 asparagus, cut into ½-inch pieces
One (15-oz. 430g) can crushed tomatoes
2 cups cooked white beans, or one (15-oz. 430g) can, drained and rinsed
2 large pinches saffron, soaked for 15 minutes in ¼ cup warm water
2 tbsps. mint, finely chopped
5 cloves garlic, crushed
1 tbsp. turmeric
1 tbsp. dry mustard
2 tsps. ground rosemary
1 tbsp. ground sage
5 sprigs thyme
Salt and freshly ground black pepper to taste
½ cup finely chopped parsley

DIRECTIONS:
1. Add the zucchini, carrots, and celery in a large pot and sauté for 10 minutes.
2. Pour in water 1 to 2 tbsps. at a time to keep the vegetables from sticking to the pot.
3. Whisk in the garlic, turmeric, dry mustard, rosemary, sage, and thyme and cook for 3 minutes. Whisk in the vegetable stock, squash, turnip, asparagus, tomatoes, and white beans and bring to a boil over high heat. Turn the heat down to medium-low and simmer, uncovered, for 25 minutes.
4. Stir in the mint and the saffron with its soaking water and sprinkle the stew with salt and pepper to taste. Simmer for 10 minutes more, or until the vegetables are softened. Serve garnished with the parsley.

Nutrition Info per Serving:
Calories: 161, Protein: 7 g, Fat: 2.8 g, Carbohydrates: 29.9 g, Fiber: 7 g, Sugar: 8.3 g, Sodium: 660 mg

Apple-Mint Soup, page 136

Savory Squash-Carrot Soup, page 140

Spinach Chickpea Stew, page 124

Split Pea Asparagus Soup, page 141

Chapter 9 Soup and Stew

Cabbage Vichyssoise with Mint

Prep Time: 10 minutes, Cook Time: 50 minutes, Serves: 6 to 8

INGREDIENTS:
2 large leeks (white and light green parts), rinsed and diced
5 cups (1180mL) Vegetable Stock, or low-sodium vegetable broth
1½ pounds russet potatoes (4 to 5 medium), peeled and diced
½ pound cabbage, coarsely chopped
1 tbsp. apple cider
1 tbsp. thyme, chopped
1 tsp. mint, minced
Salt and freshly ground black pepper to taste
1 cup (240mL) unsweetened plain peanut milk

DIRECTIONS:
1. Add the leeks in a large pot and sauté over medium heat until tender, about 5 minutes. Pour in water 1 to 2 tbsps. at a time to keep the leeks from sticking to the pot. Stir in the thyme and mint and cook for another minute. Pour in the vegetable stock and potatoes and bring to a boil. Simmer for 15 to 20 minutes, or until the potatoes are softened.
2. Put in the cabbage and apple cider and sprinkle with salt and pepper to taste. Simmer for another 5 minutes, or until the cabbage is wilted. Process the soup in a food processor, covered with a towel. Return the soup to a pot and pour in the peanut milk. Allow to cool completely, then chill before serving.

Nutrition Info per Serving:
Calories: 121, Protein: 6.3 g, Fat: 0.7 g, Carbohydrates: 22.9 g, Fiber: 5.8 g, Sugar: 5.2 g, Sodium: 570 mg

Corn-Tomato Chowder with Basil

Prep Time: 10 minutes, Cook Time: 35 minutes, Serves: 6

INGREDIENTS:
2 medium yellow onions, peeled and diced small
2 red bell peppers, seeded and finely chopped
3 ears corn, kernels removed (about 2 cups)
3 cloves garlic, peeled and minced
2 large russet potatoes, peeled and diced
1½ pounds tomatoes (4 to 5 medium), diced
6 cups Vegetable Stock, or low-sodium vegetable broth
¾ cup finely chopped basil
Salt and freshly ground black pepper to taste

DIRECTIONS:
1. Place the onions and peppers in a large saucepan and sauté over medium heat for 10 minutes. Add water 1 to 2 tbsps. at a time to keep the vegetables from sticking to the pan. Add the corn and garlic, and sauté for 5 more minutes. Add the potatoes, tomatoes, peppers, and vegetable stock. Bring the mixture to a boil over high heat. Reduce the heat to medium and cook, uncovered, for 25 minutes, or until the potatoes are tender.
2. Puree half of the soup in batches in a blender with a tight-fitting lid, covered with a towel. Return the pureed soup to the pot. Add the basil and season with salt and pepper.

Nutrition Info per Serving:
Calories: 100, Protein: 8.5 g, Fat: 1.4 g, Carbohydrates: 13.4 g, Fiber: 8.3 g, Sugar: 11.9 g, Sodium: 554 mg

Corn and Potato Soup with Dill

Prep Time: 10 minutes, Cook Time: 35 minutes, Serves: 4

INGREDIENTS:
1 zucchini, diced small
1 large red bell pepper, seeded and diced
2 large Yukon Gold potatoes (about 1 pound), peeled and chopped
3 ears corn, shucked (about 2 cups)
4 cups (1L) Vegetable Stock, or low-sodium vegetable broth
2 tsps. cinnamon
3 cloves garlic, crushed
1 tsp. mint
1 batch No-Cheese Sauce
2 tbsps. peanut milk
Salt and freshly ground black pepper to taste
2 tsps. scallion, cut
½ cup dill, chopped

DIRECTIONS:
1. Add the zucchini and red pepper in a large saucepan and sauté over medium-high heat for 7 to 8 minutes.
2. Pour in water 1 to 2 tbsps. at a time to keep the vegetables from sticking to the pan.
3. Stir in the garlic and cook for another minute. Stir in the potatoes, corn, vegetable stock, and cinnamon, mint, peanut milk and bring the mixture to a boil over high heat.
4. Turn the heat down to medium and simmer, covered, for 20 minutes, or until the potatoes are softened. Pour in the No-Cheese Sauce and simmer over low heat for 5 minutes.
5. Sprinkle with salt and black pepper to taste and serve garnished with the scallion and dill.

Nutrition Info per Serving:
Calories: 392, Protein: 11.9 g, Fat: 1.9 g, Carbohydrates: 81.6 g, Fiber: 13.7 g, Sugar: 27.5 g, Sodium: 306 mg

Sweet Potato Tofu Stew

Prep Time: 10 minutes, Cook Time: 65 minutes, Serves: 4

INGREDIENTS:

1 cup (220 g) split peas, dry
7-oz (200 g) pack smoked tofu, cubed
2 (120 g) small sweet potatoes, cubed
6 tbsps. (60 g) salt-free cajun spices
5 cups (1200 ml) water
2 stalks celery, sliced

DIRECTIONS:

1. Put the water, split peas and 20g cajun spices in a large pot over medium-high heat.
2. After the water is boiling, turn the heat down to medium.
3. Cook the split peas for 30 minutes without covering the pot. Remove the foam produced by the peas and stir occasionally.
4. Bring the heat down to a simmer and add the cajun spices, sweet potato cubes, celery stalk slices.
5. Cover the pot with a lid and simmer for 15 minutes, stirring occasionally.
6. Add the tofu cubes to the pot, stir well and simmer for 10 minutes.
7. Turn the heat off and let the soup cool down.
8. Divide the soup between two bowls, serve with the optional toppings.

Nutrition Info per Serving:
Calories: 165, Protein: 21 g, Fat: 4.1 g, Carbohydrates: 11 g, Fiber: 15.7 g, Sugar: 6.3 g, Sodium: 228 mg

Red Bean Soup with Shallot and Thyme

Prep Time: 10 minutes, Cook Time: 35 minutes, Serves: 6

INGREDIENTS:

2 large leeks (white and light green parts), chopped and rinsed
1 zucchini, peeled and chopped
3 cloves garlic, crushed
2 tsps. minced thyme
1 pound (450 g) Yukon Gold potatoes (about 3 medium), peeled and cubed
2 cups cooked red beans, or one (15-oz. 430 g) can, drained and rinsed
6 cups (1410mL) low-sodium vegetable broth
1 small shallot, diced
1 tsp. chives
Salt and freshly ground black pepper to taste

DIRECTIONS:

1. Add the leeks and celery in a large pot and sauté over medium heat for 10 minutes.
2. Pour water 1 to 2 tbsps. at a time to keep the vegetables from sticking to the pot.
3. Whisk in the garlic and thyme and cook for another minute, then stir in the potatoes, beans, shallot and vegetable broth. Bring to a boil over high heat, lower the heat to medium, and simmer, covered, for 20 minutes, or until the potatoes are softened.
4. Spread the chives, season with salt and pepper, and simmer for another 5 minutes.

Nutrition Info per Serving:
Calories: 139, Protein: 6.2 g, Fat: 0.7 g, Carbohydrates: 26.8 g, Fiber: 7.5 g, Sugar: 5.7 g, Sodium: 350 mg

Onion-Black Beans Vegetable Soup with Parsley

Prep Time: 10 minutes, Cook Time: 1 hour, Serves: 8 to 10

INGREDIENTS:

1 large onion, peeled and sliced
2 large carrots, peeled and shredded
1 zucchini, diced small
6 cloves garlic, crushed
8 cups (1880mL) Vegetable Stock, or low-sodium vegetable broth
One (28-oz. 780g) can cherry tomatoes, halved
2 medium potatoes, scrubbed and cubed
4 cups packed cabbage, chopped
½ cup uncooked brown basmati rice
6 cups cooked black beans, or three (15-oz. 430g) cans, drained and rinsed
2 tsps. cumin
2 tbsps. lemon juice
Salt and freshly ground black pepper to taste
1 cup finely chopped parsley

DIRECTIONS:

1. Add the onion, carrots, and zucchini in a large saucepan over medium heat and sauté for 10 minutes.
2. Pour in water 1 to 2 tbsps. at a time to keep the vegetables from sticking to the pan.
3. Stir in the garlic and cook for another minute. Pour in the vegetable stock, lemon juice, cherry tomatoes, cumin, potatoes, cabbage, and rice.
4. Bring the pot to a boil over high heat, turn the heat down to medium-low, and cook for 30 minutes.
5. Whisk in the beans and cook for 15 minutes, until the rice is softened. Sprinkle with salt and pepper to taste and add the parsley.

Nutrition Info per Serving:
Calories: 134, Protein: 6.4 g, Fat: 2.1 g, Carbohydrates: 25.1 g, Fiber: 8.2 g, Sugar: 7.6 g, Sodium: 249 mg

Potato Soup with Tahini

Prep Time: 10 minutes, Cook Time: 35 minutes, Serves: 4

INGREDIENTS:
1 zucchini, diced
4 cups (1L) Vegetable Stock, or low-sodium vegetable broth
3 large Yukon Gold potatoes (about 1½ pounds), peeled and chopped
1 batch No-Cheese Sauce
3 cloves garlic, crushed
1 tsp. allspice
2 tbsps. tahini
Salt and freshly ground black pepper to taste
1 tsp. scallion
2 tbsps. chopped sage

DIRECTIONS:
1. Sauté the zucchini in a large saucepan over medium heat for 10 minutes. Pour in water 1 to 2 tbsps. at a time to keep the zucchini from sticking to the pan. Stir in the garlic and cook for another minute. Pour in the vegetable stock, allspice, tahini and potatoes. Bring the mixture to a boil over high heat. Turn the heat down to medium and simmer, covered, for 20 to 25 minutes, or until the potatoes are softened. Process the soup in a food processor, covered with a towel.
2. Return the soup to the pot if necessary, whisk in the No-Cheese Sauce, and sprinkle with salt and pepper to taste. Cook over low heat, stirring often, for 5 minutes. Serve garnished with the scallion and sage.

Nutrition Info per Serving:
Calories: 294, Protein: 10.1 g, Fat: 0.9 g, Carbohydrates: 66 g, Fiber: 12 g, Sugar: 10.4 g, Sodium: 512 mg

Pumpkin and Cucumber Stew with Lime Juice

Prep Time: 15 minutes, Cook Time: 35 minutes, Serves: 6 to 8

INGREDIENTS:
1 small pumpkin (about 1 pound/450 g), peeled, seeded, and cut into 1-inch cubes
4 cups cooked black beans, or two (15-oz. 430g) cans, drained and rinsed
6 cups (1410mL) Vegetable Stock, or low-sodium vegetable broth
1 large red onion, peeled and diced
2 large carrots, peeled and diced
2 cucumber, diced
2 cloves garlic, peeled and minced
2 tbsps. coriander powder
2 tbsps. lime juice
Salt and freshly ground black pepper to taste
2 tbsps. fresh sage

DIRECTIONS:
1. In a large saucepan, add the onion, carrots, and cucumber and sauté over medium heat for 10 minutes.
2. Pour in water 1 to 2 tbsps. at a time to keep the vegetables from sticking to the pan.
3. Stir in the garlic and cook for another minute. Whisk in the coriander, lime juice, pumpkin, beans, and vegetable stock and bring to a boil over high heat.
4. Turn the heat down to medium and simmer, covered, for 25 minutes, or until the pumpkin is soft. Sprinkle with salt and pepper to taste and serve garnished with the sage.

Nutrition Info per Serving:
Calories: 113, Protein: 4.9 g, Fat: 2.1 g, Carbohydrates: 21.3 g, Fiber: 4.1 g, Sugar: 6.8 g, Sodium: 447 mg

White Bean Hummus Stew with Mint

Prep Time: 15 minutes, Cook Time: 1.5 hours, Serves: 6

INGREDIENTS:
1½ cups white beans, soaked for 8 to 10 hours (or overnight) and drained
1 cucumber, chopped
¼ cup hummus
1 asparagus, trimmed and chopped
2 medium carrots, peeled and chopped
1 green bell pepper, seeded and sliced
1 tsp. tarragon leaves
3 sprigs mint
1 tsp. nutmeg
5 cloves garlic, smashed and skin removed
Salt and freshly ground black pepper to taste

DIRECTIONS:
1. In a pot, add the soaked white beans and cover with 4 cups water and stir in the mint, nutmeg, and garlic. Cook for 1 hour, or until the beans are just soft, pour more water as needed to cover the beans well. Remove the mint, nutmeg, and garlic.
2. Meanwhile, in a large saucepan, add the cucumber, asparagus, and carrots and sauté over medium heat for 10 minutes. Pour water 1 to 2 tbsps. at a time to keep the vegetables from sticking to the pan. Whisk in the green pepper and tarragon and simmer for 4 minutes. Stir in the hummus and simmer for 1 minute.
3. Pour the vegetable mixture to the cooked beans and simmer for 15 minutes over medium heat. Sprinkle with salt and pepper to taste.

Nutrition Info per Serving:
Calories: 89, Protein: 4.1 g, Fat: 0.6 g, Carbohydrates: 17.1 g, Fiber: 4.1 g, Sugar: 4.4 g, Sodium: 30 mg

Cream of Cauliflower Soup

Prep Time: 10 minutes, Cook Time: 25 minutes, Serves: 6

INGREDIENTS:
3 large leeks (white parts only), sliced and rinsed
4 cups cauliflower florets (from about 2 large heads)
4½ cups (1060mL) Vegetable Stock, or low-sodium vegetable broth, plus more as needed
3 tbsps. apple cider
1 tsp. tarragon, minced
Salt and freshly ground black pepper to taste

DIRECTIONS:
1. Add the leeks in a large saucepan and sauté over medium heat for 10 minutes. Pour in water 1 to 2 tbsps. at a time to keep the leeks from sticking to the pan. Stir in the tarragon and cook for another minute, then stir in the cauliflower, vegetable stock, and apple cider. Bring to a boil over high heat, turn the heat down to medium, and simmer, covered, until the cauliflower is softened, about 10 minutes.
2. Process the soup in a food processor, covered with a towel. Return the soup to the pot and sprinkle with salt and pepper to taste.

Nutrition Info per Serving:
Calories: 97, Protein: 5.4 g, Fat: 1 g, Carbohydrates: 16.5 g, Fiber: 3.2 g, Sugar: 7.3 g, Sodium: 389 mg

Split Pea and Tofu Soup

Prep Time: 10 minutes, Cook Time: 60 minutes, Serves: 4

INGREDIENTS:
2 cups (440 g) split peas, dry
7-oz (200 g) pack smoked tofu, cubed
5 cups (1200 ml) vegetable stock
2 small onions, minced
4 carrots, sliced

DIRECTIONS:
1. Put the vegetable stock and split peas in a large pot over medium-high heat.
2. When the stock is boiling, turn the heat down to medium.
3. Cook the split peas for about 40 minutes without covering the pot.
4. Stir occasionally and remove the foam produced by the peas.
5. Add carrots, smoked tofu cubes and onions to the pot, then turn down the heat to a simmer, cover the pot with a lid and simmer for 20 minutes and stir occasionally.
6. Turn the heat off and cool down for 5 minutes.
7. Divide the soup between two bowls, serve with the optional toppings.

Nutrition Info per Serving:
Calories: 178, Protein: 21.2 g, Fat: 4.3 g, Carbohydrates: 13.7 g, Fiber: 16.7 g, Sugar: 8.9 g, Sodium: 556 mg

Roasted Curry Acorn Squash Soup

Prep Time: 20 minutes, Cook Time: about 1 hour, Serves: 6

INGREDIENTS:
1 acorn squash
2 garlic cloves, chopped
1 yellow onion, chopped
2 celery stalks, coarsely chopped
1 tbsp. water, plus more as needed
2 tbsps. whole wheat flour
2 cups no-sodium vegetable broth
½ tsp. dill
1 tsp. curry powder, plus more for seasoning
⅛ tsp. cayenne pepper
1 (14-ounce, 397 g) can full-fat coconut milk
Chopped scallions, green parts only, for serving

DIRECTIONS:
1. Preheat the oven to 350°F(180°C).
2. Cut the acorn squash in half lengthwise and scoop out the seeds and stringy center. Put the squash halves in a 9-by-13-inch baking dish, cut-side down, and add enough water to come up about 1 inch all around.
3. Bake for 30 to 45 minutes, or until the squash can be easily pierced with a fork. Take the squash out from the baking dish and allow to cool for 10 minutes. Scoop out the soft flesh and set aside in a bowl.
4. Combine the garlic, onion, and celery in an 8-quart pot, sauté over high heat for 2 to 3 minutes, add the water, 1 tbsp. at a time, to prevent burning, until the onion is translucent but not browned.
5. Sprinkle over with the flour and stir to coat the vegetables.
6. Add the roasted squash, vegetable broth, dill, curry powder and cayenne pepper. Bring the mixture to a boil. Lower the heat to maintain a simmer, cover and cook for 10 minutes.
7. Pour in the coconut milk. Blend the soup until smooth with an immersion blender. Serve immediately or place in an airtight container and refrigerate for up to 1 week.
8. Place the scallions and a sprinkle of curry powder on the top and serve.

Nutrition Info per Serving:
Calories: 181, Protein: 2 g, Fat: 13 g, Carbohydrates: 14 g, Fiber: 2 g, Sugar: 14.3 g, Sodium: 449 mg

Roasted Eggplant, Carrot and Lentil Stew

Prep Time: 20 minutes, Cook Time: 1 hour, 10 minutes, Serves: 4

INGREDIENTS:
- 1 large eggplant
- 4 carrots, coarsely chopped
- 4 cups no-sodium vegetable broth
- 1 cup dried brown or green lentils
- 3 garlic cloves, diced
- 1 bunch chopped scallions, white and green parts, divided
- 1 large yellow onion, diced
- 1 tbsp. water, plus more as needed
- 1 tbsp. red miso paste
- 1 (14-ounce, 397 g) can full-fat coconut milk
- 1 tbsp. low-sodium soy sauce
- 4 tsps. ground cumin
- 1 (28-ounce, 784 g) can diced tomatoes
- 1 celery stalk, coarsely chopped
- 1 tsp. adobo chili powder or smoked paprika
- Fresh cilantro leaves, for serving

DIRECTIONS:
1. Preheat the oven to 350°F(180°C).
2. Cut the eggplant in half lengthwise and place it on a baking sheet, flesh-side up. Spread around the eggplant on the same baking sheet with the carrots.
3. Roast for 30 minutes, or until the carrots and eggplant are lightly browned or caramel colored and the carrots are fork-tender.
4. Set the carrots aside. Allow the eggplant to cool before handling it. Scoop out as much flesh as possible without scooping into the skin and set aside in a bowl.
5. Add the vegetable broth into an 8-quart pot, bring to a boil over high heat. Reduce the heat to maintain a simmer and add the lentils. Cover and cook for 20 to 30 minutes, or until the lentils are soft yet retain their shape.
6. Meanwhile, add the garlic, white parts of the scallion and onion in a small sauté pan or skillet, cook over medium heat for 7 to 10 minutes, adding water, 1 tbsp. at a time, to prevent burning, until darkly browned.
7. Combine the roasted eggplant, onion mixture, miso paste, coconut milk, and soy sauce in a blender. Puree for 2 to 3 minutes until smooth.
8. When the lentils are finished cooking, add the cumin, tomatoes, celery and chili powder. Bring the mixture to a simmer. Add the eggplant sauce and roasted carrots. Cook until warmed to your liking.
9. Top with a few fresh cilantro leaves and scallion greens and serve.

Nutrition Info per Serving:
Calories: 370, Protein: 10 g, Fat: 10 g, Carbohydrates: 35 g, Fiber: 9 g, Sugar: 23.9 g, Sodium: 716 mg

Apple-Mint Soup

Prep Time: 5 minutes, Cook Time: 20 minutes, Serves: 4

INGREDIENTS:
- 4 cups (1L) vegetable broth
- ¼ cup fresh mint leaves, roughly chopped
- ¼ cup chopped scallions, white and green parts
- 3 garlic cloves, minced
- 2 tbsps. coconut yogurt
- 3 tbsps. fresh apple cider

DIRECTIONS:
1. Mix together the broth, mint, scallions, garlic, coconut yogurt and apple cider in a large stockpot. Bring to a boil over medium-high heat.
2. Cover, reduce the heat to low, simmer for 15 minutes, and serve.

Nutrition Info per Serving:
Calories: 58, Protein: 5 g, Fat: 2 g, Carbohydrates: 5 g, Fiber: 1 g, Sugar: 4.5 g, Sodium: 358 mg

Cabbage, Corn and Bean Soup

Prep Time: 10 minutes, Cook Time: 35 minutes, Serves: 8

INGREDIENTS:
- 1 large yellow onion, peeled and diced
- 8 cups (1180mL) low-sodium vegetable broth
- 1 pound (450 g) cabbage
- 1 pound (450 g) fava beans
- 6 ears corn, kernels removed (about 3½ cups)
- 4 cups cooked black beans, or two (15-oz. 430 g) cans, drained and rinsed
- 3 cloves garlic, peeled and minced
- 1 tbsp. minced tarragon
- Salt and freshly ground black pepper to taste

DIRECTIONS:
1. Add the onion in a large pot and sauté over medium heat for 10 minutes.
2. Pour water 1 to 2 tbsps. at a time to keep the onion from sticking to the pot. Whisk in the garlic and tarragon and cook for another minute.
3. Put in the vegetable broth, potatoes, cabbage, fava beans and corn and cook, covered, over medium heat, for 15 minutes.
4. Add the black beans, drizzle with salt and pepper to taste, and simmer for another 10 minutes, or until the vegetables are softened.

Nutrition Info per Serving:
Calories: 172, Protein: 7.8 g, Fat: 1.6 g, Carbohydrates: 36.5 g, Fiber: 8.9 g, Sugar: 9.5 g, Sodium: 354 mg

Kombo Soup with Almond Butter

Prep Time: 5 minutes, Cook Time: 5 minutes, Serves: 4

INGREDIENTS:
6 cups Kombu Broth
½ cup almond butter
½ cup parsley, chopped

DIRECTIONS:
1. Bring the kombu broth to a boil over high heat.
2. Turn the heat down to medium-low and cook for 2 minutes. Off heat and scoop 1 cup of the broth to a small bowl.
3. Whisk in the almond butter to the bowl and stir the mixture until is smooth and creamy. Pour the miso mixture to the pot.
4. Stir in the parsley and cook over low heat for another 2 minutes, or until heated through.

Nutrition Info per Serving:
Calories: 122, Protein: 6.1 g, Fat: 2.8 g, Carbohydrates: 21.1 g, Fiber: 3.6 g, Sugar: 3.2 g, Sodium: 662 mg

Provencal Green Lentil Soup

Prep Time: 10 minutes, Cook Time: 35 minutes, Serves: 4

INGREDIENTS:
⅔ cup (130 g) green lentils, dry
1 cup (180 g) tomato cubes, canned or fresh
4 carrots, sliced
4 cups (960 ml) vegetable stock
¼ cup (40 g) Provencal herbs

DIRECTIONS:
1. Put the vegetable stock and green lentils in a large pot over medium-high heat.
2. Boil the stock, then turn the heat down to medium.
3. Cook the lentils for 15 minutes without covering the pot. Remove any foam produced by the lentils and stir occasionally.
4. Put the carrots and Provencal herbs in the pot, cover the pot with a lid and let it simmer for 10 minutes.
5. Add the tomato cubes and stir well, let it simmer for another 5 minutes.
6. Turn the heat off and cool down for 5 minutes.
7. Transfer the soup to a blender and blend until it's smooth.
8. Divide between two bowls, serve with the optional toppings.

Nutrition Info per Serving:
Calories: 145, Protein: 9 g, Fat: 0.2 g, Carbohydrates: 26 g, Fiber: 7.2 g, Sugar: 5.3 g, Sodium: 571 mg

Fresh-Flavored Asparagus Soup

Prep Time: 10 minutes, Cook Time: 35 minutes, Serves: 6

INGREDIENTS:
2 pounds (907g) fresh asparagus, trimmed and cut into ½-inch pieces
1 large yellow onion, peeled and diced
4 cups Vegetable Stock, or low-sodium vegetable broth
2 tsps. thyme
1 tbsp. minced tarragon
Salt and freshly ground black pepper to taste

DIRECTIONS:
1. Prepare a large stockpot, put the onion in it and sauté over medium heat for 10 minutes. Add 1 to 2 tbsps. of water at a time to prevent the onion from sticking to the pot. Add the thyme, tarragon, vegetable stock and asparagus and cook on medium-low heat for 20 to 25 minutes, until the asparagus is soft.
2. Use an immersion blender or in a blender to puree the soup in batches. Close the lid and cover with a towel. Salt and pepper, to taste.

Nutrition Info per Serving:
Calories: 85, Protein: 5.6 g, Fat: 0.5 g, Carbohydrates: 14.4 g, Fiber: 6.2 g, Sugar: 6.6 g, Sodium: 727 mg

Taro Bean Stew

Prep Time: 15 minutes, Cook Time: 35 minutes, Serves: 6

INGREDIENTS:
2 large potatoes, peeled and diced small
1 taro, peeled, and cut into ½-inch pieces
2 cups cooked black beans, or one (15-oz. 430g) can, drained and rinsed
6 ears corn, shucked (about 3½ cups)
4 cloves garlic, crushed
Salt and freshly ground black pepper to taste
1 cup fresh sage, finely chopped

DIRECTIONS:
1. Add the potatoes in a large saucepan and sauté over medium heat for 10 minutes.
2. Pour in water 1 to 2 tbsps. at a time to keep the potatoes from sticking to the pan.
3. Whisk in the garlic, taro, beans, corn, and 2 cups of water and simmer for 25 minutes, or until the taro is soft.
4. Sprinkle with salt and pepper to taste and add in the sage.

Nutrition Info per Serving:
Calories: 155, Protein: 6.3 g, Fat: 1.8 g, Carbohydrates: 30.8 g, Fiber: 4.9 g, Sugar: 9.6 g, Sodium: 520 mg

Lentil Brown Rice Soup

Prep Time: 10 minutes, Cook Time: 30 minutes, Serves: 4

INGREDIENTS:

⅓ cup (60 g) quick-cooking brown rice, dry
⅔ cup (130 g) green lentils, dry
1 cup (180 g) tomato cubes, canned or fresh
3 cups (720 ml) vegetable stock
¼ cup (60 g) tahini

DIRECTIONS:

1. Put the vegetable stock and green lentils into a large pot over medium-high heat.
2. When the stock is boiling, turn the heat down to medium.
3. Cook the lentils for 15 minutes without covering the pot. Remove the foam produced by the lentils and stir.
4. Add the brown rice and bring to a simmer, then cover the pot with a lid and simmer for another 10 minutes.
5. Combine tahini and tomato cubes, stir well and let it simmer for 5 minutes.
6. Turn the heat off and let the soup cool down.
7. Divide between two bowls, serve with the optional toppings.

Nutrition Info per Serving:
Calories: 284, Protein: 14.8 g, Fat: 10.1 g, Carbohydrates: 33.3 g, Fiber: 11.9 g, Sugar: 3.1 g, Sodium: 385 mg

Vegetable Broth

Prep Time: 10 minutes, Cook Time: 15 minutes, Serves: 2

INGREDIENTS:

1 pound (454 g) leeks, white and light green parts only, chopped and washed thoroughly (2½ cups)
2 carrots, peeled and cut into ½-inch pieces (⅔ cup)
3 tbsps. dried minced onion
3 tbsps. kosher salt
½ small celery root, peeled and cut into ½-inch pieces (¾ cup)
½ cup (½ ounce, 14 g) fresh parsley leaves and thin stems
1½ tbsp. tomato paste

DIRECTIONS:

1. Process celery root, leeks, carrots, dried minced onion, parsley, and salt in food processor for 3 to 4 minutes, pausing to scrape down sides of bowl frequently, until finely mixed.
2. Add tomato paste and process for 2 minutes, scraping down sides of bowl every 30 seconds. Transfer mixture to an airtight container and tap firmly to remove bubbles. Press small piece of parchment paper flush against surface of mixture and cover tightly.

Nutrition Info per Serving:
Calories: 195, Protein: 5.1 g, Fat: 1 g, Carbohydrates: 42.7 g, Fiber: 7.1 g, Sugar: 3.5 g, Sodium: 272 mg

Green Lentil Chickpea Stew

Prep Time: 20 minutes, Cook Time: 30 minutes, Serves: 4

INGREDIENTS:

⅔ cup (130 g) green lentils, dry
1 cup (200 g) chickpeas, cooked or canned
4 carrots, sliced
2 stalks celery, sliced
4 cups (960 ml) vegetable stock

DIRECTIONS:

1. Soak and cook 66 g dry chickpeas according to the method if necessary.
2. Put the vegetable stock and green lentils in a large pot over medium-high heat.
3. Boil the stock and turn the heat down to medium.
4. Cook the lentils for 15 minutes without covering the pot. Remove any foam produced by the lentils and stir occasionally.
5. Add the carrots and celery, cover the pot with a lid and simmer for 10 minutes.
6. Turn the heat off and cool down for 5 minutes.
7. Divide between two bowls, serve with the optional toppings.

Nutrition Info per Serving:
Calories: 234, Protein: 14 g, Fat: 1.6 g, Carbohydrates: 41 g, Fiber: 11.3 g, Sugar: 7.2 g, Sodium: 542 mg

Zucchini Vegetable Soup with Tahini

Prep Time: 10 minutes, Cook Time: 30 minutes, Serves: 4

INGREDIENTS:

½ medium onion, peeled and chopped
4 cups (940mL) low-sodium vegetable broth
2 medium zucchini, peeled and chopped
2 pears, chopped
7 small red-skin potatoes, scrubbed and chopped
1 taro, peeled and chopped
2 cloves garlic, crushed
1 tsp. nutmeg
3 tbsps. low-sodium tahini

DIRECTIONS:

1. Sauté the onion and garlic in ½ cup of vegetable broth in a medium saucepan over medium-high heat until the

onion is tender.
2. Whisk in the zucchini, pears, potatoes, taro, nutmeg and the reserving 3½ cups of vegetable broth and bring to a boil. When the pot is boiling, reduce the heat and cook until the vegetables are tender, 25 to 30 minutes.
3. Pour the tahini, toss to combine, and serve hot.

Nutrition Info per Serving:
Calories: 365, Protein: 16 g, Fat: 4.5 g, Carbohydrates: 69.7 g, Fiber: 13.7 g, Sugar: 14.2 g, Sodium: 612 mg

Green Lentil Mushroom Soup

Prep Time: 10 minutes, Cook Time: 35 minutes, Serves: 4

INGREDIENTS:
⅔ cup (130 g) green lentils, dry
2 cups (150 g) button mushrooms, sliced
1 red bell pepper
4 cups (960 ml) vegetable stock
¼ cup (40 g) dried thyme

DIRECTIONS:
1. Put the vegetable stock and green lentils in a large pot over medium-high heat.
2. Boil the water and turn the heat down to medium.
3. Cook the lentils for 15 minutes without covering the pot. Remove any foam produced by the lentils and stir occasionally.
4. Add mushrooms and thyme to the pot, cover the pot with a lid and simmer for 10 minutes.
5. Remove the placenta, stem and seeds of the bell pepper and dice it.
6. Add the bell pepper to the pot, stir well and let it simmer for 5 minutes.
7. Turn the heat off and cool down for 5 minutes.
8. Divide between two bowls, serve with the optional toppings.

Nutrition Info per Serving:
Calories: 156, Protein: 10.1 g, Fat: 0.7 g, Carbohydrates: 24.9 g, Fiber: 12.4 g, Sugar: 0.6 g, Sodium: 625 mg

Moroccan Chickpea and Tomato Soup

Prep Time: 10 minutes, Cook Time: 20 minutes, Serves: 4

INGREDIENTS:
3 cups (600 g) chickpeas, cooked or canned
1 medium onion, minced
1 clove garlic, minced
2 cups (360 g) tomato cubes, canned or fresh
2 tbsps. (20 g) Ras El Hanout
2 cups (480 ml) water

DIRECTIONS:
1. Soak and cook 200 g dry chickpeas according to the method if necessary.
2. Put water, minced onions and garlic in a large pot over medium-high heat.
3. When the water is boiling, turn the heat down to medium.
4. Add the chickpeas and the Ras El Hanout spices and continue to cook and stir.
5. Bring the heat down to a simmer after about 5 minutes.
6. Add tomato cubes, cover the pot with a lid and simmer for 10 minutes.
7. Turn the heat off and cool down for 5 minutes.
8. Divide between two bowls, serve with the optional toppings.

Nutrition Info per Serving:
Calories: 260, Protein: 15.3 g, Fat: 2.4 g, Carbohydrates: 44.2 g, Fiber: 16.7 g, Sugar: 6.6 g, Sodium: 526 mg

Garlicky Vegetable Soup

Prep Time: 10 minutes, Cook Time: 35 minutes, Serves: 6

INGREDIENTS:
1 large yellow onion, peeled and chopped
5 radish, peeled and chopped
1 medium cucumber, diced
1 yellow squash, diced
3 ears corn, kernels removed (about 2 cups)
6 cups low-sodium vegetable broth
½ cup finely chopped dill
Zest and juice of 1 lemon
5 cloves garlic, crushed
Salt and freshly ground black pepper to taste

DIRECTIONS:
1. Add the onion in a medium saucepan and sauté over medium heat for 7 to 8 minutes. Pour water 1 to 2 tbsps. at a time to keep the onion from sticking to the pan.
2. Whisk in the garlic and sauté for another minute. Stir in the radish and cook for 10 minutes, or until the radish starts to soft. Whisk the cucumber, yellow squash, corn, and vegetable broth.
3. Bring the pot to a boil over high heat, reduce the heat to medium, and cook until the vegetables are tender, about 15 minutes.
4. Spread with the dill and lemon zest and juice. Sprinkle with salt and pepper to taste.

Nutrition Info per Serving:
Calories: 137, Protein: 6 g, Fat: 1.3 g, Carbohydrates: 25.4 g, Fiber: 7.2 g, Sugar: 11.3 g, Sodium: 649 mg

Cucumber Bisque

Prep Time: 10 minutes, Cook Time: 25 minutes, Serves: 4

INGREDIENTS:

1 medium red onion, peeled and finely chopped
4 medium cucumbers, finely chopped
2 cups (480mL) Vegetable Stock, or low-sodium vegetable broth
½ (120mL) to 1 cup (240mL) unsweetened plain peanut milk
½ tsp. ground mint
¼ tsp. ground rosemary
½ tsp. lemon zest
Salt and freshly ground black pepper to taste.

DIRECTIONS:

1. Add the onion in a large saucepan and sauté over medium heat for 7 to 8 minutes, or until the onion is softened. Pour in water 1 to 2 tbsps. at a time to keep the onion from sticking to the pan. Stir in the cucumber, vegetable stock, mint, rosemary, and lemon zest and simmer for 15 minutes, or until the zucchini is softened.
2. Process the soup in a food processor, covered with a towel. Return the soup to the pot and whisk in the peanut milk. Sprinkle with salt and pepper to taste and simmer until cooked through.

Nutrition Info per Serving:
Calories: 54, Protein: 3.1 g, Fat: 0.6 g, Carbohydrates: 9.3 g, Fiber: 2.7 g, Sugar: 4.8 g, Sodium: 332 mg

Garlicky Broccoli Bisque

Prep Time: 10 minutes, Cook Time: 35 minutes, Serves: 4

INGREDIENTS:

2 celery stalks, diced
1 large head broccoli, cut into florets
4 cups (1L) Vegetable Stock, or low-sodium vegetable broth
¼ cup chopped parsley
1 oregano leaf
2 tsps. ground sumac
1 tsp. cayenne pepper
3 cloves garlic, crushed
2 tbsps. apple cider

DIRECTIONS:

1. Add the celery in a large saucepan and sauté over medium heat for 10 minutes. Pour in water 1 to 2 tbsps. at a time to keep the celery from sticking to the pan. Stir in the oregano, sumac, cayenne pepper, garlic, and apple cider and cook for 30 seconds. Stir in the broccoli and vegetable stock and bring the pot to a boil over high heat. Turn the heat down to medium and simmer, covered, for 20 to 25 minutes, or until the broccoli is softened.
2. Process the soup in a food processor, cover with a towel to avoid splatter. Return to the pot and sprinkle with salt and pepper to taste. Serve garnished with the parsley.

Nutrition Info per Serving:
Calories: 98, Protein: 5.1 g, Fat: 0.8 g, Carbohydrates: 18.6 g, Fiber: 6.6 g, Sugar: 8 g, Sodium: 458 mg

Kombu-Tomato Broth

Prep Time: 10 minutes, Cook Time: 20 minutes, Serves: 6

INGREDIENTS:

One 6-inch piece kombu
1 tsp. lime juice
2 tomatoes, chopped

DIRECTIONS:

1. Bring 8 cups of water to a boil in a large saucepan.
2. Add the kombu, lime juice, tomatoes, simmer, uncovered, over medium heat for 20 minutes.
3. Allow to cool, then store in an airtight container for up to 2 weeks.

Nutrition Info per Serving:
Calories: 43, Protein: 1.4 g, Fat: 0.5 g, Carbohydrates: 8 g, Fiber: 1.1 g, Sugar: 0.5 g, Sodium: 194 mg

Savory Squash-Carrot Soup

Prep Time: 10 minutes, Cook Time: 30 minutes, Serves: 4

INGREDIENTS:

2½ cups butternut squash, peeled, halved, seeded, and diced (from about 1 medium)
1 carrot, peeled and diced (about 1 cup)
1 medium yellow onion, peeled and chopped
(about ½ cup)
¼ cup edamame
3 clove garlic, crushed
¼ tsp. thyme
Pinch freshly ground black pepper
¼ tsp. ground nutmeg
Fresh dill, finely chopped

DIRECTIONS:

1. Pour 3 cups of water to a large pot over high heat and bring to a boil. Whisk in the squash, carrot, onion, garlic, thyme, and pepper. Turn the heat down to medium and cook, covered, for 20 minutes, or until the vegetables are softened.
2. Process the soup in a processor, covered with a towel. Return the soup to the pot and pour in the edamame and nutmeg. Cook for an additional 5 to 7 minutes, or until the peas are tender. Serve hot, garnished with the dill.

Nutrition Info per Serving:
Calories: 139, Protein: 4.2 g, Fat: 0.4 g, Carbohydrates: 32.3 g, Fiber: 4.6 g, Sugar: 4.1 g, Sodium: 248 mg

Tomato and Zucchini Soup

Prep Time: 10 minutes, Cook Time: 35 minutes, Serves: 4

INGREDIENTS:

2 medium zucchinis, diced
2 large red bell peppers, seeded and coarsely chopped
3 cloves garlic, crushed
1 tsp. cinnamon leaves
1 pound (450 g) fresh tomatoes (about 3 medium), coarsely chopped
Salt and freshly ground black pepper to taste
¼ cup sage

DIRECTIONS:

1. Place the zucchinis and red peppers in a large saucepan and sauté over medium heat for 10 minutes.
2. Pour in water 1 to 2 tbsps. at a time to keep the vegetables from sticking to the pan.
3. Stir in the garlic and cinnamon and cook for another minute, then stir in the tomatoes and simmer, covered, for 20 minutes.
4. Process the soup in a food processor, covered with a towel. Sprinkle with salt and pepper to taste and serve garnished with the sage.

Nutrition Info per Serving:
Calories: 63, Protein: 2.2 g, Fat: 0.4 g, Carbohydrates: 12.6 g, Fiber: 3 g, Sugar: 6.6 g, Sodium: 437 mg

Split Pea Asparagus Soup

Prep Time: 10 minutes, Cook Time: 1 hour, Serves: 6

INGREDIENTS:

1 asparagus, diced
1 medium zucchini, diced
1 celery stalk, diced
1 cup leek, trimmed and chopped
1½ cups split peas
6 cups (1410mL) Vegetable Stock, or low-sodium vegetable broth
3 cloves garlic, crushed
1 bay leaf
2 tsps. mint, minced
2 tsps. tarragon leaves
1 tsp. allspice
Salt and freshly ground black pepper to taste

DIRECTIONS:

1. Add the asparagus, zucchini, and celery in a large saucepan and sauté over medium heat for 10 minutes, or until the asparagus is soft.
2. Pour in water 1 to 2 tbsps. at a time to keep the vegetables from sticking to the pan.
3. Stir in the garlic, bay leaf, tarragon, mint, allspice, leek, split peas, and vegetable stock and bring the pot to a boil over high heat.
4. Turn the heat down to medium and simmer until the peas are soft, about 50 minutes. Sprinkle with salt and pepper to taste.

Nutrition Info per Serving:
Calories: 106, Protein: 4.5 g, Fat: 0.6 g, Carbohydrates: 20.7 g, Fiber: 6.3 g, Sugar: 8.3 g, Sodium: 656 mg

Chapter 10 Appetizer

Baked Taco-Seasoned Chickpeas and Edamame

Prep Time: 10 minutes, Cook Time: 40 minutes, Serves: 7

INGREDIENTS:
- 12 ounces (340 g) frozen edamame
- 1 (15-ounce, 425 g) can chickpeas, drained (save the liquid to use as aquafaba) and rinsed
- 4 tbsps. taco seasoning
- 3 tbsps. aquafaba

DIRECTIONS:
1. Preheat the oven to 400°F(205°C).
2. According to directions on package to cook the edamame.
3. On a baking sheet, spread with the cooked edamame and chickpeas. Bake for 20 minutes.
4. In a medium bowl, add the taco seasoning.
5. Take the edamame and chickpeas out from the oven and toss with the aquafaba. Add to the bowl of taco seasoning and coat well.
6. Place back to the oven and bake for another 10 minutes.
7. Allow to cool and serve, but let them cool in the oven for at least 2 hours to overnight before packing away. Store in an airtight container for up to 2 weeks.

Nutrition Info per Serving:
Calories: 147, Protein: 9.6 g, Fat: 4.1 g, Carbohydrates: 19.7 g, Fiber: 6.6 g, Sugar: 3.9 g, Sodium: 255 mg

Chilled Creamy Tofu Cheese

Prep Time: 35 minutes, Cook Time: 0, Serves: 2 cups

INGREDIENTS:
- 1 (14-ounce, 397 g) package water-packed extra-firm tofu
- 1 tbsp. nutritional yeast
- 1 tsp. yellow (mellow) miso paste
- 1 tbsp. apple cider vinegar
- 1 tsp. pure maple syrup or agave syrup
- ½ tsp. salt (optional)

DIRECTIONS:
1. Drain and press the tofu to remove excess moisture: Use a clean kitchen towel or several paper towels to wrap the tofu and place a cutting board on top. Place 2 (28-ounce) cans directly on the cutting board above the tofu to add weight, which will expel the liquid. Allow to sit for at least 30 minutes.
2. Combine the nutritional yeast, pressed tofu, miso paste, vinegar, maple syrup, and salt, if using in a high-speed blender or food processor. Puree until smooth.
3. If you are adding flavorings, stir them in and place in the refrigerator and chill for at least 1 hour or overnight to develop the flavors.
4. Serve right away, or refrigerate in a sealable container for up to 2 weeks.

Nutrition Info per Serving:
Calories: 29, Protein: 3 g, Fat: 1 g, Carbohydrates: 1 g, Fiber: 1 g, Sugar: 0.5 g, Sodium: 35 mg

Baked Seitan Swirls with Mustard

Prep Time: 15 minutes, Cook Time: 15 minutes, Serves: 6

INGREDIENTS:
- 1 tbsp. coconut sugar
- ½ cup all-purpose flour
- ½ cup whole wheat flour
- 1 tsp. baking powder
- ½ tsp. baking soda
- ¼ tsp. salt
- 6 tbsps. plant-based milk
- 5 tbsps. coconut oil, melted
- 8 ounces (227 g) seitan
- Mustards, for serving

DIRECTIONS:
1. Preheat the oven to 350°F(180°C).
2. In a medium bowl, add the sugar, flours, baking powder, baking soda, and salt. Mix together well.
3. Combine the milk and oil in a small bowl. Stir into the dry mixture to make a stiff dough.
4. Roll the dough out into about an 8-inch square. Cut lengthwise down the center so that there are two rectangles measuring 4 by 8 inches.
5. In a food processor, add the seitan and process for crumbles. Divide the seitan in half and spread across each dough rectangle leaving 1 inch on the long side of each rectangle. Start rolling up, lengthwise, and end at the edge that has no seitan. Roll firmly but not tightly. Leave seam side. Cut each roll into ¾-inch rounds. You will end up with twelve rounds for each roll. Arrange about 1½ inches apart on a baking sheet and bake for 15 minutes.
6. Serve with assorted mustard.

Nutrition Info per Serving:
Calories: 251, Protein: 17.1 g, Fat: 12 g, Carbohydrates: 20.2 g, Fiber: 1.5 g, Sugar: 2.1 g, Sodium: 217 mg

Chile Lime Chutney

Prep Time: 10 minutes, Cook Time: 0, Serves: 1 cup

INGREDIENTS:

1 tbsp. grated peeled fresh ginger
2 green chiles, stemmed
2 tbsps. water, plus more as needed
1 tsp. lime zest
Juice of 1 large lime
1 tbsp. agave syrup, or pure maple syrup
2 cups fresh cilantro, washed and shaken dry
¼ tsp. ground coriander
½ tsp. ground cumin

DIRECTIONS:

1. Combine the ginger, green chiles, 2 tbsps. of water and lime zest and juice in a blender. Puree until smooth.
2. Add the agave syrup, cilantro, coriander and cumin. Puree again until smooth. Scrape down the sides, as needed, and add up to 2 tbsps. more water to reach your desired consistency.
3. Place in an airtight container and store in the refrigerator for up to 2 weeks or freeze for up to 6 months.

Nutrition Info per Serving:
Calories: 10, Protein: 0.5 g, Fat: 0 g, Carbohydrates: 2 g, Fiber: 0.6 g, Sugar: 1.7 g, Sodium: 64 mg

Creamy Garlic Mushroom Gravy

Prep Time: 10 minutes, Cook Time: 15 minutes, Serves: 3 cups

INGREDIENTS:

4 ounces (113 g) shiitake mushrooms, stemmed and diced
8 ounces (227 g) baby portabella mushrooms, diced
1 garlic clove, minced
1 small yellow onion, diced
1 tbsp. water, plus more as needed
2 tbsps. tamari or coconut aminos
3 tbsps. whole wheat flour
½ tsp. freshly ground black pepper
¼ tsp. ground white pepper
2 cups oat milk

DIRECTIONS:

1. Cook the shiitake and portabella mushrooms in a large sauté pan or skillet over medium-high heat for 3 to 5 minutes, or until all their moisture evaporates and the edges of the mushrooms begin to blacken. Add the garlic and onion. Cook for another 5 minutes, adding water, 1 tbsp. at a time, to prevent burning. The onion should be browned.
2. Stir in the tamari, flour, black pepper, and white pepper, stirring to coat and combine the cooked vegetables.
3. Add the milk. Cook, whisking, until the gravy bubbles. Lower the heat to low and cook for 5 minutes, whisking occasionally, until the gravy thickens.
4. Serve fresh or reheat as needed. Place in a sealable glass container and chill in the refrigerator for up to 1 week or freeze for up to 4 months. (Glass is preferred for freezing liquids because metal containers tend to leach a metallic taste.)

Nutrition Info per Serving:
Calories: 81, Protein: 4 g, Fat: 1 g, Carbohydrates: 15 g, Fiber: 3 g, Sugar: 10.8 g, Sodium: 126 mg

Homemade Shakshuka

Prep Time: 10 minutes, Cook Time: 20 minutes, Serves: 6

INGREDIENTS:

3 garlic cloves, finely chopped
1 yellow onion, diced
1 green bell pepper, diced
1 jalapeño pepper, seeded and diced
1 tbsp. water, plus more as needed
2 bay leaves
2 to 3 tbsps. tomato paste
1 tbsp. ground cumin
1½ tbsps. paprika
1 tsp. freshly ground black pepper
1 tsp. chili powder
1 (28-ounce, 784 g) can crushed tomatoes
1 (15-ounce, 425 g) can chickpeas, drained and rinsed
2 tbsps. finely chopped fresh cilantro
¼ to ½ cup kalamata olives or green olives, coarsely chopped (optional)

DIRECTIONS:

1. Add the garlic, onion, bell pepper, and jalapeño pepper into a large skillet, sauté over medium-high heat for about 3 minutes, until soft but not browned. Add the water, 1 tbsp. at a time, to prevent burning. Add the bay leaves and sauté for 30 seconds.
2. Stir in 2 tbsps. of tomato paste. Cook for 2 minutes, stirring constantly. If you want a thicker sauce, add another 1 tbsp. of tomato paste.
3. Add the cumin, paprika, pepper and chili powder, stir well and cook for 1 minute. Pour in the tomatoes with their juices. Cover the skillet and reduce the heat to low. Cook for 10 minutes, stirring occasionally.
4. Remove from the heat and discard the bay leaves. Stir in the chickpeas, cilantro, and olives (if using), and serve warm.

Nutrition Info per Serving:
Calories: 146, Protein: 7 g, Fat: 2 g, Carbohydrates: 26 g, Fiber: 7 g, Sugar: 15.5 g, Sodium: 470 mg

Mango Plantain and Dates Cream

Prep Time: 15 minutes, Cook Time: 0, Serves: 4

INGREDIENTS:
1 cup frozen mango pieces
2 plantains, peeled, cut into slices, and frozen
2 pitted dates or 1 tbsp. pure maple syrup
½ cup plant-based milk, plus more as needed
1 tsp. vanilla extract
Juice of 1 lime

DIRECTIONS:
1. Combine the mango, frozen plantains, dates, milk, vanilla, and lime juice in a high-speed blender or food processor. Blend for 30 seconds. Scrape down the sides and blend again until smooth, scraping down the sides again if the mixture doesn't look smooth. Add more milk, 1 tbsp. at a time, as necessary.
2. Place leftovers in an airtight container and store in the refrigerator for a smoothie-like consistency, or freeze for a firm ice cream texture. If frozen, thaw slightly before serving.

Nutrition Info per Serving:
Calories: 218, Protein: 2 g, Fat: 1 g, Carbohydrates: 52 g, Fiber: 3 g, Sugar: 6.9 g, Sodium: 88 mg

Garlic Sweet Potato Gnocchi with Cashews

Prep Time: 50 minutes, Cook Time: 10 minutes (microwave), 1 hour (oven), plus 10 minutes, Serves: 2

INGREDIENTS:
1 large sweet potato
¾ cup whole wheat flour, plus more for the work surface
4 quarts water, plus 1 tbsp.
3 garlic cloves, minced
2 handfuls fresh spinach
1 tsp. crushed cashews

DIRECTIONS:
1. Poke holes in the skin of the sweet potato with a fork or the tip of a knife. Microwave with the skin on, on high power for 10 minutes, or bake at 350°F(180°C) for 1 hour. The flesh of the sweet potato should be soft.
2. Halve the potato lengthwise and scoop the flesh into a bowl. Use a fork to mash well. Add the flour and use a fork to combine well.
3. Transfer the dough to a lightly dusted work surface. Knead for 2 to 3 minutes. Roll the dough into a rope about ½ inch thick. Cut the rope into ¼-inch pieces. Roll the tines of a fork lightly across each piece to create grooves.
4. Fill 4 quarts of water into a pot and bring to a boil over high heat. Lower the heat to maintain a simmer and place the gnocchi in the water carefully. Cook for about 2 minutes, or until they float.
5. Heat 1 tbsp. water in a medium skillet over medium-high heat. Add the garlic and sauté for 1 minute. Stir in the spinach and cook until it wilts. Add the cooked gnocchi and cook for 1 minute, stirring. Remove from the heat and sprinkle with cashews and serve.

Nutrition Info per Serving:
Calories: 258, Protein: 9 g, Fat: 2 g, Carbohydrates: 55 g, Fiber: 8 g, Sugar: 0.5 g, Sodium: 82 mg

Easy Chilled Pickles

Prep Time: 20 minutes, plus overnight to chill, Cook Time: 0, Serves: 10 pints

INGREDIENTS:
1 pound (454 g) small cucumbers, preferably pickling cucumbers, washed and dried
1 small yellow onion, chopped or cut into rings
1 cup water
1 cup apple cider vinegar
1 tbsp. kosher salt
¼ cup beet sugar
1 tbsp. pickling spice

DIRECTIONS:
1. Cut the unpeeled cucumbers into ¼-inch-thick rounds with a sharp knife or mandoline.
2. Evenly toss together the onion and cucumbers in a large bowl. Place the mixture into 2 widemouthed 1-pint canning jars with lids, leaving ½ inch of headspace at the top where the lid rings begin, and use your clean hand or a heavy spoon to pack them in. Not to break the cucumbers.
3. Add the water, vinegar, salt, beet sugar and pickling spice into a small pot, bring to a boil over high heat, stirring, and cook until the sugar and salt dissolve. Pour over the vegetables with the brine, leaving ½ inch of headspace at the top. You might not use all the brine. Loosely screw on the lids and gently tap the jars on the counter a couple of times to remove any air bubbles. Add more brine to fill the jars to the ½-inch line if needed, then secure the lids tightly. Allow the jars to cool to room temperature.
4. Place in the refrigerator to chill for at least 24 hours before serving.
5. You can keep these pickles refrigerated for 1 month or longer, however, because they did not go through a canning process, they are not shelf-stable.

Nutrition Info per Serving:
Calories: 218, Protein: 4 g, Fat: 1 g, Carbohydrates: 50 g, Fiber: 7 g, Sugar: 8.3 g, Sodium: 274 mg

Garlicky Cauliflower Wings

Prep Time: 10 minutes, Cook Time: 40 minutes, Serves: 6

INGREDIENTS:

¾ cup gluten-free or whole-wheat flour
1 cup oat milk
2 tsps. onion powder
2 tsps. garlic powder
½ tsp. paprika
¼ tsp. freshly ground black pepper
1 head cauliflower, cut into bite-size florets

DIRECTIONS:

1. Preheat the oven to 425°F(220°C). Use parchment paper to line a baking sheet.
2. Add the flour, milk, onion powder, garlic powder, paprika, and pepper in a large bowl, whisk them together. Add the cauliflower florets, toss until the florets are completely coated.
3. On the baking sheet, add the coated florets in an even layer, and bake until golden brown and crispy, about 40 minutes, turning once halfway through the cooking process.
4. After baking, serve warm.

Nutrition Info per Serving:

Calories: 101, Protein: 3 g, Fat: 1 g, Carbohydrates: 20 g, Fiber: 2 g, Sugar: 10.2 g, Sodium: 197 mg

Garlicky Red Pepper Farro and Kidney Bean Bowl

Prep Time: 15 minutes, Cook Time: 40 minutes, Serves: 4

INGREDIENTS:

1½ cups dried farro
4 cups water, plus 1 tbsp. and more as needed
5 garlic cloves, minced
1 onion, diced
2 roasted red peppers
1 (15-ounce, 425 g) can diced tomatoes
1 tbsp. tamari
1 cup no-sodium vegetable broth
1 tsp. paprika
1 tbsp. dried parsley
½ tsp. dried thyme
½ tsp. cayenne pepper
1 (15-ounce, 425 g) can red kidney beans, drained and rinsed

DIRECTIONS:

1. Combine the farro and 4 cups of water in an 8-quart pot, bring to a boil over high heat. Reduce the heat to medium-low, cover and cook for 25 minutes. If the farro looks too dry, add more water, ½ cup at a time,
2. Meanwhile, cook the garlic and onion in a sauté pan or skillet over medium-high heat for 5 minutes, adding water, 1 tbsp. at a time, to prevent burning. The onion should be browned but not burned.
3. Transfer to a blender and add the roasted red peppers, tomatoes with their juices, tamari, vegetable broth, paprika, parsley, thyme, and cayenne pepper. Puree until smooth.
4. Stir the kidney beans and sauce into the cooked farro. Cook over medium-low heat, stirring, until the sauce starts to bubble. Turn off the heat, cover and allow to sit for 10 minutes and serve.

Nutrition Info per Serving:

Calories: 412, Protein: 19 g, Fat: 2 g, Carbohydrates: 85 g, Fiber: 17 g, Sugar: 12.2 g, Sodium: 366 mg

Chia Onion Crackers

Prep Time: 20 minutes, Cook Time: 20 minutes, Serves: 36 crackers

INGREDIENTS:

½ cup oat flour
½ cup brown rice flour
2 tsps. nutritional yeast
¼ cup water
¼ tsp. freshly ground black pepper
1 tsp. chia seeds
¼ tsp. onion powder

DIRECTIONS:

1. Preheat the oven to 350°F(180°C). Cut 2 sheets of parchment paper the size of your baking sheet. Add them onto a work surface.
2. Combine the oat and brown rice flours, nutritional yeast, water, pepper, chia seeds, and onion powder in a food processor. Process for 1 to 2 minutes to combine into a dough. You should be able to pinch the dough between two fingers without it sticking to you.
3. On one of the sheets of parchment paper, add the dough. Press the dough together into a mound with your clean hands, then press to flatten and shape into a thick square. Then top with the other sheet of parchment paper. Evenly flatten the dough to ⅛ inch thick with a rolling pin. If your dough is too thick, the crackers won't be crispy. Remove the top sheet of parchment paper and save it for another use.
4. Cut the dough into 36 (1-by-2-inch) rectangles with a knife or pizza cutter. Lightly prick holes in the center of each cracker with a fork. Carefully transfer the parchment paper with the dough on it to a baking sheet.
5. Bake for 10 minutes. Flip the crackers carefully and bake for another 10 minutes until golden brown on the edges. Transfer the crackers to a wire rack to cool. They will crisp as they cool.
6. Place in an airtight container and store at room temperature for up to 1 week or freeze for up to 1 month.

Nutrition Info per Serving:

Calories: 61, Protein: 2 g, Fat: 1 g, Carbohydrates: 12 g, Fiber: 1 g, Sugar: 2.5 g, Sodium: 92 mg

Lemon Chickpea and White Bean Hummus

Prep Time: 5 minutes, Cook Time: 0, Serves: 3 cups

INGREDIENTS:
1 (15-ounce, 425 g) can white beans (cannellini or great northern)
1 (15-ounce, 425 g) can chickpeas
2 tsps. garlic powder
3 tbsps. freshly squeezed lemon juice
1 tsp. onion powder

DIRECTIONS:
1. Drain and rinse the white beans and chickpeas.
2. Combine the beans, chickpeas, garlic powder, lemon juice, and onion powder in a food processor or blender. Process for 1 to 2 minutes, or until the texture is creamy and smooth and creamy.
3. Serve immediately, or keep in a refrigerator-safe container for up to 5 days.

Nutrition Info per Serving:
Calories: 73, Protein: 4 g, Fat: 1 g, Carbohydrates: 12 g, Fiber: 4 g, Sugar: 2.3 g, Sodium: 34 mg

Mixed Vegetable Wraps

Prep Time: 20 minutes, Cook Time: 1 minute, Serves: 4

INGREDIENTS:
2 tbsps. rice vinegar
¼ cup smooth peanut butter
1 tbsp. minced peeled fresh ginger
1 tbsp. coconut aminos
½ tsp. garlic powder
4 large collard green leaves
½ cup hummus
1 English cucumber, cut into matchsticks
4 carrots, cut into matchsticks
1 celery stalk, cut into thin strips
1 red bell pepper, cut into thin strips
1 small red cabbage, cut into strips
2 avocados, pitted and thickly cut
1 cup chopped fresh cilantro

DIRECTIONS:
1. Add the vinegar, peanut butter, ginger, coconut aminos, and garlic powder in a small bowl, whisk them together to blend. Set aside.
2. Fill the water into an 8-quart pot, and bring to a boil over high heat. Drop each collard green leaf in the water for 30 seconds. Then place onto a clean kitchen towel and pat dry. Trim the thick, tough rib of each collard green leaf with a sharp kitchen knife, cutting it so the stem is flush with the rest of the leaf, rather than cutting out the stem completely.
3. In the center of each prepared leaf, spread with 2 tbsps. of hummus. Place over the hummus with one-quarter of the cucumber, carrots, celery, bell pepper, red cabbage, and avocados. Top with a sprinkle of cilantro and a drizzle of peanut butter sauce.
4. Fold each leaf like a burrito, rolling it and folding in the sides to contain the vegetables and filling. Tightly roll the wraps so they are easier to enjoy. Halve and serve.

Nutrition Info per Serving:
Calories: 399, Protein: 11 g, Fat: 23 g, Carbohydrates: 37 g, Fiber: 14 g, Sugar: 4.7 g, Sodium: 339 mg

Mashed Potatoes with Vegetable Gravy

Prep Time: 10 minutes, Cook Time: 15 minutes, Serves: 6

INGREDIENTS:
FOR THE MASHED POTATOES:
8 red or yukon gold potatoes, cut into 1-inch cubes
1 tsp. garlic powder
1 tsp. onion powder
½ cup plant-based milk
FOR THE GRAVY:
2 cups vegetable broth, divided
¼ cup gluten-free or whole-wheat flour
¼ tsp. dried thyme
½ tsp. onion powder
½ tsp. garlic powder
¼ tsp. freshly ground black pepper
¼ tsp. dried sage

DIRECTIONS:
TO MAKE THE MASHED POTATOES:
1. In a large stockpot, pour in the water and bring to a boil over high heat, then immerse the potatoes gently. Cover, lower the heat to medium, and boil until the potatoes are easily pierced with a fork, about 15 minutes.
2. Drain the liquid, and place the potatoes back to the pot. Mash the potatoes with a potato masher or large mixing spoon until smooth.
3. Stir in the garlic powder, onion powder and milk.
TO MAKE THE GRAVY:
1. Meanwhile, whisk together ½ cup of broth and the flour in a medium saucepan. When no dry flour is left, whisk in the remaining 1½ cups of broth.
2. Stir in the thyme, onion powder, garlic powder, pepper and sage. Bring the gravy to a boil over medium-high heat, then reduce the heat to low.
3. Simmer for 10 minutes, stirring every other minute, and serve with the mashed potatoes.

Nutrition Info per Serving:
Calories: 260, Protein: 8 g, Fat: 1 g, Carbohydrates: 56 g, Fiber: 4 g, Sugar: 9.4 g, Sodium: 375 mg

Garlic Sautéed Collard Greens

Prep Time: 10 minutes, Cook Time: 25 minutes, Serves: 4

INGREDIENTS:
1½ pounds (680 g) collard greens
1 cup vegetable broth
½ tsp. onion powder
½ tsp. garlic powder
⅛ tsp. freshly ground black pepper

DIRECTIONS:
1. Remove the hard middle stems from the greens, and chop the leaves into 2-inch pieces.
2. Mix together the remaining ingredients in a large saucepan. Bring to a boil over medium-high heat, then stir in the chopped greens.
3. Reduce the heat to low, cover and cook for 20 minutes, stirring well every 4 to 5 minutes, and serve. (Stir in a few extra tbsps. of vegetable broth or water if the liquid has completely evaporated and the greens are beginning to stick to the bottom of the pan.)

Nutrition Info per Serving:
Calories: 28, Protein: 3 g, Fat: 1 g, Carbohydrates: 4 g, Fiber: 2 g, Sugar: 0.3 g, Sodium: 134 mg

Mustard Spiced Creamy Potato Salad

Prep Time: 10 minutes, Cook Time: 20 minutes, plus 50 minutes to cool and chill, Serves: 4

INGREDIENTS:
5 large red or golden potatoes, cut into 1-inch cubes
1 cup silken tofu or 1 large avocado
2 tbsps. Dijon mustard
¼ cup chopped fresh chives
½ tsp. dried dill
½ tbsp. freshly squeezed lemon juice
½ tsp. garlic powder
½ tsp. onion powder
¼ tsp. freshly ground black pepper

DIRECTIONS:
1. In a large pot, pour in the water and bring to a boil over high heat. Gently immerse the potatoes in the hot water. Boil for 10 minutes, or until the potatoes can be easily pierced with a fork. Drain.
2. Place the potatoes in a large bowl, and refrigerate for at least 20 minutes.
3. While the potatoes refrigerate, in another bowl, add the tofu. Smash the tofu until creamy with a fork or mixing spoon. Add the mustard, chives, dill, lemon juice, garlic powder, onion powder, and pepper, whisk until well combined.
4. Place the cooled potatoes into the creamy dressing. Mix gently until the potatoes are well coated. Place the dish in the refrigerator to chill for at least 30 minutes or until ready to serve.

Nutrition Info per Serving:
Calories: 341, Protein: 10 g, Fat: 1 g, Carbohydrates: 74 g, Fiber: 12 g, Sugar: 0.5 g, Sodium: 1o7 mg

Garlicky Vegetable Burgers

Prep Time: 15 minutes, Cook Time: 30 minutes, Serves: 12 patties

INGREDIENTS:
3 garlic cloves, coarsely chopped
1 yellow onion, coarsely chopped
½ cup walnuts
1 sweet potato, skin on, cubed
2 cups precooked green lentils or brown lentils
1 cup precooked brown rice
1 tbsp. tamari
1 tbsp. paprika
¼ cup water
2 tbsps. tomato paste
¼ cup ground flaxseed
1 tbsp. Dijon mustard or yellow mustard
¾ to 1 cup coarse cornmeal

DIRECTIONS:
1. Preheat the oven to 450°F(235°C). Use parchment paper to line a baking sheet.
2. Combine the garlic, onion, walnuts and sweet potato in a food processor. Process for 1 to 2 minutes, or until the ingredients are combined and have the consistency of rice.
3. Add the cooked lentils, brown rice, tamari and paprika. Pulse several times to incorporate the ingredients.
4. Add the water, tomato paste, flaxseed and mustard in a large bowl, stir them together. Add the blended ingredients to the bowl and mix to combine fully.
5. Starting with ¾ cup, add the cornmeal, stirring in more if the mixture looks too wet. The dough should shape a ball without sticking to your hands too much. Divide the dough into 12 equal portions, roughly ¼ cup each. Roll the portions into balls and flatten onto the prepared baking sheet.
6. Bake for 15 minutes. Flip the patties and bake for another 15 minutes. The patties should be browned on the outside and firm to the touch. Serve immediately or allow to cool completely before freezing in an airtight container for up to 3 months.

Nutrition Info per Serving:
Calories: 161, Protein: 6 g, Fat: 5 g, Carbohydrates: 24 g, Fiber: 6 g, Sugar: 1.9 g, Sodium: 317 mg

Chia Onion Crackers, page 146

Easy Lemon and Almond Ricotta, page 153

Lemon Chickpea and White Bean Hummus, page 147

Garlic Sautéed Collard Greens, page 148

Chapter 10 Appetizer   149

Italian Oats Rice Bean Balls

Prep Time: 10 minutes, Cook Time: 30 minutes, Serves: 6

INGREDIENTS:

1½ cups cooked red kidney beans
1½ cups cooked black beans
1 cup quick-cooking oats
1 cup cooked brown rice
¼ cup easy one-pot vegan marinara
1 tbsp. Italian seasoning
1 tsp. onion powder
1 tsp. garlic powder
¼ tsp. freshly ground black pepper

DIRECTIONS:

1. Preheat the oven to 400°F(205°C). Use the parchment paper to line a baking sheet.
2. Mash the kidney beans and black beans together with a fork or mixing spoon in a large bowl.
3. Stir in the oats, rice, marinara, Italian seasoning, onion powder, garlic powder, and pepper. Mix well.
4. Scoop out ¼ cup of the bean mixture, and shape into a ball. Put the bean ball on the baking sheet. Repeat with the remaining bean mixture.
5. Bake the bean balls for 30 minutes, or until lightly browned and heated through, turning once after about 15 minutes.

Nutrition Info per Serving:
Calories: 144, Protein: 6 g, Fat: 2 g, Carbohydrates: 26 g, Fiber: 5 g, Sugar: 2.5 g, Sodium: 282 mg

Quick French Fries

Prep Time: 10 minutes, Cook Time: 1 hour, plus 30 minutes to cool, Serves: 6

INGREDIENTS:

2 pounds (907 g) medium white potatoes
1 to 2 tbsps. no-salt seasoning

DIRECTIONS:

1. Preheat the oven to 400°F(205°C). Use parchment paper to line a baking sheet.
2. Wash and scrub the potatoes, and put them on the baking sheet, bake for 45 minutes, or until easily pierced with a fork.
3. Take the potatoes out from the oven, let cool in the refrigerator for about 30 minutes, or until you're ready to make a batch of fries.
4. Preheat the oven to 425°F(220°C). Use parchment paper to line a baking sheet.
5. Slice the cooled potatoes into the shape of wedges or fries, then place them in a large bowl, add the no-salt seasoning and toss well.
6. On the baking sheet, spread with the coated fries in an even layer. Bake for about 7 minutes, then take them out from the oven, flip the fries over, and redistribute them in an even layer. Bake for an additional 8 minutes, or until the fries are crisp and golden brown. Then serve.

Nutrition Info per Serving:
Calories: 108, Protein: 3 g, Fat: 0 g, Carbohydrates: 24 g, Fiber: 4 g, Sugar: 1.5 g, Sodium: 150 mg

Vegetable Spring Rolls with Peanut Dipping Sauce

Prep Time: 15 minutes, Cook Time: 0, Serves: 2

INGREDIENTS:
FOR THE SPICY PEANUT DIPPING SAUCE:
2 tbsps. defatted peanut powder
1 tbsp. rice vinegar
1 tbsp. maple syrup
½ tsp. garlic powder
½ tsp. onion powder
½ tsp. red pepper flakes
FOR THE SPRING ROLLS:
6 (8- to 10-inch) rice paper wraps
6 large lettuce leaves
1 cup shredded carrots
1½ cups brown rice, cooked
1 bunch fresh cilantro
1 bunch fresh mint
1 bunch fresh basil

DIRECTIONS:
TO MAKE THE SPICY PEANUT DIPPING SAUCE:
1. Combine all of the peanut dipping sauce ingredients in a small saucepan, cook over medium heat for 10 minutes, stirring occasionally. Remove the sauce from the heat, and set aside to cool.
TO MAKE THE SPRING ROLLS:
1. Fill the warm water in a shallow bowl or pan, and dip a rice paper wrap in the water for 10 to 15 seconds. Remove and place on a cutting board or other clean, smooth surface. It's okay that the rice paper may not be completely soft right away, but it will soften as you add the filling.
2. Lay a lettuce leaf down flat on a rice paper wrap, then add 2 to 3 tbsps. of shredded carrots, ¼ cup of brown rice, and a few leaves each of mint, cilantro, and basil.
3. Wrap the sides of the rice paper halfway into the center, then roll the wrap from the bottom to the top to form a tight roll.
4. Repeat for the remaining spring rolls. Serve with the sauce in a dipping bowl.

Nutrition Info per Serving:
Calories: 263, Protein: 11 g, Fat: 3 g, Carbohydrates: 46 g, Fiber: 5 g, Sugar: 0.5 g, Sodium: 92 mg

Asian Veggie Slaw with Maple-Ginger Dressing

Prep Time: 10 minutes, Cook Time: 0, Serves: 6

INGREDIENTS:
- 1 tsp. freshly grated garlic
- 1 tbsp. freshly grated ginger
- 1 tbsp. maple syrup
- 2 tbsps. rice vinegar
- ¼ tsp. red pepper flakes (optional)
- 1 cup shredded carrots
- 4 cups chopped purple cabbage
- ¼ cup chopped scallions, white and green parts
- 1 red or yellow bell pepper, sliced
- ¼ cup roughly chopped fresh cilantro

DIRECTIONS:
1. Add the garlic, ginger, maple syrup, vinegar, and red pepper flakes (if using) in a large bowl, whisk them together.
2. Add the carrots, cabbage, scallions, bell pepper, and cilantro. Mix until the vegetables are well coated with dressing, and serve.

Nutrition Info per Serving:
Calories: 43, Protein: 1 g, Fat: 0 g, Carbohydrates: 9 g, Fiber: 2 g, Sugar: 1 g, Sodium: 69 mg

Quinoa Stuffed Peppers with Pesto

Prep Time: 10 minutes, Cook Time: 30 minutes, Serves: 4

INGREDIENTS:
- 4 red bell peppers, halved lengthwise and cored
- 1 (15-ounce, 425 g) can no-salt-added diced tomatoes
- 1 cup no-sodium vegetable broth
- 8 ounces (227 g) fresh baby spinach
- ¾ cup dried quinoa, rinsed
- 2 tbsps. everyday pesto

DIRECTIONS:
1. Preheat the oven to broil. Use parchment paper to line a baking sheet.
2. Place the bell pepper halves on the prepared baking sheet, skin-side up.
3. Broil until the pepper skins begin to blister and slightly blacken, about 2 to 5 minutes. Remove from the oven and preheat to 350°F(180°C).
4. Add the tomatoes and vegetable broth into an 8-quart pot, bring to a boil over high heat. Stir in the spinach and quinoa. Reduce the heat to medium-low, cover and cook for 10 minutes, stirring occasionally.
5. Fill the the quinoa mixture into the pepper halves.
6. Bake for 10 minutes. Top with the pesto and serve warm.

Nutrition Info per Serving:
Calories: 257, Protein: 13 g, Fat: 6 g, Carbohydrates: 40 g, Fiber: 9 g, Sugar: 18.2 g, Sodium: 597 mg

Vanilla Seedy Granola

Prep Time: 15 minutes, Cook Time: 25 minutes, Serves: 8 cups

INGREDIENTS:
- ½ tsp. cream of tartar
- ½ cup aquafaba (canned chickpea water)
- 1 tbsp. chia seeds
- ½ cup pitted Medjool dates
- ½ tsp. vanilla extract
- 1 cup unsweetened coconut flakes
- 3 cups old-fashioned rolled oats or certified gluten-free oats
- ¼ cup sliced almonds
- ¼ cup pecans, coarsely chopped
- 1 tbsp. ground flaxseed
- 1 tsp. ground cinnamon
- ½ cup dried cranberries or dried-fruit blend
- ¼ cup sunflower seeds
- ¼ cup pumpkin seeds

DIRECTIONS:
1. Preheat the oven to 350°F(180°C). Use parchment paper to line a baking sheet.
2. Combine the cream of tartar and aquafaba in a food processor or high-speed blender. Process for 1 to 2 minutes until foamy and thick. Add the chia seeds and dates. Puree for about 1 minute until completely incorporated. Scrape down the sides and add the vanilla. Process for 30 seconds. Set aside.
3. Stir together the coconut, oats, almonds, pecans, flaxseed, and cinnamon in a large bowl, stirring well. Pour in the date mixture and stir until the oats are covered. Spread the granola onto the prepared baking sheet, but allow it to have some clumps.
4. Bake for 15 minutes. Turn over the granola with a spatula and gently mix it without breaking up the clumps. Flipping it helps the granola crisp without burning. Bake for another 10 minutes. The granola might feel slightly damp, but it will crisp as it cools. Allow the granola to cool completely.
5. Add the sunflower seeds, cranberries, and pumpkin seeds, and stir well.
6. Place in an airtight container and store at room temperature for up to 2 weeks or freeze for up to 2 months. Do not refrigerate, as it cause the oats to soften.

Nutrition Info per Serving:
Calories: 358, Protein: 8 g, Fat: 18 g, Carbohydrates: 46 g, Fiber: 9 g, Sugar: 8.3 g, Sodium: 313 mg

Homemade Deconstructed Malai Kofta

Prep Time: 20 minutes, Cook Time: 30 minutes, Serves: 4

INGREDIENTS:

2 carrots, diced
2 russet potatoes, diced
1¼ cups water, plus 2 tbsps. and more as needed, divided
1 (15-ounce, 425 g) package frozen sweet peas, or canned, drained
1 (28-ounce, 784 g) can crushed tomatoes
1 tbsp. minced peeled fresh ginger
3 garlic cloves, minced
1 (4-ounce, 113 g) can diced green chiles
1 tsp. ground cumin
1 tbsp. ground coriander
¼ tsp. onion powder
1 tsp. ground turmeric
¼ to ½ tsp. cayenne pepper
2 tbsps. tomato paste
¼ cup coconut cream
¼ tsp. garam masala
¼ cup minced fresh cilantro

DIRECTIONS:

1. Combine the carrots, potatoes, and ¼ cup of water in a sauté pan or skillet, cover and simmer over medium-high heat for about 5 minutes, or until the carrots begin to soften. Place the sweet peas on top. Remove from the heat and keep covered.
2. Combine the tomatoes with their juices, ginger, garlic and green chiles in a high-speed blender, puree into a thick sauce. Set aside.
3. Add the cumin, coriander, onion powder, turmeric, cayenne pepper, and 2 tbsps. of water in a small bowl, whisk together to combine.
4. Pour the spice mixture in an 8-quart pot, cook over medium heat for 1 minute, stirring. If the mixture looks dry, add more water, 2 tbsps. at a time. Tempering the spices by heating brings out a different flavor and is common in Indian recipes.
5. Combine the tomato paste into the tempered spices, stir to mix well. Cook for 2 minutes, adding more water as needed.
6. Stir in the pureed tomato sauce, mix well, and bring to a simmer. Lower the heat and cook, partially covered, for 10 minutes.
7. Add the remaining 1 cup of water, coconut cream, garam masala, and cilantro. Mix to incorporate the coconut cream. Stir in the cooked carrots, potatoes, and peas. Bring to a simmer and serve warm as a rich stew or paired with basmati rice. Serve with chickpeas or baked tofu for added protein.

Nutrition Info per Serving:
Calories: 308, Protein: 13 g, Fat: 5 g, Carbohydrates: 59 g, Fiber: 13 g, Sugar: 19 g, Sodium: 414 mg

Seasoned Vegan Bouillon Base

Prep Time: 5 minutes, Cook Time: 0, Serves: 2 cups

INGREDIENTS:

2 tbsps. onion powder
2 cups nutritional yeast
1 tbsp. Italian seasoning
2 tsps. garlic powder
¼ cup sea salt (optional)
1 tsp. celery salt
1 tsp. ground turmeric
1 tsp. dried thyme

DIRECTIONS:

1. Combine the onion powder, nutritional yeast, Italian seasoning, garlic powder, salt (if using), celery salt, turmeric, and thyme in a small blender, food processor, spice grinder, or mortar and pestle. Blend to a powder.
2. Place the bouillon powder in a sealable jar or container and store at room temperature. Use 1 tbsp. per 1 cup of water for a flavorful stock.

Nutrition Info per Serving:
Calories: 24, Protein: 3 g, Fat: 0 g, Carbohydrates: 3 g, Fiber: 1 g, Sugar: 0 g, Sodium: 80 mg

Tempeh Onion Stuffed Cremini Mushrooms

Prep Time: 15 minutes, Cook Time: 20 minutes, Serves: 6

INGREDIENTS:

18 cremini mushrooms
2 tbsps. diced red onion, small dice
3 ounces (85 g) tempeh, diced very small, or pulsed small
Pinch of cayenne pepper
Pinch of onion powder
¼ cup rice, cooked
1 tbsp. tamari

DIRECTIONS:

1. Remove stems from the mushrooms and set the caps aside. Chop the stems finely and set aside.
2. In a medium skillet, add 3 tbsps. of water and heat it. Add the chopped mushroom stems and onion. Sauté for 10 to 15 minutes or until the onion is translucent. Stir in the tempeh and cook for another 5 minutes. Add the cayenne pepper, onion powder, rice, and tamari. Cook for 2 minutes, stirring occasionally.
3. Preheat the oven to 350°F(180°C).
4. Stuff the mixture into mushroom caps and place on baking sheet. Bake for 20 minutes.

Nutrition Info per Serving:
Calories: 71, Protein: 5.3 g, Fat: 2.8 g, Carbohydrates: 6.2 g, Fiber: 1.7 g, Sugar: 1.3 g, Sodium: 172 mg

Roasted Jalapeño, Lime and Avocado Guacamole

Prep Time: 5 minutes, Cook Time: 10 minutes, Serves: 4

INGREDIENTS:
1 to 3 jalapeños (depending on your preferred level of spiciness)
1 avocado, peeled and pitted
1 tbsp. freshly squeezed lime juice

DIRECTIONS:
1. Preheat the oven to 400°F(205°C). Use parchment paper to line a baking sheet.
2. On the baking sheet, add the jalapeños and roast for 8 minutes. (Or roast the jalapeños on a grill for 5 minutes, if you already have it fired up.)
3. Slice the jalapeños down the center, and remove the seeds. Then cut the top stem off, and dice into ⅛-inch pieces. Be caureful to wash your hands.
4. Use a fork to mash together the jalapeño pieces, avocado, and lime juice in a medium bowl. Continue mashing and mixing until the guacamole reaches your desired consistency, and serve.

Nutrition Info per Serving:
Calories: 87, Protein: 1 g, Fat: 7 g, Carbohydrates: 5 g, Fiber: 3 g, Sugar: 2.6 g, Sodium: 122 mg

Toasted Cashew and Mushroom Rolls

Prep Time: 1 hour 20 minutes, Cook Time: 15 minutes, Serves: 6

INGREDIENTS:
1 tbsp. plus 2 tsps. plant-based milk
¼ cup raw cashews, soaked for 1 hour
1 tsp. lemon juice
¼ tsp. salt
Pinch of ground black pepper
4 ounces (113 g) button mushrooms
¼ cup dairy-free butter, divided
2 tbsps. raw shelled hempseed
9 slices whole-grain bread

DIRECTIONS:
1. In a food processor, add the milk, cashews, lemon juice, salt, and pepper. Process until smooth.
2. Clean mushrooms well and finely chop.
3. In a small skillet, heat 1 tbsp. butter over medium-high heat. Add the chopped mushrooms and sauté for 5 minutes. Remove from the heat and add the cashew mixture and hempseed. Stir well.
4. Preheat the oven to 425°F(220°C).
5. Cut crusts off of the bread and leave in a square shape. Use a rolling pin to roll each square thin. You will be rolling up these squares. Spread 1 tbsp. mushroom mixture onto each square and roll up.
6. Melt the remaining butter.
7. Cut rolls in half and roll in melted butter. Arrange the rolls on the cookie sheets and bake for 8 minutes or until browned.

Nutrition Info per Serving:
Calories: 207, Protein: 6.7 g, Fat: 11.6 g, Carbohydrates: 20.2 g, Fiber: 3.6 g, Sugar: 3.4 g, Sodium: 311 mg

Sweet Tofu Cream

Prep Time: 5 minutes, Cook Time: 10 minutes, Serves: 1½ cups

INGREDIENTS:
One (12-oz. 340 g) package extra firm silken tofu, drained
1 tbs. fresh cider
1 tbsp. maple syrup
Salt to taste

DIRECTIONS:
1. Mix all ingredients in a food processor and pulse until smooth and creamy. Chill before serving.

Nutrition Info per Serving:
Calories: 346, Protein: 33.7 g, Fat: 19.8 g, Carbohydrates: 7.9 g, Fiber: 1.4 g, Sugar: 2.1 g, Sodium: 254 mg

Easy Lemon and Almond Ricotta

Prep Time: 5 minutes, Cook Time: 0, Serves: 1 cup

INGREDIENTS:
2 cups blanched slivered almonds (not sliced)
1 tbsp. pure maple syrup
2 tsps. nutritional yeast
½ tsp. almond extract
2 tbsps. freshly squeezed lemon juice
¾ cup cold water
1 tbsp. lemon zest

DIRECTIONS:
1. Add all of the ingredients into a food processor or high-speed blender. Pulse to combine, scrape down the sides, and puree until mostly smooth.
2. Place in an airtight container and refrigerate for up to 2 weeks, or freeze for up to 6 months.

Nutrition Info per Serving:
Calories: 166, Protein: 6 g, Fat: 14 g, Carbohydrates: 8 g, Fiber: 4 g, Sugar: 3 g, Sodium: 155 mg

Mashed Sweet Potato Bake

Prep Time: 15 minutes, Cook Time: 30 minutes, Serves: 6

INGREDIENTS:
8 sweet potatoes, cooked
1 tbsp. dried sage
½ cup vegetable broth
1 tsp. dried thyme
1 tsp. dried rosemary

DIRECTIONS:
1. Preheat the oven to 375°F(190°C).
2. Remove and discard the skin from the cooked sweet potatoes, place them in a baking dish. Use a fork or potato masher to mash the sweet potatoes, then stir in the remaining ingredients.
3. Bake for 30 minutes, after baking, serve warm.

Nutrition Info per Serving:
Calories: 154, Protein: 3 g, Fat: 0 g, Carbohydrates: 35 g, Fiber: 6 g, Sugar: 0.7 g, Sodium: 128 mg

Rosemary Garlic New Potatoes

Prep Time: 15 minutes, Cook Time: 2-6 hours, Serves: 4 to 6

INGREDIENTS:
1½ lbs. (680 g) new red potatoes, unpeeled
1 tbsp. olive oil
1 tsp. garlic and pepper seasoning, or 1 large clove garlic, minced
1 tbsp. fresh chopped rosemary, or 1 tsp. dried rosemary
½ tsp. salt
¼ tsp. pepper

DIRECTIONS:
1. Cut the potatoes in half or in quarters, if they are larger than golf balls.
2. Toss potatoes with olive oil in a bowl or plastic bag, coating well.
3. Add the garlic and pepper seasoning and rosemary (or the minced garlic, salt, and pepper). Toss again until the potatoes are well coated.
4. In the slow cooker, add the potatoes. Cook on High for 2 to 3 hours, or on Low for 5 to 6 hours, or until the potatoes are tender but not mushy or dry.

Nutrition Info per Serving:
Calories: 102, Protein: 2.3 g, Fat: 2.4 g, Carbohydrates: 18.8 g, Fiber: 6 g, Sugar: 4 g, Sodium: 328 mg

Chapter 11 Snack and Dessert

Vanilla Cranberry Thumbprints Cookies

Prep Time: 20 minutes, Cook Time: 20 minutes, plus overnight to chill, Serves: 16 cookies

INGREDIENTS:
FOR THE CHIA CRANBERRY JAM:
¼ cup water
2 cups fresh or frozen cranberries
1 tsp. vanilla extract, plus more as needed
¼ cup pure maple syrup, plus more as needed
2 tbsps. chia seeds
FOR THE COOKIES:
¼ cup avocado oil (optional)
¼ cup pure maple syrup
2 tsps. vanilla extract
2 cups almond flour
¼ cup slivered almonds, crushed or chopped

DIRECTIONS:
TO MAKE THE CHIA CRANBERRY JAM:
1. Before starting the cookies, make the jam, because the jam needs some time to set. The jam is best refrigerated overnight. If you are using a premade jam, skip to step 4.
2. Add the water, cranberries, vanilla and maple syrup into a saucepan, stir them together over medium heat. Cook for 6 to 8 minutes, stirring occasionally. Once the cranberries begin to burst and split open, turn off the heat and break the rest of the cranberries with the back of a heavy wooden spoon or potato masher. If you want a smoother jam, transfer the mixture to a blender and blend until smooth, or puree with an immersion blender in the pot. Taste and adjust the maple syrup or vanilla, as you like.
3. Stir in the chia seeds and transfer the jam to a glass jar or dish, cover, and chill in the refrigerator for a few hours, or overnight. The jam will thicken as it cools as the chia seeds soak up liquid and expand.
TO MAKE THE COOKIES:
4. Preheat the oven to 350°F(180°C). Use parchment paper or a silicone mat to line a baking sheet.
5. Combine the oil, maple syrup and vanilla in a medium bowl, whisk them together to blend. Add the almond flour and mix until a soft dough forms.
6. In a shallow dish, add the almonds.
7. Divide the dough into 16 equal pieces. Rolling each piece into a small ball. Roll each ball in the almonds, then press them down on the prepared baking sheet. Each cookie should be roughly ½ inch thick.
8. Make an indentation in each pressed cookie with the back of a tablespoon-size measuring spoon, or go classic and use your thumb to make. Don't press all the way through.
9. Fill the chia cranberry jam into each indentation, so it just lines up with the top of the cookie.
10. Bake for 12 to 15 minutes. The cookies should be just turning golden brown.
11. Place the cookies in a covered dish and store at room temperature for up to 3 days, or refrigerate for up to 2 weeks.

Nutrition Info per Serving:
Calories: 170, Protein: 4 g, Fat: 12 g, Carbohydrates: 12 g, Fiber: 3 g, Sugar: 14.5 g, Sodium: 130 mg

Vanilla Chickpea Cookie Dough with Pecans

Prep Time: 20 minutes, Cook Time: 0, Serves: 8

INGREDIENTS:
1 (15-ounce, 425 g) can chickpeas
½ cup smooth natural peanut butter
1½ tsps. vanilla extract
2 tbsps. pure maple syrup
½ tsp. ground cinnamon
2 tbsps. pecans

DIRECTIONS:
1. In a bowl, add the chickpeas and fill water into the bowl. Gently rub the chickpeas between your hands until you feel the skins coming off. Add more water to the bowl and allow the skins to float to the surface. Scoop out the skins with your hand. Drain some of the water and repeat this step once more to remove as many of the chickpea skins as possible. Drain to remove all the water. Set the chickpeas aside. Doing this gives the final product a smooth consistency.
2. Combine the peanut butter, chickpeas, vanilla, maple syrup, and cinnamon in a food processor. Process for 2 minutes. Scrape down the sides and process for another 2 minutes, or until the dough is smooth and the ingredients are evenly distributed.
3. Add the pecans and pulse to combine but not fully process.
4. Place in an airtight container and keep for up to 1 week.

Nutrition Info per Serving:
Calories: 170, Protein: 6 g, Fat: 10 g, Carbohydrates: 15 g, Fiber: 3 g, Sugar: 7.4 g, Sodium: 83 mg

Coconut Protein Bars

Prep Time: 5 minutes, Cook Time: 15 minutes, Serves: 8

INGREDIENTS:

2 cups (280 g) almonds, raw and unsalted
10 dates, pitted
2 scoops (60 g) soy protein isolate, chocolate flavor
½ cup (50 g) cocoa powder
½ cup (50 g) shredded coconut

DIRECTIONS:

1. Preheat the oven to 257°F(125°C) and line with parchment paper.
2. Put the almonds on the baking sheet and roast for 10 to 15 minutes or until they're fragrant.
3. Cover the dates with water in a small bowl and soak for 10 minutes. Drain the dates and make sure no water is left.
4. Add the almonds, dates, cocoa powder and chocolate protein to a food processor and combine into a chunky mixture.
5. Line a loaf pan with parchment paper. Put mixture on the loaf pan, spread it out and press down firmly until it's 2.5 cm thick all over.
6. Add the shredded coconut in an even layer on top and press it down firmly.
7. Divide into 8 bars, serve.

Nutrition Info per Serving:
Calories: 151, Protein: 17.6 g, Fat: 5 g, Carbohydrates: 9 g, Fiber: 5 g, Sugar: 7.3 g, Sodium: 105 mg

Homemade Whole Wheat Pita Pockets

Prep Time: 30 minutes, plus 2 hours for the dough to rise, Cook Time: 5 minutes, Serves: 4

INGREDIENTS:

1 (¼-ounce, 7 g) packet fast-acting bread yeast
2 cups whole-wheat flour
1 cup water

DIRECTIONS:

1. Combine the yeast and whole-wheat flour in a large bowl. Then slowly pour in the water while continually mixing until there is no dry flour left.
2. Place the dough on a clean surface, and knead it for 8 to 10 minutes, or until slightly springy and soft.
3. Shape the dough into a ball and transfer it to another large bowl. Use a kitchen towel to cover the bowl. Allow to proof at room temperature for 2 hours, or until the dough has doubled in size.
4. Place the baking sheet or baking stone in the oven, and preheat the oven to 450°F(235°C).
5. Divide the dough ball evenly into 4 pieces. Roll out each ball until the dough is roughly ¼ inch thick.
6. Remove the baking sheet from the oven with a hot pad, and use parchment paper to line it. Place the disks of dough on the baking sheet. Bake until the pitas puff up and turn slightly golden brown, about 3 to 5 minutes.

Nutrition Info per Serving:
Calories: 266, Protein: 10 g, Fat: 2 g, Carbohydrates: 53 g, Fiber: 8 g, Sugar: 1 g, Sodium: 46 mg

Nutty Lemon Oatmeal Cacao Cookies

Prep Time: 30 minutes, Cook Time: 35 minutes, Serves: 14 cookies

INGREDIENTS:

12 pitted Medjool dates
Boiling water, for soaking the dates
1 tbsp. freshly squeezed lemon juice
1 cup unsweetened applesauce
1 tsp. vanilla extract
1 tbsp. water, plus more as needed (optional)
1 cup oat flour
1½ cups old-fashioned oats
2 tbsps. lemon zest
¾ cup coarsely chopped walnuts
1 tbsp. cacao powder
½ tsp. baking soda

DIRECTIONS:

1. Add the dates into a small bowl, cover with enough boiling water. Allow to sit for 15 to 20 minutes to soften.
2. Meanwhile, preheat the oven to 300°F(150°C). Use parchment paper or silicone mats to line 2 baking sheets.
3. Drain the excess liquid from the dates and place them into a blender, then add the lemon juice, applesauce, and vanilla. Puree until a thick paste forms. If the mixture isn't getting smooth, add the water, 1 tbsp. at a time.
4. Add the oat flour, oats, lemon zest, walnuts, cacao powder, and baking soda in a large bowl, stir them together. Pour in the date mixture and stir to combine. One at a time, scoop ¼-cup portions of dough, gently roll into a ball, and lightly press down on the prepared baking sheets. The cookie is about 1 inch thick and roughly 3 inches in diameter.
5. Bake until the tops of the cookies look crispy and dry, about 30 to 35 minutes. After baking, transfer to a wire rack to cool.
6. Keep in an airtight container at room temperature for up to 1 week.

Nutrition Info per Serving:
Calories: 174, Protein: 4 g, Fat: 6 g, Carbohydrates: 30 g, Fiber: 4 g, Sugar: 6.9 g, Sodium: 120 mg

Chocolate Protein Bars

Prep Time: 5 minutes, Cook Time: 15 minutes, Serves: 4

INGREDIENTS:
1 cup (140 g) almonds, raw and unsalted
5 dates, pitted
1 scoop (30 g) soy protein isolate, chocolate flavor

DIRECTIONS:
1. Preheat the oven to 257°F(125°C) and line with parchment paper.
2. Put the almonds on the baking sheet and roast for 10 to 15 minutes or until they're fragrant.
3. Cover the dates with water in a small bowl and soak for 10 minutes. Drain the dates and make sure no water is left.
4. Take the almonds out of the oven and cool down for 5 minutes.
5. Add all ingredients to a medium bowl, cover it, and mix with a handheld blender.
6. Put the almond mixture on the loaf pan with parchment paper, spread it out and press it down firmly until it is 1 inch thick all over.
7. Divide into 4 bars, serve cold with the optional toppings.

Nutrition Info per Serving:
Calories: 286, Protein: 16 g, Fat: 17.5 g, Carbohydrates: 16 g, Fiber: 3.6 g, Sugar: 7 g, Sodium: 51 mg

Almond Protein Bars

Prep Time: 45 minutes, Cook Time: 15 minutes, Serves: 8

INGREDIENTS:
2 cups (280 g) almonds, raw and unsalted
10 dates, pitted
4 tbsps. (40 g) 5-spice powder
2 scoops (60 g) soy protein isolate (chocolate flavor)
4-inch piece (40 g) ginger, minced

DIRECTIONS:
1. Preheat the oven to 257°F(125°C) and line with parchment paper.
2. Put the almonds on the baking sheet and roast for 10 to 15 minutes or until they're fragrant.
3. Cover the dates with water in a small bowl and soak for 10 minutes. Drain the dates and make sure no water is left.
4. Add the almonds, dates, protein powder, 5-spice powder, and ginger to a medium bowl, cover it, and process with a handheld blender.
5. Line a loaf pan with parchment paper. Place the almond mixture on the loaf pan, spread it out and press it down firmly until it is 1 inch thick all over.
6. Put the loaf pan in the fridge for 45 minutes, until it has firmed up.
7. Divide into 8 bars, serve cold with optional toppings.

Nutrition Info per Serving:
Calories: 263, Protein: 16.1 g, Fat: 18.2 g, Carbohydrates: 8.9 g, Fiber: 3.7 g, Sugar: 6.9 g, Sodium: 86 mg

Roasted Vegetable Chips

Prep Time: 20 minutes, Cook Time: 35 minutes, Serves: 6

INGREDIENTS:
1 pound (454 g) high-water vegetables, such as zucchini or summer squash
Kosher salt, for absorbing moisture
1 pound (454 g) starchy root vegetables, such as russet potato, sweet potato, rutabaga, parsnip, red or golden beet, or taro
1 tsp. paprika
1 tsp. garlic powder
½ tsp. onion powder
½ tsp. freshly ground black pepper
1 tsp. avocado oil or other oil (optional)

DIRECTIONS:
1. Preheat the oven to 300°F(150°C). Use parchment paper to line 2 baking sheets. Set aside.
2. Wash and dry the high-water vegetables. Scrub the root vegetables well to remove the dirt.
3. Cut all the vegetables into ⅛-inch-thick slices with a mandoline or sharp kitchen knife. The thinner you slice them, the crispier they will be.
4. Place the sliced high-water vegetables on a clean kitchen towel or paper towel. Sprinkle with a generous amount of kosher salt, which draws out moisture. Allow to sit for 15 minutes. Dab off excess moisture and salt with a paper towel.
5. Add the paprika, garlic powder, onion powder, and pepper in a small bowl, stir them together.
6. Place all the vegetables to the prepared baking sheets in a single layer. Brush with oil, if using. Evenly sprinkle over with the spice mix.
7. Bake for 15 minutes. Switch the pans between the oven racks and bake for another 20 minutes, or until the vegetables are darker in color and crispy on the edges.
8. Place the chips onto a wire rack to cool with a spatula. The baked chips will crisp within a few minutes of cooling.

Nutrition Info per Serving:
Calories: 250, Protein: 8 g, Fat: 3 g, Carbohydrates: 51 g, Fiber: 6 g, Sugar: 0.6 g, Sodium: 218 mg

Vanilla Oat Apple Crisp

Prep Time: 10 minutes, Cook Time: 35 minutes, Serves: 6

INGREDIENTS:
¾ cup apple juice
3 medium apples, cored and cut into ¼-inch pieces
1 tsp. vanilla extract
1 tsp. ground cinnamon, divided
2 cups rolled oats
¼ cup maple syrup

DIRECTIONS:
1. Preheat the oven to 375°F(190°C).
2. Add the apple juice, apple slices, vanilla, and ½ tsp. of cinnamon in a large bowl. Mix well to thoroughly coat the apple slices.
3. Layer the apple slices on the bottom of a round or square baking dish. Pour any leftover liquid over the apple slices.
4. Add the maple syrup, oats, and the remaining ½ tsp. of cinnamon in a large bowl, stir them together until the oats are completely coated.
5. Sprinkle over the apples with the oat mixture, make sure to evenly spread it out so that none of the apple slices are visible.
6. Bake until the oats begin to turn golden brown, about 35 minutes, and serve.

Nutrition Info per Serving:
Calories: 222, Protein: 4 g, Fat: 2 g, Carbohydrates: 47 g, Fiber: 6 g, Sugar: 18 g, Sodium: 84 mg

Lemony Vanilla Pie Bars

Prep Time: 35 minutes, Cook Time: 15 minutes, Serves: 8

INGREDIENTS:
2 cups (200 g) cashews, raw and unsalted
10 dates, pitted
2 scoops (60 g) organic pea protein
1 organic lemon
1 tsp. (10 ml) vanilla extract

DIRECTIONS:
1. Preheat the oven to 257°F(125°C) and line with parchment paper.
2. Place the cashews on the baking sheet and roast them for 10 to 15 minutes or until they're fragrant.
3. Cover the dates with water in a small bowl and let them soak for 10 minutes. Drain the dates and make sure no water is left.
4. Rinse and scrub the lemon lightly.
5. Add the cashews, pea protein, dates, vanilla extract and the whole lemon to a food processor and blend into a smooth mixture.
6. Put the cashew mixture on the loaf pan with parchment paper, spread it out and press it down firmly until it's 1-inch thick.
7. Put the loaf pan in the fridge for 45 minutes, until it firms up.
8. Divide into 8 bars, serve cold with the optional toppings.

Nutrition Info per Serving:
Calories: 209, Protein: 11.2 g, Fat: 13.1 g, Carbohydrates: 11.6 g, Fiber: 3.2 g, Sugar: 7.4 g, Sodium: 65 mg

Stuffed Cabbage Rolls

Prep Time: 15 minutes, Cook Time: 45 minutes, Serves: 6

INGREDIENTS:
1 large head savoy cabbage, separated into individual leaves
1 large yellow onion, peeled and diced small
2 carrots, peeled and finely diced
1 tbsp. minced sage
¼ cup dry sherry
3 cups cooked wild rice blend
2 celery stalks, diced small
2 cloves garlic, peeled and minced
½ cup (120 ml) low-sodium vegetable broth
2 cups Tomato Sauce
Salt and freshly ground black pepper

DIRECTIONS:
1. Boil a pot of salted water. Blanch the cabbage leaves in the boiling water for 5 to 6 minutes. Remove them from the pot and rinse. Set aside.
2. Put the carrots, onion, and celery in a large saucepan and sauté over medium heat for 7 to 8 minutes. Add water 1 tbsp. at a time to keep the vegetables from sticking to the pan. Add the sage and garlic, cook for 3 minutes. Add the sherry and cook until the liquid is almost evaporated. Remove the pan from the heat, add the wild rice and season with salt and pepper.
3. Preheat the oven to 350°F(180ºC).
4. Lay 2 cabbage leaves with a ½-inch overlap. Place ½ cup of the rice in the center of the leaves. Fold in the leaves from the sides over the filling, then roll the leaves into a cylinder. Place the roll, seam side down, in a baking dish. Repeat until all the filling is used, reserving any leftover leaves for another use. Add the vegetable stock to the baking dish, cover with aluminum foil, and bake for 10 minutes. Uncover the dish and pour the tomato sauce over the rolls. Bake for another 15 minutes.

Nutrition Info per Serving:
Calories: 170, Protein: 6.7 g, Fat: 0.8 g, Carbohydrates: 38 g, Fiber: 6.7 g, Sugar: 12 g, Sodium: 668 mg

Hazelnut Choco Balls

Prep Time: 10 minutes, Cook Time: 50 minutes, Serves: 12

INGREDIENTS:
2 cups (200 g) Hazelnuts, roasted
8 dried plums, pitted
1 cup (90 g) soy protein isolate (chocolate flavor)
½ cup (50 g) cocoa powder

DIRECTIONS:
1. Put the hazelnuts, plums and soy protein isolate in a food processor and process into a smooth mixture.
2. Line a baking sheet with parchment paper to prevent sticking to the plate.
3. Scoop out a tbsp. of the chocolate hazelnut mixture and roll it into a firm ball using your hands. Repeat the same process for the other 11 balls.
4. Roll the balls in the cocoa powder, then place them to the baking sheet.
5. Put the baking sheet in the fridge for about 45 minutes, until all the balls have firmed up.
6. Take the baking dish out of the fridge and store the hazelnut chocolate balls or serve them right away with the optional toppings.

Nutrition Info per Serving:
Calories: 169, Protein: 10.1 g, Fat: 11 g, Carbohydrates: 7.5 g, Fiber: 3.6 g, Sugar: 2.7 g, Sodium: 53 mg

Almond and Coconut Cookie Balls

Prep Time: 45 minutes, Cook Time: 15 minutes, Serves: 12

INGREDIENTS:
2 cups (280 g) almonds, raw and unsalted
8 dates, pitted
¼ cup (40 g) raisins
2 scoops (60 g) organic pea protein
½ cup (50 g) shredded coconut

DIRECTIONS:
1. Preheat the oven to 257°F(125°C) and line with parchment paper.
2. Put the almonds on the baking sheet and roast for 10 to 15 minutes or until they're fragrant.
3. Cover the dates with water in a small bowl and soak for 10 minutes. Drain the dates and make sure no water is left.
4. Add the pea protein, almonds, dates, raisins and shredded coconut to a food processor and blend into a chunky mixture.
5. Scoop out a tbsp. of the mixture and roll it into a firm ball using your hands and place them on the baking sheet.
6. Repeat the same process for the other 11 balls.
7. Put the baking sheet in the fridge for about 45 minutes, until all the balls have firmed up.
8. Serve the cookie balls with the optional toppings.

Nutrition Info per Serving:
Calories: 294, Protein: 15.3 g, Fat: 20.8 g, Carbohydrates: 11.3 g, Fiber: 4.4 g, Sugar: 9.2 g, Sodium: 26 mg

Stuffed Chard Rolls

Prep Time: 10 minutes, Cook Time: 55 minutes, Serves: 6

INGREDIENTS:
12 large Swiss chard leaves, ribs removed
3 tbsps. minced basil
1 tbsp. thyme
1½ cups millet
5 cups (1200 ml) low-sodium vegetable broth
½ cup pine nuts, toasted
¼ cup nutritional yeast
1 large onion, peeled and finely diced
6 cloves garlic, peeled and minced
1 batch Roasted Red Pepper Sauce
Salt and freshly ground black pepper

DIRECTIONS:
1. Prepare a large bowl with ice and cold water. Boil a pot of water, large enough to hold the chard leaves without bending them. Add the chard and blanch the leaves for 20 to 30 seconds until they soften. Submerge the softened leaves in the ice water. Set aside.
2. Preheat the oven to 350°F (180ºC).
3. Put the onion in a large saucepan and sauté over medium heat for 8 minutes. Add water 1 tbsp. at a time to keep the onion from sticking to the pan. Add the garlic and cook for 2 minutes. Add the thyme, basil, millet, and 4½ cups of vegetable stock and boil over high heat. Lower the heat to medium and cook, covered, for 20 minutes. Remove from the heat. Add the pine nuts and nutritional yeast and season with salt and pepper.
4. Put a chard leaf on a flat surface. Spoon some of the millet mixture in the middle of the chard leaf. Fold the large end of the chard over the filling, then fold in the sides and roll up like a cigar. Place the roll, seam side down, in a baking dish. Repeat with the remaining chard leaves. Pour the remaining vegetable stock into the pan. Cover the dish with aluminum foil and bake for 25 minutes. Serve topped with the roasted red pepper sauce.

Nutrition Info per Serving:
Calories: 362, Protein: 14.1 g, Fat: 10.8 g, Carbohydrates: 55.8 g, Fiber: 8.7 g, Sugar: 8.5 g, Sodium: 681 mg

Vanilla Protein Muffins

Prep Time: 5 minutes, Cook Time: 25 minutes, Serves: 8

INGREDIENTS:
1½ cups (150 g) pea protein isolate
½ cup (100 g) whole wheat flour
1½ cups (375 ml) water
¼ cup (40 g) raisins
2 tsps. (8 g) baking powder
2 tsps. (20 ml) vanilla extract

DIRECTIONS:
1. Preheat the oven to 320°F(160°C), line with muffin liners and set it aside.
2. Add all ingredients to a blender and mix until smooth, scraping down the sides of the blender to prevent any lumps.
3. Spoon the mixture into the muffin liners about three-quarters filled.
4. Bake the muffins for 20-25 minutes, then test to see if they are done by sticking a toothpick in.
5. Take the muffins out of the oven and cool down completely before taking the muffin liners off.
6. Serve the muffins with the optional toppings.

Nutrition Info per Serving:
Calories: 123, Protein: 16.2 g, Fat: 1.1 g, Carbohydrates: 12.1 g, Fiber: 1.4 g, Sugar: 3 g, Sodium: 66 mg

Peanut Butter Protein Bars

Prep Time: 55 minutes, Cook Time: 25 minutes, Serves: 8

INGREDIENTS:
1 cup (260 g) peanut butter
10 medjool dates, pitted
1 cup (90 g) instant oats
2 scoops (60 g) organic pea protein
½ cup (100 g) dark chocolate, crushed
½ cup (120 ml) water

DIRECTIONS:
1. Preheat the oven to 257°F(125°C).
2. Combine the oats, half of the water and 5 medjool dates in a food processor and blend into a smooth mixture.
3. Line a loaf pan with parchment paper. Place the oats mixture on the loaf pan, spread it out and press it down firmly until it is 1 cm thick all over.
4. Add the ingredients to a medium bowl, cover it, and process with a handheld blender.
5. Add the peanut butter mixture in an even layer about 1-inch thick on top of the oats layer and press it down firmly.
6. Put the loaf pan into the oven and bake for 15 minutes.
7. Take the loaf pan out of the oven and add an even layer of the crushed chocolate on top.
8. Bake for another 10 minutes, take the loaf pan out of the oven, cool down and transfer to the fridge to let the mixture completely firm up for 45 minutes.
9. Divide into 8 bars, serve cold with the optional peanut butter.

Nutrition Info per Serving:
Calories: 374, Protein: 17 g, Fat: 23.8 g, Carbohydrates: 23 g, Fiber: 6.4 g, Sugar: 5.4 g, Sodium: 91 mg

Vanilla Ginger Cookies

Prep Time: 15 minutes, Cook Time: 10 minutes, Serves: 12 cookies

INGREDIENTS:
2 tbsps. pure maple syrup
¼ cup tahini
1½ tbsps. oat milk
2 tbsps. date sugar
½ tsp. vanilla extract
1 tsp. ground ginger
¾ cup whole wheat flour, or a 1:1 gluten-free blend, plus more as needed
1 tsp. baking powder
¼ tsp. baking soda
½ tsp. ground cinnamon
⅛ tsp. ground cloves
⅛ tsp. ground nutmeg
2 tbsps. finely chopped dried ginger pieces

DIRECTIONS:
1. Preheat the oven to 350°F(180°C). Use parchment paper or a silicone mat to line a baking sheet.
2. Add the maple syrup, tahini, oat milk, date sugar, and vanilla in a small bowl, whisk together until smooth.
3. Combine the ginger, flour, baking powder, baking soda, cinnamon, cloves, and nutmeg in a large bowl, whisk them together until fully combined. Add the dried ginger.
4. Fold the wet ingredients into the dry ingredients, mixing until the dough seems smooth and isn't too sticky. Add more flour as needed, 1 tbsp. at a time, but do not overmix. Divide the dough into 12 equal portions. Roll each piece into a ball and press them on the prepared baking sheet to about 1 inch thick.
5. Bake on the middle rack until the tops are lightly golden brown, about 8 to 10 minutes. After baking, place onto a wire rack to cool. They will firm up as they cool but will remain slightly soft.
6. Place in an airtight container and store at room temperature for up to 1 week, or freeze for up to 6 months.

Nutrition Info per Serving:
Calories: 75, Protein: 2 g, Fat: 3 g, Carbohydrates: 10 g, Fiber: 1 g, Sugar: 7.8 g, Sodium: 85 mg

Oat and Mint Brownie Date Bars

Prep Time: 10 minutes, plus 15 minutes to chill, Cook Time: 0, Serves: 4

INGREDIENTS:
1 cup old-fashioned oats
1 cup pitted Medjool dates
¼ tsp. mint extract
2 tbsps. cacao powder
¼ cup cacao nibs or vegan chocolate chips

DIRECTIONS:
1. Sort through the dates and ensure there are no pits.
2. Combine the oats, dates, mint extract, cacao powder, and cacao nibs in a food processor. Pulse a few times to combine, scrape down the sides, and process until a ball forms. Form the dough into a rectangle roughly ½ inch thick and cut it into 6 bars.
3. Use a sheet of parchment paper or wax paper to stack the bars between them to avoid sticking. Place in a sealable bag and store in the refrigerator for up to 2 weeks, or freeze in an airtight container for 4 to 6 months.

Nutrition Info per Serving:
Calories: 200, Protein: 3 g, Fat: 4 g, Carbohydrates: 39 g, Fiber: 7 g, Sugar: 12.7 g, Sodium: 119 mg

Sweet Potato Whole Wheat Cake

Prep Time: 5 minutes, Cook Time: 45 minutes, Serves: 6

INGREDIENTS:
1 sweet potato, cooked and peeled
½ cup plant-based milk
½ cup unsweetened applesauce
1 tsp. vanilla extract
¼ cup maple syrup
½ tsp. baking soda
2 cups whole-wheat flour
¼ tsp. ground ginger
½ tsp. ground cinnamon

DIRECTIONS:
1. Preheat the oven to 350°F(180°C).
2. Mash the sweet potato with a fork or potato masher in a large mixing bowl.
3. Add the milk, applesauce, vanilla and maple syrup, stir well.
4. Stir in the baking soda, flour, ginger and cinnamon until the dry ingredients have been thoroughly combined with the wet ingredients.
5. Pour the batter into a nonstick baking dish or one lined with parchment paper. Bake until you can stick a knife into the middle of the cake and it comes out clean, about 45 minutes.
6. After baking, allow to cool, slice, and serve.

Nutrition Info per Serving:
Calories: 238, Protein: 5 g, Fat: 1 g, Carbohydrates: 52 g, Fiber: 2 g, Sugar: 13.7 g, Sodium: 62 mg

Moroccan Shepherd's Pie

Prep Time: 20 minutes, Cook Time: 1½ hours, Serves: 6 to 8

INGREDIENTS:
1 large onion, peeled and diced
2 medium carrots, peeled and diced
2 celery stalks, diced
6 cloves garlic, peeled and minced
2 tbsps. sweet paprika
2 cups green lentils, rinsed
1 tbsp. cumin seeds, toasted and ground
1 tsp. turmeric
1 tsp. crushed red pepper flakes
3 large yams, peeled and diced
2 cinnamon sticks
12 cups packed spinach (about 2 pounds, 907 g)
1 cup chopped cilantro
8 cups (1440 ml) low-sodium vegetable broth
Zest and juice of 2 lemons
Salt and freshly ground black pepper

DIRECTIONS:
1. Put carrots, onion, and celery in a large saucepan and sauté for 10 minutes over medium heat. Add water 1 tbsp. at a time to keep the vegetables from sticking to the pan. Add the garlic and cook for one more minute. Add the paprika, turmeric, cumin, lentils, crushed red pepper flakes, and vegetable stock. Boil over high heat, lower the heat to medium, and cook with lid covered, for 45 minutes until the lentils are tender.
2. Meanwhile, put the yams and the cinnamon sticks in another saucepan. Add enough water to cover, boil, and cook over medium heat for about 15 minutes until tender. Remove from the heat, drain the excess water, and discard the cinnamon sticks. Mash the yams until creamy and set aside.
3. Preheat the oven to 350°F (180°C).
4. Add the spinach and cilantro to the lentil mixture and cook for about 5 minutes until the spinach is wilted. Season with salt and pepper and mix in the lemon zest and juice. Pour the mixture into a baking dish.
5. Spread the mashed yams evenly over the lentil mixture and bake the casserole for 20 minutes. Set aside for 10 minutes before serving.

Nutrition Info per Serving:
Calories: 217, Protein: 8.5 g, Fat: 1.8 g, Carbohydrates: 48.5 g, Fiber: 8.6 g, Sugar: 10 g, Sodium: 217 mg

Homemade Maple Cinnamon Latte, page 170

Baked Garlicky Kale Chips, page 166

Chocolate Protein Bars, page 158

Homemade Popcorn, page 168

Chapter 11 Snack and Dessert

Smoked Coconut Bits

Prep Time: 15 minutes, Cook Time: 12 minutes, plus time to cool, Serves: 2 cups

INGREDIENTS:

1 tbsp. liquid hickory smoke
2 tbsps. tamari or low-sodium soy sauce
1 tbsp. pure maple syrup
¼ tsp. onion powder
½ tsp. smoked paprika
¼ tsp. ground white pepper
2 cups unsweetened coconut flakes (not desiccated)

DIRECTIONS:

1. Preheat the oven to 350°F(180°C). Use parchment paper or aluminum foil to line a baking sheet. Avoid using a silicone mat, because the ingredients will stain the surface.
2. Add the liquid smoke, tamari, maple syrup, onion powder, paprika, and ground white pepper in a large bowl, stir them together. Stir in the coconut flakes. Toss gently to combine until the coconut flakes are thoroughly coated. Allow to sit for 10 minutes. Stir again, then evenly spread the coconut on the prepared baking sheet.
3. Bake for 12 minutes, until the coconut flakes look dry and golden brown rather than dark.
4. After baking, allow to cool completely on the baking sheet.
5. Place in an airtight container and store at room temperature for 2 weeks or freeze for up to 2 months.

Nutrition Info per Serving:
Calories: 39, Protein: 1 g, Fat: 3 g, Carbohydrates: 2 g, Fiber: 1 g, Sugar: 3 g, Sodium: 45 mg

Vanilla Carrot and Coconut Cake Balls

Prep Time: 10 minutes, Cook Time: 6 minutes, Serves: 30 balls

INGREDIENTS:

2 cups unsweetened coconut flakes
1 carrot, coarsely chopped
2 cups old-fashioned oats
½ cup pure maple syrup
½ cup smooth natural peanut butter
1 tsp. ground cinnamon
¼ cup coarsely chopped pecans
½ tsp. vanilla extract
½ tsp. ground ginger

DIRECTIONS:

1. Toast the coconut in a sauté pan or skillet over medium-high heat for 3 to 6 minutes, stirring or flipping occasionally, until lightly browned. Remove from the heat.
2. Add the carrot into a food processor, pulse until finely chopped but not pureed. Place the carrot into a bowl and set aside.
3. Combine the oats and toasted coconut flakes in the food processor. Pulse until coarsely ground but not until the ingredients become a flour.
4. Place the carrots back to the processor and add the maple syrup, peanut butter, cinnamon, pecans, vanilla, and ginger. Pulse until the dough starts to form a ball. Divide the dough into 30 portions. Press and form each portion into a ball with your clean hands.
5. Store in a sealable bag or airtight container and keep for up to 2 weeks.

Nutrition Info per Serving:
Calories: 209, Protein: 4 g, Fat: 13 g, Carbohydrates: 19 g, Fiber: 4 g, Sugar: 8.6 g, Sodium: 158 mg

Tasty Vanilla Cookies

Prep Time: 15 minutes, Cook Time: 10 minutes, Serves: 36 cookies

INGREDIENTS:

1 cup oat flour
⅔ cup coconut flour
⅔ cup (160 ml) unsweetened plant-based milk
¼ cup (60 ml) almond butter
¼ cup (60 ml) unsweetened applesauce
⅔ cup dry sweetener
1 tsp. pure vanilla extract
1 vanilla bean, halved
1 tbsp. cornstarch
2 tsps. baking powder
½ tsp. salt

DIRECTIONS:

1. Preheat the oven to 350°F (180ºC). Line 2 large baking sheets with parchment paper.
2. Use a strong fork to beat together the plant-based milk, applesauce, almond butter, and dry sweetener in a large mixing bowl. When it is relatively smooth, mix in the vanilla. Scrape the seeds from the vanilla bean and put them in the batter. Mix well.
3. Add in the oat flour, cornstarch, coconut flour, baking powder, and salt. Combine well. The dough will be stiff.
4. Roll the dough into walnut-size balls and place them on the prepared baking sheets, a little over an inch apart. Flatten the cookies a bit and make them look like thick discs. Bake for 8 to 10 minutes.
5. Remove the cookies from the oven and cool down on the baking sheets for 5 minutes, and then transfer to a cooling rack to cool completely.

Nutrition Info per Serving:
Calories: 41, Protein: 1 g, Fat: 1.3 g, Carbohydrates: 6.7 g, Fiber: 0.4 g, Sugar: 4 g, Sodium: 40 mg

Berries Cobbler

Prep Time: 20 minutes, Cook Time: 1 hour, Serves: 8

INGREDIENTS:

FOR THE FILLING:
5 cups mixed berries (such as blueberries, raspberries, and strawberries)
2 tbsps. fresh lemon juice
⅓ cup dry sweetener
3 tbsps. cornstarch
Pinch salt

FOR THE BISCUIT TOPPING:
½ cup (120 ml) unsweetened plant-based milk
1 tsp. apple cider vinegar
1 tsp. pure vanilla extract
1½ cups oat flour
1 tbsp. baking powder
¼ cup dry sweetener
¼ tsp. salt
3 tbsps. unsweetened applesauce
2 tbsps. almond butter

FOR SPRINKLING:
1 tbsp. dry sweetener
¼ tsp. ground cinnamon

DIRECTIONS:
1. Preheat the oven to 425°F (220ºC). Line an 8 × 8-inch pan with parchment paper, making sure that the parchment goes up the sides of the pan, or prepare an 8 × 8-inch nonstick or silicone baking pan.
TO MAKE THE FILLING:
2. Mix together the berries, dry sweetener, cornstarch, lemon juice, and salt in a large bowl until well combined. Put the mixture in the prepared pan. Bake for 25 minutes covered with aluminum foil.
TO MAKE THE BISCUIT TOPPING:
3. Whisk together the apple cider vinegar and plant-based milk in a large measuring cup. Set aside to let curdle for a few minutes, then add the vanilla.
4. Sift together the baking powder, oat flour, dry sweetener, and salt in a large bowl.
5. Mix together the applesauce and almond butter in a small bowl.
6. Combine the applesauce mixture and the flour mixture with a fork, until crumbly. Add the milk mixture and stir until just moistened.
TO ASSEMBLE THE COBBLER:
7. Reduce the oven temperature to 350°F (180ºC). Remove the foil from the pan and drop spoonfuls of the batter over the berry filling. Mix the cinnamon and dry sweetener and sprinkle evenly over the top of the biscuit dough. Put the pan back to the oven, uncovered, and bake for another 20 minutes.
8. Take out the pan from the oven and transfer it to a cooling rack. Serve warm.

Nutrition Info per Serving:
Calories: 251, Protein: 4.1 g, Fat: 5.1 g, Carbohydrates: 50.2 g, Fiber: 2.3 g, Sugar: 30.8 g, Sodium: 401 mg

Mango Choco Protein Pudding

Prep Time: 5 minutes, Cook Time: 0, Serves: 2

INGREDIENTS:
2 cups (250 g) mango cubes
1 banana, peeled
2 scoops (60 g) soy protein isolate (chocolate flavor)
¼ cup (30 g) flaxseeds
3 cups (720 ml) water

DIRECTIONS:
1. Add all ingredients to a blender and blend until smooth. Or blend the banana, soy isolate, 2 tbsps. of flaxseeds and the water first and divide half of the mixture in two glasses.
2. Scoop out the remaining banana mix into a bowl and set it aside.
3. Blend the mango with the remaining flaxseeds.
4. Divide the mango purée between the two glasses and top with the remaining banana mix.
5. Serve with the optional toppings.

Nutrition Info per Serving:
Calories: 343, Protein: 31.1 g, Fat: 6.9 g, Carbohydrates: 39.1 g, Fiber: 7.9 g, Sugar: 25.9 g, Sodium: 69 mg

Vanilla Chocolate Whole Wheat Mug Cake

Prep Time: 5 minutes, Cook Time: 90 seconds, plus 5 minutes to cool, Serves: 1

INGREDIENTS:
3 tbsps. unsweetened applesauce
3 tbsps. whole-wheat flour
1 tbsp. cocoa powder
1 tsp. vanilla extract
1 tbsp. maple syrup
1 tbsp. plant-based milk
¼ tsp. baking powder

DIRECTIONS:
1. Add all of the ingredients in a microwave-safe coffee mug or bowl. Stir together until there are no clumps of dry flour left. Put the mug on a paper towel or plate to ensure easy cleanup.
2. Microwave on high for 90 seconds, or until the cake has risen to the top of the mug.
3. Take out from the microwave and set aside to cool for at least 5 minutes and serve.

Nutrition Info per Serving:
Calories: 185, Protein: 4 g, Fat: 1 g, Carbohydrates: 41 g, Fiber: 3 g, Sugar: 6.5 g, Sodium: 43 mg

Choco Almond Mousse Pudding

Prep Time: 5 minutes, Cook Time: 0, Serves: 2

INGREDIENTS:
2 cups (480 ml) soymilk
1 cup (170 g) pomegranate seeds
2 bananas, peeled
2 scoops (60 g) soy protein isolate (chocolate flavor)
¼ cup (60 g) almond butter
1 cup (240 ml) water

DIRECTIONS:
1. Add all ingredients to a blender and blend until smooth.
2. Add a tbsp. of the almond butter mixture to 2 large glasses.
3. Add ¼ cup of soymilk and a tbsp. of pomegranate seeds to each glass.
4. Repeat steps 3 until all of the almond mixture, pomegranate seeds and soymilk has been used.
5. Serve with the optional toppings.

Nutrition Info per Serving:
Calories: 597, Protein: 42.9 g, Fat: 22.7 g, Carbohydrates: 55.3 g, Fiber: 12.2 g, Sugar: 28.9 g, Sodium: 110 mg

Baked Garlicky Kale Chips

Prep Time: 5 minutes, Cook Time: 20 minutes, Serves: 4

INGREDIENTS:
1 tbsp. nutritional yeast
¼ cup vegetable broth
½ tsp. onion powder
½ tsp. garlic powder
6 ounces (170 g) kale, stemmed and cut into 2- to 3-inch pieces

DIRECTIONS:
1. Preheat the oven to 300°F(150°C). Use parchment paper to line a baking sheet.
2. Mix together the nutritional yeast, broth, onion powder, and garlic powder in a small bowl.
3. In a large bowl, add the kale. Pour the broth mixture over the kale, and toss well to thoroughly coat.
4. Arrange the kale pieces on the baking sheet in an even layer. Bake until crispy, about 20 minutes, turning the kale halfway through.

Nutrition Info per Serving:
Calories: 41, Protein: 4 g, Fat: 0 g, Carbohydrates: 7 g, Fiber: 2 g, Sugar: 0.5 g, Sodium: 73 mg

Quinoa Almond Cookies

Prep Time: 8 minutes, Cook Time: 12 minutes, Serves: 8

INGREDIENTS:
1½ cups (210 g) almonds, raw and unsalted
10 dates, pitted
¼ cup (45 g) quinoa, dry
1 cup (90 g) instant oats
¼ cup (40 g) chia seeds
½ cup (120 ml) water

DIRECTIONS:
1. Preheat the oven to 257°F(125°C), line with parchment paper and set it aside.
2. Add all ingredients to a food processor and blend until smooth, scraping down the sides of the container if necessary.
3. Take a tbsp. of the mixture, put it on the baking tray and press it down to form a 2 cm thick cookie.
4. Repeat the process for the remaining cookie dough.
5. Put the baking tray in the oven and bake the cookies for 12 minutes, until the cookies have set.
6. Take the cookies out of the oven and cool down before serving.
7. Serve the cookies with the optional toppings.

Nutrition Info per Serving:
Calories: 268, Protein: 10.1 g, Fat: 16.1 g, Carbohydrates: 20.7 g, Fiber: 5.9 g, Sugar: 6.7 g, Sodium: 214 mg

Raisin and Oat Cookies

Prep Time: 15 minutes, Cook Time: 15 minutes, Serves: 8

INGREDIENTS:
1 cup (90 g) instant oats
4 bananas
¼ cup (40 g) raisins
2 scoops (60 g) soy protein isolate (chocolate flavor)
1 tsp. (10 ml) vanilla extract

DIRECTIONS:
1. Preheat the oven to 325°F(170°C), line with parchment paper and set it aside.
2. Add all ingredients to a food processor and blend until smooth, scraping down the sides of the container if necessary.
3. Take a tbsp. of the mixture, put it on the baking tray and press it down to form a 1 cm thick cookie. Repeat the process and make sure there is a bit of space between each cookie.
4. Bake the cookies for 15 minutes in the oven, until they have set.
5. Take the cookies out of the oven and cool down before serving.
6. Serve the cookies with the optional toppings.

Nutrition Info per Serving:
Calories: 146, Protein: 9 g, Fat: 1.1 g, Carbohydrates: 25.1 g, Fiber: 2.8 g, Sugar: 10.5 g, Sodium: 36 mg

Baked Maple-Glazed Mixed Nuts

Prep Time: 5 minutes, Cook Time: 15 minutes, Serves: 6

INGREDIENTS:
1½ cups maple syrup
1 cup walnuts
1 cup cashews
1 cup pecans

DIRECTIONS:
1. Preheat the oven to 325°F(165°C).
2. In a medium bowl, add the maple syrup and nuts, mix them together. Be sure that each nut has been coated well. Spread out on a baking sheet so they are in one layer but still close to each other. Bake for 7 minutes.
3. Remove from oven and use a spatula to flip. They can overlap some at this point. Return in the oven and bake for another 6 minutes or so. Watch closely, do not burn.
4. Remove the baking sheet from the oven, flip the nuts again, and allow to cool completely. Eat right away or pack in an airtight container. Store the nuts in your pantry for quite a few weeks and will keep in the refrigerator about 2 to 3 months, or keep in the freezer for 6 months.

Nutrition Info per Serving:
Calories: 666, Protein: 8.7 g, Fat: 43.2 g, Carbohydrates: 69.8 g, Fiber: 3.8 g, Sugar: 42.5 g, Sodium: 136 mg

Vanilla Sweet Potato Pie Cream

Prep Time: 5 minutes, plus at least 4 hours to freeze, Cook Time: 0, Serves: 2

INGREDIENTS:
2 medium sweet potatoes, cooked
½ cup plant-based milk
1 tsp. vanilla extract
1 tbsp. maple syrup
½ tsp. ground cinnamon

DIRECTIONS:
1. Use parchment paper to line a baking sheet.
2. Peel and discard the skin from the cooked sweet potatoes, and cut the flesh into 1-inch cubes. Put on the baking sheet in an even layer, then place in the freezer overnight, or for at least 4 hours.
3. Combine the milk, frozen sweet potato, vanilla, maple syrup and cinnamon in a food processor.
4. Process on medium speed for 1 to 2 minutes, or until smooth, and serve. (If there are any sweet potato pieces stuck toward the top and sides of the food processor, stop and scrape them down with a spatula, then pulse until smooth.)

Nutrition Info per Serving:
Calories: 155, Protein: 2 g, Fat: 1 g, Carbohydrates: 34 g, Fiber: 5 g, Sugar: 13.3 g, Sodium: 57 mg

Chocolate-Peppermint Banana Cream

Prep Time: 5 minutes, Cook Time: 0, Serves: 2

INGREDIENTS:
3 tbsps. plant-based milk
3 frozen ripe bananas, broken into thirds
⅛ tsp. peppermint extract
2 tbsps. cocoa powder

DIRECTIONS:
1. Add all of the ingredients in a food processor.
2. Process on medium speed for 30 to 60 seconds, or until smooth, and serve. (If there is any banana pieces stuck toward the top and sides of the food processor, stop and scrape them down with a spatula, then pulse until smooth.)

Nutrition Info per Serving:
Calories: 203, Protein: 3 g, Fat: 2 g, Carbohydrates: 43 g, Fiber: 6 g, Sugar: 7.5 g, Sodium: 61 mg

Cheesy Zucchini Pancake

Prep Time: 5 minutes, Cook Time: 30 minutes, Serves: 8

INGREDIENTS:
1 cup whole wheat or all-purpose flour
2 tsps. baking powder
½ tsp. salt
2 tbsps. canola or vegetable oil, plus more for greasing
1 cup vegan cheese
½ cup grated zucchini
(about 1 small zucchini)
1 cup plant-based milk
1½ tsps. vanilla extract
1 tbsp. agave, brown sugar, or maple syrup
¼ tsp. Lemon zest
½ tbsp. flaxseed meal added in step 2
Vegan butter

DIRECTIONS:
1. Preheat a nonstick pan over medium-high heat. If you don't have a nonstick pan (or your nonstick pan needs a bit more slip), you can lightly grease the pan.
2. Combine all the ingredients in a medium bowl. Gently toss until the batter is smooth, but there's no need to remove all the lumps.
3. Scoop out the batter using a ¼-cup measuring cup and pour onto the preheated pan. Once bubbles begin to form in the center of the pancake, turn the pancake over to cook the other side until light brown. Remove from the heat and repeat with the rest of batter.

Nutrition Info per Serving:
Calories: 183, Protein: 6.7 g, Fat: 10.2 g, Carbohydrates: 15.9 g, Fiber: 0.5 g, Sugar: 3.3 g, Sodium: 261 mg

Coconut Whipped Cream

Prep Time: 5 minutes, Cook Time: 0, Serves: 5

INGREDIENTS:
1 cup (300 g) coconut cream
1 tsp. vanilla extract
2 tbsps. cocoa powder(optional)

DIRECTIONS:
1. Add all ingredients to large bowl and mix for about 5 minutes with an electrical mixer.
2. Serve the whipped cream chilled as a topping or a side!

Nutrition Info per Serving:
Calories: 40, Protein: 0 g, Fat: 1.5 g, Carbohydrates: 6.7 g, Fiber: 0 g, Sugar: 6.1 g, Sodium: 52 mg

Quick Hummus

Prep Time: 5 minutes, Cook Time: 5 minutes, Serves: 2 cups

INGREDIENTS:
1 (15-oz. 430g) can chickpeas, drained and rinsed
2 cloves garlic
¼ cup tahini
2 tbsps. apple cider
3 tbsps. water
1 tsp. ground cinnamon
Salt, to taste

DIRECTIONS:
1. Process all the ingredients on high in a food processor until completely smooth.

Nutrition Info per Serving:
Calories: 184, Protein: 7.1 g, Fat: 9.6 g, Carbohydrates: 19.6 g, Fiber: 5.8 g, Sugar: 3.4 g, Sodium: 250 mg

Homemade Popcorn

Prep Time: 1 minute, Cook Time: 5 minutes, Serves: 2

INGREDIENTS:
¼ cup popcorn kernels
¼ tsp. garlic powder
1 tbsp. nutritional yeast
¼ tsp. onion powder

DIRECTIONS:
1. In a paper lunch bag, add the popcorn kernels, folding over the top of the bag so the kernels won't spill out.
2. Microwave on high for 2 to 3 minutes, or until you hear a pause of 2 seconds in between kernels popping.
3. Take the bag out from the microwave, and add the garlic powder, nutritional yeast, and onion powder. Fold the top of the bag back over, shake to thoroughly coat.
4. Pour into a bowl and enjoy.

Nutrition Info per Serving:
Calories: 49, Protein: 4 g, Fat: 1 g, Carbohydrates: 6 g, Fiber: 2 g, Sugar: 3.2 g, Sodium: 30 mg

Easy Slow Cooker Spicy Peanuts

Prep Time: 10 minutes, Cook Time: 1 hour 15 minutes, Serves: 6

INGREDIENTS:
3 cups peanuts
2 tsps. extra virgin olive oil
½ tsp. smoked paprika
½ tsp. powdered garlic
½ tsp. cayenne powder
½ tsp. ground cumin
½ tsp. salt

DIRECTIONS:
1. In a slow cooker, add the peanuts and the oil, stir to make a little bit of oil on all the peanuts. It will be enough.
2. Place the spices in the cooker and stir.
3. Set on low and cook for 1 hour.
4. Uncover and then cook for another 15 minutes.

Nutrition Info per Serving:
Calories: 430, Protein: 19 g, Fat: 37.5 g, Carbohydrates: 12.2 g, Fiber: 6.4 g, Sugar: 3.5 g, Sodium: 208 mg

Pistachio and Coconut Ice Cream

Prep Time: 20 minutes, Cook Time: 60 minutes, Serves: 8

INGREDIENTS:
1 can (400 ml) low-fat coconut milk
10 medjool dates, pitted
2 scoops (60 g) organic pea protein
1 tbsp. (15 ml) vanilla extract
½ cup (50 g) pistachios, shelled

DIRECTIONS:
1. Add all ingredients to a medium bowl, cover it, and process with a handheld blender.
2. Freeze the mixture for 15 minutes, then stir it and freeze for another 10 minutes.
3. Add any desired toppings and freeze for at least 2 hours. Thaw for 5 minutes at room temperature before serving.

Nutrition Info per Serving:
Calories: 115, Protein: 8.8 g, Fat: 4.5 g, Carbohydrates: 10 g, Fiber: 1.9 g, Sugar: 3.8 g, Sodium: 46 mg

Easy Cold-Brew Peach Iced Tea

Prep Time: 10 minutes, plus 8 hours or overnight to steep, Cook Time: 0, Serves: 6

INGREDIENTS:
4 ripe peaches, sliced
8 cups water
5 tea bags (black, green, or white)

DIRECTIONS:
1. Combine the water, peach slices, and tea bags in a pitcher.
2. Place in the refrigerator, and allow to steep overnight, about 8 to 12 hours.
3. Keep in the refrigerator for up to 5 days.

Nutrition Info per Serving:
Calories: 39, Protein: 1 g, Fat: 0 g, Carbohydrates: 9 g, Fiber: 2 g, Sugar: 6.1 g, Sodium: 113 mg

Maple Lemon Ginger Tea

Prep Time: 5 minutes, Cook Time: 15 minutes, Serves: 2

INGREDIENTS:
4 cups water
1 tbsp. minced ginger
2 tbsps. freshly squeezed lemon juice
1 tbsp. maple syrup

DIRECTIONS:
1. Fill the water in a medium saucepan, bring to a boil. Remove from the heat and stir in the ginger, lemon juice and maple syrup. Cover and steep for 15 minutes.
2. Pour through a sieve to strain and enjoy hot, or allow to cool and pour over a glass filled with ice to enjoy as a cold drink.

Nutrition Info per Serving:
Calories: 36, Protein: 0 g, Fat: 0 g, Carbohydrates: 9 g, Fiber: 0 g, Sugar: 6.1 g, Sodium: 42 mg

Easy Watermelon Lemonade

Prep Time: 5 minutes, Cook Time: 0, Serves: 6

INGREDIENTS:
4 cups diced watermelon
2 tbsps. freshly squeezed lemon juice
1 tbsp. freshly squeezed lime juice
4 cups cold water

DIRECTIONS:
1. Add all of the ingredients in a blender, and blend for 1 minute.
2. Pour the contents through a fine-mesh sieve or nut-milk bag to strain.
3. Serve chilled.
4. Keep the lemonade in the refrigerator for up to 3 days.

Nutrition Info per Serving:
Calories: 64, Protein: 1 g, Fat: 0 g, Carbohydrates: 15 g, Fiber: 1 g, Sugar: 9.8 g, Sodium: 47 mg

Strawberry and Watermelon Ice Pops

Prep Time: 5 minutes, plus at least 6 hours to freeze, Cook Time: 0, Serves: 6

INGREDIENTS:
4 strawberries, tops removed
4 cups diced watermelon
2 tbsps. freshly squeezed lime juice

DIRECTIONS:
1. Add the strawberries, watermelon, and lime juice in a blender. Blend for 1 to 2 minutes, or until well combined.
2. Evenly pour into 6 ice-pop molds, insert the ice-pop sticks, and freeze for at least 6 hours and serve.

Nutrition Info per Serving:
Calories: 64, Protein: 1 g, Fat: 0 g, Carbohydrates: 15 g, Fiber: 1 g, Sugar: 7.2 g, Sodium: 23 mg

Mixed Berry Pudding

Prep Time: 5 minutes, Cook Time: 0, Serves: 2

INGREDIENTS:
3 bananas (peeled)
2 scoops (60 g) soy protein isolate (chocolate flavor)
¼ cup (32 g) flaxseeds
1 cup (140 g) mixed berries
3 cups (720 ml) water

DIRECTIONS:
1. Add all ingredients to a blender and blend until smooth. Or blend the berries and 2 tbsps. of flaxseeds first and half fill two glasses with the berry mix.
2. Blend the remaining ingredients later, and top the berry mix with the banana protein mix.
3. Serve with optional toppings.

Nutrition Info per Serving:
Calories: 427, Protein: 32.3 g, Fat: 7.3 g, Carbohydrates: 53.3 g, Fiber: 11.2 g, Sugar: 26.9 g, Sodium: 93 mg

Homemade Easy Cashew Milk

Prep Time: 5 minutes, Cook Time: 2 minutes, Serves: 8

INGREDIENTS:
¼ cup raw cashews, soaked overnight
4 cups water

DIRECTIONS:
1. Combine the cashews and water in a blender, and blend on high speed for 2 minutes, until creamy.
2. Pour through a nut-milk bag or cheesecloth to strain, and keep in the refrigerator for up to 5 days.

Nutrition Info per Serving:
Calories: 26, Protein: 1 g, Fat: 2 g, Carbohydrates: 1 g, Fiber: 0 g, Sugar: 1 g, Sodium: 27 mg

Homemade Maple Cinnamon Latte

Prep Time: 5 minutes, Cook Time: 5 minutes, Serves: 2

INGREDIENTS:
3 cups plant-based milk
1 tbsp. maple syrup
1 tsp. ground cinnamon

DIRECTIONS:
1. Add the milk in a medium saucepan on the stovetop, heat until it just begins to boil, or microwave in a microwave-safe bowl on high for 2 minutes.
2. In a blender, add the warmed milk, cinnamon and maple syrup, and blend for 1 to 2 minutes, or until the mixture turns frothy.
3. Serve warm.

Nutrition Info per Serving:
Calories: 97, Protein: 2 g, Fat: 5 g, Carbohydrates: 11 g, Fiber: 2 g, Sugar: 22.8 g, Sodium: 89 mg

Lemony Tahini Cream

Prep Time: 5 minutes, Cook Time: 0, Serves: 6

INGREDIENTS:
½ cup (120 g) Tahini
3 dates (pitted)
½ cup (120 ml) water
¼ cup (60 ml) lemon juice
2 cloves garlic
6 leaves mint

DIRECTIONS:
1. Add all ingredients to a food processor and blend to form a thick and smooth sauce.

Nutrition Info per Serving:
Calories: 141, Protein: 5.1 g, Fat: 11.3 g, Carbohydrates: 4.8 g, Fiber: 1 g, Sugar: 3.7 g, Sodium: 56 mg

Homemade Bubbly Orange Soda

Prep Time: 5 minutes, Cook Time: 0, Serves: 4

INGREDIENTS:
2 cups pulp-free orange juice (4 oranges, freshly squeezed and strained)
4 cups carbonated water

DIRECTIONS:
1. For each serving, pour 2 parts carbonated water and 1 part orange juice over the ice in the glass right before serving.
2. Stir well and serve.

Nutrition Info per Serving:
Calories: 56, Protein: 1 g, Fat: 0 g, Carbohydrates: 13 g, Fiber: 0 g, Sugar: 16.3 g, Sodium: 86 mg

Easy Oat Milk

Prep Time: 5 minutes, plus 15 minutes to soak, Cook Time: 3 minutes, Serves: 8

INGREDIENTS:
1 cup rolled oats
4 cups water

DIRECTIONS:
1. In a medium bowl, add the oats, pour in the water to cover. Allow the oats to soak for 15 minutes, then drain and rinse.
2. In a blender, add the soaked oats and cold water. Blend for 60 to 90 seconds, or just until the mixture is a creamy white color throughout. (Overblend the oats, resulting in a gummy milk.)
3. Pour through a nut-milk bag or colander to strain, and keep in the refrigerator for up to 5 days.

Nutrition Info per Serving:
Calories: 41, Protein: 1 g, Fat: 1 g, Carbohydrates: 7 g, Fiber: 1 g, Sugar: 0.6 g, Sodium: 77 mg

Chapter 12 Smoothie 171

Chapter 12 Smoothie

Blueberry Lychee Smoothie

Prep Time: 10 minutes, Cook Time: 10 minutes, Serves: 1

INGREDIENTS:
- ½ cup chopped frozen blueberries
- ½ cup frozen lychee, peeled and seeded
- 1½ cups unsweetened peanut milk, plus more as needed
- ½ cup raisins

DIRECTIONS:
1. Mix all ingredients in a food processor and process until smooth and creamy. Add more peanut milk, if needed, to achieve a smooth consistency.

Nutrition Info per Serving:
Calories: 204, Protein: 13.1 g, Fat: 0.4 g, Carbohydrates: 39.2 g, Fiber: 3.3 g, Sugar: 33.4 g, Sodium: 157 mg

Pineapple Mango Smoothie Bowl

Prep Time: 5 minutes, Cook Time: 0, Serves: 2

INGREDIENTS:
- 1 cup frozen mango chunks
- 2 bananas, sliced and frozen
- 1 (20-ounce, 567 g) can pineapple chunks, drained
- 1 tsp. vanilla extract
- 1 (14-ounce, 397 g) can full-fat coconut milk
- Water, for thinning (optional)
- Cashew butter, for garnish
- Hemp seeds, for garnish
- Chia seeds, for garnish (optional)
- Fresh pitted cherries, for garnish (optional)
- Starfruit slices, for garnish (optional)

DIRECTIONS:
1. Add the mango, bananas, pineapple, vanilla and coconut milk in a high-speed blender or food processor, blend until smooth. This smoothie will be thick and may require several starts and stops to scrape the sides down. Add water to thin if it seems too thick.
2. Serve in a bowl, and place the cashew butter, hemp seeds, chia seeds, cherries and starfruit (if using) on the top.

Nutrition Info per Serving:
Calories: 718, Protein: 5 g, Fat: 38 g, Carbohydrates: 89 g, Fiber: 8 g, Sugar: 18.3 g, Sodium: 291 mg

Fruity Vitamin C Smoothie

Prep Time: 5 minutes, Cook Time: 0, Serves: 2

INGREDIENTS:
- 2 cups frozen spinach
- 1 large navel orange, peeled and segmented
- 1 cup frozen mango chunks
- 2 bananas
- 2 celery stalks, broken into pieces
- 2 tbsps. cashew butter or almond butter
- 1 tbsp. ground flaxseed
- 1 tbsp. spirulina
- 1 cup plant-based milk, plus more as needed
- Water, for thinning (optional)

DIRECTIONS:
1. Combine all of the ingredients except the water in a high-speed blender or food processor.
2. Blend until creamy, if the smoothie is too thick, add more milk or water.
3. Serve immediately.

Nutrition Info per Serving:
Calories: 432, Protein: 13 g, Fat: 12 g, Carbohydrates: 68 g, Fiber: 13 g, Sugar: 14.8 g, Sodium: 156 mg

Raspberry Acai Smoothie Bowl

Prep Time: 5 minutes, Cook Time: 0, Serves: 1

INGREDIENTS:
- 1 medium ripe banana
- 2 (100g) packets açaí pureé
- ½ cup (125ml) coconut yogurt
- Maple Cinnamon Granola
- Raspberries
- Hazelnuts
- Shredded coconut

DIRECTIONS:
1. Slice the banana into chunks and store in a small freezer-safe container or plastic zip-top bag. Transfer to the freezer until frozen, at least 30 minutes. (Slice and freeze as many bananas as you will need for the week.)
2. To prepare, mix the frozen banana, açaí pureé, and coconut yogurt in a processor. Process until smooth. Pour into a bowl or glass and top with granola, raspberries, hazelnuts, shredded coconut. Serve immediately.

Nutrition Info per Serving:
Calories: 320, Protein: 3 g, Fat: 8 g, Carbohydrates: 59 g, Fiber: 7 g, Sugar: 40 g, Sodium: 73 mg

Vanilla Fruit Smoothie

Prep Time: 5 minutes, Cook Time: 0, Serves: 2

INGREDIENTS:

1 frozen banana
2 cups plant-based milk
½ cup frozen pineapple chunks
½ cup frozen mango chunks
1 tsp. vanilla extract

DIRECTIONS:
1. Combine all of the ingredients in a blender.
2. Blend on high for 1 to 2 minutes, or until smooth and creamy.
3. Serve immediately.

Nutrition Info per Serving:
Calories: 186, Protein: 2 g, Fat: 4 g, Carbohydrates: 36 g, Fiber: 4 g, Sugar: 20.6 g, Sodium: 149 mg

Snow Pear Mint Smoothie

Prep Time: 10 minutes, Cook Time: 10 minutes, Serves: 1

INGREDIENTS:

1 cup (240mL) unsweetened peanut milk, or water
½ cup (120mL) snow pear puree
½ cup ice cubes
4 Medjool dates, pitted and chopped, or to taste
¼ tsp. maple syrup
¼ tsp. ground mint
Pinch ground nutmeg

DIRECTIONS:
1. Mix all ingredients in a food processor and process until smooth and creamy.

Nutrition Info per Serving:
Calories: 422, Protein: 11 g, Fat: 1.2 g, Carbohydrates: 91.9 g, Fiber: 8.6 g, Sugar: 79 g, Sodium: 106 mg

Vanilla Green Chocolate Smoothie

Prep Time: 5 minutes, Cook Time: 0, Serves: 2

INGREDIENTS:

2 very ripe frozen bananas, halved
6 ounces (170 g) greens (kale, collards, or spinach)
3 cups plant-based milk
1 tsp. vanilla extract
2 tbsps. cocoa powder

DIRECTIONS:
1. Add all of the ingredients in a blender.
2. Blend on high for 1 to 2 minutes, or until smooth and creamy.
3. Serve immediately.

Nutrition Info per Serving:
Calories: 246, Protein: 6 g, Fat: 6 g, Carbohydrates: 42 g, Fiber: 8 g, Sugar: 34.3 g, Sodium: 152 mg

Vanilla Apple Pie Smoothie

Prep Time: 5 minutes, Cook Time: 2 minutes, Serves: 2

INGREDIENTS:

2 sweet crisp apples, cut into 1-inch cubes
2 cups plant-based milk
1 tsp. ground cinnamon
1 tbsp. maple syrup
1 tsp. vanilla extract
1 cup ice

DIRECTIONS:
1. Combine all of the ingredients in a blender.
2. Blend on high for 1 to 2 minutes, or until smooth and creamy.
3. Serve immediately.

Nutrition Info per Serving:
Calories: 208, Protein: 3 g, Fat: 6 g, Carbohydrates: 32 g, Fiber: 8 g, Sugar: 22.5 g, Sodium: 97 mg

Tropical Smoothie Bowl with Pine nuts

Prep Time: 5 minutes, Cook Time: 2 minutes, Serves: 1 bite

INGREDIENTS:

1 cups frozen mango chunks
½ cup frozen pineapple chunks
2 frozen guava chunks
½–1 cup plant-based milk
2 tbsps. chopped nuts of your choice
¼ cup chopped fruit of your choice
1 tbsp. raisins
1½ tbsps. Pine nuts

DIRECTIONS:
1. Add the mango, pineapple, guava, and milk (1 cup makes it a thinner smoothie and ½ cup makes it thicker) to a food processor and process until smooth.
2. Transfer the smoothie into a bowl and top with the nuts and fruit.

Nutrition Info per Serving:
Calories: 312, Protein: 7 g, Fat: 5.6 g, Carbohydrates: 63.8 g, Fiber: 4.9 g, Sugar: 58.2 g, Sodium: 62 mg

Banana Mint Smoothie

Prep Time: 5 minutes, Cook Time: 0, Serves: 2

INGREDIENTS:
2 frozen bananas, halved
2 cups plant-based milk
1 tsp. vanilla extract
1 tbsp. fresh mint leaves or ¼ tsp. peppermint extract

DIRECTIONS:
1. Add all of the ingredients in a blender.
2. Blend on high for 1 to 2 minutes, or until smooth and creamy.
3. Serve immediately.

Nutrition Info per Serving:
Calories: 164, Protein: 2 g, Fat: 4 g, Carbohydrates: 30 g, Fiber: 4 g, Sugar: 10 g, Sodium: 49 mg

Strawberry Banana Smoothie

Prep Time: 5 minutes, Cook Time: 0, Serves: 2

INGREDIENTS:
1 cup (150 g) strawberries
1 cup (225 g) spinach
2 bananas
2 scoops (60 g) pea protein
¼ cup (30 g) flaxseeds
2 cups (480 ml) water

DIRECTIONS:
1. Add all ingredients to a blender and blend until smooth.
2. Serve with the optional toppings.

Nutrition Info per Serving:
Calories: 379, Protein: 30.8 g, Fat: 9.7 g, Carbohydrates: 42.3 g, Fiber: 11.2 g, Sugar: 18.6 g, Sodium: 132 mg

Banana, Peanut Butter and Chia Smoothie

Prep Time: 5 minutes, Cook Time: 3 minutes, Serves: 2

INGREDIENTS:
3 frozen bananas, halved
2 tbsps. defatted peanut powder
1 cup plant-based milk
1 tsp. vanilla extract
½ tbsp. chia seeds

DIRECTIONS:
1. Place all of the ingredients except the chia seeds in a blender or food processor. Blend on high for 1 to 2 minutes.
2. Add the chia seeds, pulse 2 to 4 times, or until the chia seeds have evenly dispersed without being blended up, and serve.

Nutrition Info per Serving:
Calories: 271, Protein: 11 g, Fat: 5 g, Carbohydrates: 47 g, Fiber: 8 g, Sugar: 12.9 g, Sodium: 83 mg

Raspberry Banana Smoothie

Prep Time: 5 minutes, Cook Time: 0, Serves: 1

INGREDIENTS:
1 medium banana
½ cup frozen wild raspberries
½ cup frozen kiwifruit chunks
1 cup (240ml) almond milk

DIRECTIONS:
1. Cut the banana into chunks and place in a small freezer-safe container or plastic zip-top bag along with the raspberries and kiwifruit. Keep frozen until ready to use. (Prepare as many bags as you will need for the week.)
2. To prepare, place all ingredients in a processor and process until smooth. Serve immediately.

Nutrition Info per Serving:
Calories: 253, Protein: 2 g, Fat: 1 g, Carbohydrates: 59 g, Fiber: 7 g, Sugar: 39 g, Sodium: 95 mg

Peanut Butter Creamy Banana Smoothie

Prep Time: 5 minutes, Cook Time: 0, Serves: 2

INGREDIENTS:
3 tbsps. plant-based milk
3 frozen ripe bananas, broken into thirds
2 tbsps. defatted peanut powder
1 tsp. vanilla extract

DIRECTIONS:
1. Add the milk, bananas, peanut powder, and vanilla in a food processor.
2. Process on medium speed for 30 to 60 seconds, or until smooth, and serve. (If there is any banana pieces stuck toward the top and sides of the food processor, stop and use a spatula to scrape them down, then pulse until smooth.)

Nutrition Info per Serving:
Calories: 247, Protein: 10 g, Fat: 3 g, Carbohydrates: 45 g, Fiber: 7 g, Sugar: 8.6 g, Sodium: 125 mg

Blueberry Lychee Smoothie, page 172

Chocolate Peanut Milk Smoothie, page 176

Orange Pineapple Smoothie, page 177

Strawberry Banana Smoothie, page 174

Chapter 12 Smoothie 175

Chocolate Avocado Smoothie

Prep Time: 5 minutes, Cook Time: 0, Serves: 2

INGREDIENTS:

1 cup (225 g) Spinach (fresh or frozen)
2 scoops (60 g) soy protein isolate (chocolate flavor)
2 bananas peeled
1 small avocado, peeled, stoned
¼ cup (30 g) flaxseeds
3 cups (720 ml) water

DIRECTIONS:

1. Add all ingredients to a blender and blend until smooth.
2. Serve with the optional toppings.

Nutrition Info per Serving:
Calories: 433, Protein: 35.6 g, Fat: 16.2 g, Carbohydrates: 36.1 g, Fiber: 12.9 g, Sugar: 15.8 g, Sodium: 136 mg

Ginger Raisin Smoothie

Prep Time: 5 minutes, Cook Time: 5 minutes, Serves: 1

INGREDIENTS:

1½ cups unsweetened peanut milk, or water
1 tsp. unsulfured molasses, or to taste (see more about sulfites and sulfur dioxide)
1 tbsp. raisins
½-inch piece ginger, peeled and grated
Dash ground cinnamon
2 to 3 ice cubes

DIRECTIONS:

1. Mix all ingredients in a food processor and process until smooth and creamy.

Nutrition Info per Serving:
Calories: 223, Protein: 15.6 g, Fat: 1.8 g, Carbohydrates: 36.1 g, Fiber: 11.7 g, Sugar: 69.2 g, Sodium: 199 mg

Chocolate Peanut Milk Smoothie

Prep Time: 5 minutes, Cook Time: 0, Serves: 1

INGREDIENTS:

2 bananas, about 7 oz. (200g) total
1 cup (240ml) peanut milk
2 tbsps. maple syrup
1 tsp. cacao powder

DIRECTIONS:

1. Cut the bananas into chunks and transfer to a small freezer-safe container or plastic zip-top bag. Keep in the freezer until frozen, at least 30 minutes. (Slice and freeze as many bananas as you will need for the week.)
2. To prepare, mix all ingredients in a food processor and process until smooth. Serve immediately.

Nutrition Info per Serving:
Calories: 500, Protein: 14 g, Fat: 24 g, Carbohydrates: 57 g, Fiber: 11 g, Sugar: 26 g, Sodium: 218 mg

Gingerbread Smoothie

Prep Time: 5 minutes, Cook Time: 0, Serves: 2

INGREDIENTS:

2 scoops (60 g) soy protein isolate (chocolate flavor)
2 bananas, peeled
1 medium avocado, peeled, stoned
2 tbsps. chia seeds
2 tbsps. 5-spice powder
3 cups (720 ml) water

DIRECTIONS:

1. Add all ingredients to a blender and blend until smooth.
2. Serve with the optional toppings.

Nutrition Info per Serving:
Calories: 392, Protein: 31.2 g, Fat: 13.4 g, Carbohydrates: 36.4 g, Fiber: 10.2 g, Sugar: 14.4 g, Sodium: 94 mg

Vanilla Banana Breakfast Smoothie

Prep Time: 10 minutes, Cook Time: 0, Serves: 1

INGREDIENTS:

1 cup vanilla almond milk
1 frozen banana, sliced
¼ cup old-fashioned oats
¼ cup raisins
3 tbsps. vanilla protein powder
1 tbsp. flaxseed meal
¼ tsp. cinnamon

DIRECTIONS:

1. In a blender, add all of the ingredients.
2. Blend until very smooth.
3. Serve immediately.

Nutrition Info per Serving:
Calories: 375, Protein: 22.5 g, Fat: 9.2 g, Carbohydrates: 63 g, Fiber: 11.4 g, Sugar: 30 g, Sodium: 185 mg

Papaya Smoothie

Prep Time: 3 minutes, Cook Time: 1 minute, Serves: 2 bites

INGREDIENTS:
1 sliced frozen papaya
1½ cups kale, stems removed
1½ cups plant-based milk
1 tbsp. flaxseed meal

DIRECTIONS:
1. Process all the ingredients on high in a food processor until smooth.

Nutrition Info per Serving:
Calories: 293, Protein: 9.3 g, Fat: 6.9 g, Carbohydrates: 53.6 g, Fiber: 8.5 g, Sugar: 40.1 g, Sodium: 123 mg

Orange Pineapple Smoothie

Prep Time: 5 minutes, Cook Time: 0, Serves: 2

INGREDIENTS:
1 cup (225 g) pineapple chunks
2 oranges, peeled and quartered
2 scoops (60 g) pea protein
¼ cup (30 g) flaxseeds
2 cups (480 ml) water

DIRECTIONS:
1. Put all ingredients to a blender and blend until smooth.
2. Serve with the optional toppings.

Nutrition Info per Serving:
Calories: 335, Protein: 27.8 g, Fat: 8.8 g, Carbohydrates: 36.1 g, Fiber: 8.2 g, Sugar: 23.7 g, Sodium: 85 mg

Mango Raisin Smoothie

Prep Time: 10 minutes, Cook Time: 10 minutes, Serves: 1

INGREDIENTS:
1 cup (240mL) unsweetened almond butter, plus more as needed
2 medium frozen mangoes, peeled, seeded and cut into chunks
1 tbsp. mint
½ cup raisins
1 tbsp. apple cider

DIRECTIONS:
1. Combine all ingredients in a blender and process until smooth and creamy. Add more almond milk as needed to achieve a smooth consistency.

Nutrition Info per Serving:
Calories: 408, Protein: 13.3 g, Fat: 4.8 g, Carbohydrates: 82 g, Fiber: 8.9 g, Sugar: 52 g, Sodium: 373 mg

Savory Tropical Green Smoothie

Prep Time: 10 minutes, Cook Time: 10 minutes, Serves: 1

INGREDIENTS:
2 cups tightly packed radicchio
1 cup frozen lychee
1 cup frozen mango chunks
1 small orange, peeled and pitted,
1 cup (240mL) apple cider
¼ tsp. cayenne pepper

DIRECTIONS:
1. Mix all ingredients in a food processor and process on high until smooth. Enjoy cold.

Nutrition Info per Serving:
Calories: 283, Protein: 6.4 g, Fat: 1.8 g, Carbohydrates: 67.9 g, Fiber: 10.4 g, Sugar: 53.4 g, Sodium: 304 mg

Chapter 13 Sauce and Dressing

Garlicky Harissa Sauce

Prep Time: 10 minutes, Cook Time: 20 minutes, Serves: 3 to 4 cups

INGREDIENTS:

1 large red bell pepper, seeded, cored, and cut into chunks
4 garlic cloves, peeled
1 yellow onion, cut into thick rings
2 tbsps. tomato paste
1 cup no-sodium vegetable broth or water
1 tsp. ground cumin
1 tbsp. low-sodium soy sauce or tamari
1 tbsp. Hungarian paprika

DIRECTIONS:

1. Preheat the oven to 450°F(235°C). Use parchment paper or aluminum foil to line a baking sheet.
2. On the prepared baking sheet, add the bell pepper, flesh-side up, and space out the garlic and onion around the pepper.
3. Roast on the middle rack for 20 minutes. Then transfer to a blender.
4. Add the remaining ingredients to the blender, puree until smooth. Serve cold or warm.
5. Place in an airtight container and refrigerate for up to 2 weeks or freeze for up to 6 months.

Nutrition Info per Serving:
Calories: 21, Protein: 1 g, Fat: 0.5 g, Carbohydrates: 3 g, Fiber: 1 g, Sugar: 1 g, Sodium: 72 mg

Cabbage Alfredo Sauce

Prep Time: 2 minutes, Cook Time: 0, Serves: 4 cups

INGREDIENTS:

3 cups (710mL) unsweetened peanut milk
2 cups cabbage
1 tsp. Salt
2 tbsps. olive oil
5 garlic cloves, mince
¼ tsp. freshly ground black pepper
Juice of 1 lime
4 tbsps. nutritional yeast

DIRECTIONS:

1. Heat the olive oil in a medium saucepan over medium-high heat. Sprinkle the garlic and sauté for 1 minute or until fragrant. Pour in the peanut milk, stir, and bring to a boil.
2. Carefully add the cabbage. Drizzle with the salt and pepper and bring to a boil. Continue to cook over medium-high heat for 5 minutes or until the cabbage is tender. Stir often and lower the heat if needed to keep the liquid from boiling over.
3. Carefully transfer the cabbage and cooking liquid to a blender, scoop out the larger pieces of cabbage using a slotted spoon before pouring in the liquid. Pour in the lime and nutritional yeast and puree for 1–2 minutes, until smooth and creamy.

Nutrition Info per Serving:
Calories: 107, Protein: 4 g, Fat: 7 g, Carbohydrates: 7 g, Fiber: 3 g, Sugar: 1 g, Sodium: 71 mg

Garlicky Roasted Red Pepper Hummus

Prep Time: 20 minutes, Cook Time: 0, Serves: 8

INGREDIENTS:

1 (15-ounce, 425 g) can chickpeas, 3 tbsps. aquafaba (chickpea liquid from the can) reserved, remaining liquid drained, rinsed
1 tbsp. freshly squeezed lemon juice
¼ cup tahini
½ tsp. ground cumin
1 tsp. Hungarian paprika
2 garlic cloves, peeled and stemmed
¼ tsp. freshly ground black pepper
2 roasted red peppers

DIRECTIONS:

1. In a bowl, add the chickpeas and fill in the water. Gently rub the chickpeas between your hands until you feel the skins coming off. Add more water and allow the skins to float to the surface. Scoop out the skins with your hand. Drain some of the water and repeat this step once more to remove as many of the chickpea skins as possible. Drain well and set the chickpeas aside.
2. Combine the reserved aquafaba, lemon juice and tahini in a food processor or high-speed blender. Process for 2 minutes.
3. Add the cumin, paprika, garlic, black pepper, and red peppers. Puree until the red peppers are incorporated.
4. Mix in the chickpeas and blend for 2 to 3 minutes, or until the hummus is smooth.
5. Serve immediately and refrigerate the leftovers in an airtight container for up to 1 week.

Nutrition Info per Serving:
Calories: 109, Protein: 4 g, Fat: 5 g, Carbohydrates: 11 g, Fiber: 3 g, Sugar: 1.5 g, Sodium: 37 mg

Refried Lentil Pepper Dip

Prep Time: 25 minutes, Cook Time: 25 minutes, Serves: 4

INGREDIENTS:
2 cups water
½ cup dried brown or green lentils, rinsed
1 jalapeño pepper, stemmed
1 (4-ounce, 113 g) can diced green chiles
½ cup cashew sour cream
½ tsp. garlic powder
1 tsp. onion powder

DIRECTIONS:
1. Preheat the broiler.
2. Fill the water in an 8-quart pot, bring to a boil over high heat. Add the lentils, lower the heat to maintain a simmer, cover and cook for 15 to 20 minutes. The lentils should be soft and squishable. Drain and set aside.
3. Meanwhile, use aluminum foil to wrap the jalapeño pepper to prevent it from burning. Place it under the broiler for 5 minutes. Turn the jalapeño pepper and cook for another 2 minutes. Remove and set aside.
4. Combine the cooked lentils, roasted jalapeño pepper, green chiles, cashew sour cream, garlic powder, and onion powder in a high-speed blender or food processor. Puree until the dip achieves desired smoothness.
5. Serve warm or cold with pita, chips, spread on a wrap, or as a dip for crudités, as desired.

Nutrition Info per Serving:
Calories: 183, Protein: 9 g, Fat: 7 g, Carbohydrates: 21 g, Fiber: 5 g, Sugar: 4.8 g, Sodium: 74 mg

Chickpea Avocado Guacamole

Prep Time: 15 minutes, plus 1 hour to chill, Cook Time: 0, Serves: 4

INGREDIENTS:
1 (15-ounce, 425 g) can chickpeas
2 large ripe avocados, halved and pitted
½ small red onion, diced
3 garlic cloves, minced
¼ cup packed chopped fresh cilantro
½ small red bell pepper, diced
Juice of 1 lime
½ tsp. ground cumin
1 jalapeño pepper, seeded and minced (optional)

DIRECTIONS:
1. Drain, rinse, and peel the chickpeas. You can leave the skins on for added fiber, but your guacamole will be smoother if you remove the skins. Transfer to a large bowl. Crush the chickpeas with a potato masher.
2. Scoop the avocado flesh into the chickpeas bowl and mash to your preferred texture.
3. Stir in the red onion, garlic, cilantro, bell pepper, cumin, lime juice, and jalapeño pepper (if using) with a spatula or spoon. Scoop the guacamole into a sealable container and refrigerate for at least 1 hour to allow the flavors to combine.
4. Place the leftovers in an airtight container and store in the refrigerator. It is best if eaten within 2 to 3 days but will keep for up 1 week.

Nutrition Info per Serving:
Calories: 266, Protein: 7 g, Fat: 17 g, Carbohydrates: 27 g, Fiber: 12 g, Sugar: 3.1 g, Sodium: 315 mg

Mixed Vegetable and Cashew Sauce

Prep Time: 10 minutes, Cook Time: 25 minutes, Serves: 4 cups

INGREDIENTS:
1 russet potato, peeled and cubed
1 cup raw cashews
2 carrots, cubed
½ cup nutritional yeast
2 cups unsweetened oat milk (or almond or cashew if gluten-free)
1 tsp. ground mustard
2 tbsps. yellow (mellow) miso paste
1 tbsp. arrowroot powder, cornstarch, or tapioca starch
1 onion, chopped
3 garlic cloves, minced
1 tbsp. water, plus more as needed

DIRECTIONS:
1. Combine the potato, cashews, and carrots in an 8-quart pot. Fill in the water to cover by 2 inches. Bring to a boil over high heat, then lower the heat to simmer. Cook for 15 minutes.
2. Add the nutritional yeast, milk, ground mustard, miso paste, and arrowroot powder in a blender.
3. Drain the potato, cashews, and carrot well and add to the blender but don't blend yet.
4. Rinse the pot, heat it over high heat, and add the garlic and onion. Cook for 3 to 4 minutes, adding water 1 tbsp. at a time to prevent burning. Transfer to the blender. Puree everything until smooth. Scrape the sides and continue blending as needed. Pour the cheese sauce into the pot and place it over medium heat. Cook until the sauce comes to a simmer, stirring often.
5. Use immediately, or place in a sealable container and refrigerate for up to 1 week.

Nutrition Info per Serving:
Calories: 211, Protein: 9 g, Fat: 10 g, Carbohydrates: 20 g, Fiber: 4 g, Sugar: 3.5 g, Sodium: 139 mg

Spicy Tempeh

Prep Time: 70 minutes, Cook Time: 40 minutes, Serves: 4

INGREDIENTS:

2 cups (400 g) pinto beans, cooked or canned
7-oz (200 g) pack tempeh
2 cups (360 g) tomato cubes, canned or fresh
2 cups (180 g) sweet corn, cooked or canned
6 tbsps. (60 g) Mexican chili spices
3 cups (720 ml) water

DIRECTIONS:

1. Soak and cook 133 g dry pinto beans according to the method.
2. Cut the tempeh into bits, put them into an airtight container and add 20g Mexican chili spices.
3. Shake well and put it in the fridge, let tempeh marinate for at least 1 hour, and up to 12 hours.
4. Put the water, tempeh cubes and the pinto beans in a large pot over medium-high heat.
5. After the stock is boiling, cook for 15 minutes.
6. Turn down the heat to a simmer and mix the tomato cubes, remaining Mexican spices and corn in the pot.
7. Stir well, then let it simmer for 20 minutes.
8. Turn the heat off and cool down for 5 minutes.
9. Divide between two bowls, serve with the optional toppings.

Nutrition Info per Serving:
Calories: 298, Protein: 21 g, Fat: 4.1 g, Carbohydrates: 44.2 g, Fiber: 14.8 g, Sugar: 6 g, Sodium: 261 mg

Spinach, Artichoke and Quinoa Dip

Prep Time: 20 minutes, Cook Time: 25 minutes, Serves: 4

INGREDIENTS:

½ cup quinoa
1 tbsp. extra virgin olive oil
½ cup diced onion
4 ounces (113 g) baby spinach, with stems chopped off
¼ cup raw shelled hempseed
½ tsp. garlic powder
½ tsp. onion powder
1 tsp. salt
¼ tsp. ground black pepper
1 tbsp. lemon juice
8 ounces (227 g) artichoke hearts in water, drained

DIRECTIONS:

1. Put quinoa in a sieve and rinse well. In a small saucepan, combine the quinoa and 1 cup water. Bring to a boil, cover, and reduce the heat to maintain a simmer. Cook for 10 to 15 minutes or until the liquid is absorbed. Remove from the heat, cover and set aside for 5 minutes. Remove the lid and fluff.
2. Add the oil in a large skillet and heat it over medium-high heat. Add the onion, reduce the heat to medium, and sauté for 10 minutes. Stir in the spinach and cook for 1 minutes until wilted. Add the hempseed and spices and stir in quickly. Remove from the heat.
3. Cut off the top of the artichoke hearts. Discard the toughest of the outside leaves.
4. In a food processor, add everything. Process until well combined and chopped very small.
5. Serve with the pita chips.

Nutrition Info per Serving:
Calories: 180, Protein: 15.4 g, Fat: 5.7 g, Carbohydrates: 17.9 g, Fiber: 2.8 g, Sugar: 0.9 g, Sodium: 649 mg

White Bean, Pumpkin, Spinach and Artichoke Dip

Prep Time: 10 minutes, Cook Time: 15 minutes, Serves: 8

INGREDIENTS:

3 garlic cloves, coarsely chopped
½ yellow onion, peeled and sliced
1 tbsp. water
½ cup nutritional yeast
1 (15-ounce, 425 g) can cannellini beans, drained and rinsed
1 tbsp. tapioca starch
2 tbsps. yellow (mellow) miso paste
1 cup unsweetened oat milk
1 (15-ounce, 425 g) can pumpkin
1 (1-pound, 454 g) package chopped frozen spinach
1 (14-ounce, 397 g) can quartered artichoke hearts, drained

DIRECTIONS:

1. Add the garlic, onion and water into a medium nonstick sauté pan or skillet, cook over high heat for 3 minutes, or until the onion is translucent and just beginning to brown. Transfer to a blender and add the nutritional yeast, cannellini beans, tapioca starch, miso paste, oat milk, and pumpkin. Puree until smooth. Set aside.
2. Place the pan back to medium heat and stir in the spinach. Cook for 4 to 7 minutes, stirring, to thaw the spinach.
3. Add the puree mixture, stir well. Cook for 3 to 5 minutes until the dip begins to bubble and thicken, stirring occasionally. Add the artichoke hearts and stir to combine. Serve warm.

Nutrition Info per Serving:
Calories: 158, Protein: 12 g, Fat: 2 g, Carbohydrates: 23 g, Fiber: 9 g, Sugar: 5.5 g, Sodium: 363 mg

Chapter 13 Sauce and Dressing

Almond Butter Apple Sauce

Prep Time: 10 minutes, Cook Time: 15 minutes, Serves: 16

INGREDIENTS:
4 large apples
½ cup (130 g) almond butter
¼ cup (40 g) raisins
1 tbsp. (10 g) cinnamon
½ cup (120 ml) water

DIRECTIONS:
1. Cut the core and peeled apples into small pieces and put them in the saucepan.
2. Add water and cook over low heat with saucepan lid covered and bring it to a boil.
3. Cook the apples for 15 minutes or until they are soft. Turn off the heat and mash the apples with a potato masher or a fork.
4. Add the almond butter and stir thoroughly until well mixed.
5. If the sauce is too thick, then add more water. Then put in the raisins and cinnamon.
6. Stir and make it mixed thoroughly, serve.

Nutrition Info per Serving:
Calories: 91, Protein: 2 g, Fat: 4.1 g, Carbohydrates: 11.7 g, Fiber: 2.1 g, Sugar: 7.8 g, Sodium: 43 mg

Roasted Garlic Lemon Dressing

Prep Time: 5 minutes, Cook Time: 30 minutes, Serves: 1 cup

INGREDIENTS:
1 head garlic
1 tbsp. white balsamic vinegar
½ cup water
1 tbsp. freshly squeezed lemon juice
1 tbsp. maple syrup

DIRECTIONS:
1. Preheat the oven to 400°F(205°C).
2. Remove the outermost paper-like covering from the head of garlic while still leaving the bulbs intact to the base. Slice the top of the head of garlic so that the flesh inside the bulbs is just showing.
3. Use parchment paper to double-wrap the head of garlic and place it on a baking sheet. Bake for 30 minutes.
4. Take the garlic out from the oven, and unwrap the parchment paper. Squeeze the head of garlic from the base to remove the caramelized cloves. They should slide out easily.
5. Combine the caramelized garlic cloves, vinegar, water, lemon juice, and maple syrup in a blender. Blend on high for 1 minute, or until the dressing has a creamy consistency.
6. Use immediately, or keep in a refrigerator-safe container for up to 5 days.

Nutrition Info per Serving:
Calories: 12, Protein: 0 g, Fat: 0 g, Carbohydrates: 3 g, Fiber: 0 g, Sugar: 3.9 g, Sodium: 16 mg

Homemade Mole Sauce

Prep Time: 40 minutes, Cook Time: 25 minutes, Serves: 4 cups

INGREDIENTS:
2 dried ancho chiles
4 dried pasilla chiles
Boiling water, for soaking the peppers
6 garlic cloves, coarsely chopped
1 yellow onion, cut into slices
1 tbsp. water, plus more as needed
2 tbsps. tomato paste
1 jalapeño pepper, seeded and chopped
2 tbsps. whole wheat flour
2 ounces (57 g) vegan dark chocolate
2 tbsps. almond butter
2 tbsps. cocoa powder
1 tsp. ground cumin
2 tsps. smoked paprika
½ tsp. dried oregano
1 tsp. ground cinnamon
2½ cups no-sodium vegetable broth

DIRECTIONS:
1. Cut off the stem ends from the ancho and pasilla chiles and shake out the seeds. Cut the chiles in half, place into a medium bowl, and pour in the boiling water to cover. Allow to soak for 20 minutes. Drain.
2. Add the garlic and onion into a large nonstick sauté pan or skillet, cook over medium-high heat for 5 to 7 minutes, adding water, 1 tbsp. at a time, to prevent burning. The onions should be dark brown but not burned. Add the tomato paste and stir well, cook for 2 minutes to caramelize. Transfer to a high-speed blender.
3. Add the jalapeño pepper, soaked chiles, flour, chocolate, almond butter, cocoa powder, cumin, paprika, oregano, cinnamon, and vegetable broth. Puree for about 3 minutes until smooth.
4. Place the sauté pan or skillet back to medium-high heat. Add the sauce and cover the pan. Cook until the sauce begins to bubble. Lower the heat to low, uncovered and simmer for 5 minutes, stirring occasionally.
5. Serve immediately, place in an airtight container and store in the refrigerator for up to 1 week, or freeze for up to 6 months.

Nutrition Info per Serving:
Calories: 131, Protein: 4 g, Fat: 7 g, Carbohydrates: 13 g, Fiber: 4 g, Sugar: 3.7 g, Sodium: 86 mg

BBQ Sauce, page 184

Easy Homemade Pesto, page 187

Easy Vegan Marinara, page 185

Homemade Guacamole, page 186

Chapter 13 Sauce and Dressing   183

BBQ Sauce

Prep Time: 5 minutes, Cook Time: 0, Serves: 16

INGREDIENTS:
2 cups (360 g) tomato cubes
5 dates (pitted)
3 tbsps. smoked paprika
2 tbsps. garlic powder

DIRECTIONS:
1. Add all ingredients to a food processor and blend smooth.

Nutrition Info per Serving:
Calories: 11, Protein: 0.2 g, Fat: 0 g, Carbohydrates: 2.4 g, Fiber: 0.4 g, Sugar: 2 g, Sodium: 46 mg

Tofu Sour Cream

Prep Time: 5 minutes, Cook Time: 0, Serves: 1 cup

INGREDIENTS:
8 ounces (227 g) silken tofu
2 tbsps. freshly squeezed lemon juice
1 tsp. onion powder
1 tsp. apple cider vinegar

DIRECTIONS:
1. Combine all of the ingredients in a blender, blend for 1 minute, or until creamy.
2. Store in a refrigerator-safe container and keep in the refrigerator for up to 5 days.

Nutrition Info per Serving:
Calories: 10, Protein: 1 g, Fat: 0 g, Carbohydrates: 1 g, Fiber: 0 g, Sugar: 0.5 g, Sodium: 43 mg

Black Bean Spread

Prep Time: 10 minutes, Cook Time: 0, Serves: 3½ cups

INGREDIENTS:
4 cups cooked black beans, or two (15-oz. 430g) cans, drained and rinsed
6 cloves garlic, smashed and skin removed
Zest of 1 lemon and juice of 2 lemons
1 tbsp. maple syrup
3 tsps. mint
Salt to taste

DIRECTIONS:
1. Mix together the beans, garlic, lemon zest and juice, mint, maple syrup, salt, and 1 cup of water in the bowl of a blender and pulse until smooth and creamy. Add more water as needed to achieve a smooth consistency.

Nutrition Info per Serving:
Calories: 47, Protein: 2.2 g, Fat: 0.9 g, Carbohydrates: 9.6 g, Fiber: 3.1 g, Sugar: 1.6 g, Sodium: 586 mg

Artichoke and Feta Sauce

Prep Time: 10 minutes, Cook Time: 20 minutes, Serves: 4

INGREDIENTS:
One (15-ounce, 425 g) can artichoke hearts, drained and coarsely chopped
¼ cup (1½ ounces, 43 g) crumbled low-fat feta cheese
2 tbsps. lemon juice
1 tbsp. dried tarragon
1 sun-dried tomato, minced
¼ cup chopped onion
1 garlic clove, minced
¼ tsp. white pepper

DIRECTIONS:
1. Mix all ingredients in the bowl of a food processor. Pulse until coarsely chopped.
2. Serve immediately, or chill for up to three days before serving.

Nutrition Info per Serving:
Calories: 116, Protein: 6.3 g, Fat: 5.9 g, Carbohydrates: 9.8 g, Fiber: 2.8 g, Sugar: 5.3 g, Sodium: 194 mg

Simple Sweet and Tangy Ketchup

Prep Time: 5 minutes, Cook Time: 15 minutes, plus 30 minutes to cool, Serves: 2½ cups

INGREDIENTS:
1 cup water
¼ cup maple syrup
1 cup tomato paste
3 tbsps. apple cider vinegar
1 tsp. onion powder
1 tsp. garlic powder

DIRECTIONS:
1. Pour in the water to a medium saucepan, bring to a rolling boil over high heat. Reduce the heat to low, and whisk in the maple syrup, tomato paste, vinegar, onion powder, and garlic powder. Cover the pan and simmer for 10 minutes.
2. Remove from the heat and allow to cool for about 30 minutes before transferring to a refrigerator-safe container. Keep in the refrigerator for up to 1 month.

Nutrition Info per Serving:
Calories: 48, Protein: 1 g, Fat: 0 g, Carbohydrates: 11 g, Fiber: 1 g, Sugar: 6.1 g, Sodium: 57 mg

Easy Strawberry and Peach Vinaigrette

Prep Time: 5 minutes, Cook Time: 0, Serves: 1¼ cups

INGREDIENTS:
4 strawberries
1 peach, pitted
2 tbsps. balsamic vinegar
¼ cup water

DIRECTIONS:
1. Add the strawberries, peach, vinegar and water in a blender, blend on high for 1 to 2 minutes, or until the dressing has a smooth consistency.
2. Place in a refrigerator-safe container and chill for up to 3 days.

Nutrition Info per Serving:
Calories: 10, Protein: 0 g, Fat: 0 g, Carbohydrates: 2 g, Fiber: 0 g, Sugar: 8.5 g, Sodium: 48 mg

Garlicky Sunflower "Cheese"

Prep Time: 5 minutes, Cook Time: 0, Serves: ½ cup

INGREDIENTS:
½ cup sunflower seeds
½ tsp. garlic powder
2 tbsps. nutritional yeast

DIRECTIONS:
1. Add all of the ingredients into a food processor or blender. Process on low for 30 to 45 seconds, or until the sunflower seeds have been broken down to the size of coarse sea salt.
2. Place in a refrigerator-safe container, and store in the refrigerator for up to 2 months.

Nutrition Info per Serving:
Calories: 60, Protein: 3 g, Fat: 4 g, Carbohydrates: 3 g, Fiber: 1 g, Sugar: 0.4 g, Sodium: 29 mg

Easy Vegan Marinara

Prep Time: 5 minutes, Cook Time: 15 minutes, Serves: 2¼ cups

INGREDIENTS:
1 cup water
2 tbsps. maple syrup
1 cup tomato paste
1 tsp. dried thyme
1 tsp. garlic powder
1 tsp. onion powder
1 tsp. dried oregano
½ tsp. dried basil
¼ tsp. red pepper flakes

DIRECTIONS:
1. Fill the water in a medium saucepan, bring to a rolling boil over high heat. Reduce the heat to low, and whisk in the remaining ingredients.
2. Cover the pan and simmer for 10 minutes, stirring occasionally. Serve warm.

Nutrition Info per Serving:
Calories: 80, Protein: 3 g, Fat: 0 g, Carbohydrates: 17 g, Fiber: 3 g, Sugar: 2.1 g, Sodium: 27 mg

Mexican Salsa

Prep Time: 5 minutes, Cook Time: 0, Serves: 5

INGREDIENTS:
3 large tomatoes, quartered
¼ red onion, chopped
¼ cup (10 g) fresh cilantro
1 jalapeno
1 clove garlic, minced

DIRECTIONS:
1. Remove the stem, placenta and seeds of the jalapeno and cut into slices.
2. Put all ingredients to a food processor and blend until smooth.
3. Serve the salsa chilled as a topping or a side!

Nutrition Info per Serving:
Calories: 27, Protein: 1.1 g, Fat: 0.2 g, Carbohydrates: 5.2 g, Fiber: 1.5 g, Sugar: 3.2 g, Sodium: 121 mg

Lime-Garlic Spread

Prep Time: 10 minutes, Cook Time: 0, Serves: 2 cups

INGREDIENTS:
2 cups cooked great northern beans, or one (15-oz. 430g) can, drained and rinsed
1 red bell pepper, roasted, seeded, and coarsely chopped
2 cloves garlic, smashed and skin removed
2 tsps. ground turmeric
3 tbsps. basil, finely chopped
Zest and juice of 1 lime
Salt to taste
Pinch paprika

DIRECTIONS:
1. Mix all ingredients in the bowl of a blender and pulse until smooth and creamy.

Nutrition Info per Serving:
Calories: 98, Protein: 4.8 g, Fat: 1.9 g, Carbohydrates: 17.3 g, Fiber: 4.9 g, Sugar: 2.3 g, Sodium: 153 mg

Pomegranate Ginger Sauce

Prep Time: 5 minutes, Cook Time: 0, Serves: 8

INGREDIENTS:
2 cups (320 g) pomegranate seeds
10 dried plums (pitted)
20 g 2-inch piece ginger
1 tbsp. black pepper

DIRECTIONS:
1. Add all ingredients to a food processor and blend to form a smooth sauce.

Nutrition Info per Serving:
Calories: 65, Protein: 0.8 g, Fat: 0 g, Carbohydrates: 15.4 g, Fiber: 2.8 g, Sugar: 9.7 g, Sodium: 31 mg

Spicy Tahini Dressing

Prep Time: 10 minutes, Cook Time: 0, Serves: 8

INGREDIENTS:
½ cup (120 g) Tahini
2 tbsps. Lemon juice
1 clove Garlic (minced)
1 tbsp. Paprika powder
½ cup (120 ml) Water

DIRECTIONS:
1. Put all ingredients to a small bowl and whisk or shake until smooth.
2. Serve the tahini dressing chilled as a topping or a side!

Nutrition Info per Serving:
Calories: 102, Protein: 3.8 g, Fat: 8.6 g, Carbohydrates: 2.3 g, Fiber: 0.9 g, Sugar: 1.2 g, Sodium: 35 mg

Homemade Guacamole

Prep Time: 8 minutes, Cook Time: 5 minutes, Serves: 2 cups

INGREDIENTS:
½ medium tomato, chopped
3–4 small avocados, pitted and diced
¼ cup white onion, finely diced
1 tsp. minced garlic (about 2 small cloves)
¾ tsp. ground nutmeg
½ tbsp. lime juice
2 tbsps. chopped mint
Dash of salt
Freshly ground pepper, to taste
½ tsp. minced oregano
1 tbsp. Cashew Cream

DIRECTIONS:
1. Mash the avocados in a medium bowl with a fork to the desired consistency.
2. Add the lime juice, onion, garlic, nutmeg, oregano, mint, tomato, Cashew Cream, salt and pepper, and toss to combine well.

Nutrition Info per Serving:
Calories: 540, Protein: 7.2 g, Fat: 47.1 g, Carbohydrates: 33.4 g, Fiber: 21.6 g, Sugar: 3.5 g, Sodium: 149 mg

Sour Coconut Cream

Prep Time: 5 minutes, Cook Time: 0, Serves: 10

INGREDIENTS:
1 cup (300 g) Coconut cream
2 tbsps. Lemon juice
½ tsp. Apple cider vinegar
½ tsp. Salt (optional)

DIRECTIONS:
1. Put all ingredients to a food processor and blend until smooth.
Or put all ingredients into a medium bowl and whisk by hand until smooth.
2. Serve the sour coconut cream chilled as a topping or a side!

Nutrition Info per Serving:
Calories: 20, Protein: 0 g, Fat: 0.7 g, Carbohydrates: 3.3 g, Fiber: 0 g, Sugar: 3 g, Sodium: 22 mg

Spicy Satay Sauce

Prep Time: 5 minutes, Cook Time: 10 minutes, Serves: 8

INGREDIENTS:
1 cup (260 g) peanut butter
2 tbsps. lime juice
¼ cup (60 ml) sweet soy sauce
2 small onions, minced
2 cloves garlic, minced
2 cups (480 ml) water

DIRECTIONS:
1. Put all ingredients in a food processor and blend until smooth, add more water if the sauce is too thick. Or mix with a medium bowl and a handheld mixer.
2. Heat up the sauce in a saucepan at medium heat. Cook for 10 minutes and stir continuously.
3. Turn off the heat and let the sauce cool down for a minute while stirring.
4. Serve warm with optional toppings.

Nutrition Info per Serving:
Calories: 217, Protein: 8.5 g, Fat: 15.6 g, Carbohydrates: 10.6 g, Fiber: 2.5 g, Sugar: 4.9 g, Sodium: 88 mg

Raw Healing Pesto with Apple Cider

Prep Time: 10 minutes, Cook Time: 0, Serves: 1 cup

INGREDIENTS:
¼ cup (35g) raw cashews
2 tbsps. apple cider
1 garlic cloves, chopped
⅓ red onion, about 2 oz (50g)
1 tsp. nutmeg
1 tbsp. olive oil
4 cups (80g) packed sage
1 cup (40g) wheatgrass
¼ cup (60ml) water
¼ tsp. salt

DIRECTIONS:
1. In a heatproof bowl add the cashews and cover with boiling water. Soak for 5 minutes, and then drain.
2. Mix all ingredients in a food processor and process for 2 to 3 minutes or until well combined. Serve immediately or store in an airtight container and refrigerate for later use. For maximum health benefits, do not heat the pesto.

Nutrition Info per Serving:
Calories: 99, Protein: 3 g, Fat: 7 g, Carbohydrates: 6 g, Fiber: 1 g, Sugar: 1 g, Sodium: 24 mg

Maple Lemon and Poppy Seed Dressing

Prep Time: 10 minutes, Cook Time: 2 minutes, Serves: 1 cup

INGREDIENTS:
½ cup plant-based milk
1 tbsp. apple cider vinegar
1 tbsp. maple syrup
2 tbsps. freshly squeezed lemon juice
2 tsps. cornstarch
2 tsps. dried poppy seeds
½ tsp. garlic powder

DIRECTIONS:
1. Combine all of the ingredients in a small saucepan, mix until the cornstarch has completely dissolved.
2. Bring the dressing to a rolling boil over medium heat. Whisk the dressing and then remove from the heat.
3. Let the dressing cool before storing in a refrigerator-safe container for up to 4 days.

Nutrition Info per Serving:
Calories: 21, Protein: 0 g, Fat: 1 g, Carbohydrates: 3 g, Fiber: 0 g, Sugar: 3.3 g, Sodium: 41 mg

Easy Homemade Pesto

Prep Time: 5 minutes, Cook Time: 0, Serves: 1 cup

INGREDIENTS:
4 cups packed fresh basil leaves
2 tbsps. nutritional yeast
¼ cup raw cashews
¼ tsp. freshly ground black pepper
1 garlic clove
3 tbsps. boiling water, plus more as needed

DIRECTIONS:
1. Add all of the ingredients into a food processor, blend until smooth. Add more water to thin until you have a smooth, slightly thick mixture.
2. Place pesto in a sealed jar and refrigerate for up to 1 month.

Nutrition Info per Serving:
Calories: 38, Protein: 3 g, Fat: 2 g, Carbohydrates: 2 g, Fiber: 1 g, Sugar: 1.8 g, Sodium: 44 mg

Creamy Potato Oat Sauce

Prep Time: 5 minutes, Cook Time: 15 minutes, Serves: 6 cups

INGREDIENTS:
1 medium sweet potato, cut into 1-inch cubes
1 medium Yukon Gold potato, cut into 1-inch cubes
¼ cup rolled oats
¼ cup nutritional yeast
2 tsps. garlic powder
2 tsps. onion powder
1 tbsp. freshly squeezed lemon juice
1 tsp. smoked paprika

DIRECTIONS:
1. Pour in the water in a large stockpot, bring to a boil over high heat. Immerse the sweet potato and Yukon Gold potato in the boiling water gently. Cook for 12 minutes. Strain, reserving 3 cups of cooking liquid.
2. Combine the reserved cooking liquid, boiled sweet potato and potato, and the remaining ingredients in a blender, blend on high for 3 to 5 minutes, and serve.

Nutrition Info per Serving:
Calories: 65, Protein: 4 g, Fat: 1 g, Carbohydrates: 10 g, Fiber: 2 g, Sugar: 2.4 g, Sodium: 85 mg

Appendix 1: 28-Day Meal Plan

Meal Plan	Breakfast	Lunch	Dinner	Snack & Smoothies (Optional)
DAY-1	Breakfast Quinoa with Peach (page 18)	Chickpea Hummus Lettuce Gyros (page 28)	Sweet Potato and Cauliflower Pilaf (page 61)	Blueberry Lychee Smoothie (page 172)
DAY-2	Celery Tomato Rancheros (page 9)	Rice and Bean Tostadas (page 35)	Chocolate Cherry Oats (page 64)	Easy Chilled Pickles (page 145)
DAY-3	Guava Oatmeal with Yogurt (page 15)	Roasted Golden Beet and Tofu Curry (page 31)	Sweet Potato and Zucchini (page 42)	Berries Cobbler (page 165)
DAY-4	Maple Almond Granola (page 13)	Spiralized Mixed Vegetables Lo Mein (page 27)	Bean Chili with Lime and Jalapeño (page 77)	Orange Pineapple Smoothie (page 177)
DAY-5	Hummus and Date Bagel (page 15)	Baked Potato Casserole (page 34)	Potato Samosa Chard Roll (page 56)	Mixed Vegetable Wraps (page 147)
DAY-6	Raspberry Banana Muffins (page 10)	Stuffed Portobello Mushrooms (page 32)	Miso-Glazed Winter Squash with Spinach (page 55)	Ginger Raisin Smoothie (page 176)
DAY-7	Spinach Pesto Quinoa Bowl (page 19)	Veggie Quinoa Beans Soup (page 36)	Pineapple Black Bean Salad (page 119)	Rosemary Garlic New Potatoes (page 154)

Meal Plan	Breakfast	Lunch	Dinner	Snack & Smoothies (Optional)
DAY-8	Chocolate and Almond Butter Quinoa (page 20)	Rice Stuffed Eggplant (page 37)	Garlicky Tomato Carrot Soup (page 52)	Savory Tropical Green Smoothie (page 177)
DAY-9	Cinnamon Walnut and Apple Bowl (page 12)	Black Bean, Kale and Quinoa Salad (page 106)	Black Beans and Brown Rice (page 44)	Vanilla Protein Muffins (page 161)
DAY-10	Maple Plant-Powered Pancakes (page 18)	Pesto Pasta with Lentils (page 102)	Asparagus-Onion Millet Stew (page 123)	Italian Oats Rice Bean Balls (page 150)
DAY-11	Salted Raisin Oatmeal (page 17)	Sweet Potato & Broccoli (page 40)	Mint Larb Salad (page 114)	Strawberry Banana Smoothie (page 174)
DAY-12	Apple Granola Parfait (page 15)	Spiced Corn and Yam (page 67)	Creamy Garlic Mushroom Pizza (page 51)	Stuffed Chard Rolls (page 160)
DAY-13	Brown Rice Apricot Pudding (page 22)	Rice and Tofu Scramble (page 64)	Chestnut-Zucchini Soup (page 123)	Mashed Sweet Potato Bake (page 154)
DAY-14	Maple Granola with Peaches (page 19)	Baked Cucumber Stuffed Tomatoes (page 39)	Kidney Bean, Barley and Broccoli Bowl (page 56)	Peanut Butter Creamy Banana Smoothie (page 174)

Meal Plan	Breakfast	Lunch	Dinner	Snack & Smoothies (Optional)
DAY-15	Peanut Milk Oatmeal (page 23)	Grilled Veggie Kabobs (page 38)	Slow Cooker Seitan Log (page 48)	Quick French Fries (page 150)
DAY-16	Peach Kiwifruit Steel-Cut Oats (page 23)	Fava Beans with Olives (page 74)	Mushroom Sweet Potato Soup (page 124)	Lemony Vanilla Pie Bars (page 159)
DAY-17	Apple Granola Parfait (page 15)	Carrot Date Salad with Walnuts (page 111)	Paprika Broccoli Casserole (page 52)	Raspberry Acai Smoothie Bowl (page 172)
DAY-18	Stovetop Raspberry Oatmeal (page 22)	Indian Spiced Asparagus (page 36)	Vegan Avocado Chickpea Salad (page 116)	Strawberry and Watermelon Ice Pops (page 169)
DAY-19	Pecan Crunch Banana Bread (page 17)	Penne with Asparagus and Carrot (page 94)	Creamy Eggplant Polenta Casserole (page 45)	Vanilla Oat Apple Crisp (page 159)
DAY-20	Polenta with Longans and Dates (page 18)	Summer Ratatouille (page 25)	Stir-Fry Eggplant Dengaku (page 49)	Vanilla Apple Pie Smoothie (page 173)
DAY-21	Overnight Oatmeal with Maple Syrup (page 21)	Tomato Curry Chickpeas (page 84)	Garlicky Potato Leek Soup with Onion (page 125)	Roasted Vegetable Chips (page 158)

Meal Plan	Breakfast	Lunch	Dinner	Snack & Smoothies (Optional)
DAY-22	Broccoli Mushroom Breakfast Scramble (page 14)	Creamy Asparagus & Tofu Cubes (page 40)	Radish, Potato and White Beans Salad (page 110)	Vanilla Fruit Smoothie (page 173)
DAY-23	Escarole with Portobello (page 13)	Lentils with Rice and Onions (page 69)	Baked Spaghetti Squash with Bok Choy (page 54)	Easy Slow Cooker Spicy Peanuts (page 168)
DAY-24	Cauliflower and Chickpea Scramble (page 9)	Mango and Chickpea Curry (page 84)	Thai Potato Stew with Mint (page 127)	Garlicky Cauliflower Wings (page 146)
DAY-25	Maple Almond Granola (page 13)	Grilled and Marinated Mushrooms (page 34)	Soy Mince Noodles (page 101)	Vanilla Banana Breakfast Smoothie (page 176)
DAY-26	Rainbow Vegetable Breakfast Hash (page 10)	Tomato and Fava Bean Ratatouille (page 82)	Spinach and Mushroom Pilaf (page 47)	Homemade Popcorn (page 168)
DAY-27	Spelt Berry Longan Breakfast Cereal (page 22)	Eggplant and Chickpea Pilaf (page 60)	Cabbage, Corn and Bean Soup (page 136)	Gingerbread Smoothie (page 176)
DAY-28	Apple Cashew Granola (page 14)	Fruited Pistachios Millet Salad (page 111)	Stuffed Delicata Squash (page 47)	Chocolate Protein Bars (page 158)

Appendix 2: Measurement Conversion Chart

Volume Equivalents (Dry)	
US STANDARD	METRIC (APPROXIMATE)
1/8 teaspoon	0.5 mL
1/4 teaspoon	1 mL
1/2 teaspoon	2 mL
3/4 teaspoon	4 mL
1 teaspoon	5 mL
1 tablespoon	15 mL
1/4 cup	59 mL
1/2 cup	118 mL
3/4 cup	177 mL
1 cup	235 mL
2 cups	475 mL
3 cups	700 mL
4 cups	1 L

Temperatures Equivalents	
FAHRENHEIT (F)	CELSIUS(C) (APPROXIMATE)
225 °F	107 °C
250 °F	120 °C
275 °F	135 °C
300 °F	150 °C
325 °F	160 °C
350 °F	180 °C
375 °F	190 °C
400 °F	205 °C
425 °F	220 °C
450 °F	235 °C
475 °F	245 °C
500 °F	260 °C

Volume Equivalents (Liquid)		
US STANDARD	US STANDARD (OUNCES)	METRIC (APPROXIMATE)
2 tablespoons	1 fl.oz.	30 mL
1/4 cup	2 fl.oz.	60 mL
1/2 cup	4 fl.oz.	120 mL
1 cup	8 fl.oz.	240 mL
1 1/2 cup	12 fl.oz.	355 mL
2 cups or 1 pint	16 fl.oz.	475 mL
4 cups or 1 quart	32 fl.oz.	1 L
1 gallon	128 fl.oz.	4 L

Weight Equivalents	
US STANDARD	METRIC (APPROXIMATE)
1 ounce	28 g
2 ounces	57 g
5 ounces	142 g
10 ounces	284 g
15 ounces	425 g
16 ounces (1 pound)	455 g
1.5 pounds	680 g
2 pounds	907 g

Appendix 3: Dirty Dozen and Clean Fifteen

The Environmental Working Group (EWG) is a widely known organization that has an eminent guide to pesticides and produce. More specifically, the group takes in data from tests conducted by the US Department of Agriculture (USDA) and then categorizes produce into a list titled "Dirty Dozen," which ranks the twelve top produce items that contain the most pesticide residues, or alternatively the "Clean Fifteen," which ranks fifteen produce items that are contaminated with the least amount of pesticide residues.

The EWG has recently released their 2021 Dirty Dozen list, and this year strawberries, spinach and kale – with a few other produces which will be revealed shortly – are listed at the top of the list. This year's ranking is similar to the 2020 Dirty Dozen list, with the few differences being that collards and mustard greens have joined kale at number three on the list. Other changes include peaches and cherries, which having been listed subsequently as seventh and eighth on the 2020 list, have now been flipped; the introduction – which the EWG has said is the first time ever – of bell and hot peppers into the 2021 list; and the departure of potatoes from the twelfth spot.

DIRTY DOZEN LIST

Strawberries	Apples	Pears
Spinach	Grapes	Bell and hot peppers
Kale, collards and mustard greens	Cherries	Celery
Nectarines	Peaches	Tomatoes

CLEAN FIFTEEN LIST

Avocados	Sweet peas (frozen)	Kiwi
Sweet corn	Eggplant	Cauliflower
Pineapple	Asparagus	Mushrooms
Onions	Broccoli	Honeydew melon
Papaya	Cabbage	Cantaloupe

These lists are created to help keep the public informed on their potential exposures to pesticides, which then allows for better and healthier food choices to be made.

This is the advice that ASEQ-EHAQ also recommends. Stay clear of the dirty dozen by opting for their organic versions, and always be mindful of what you are eating and how it was grown. Try to eat organic as much as possible – whether it is on the list, or not.

Appendix 4: Recipes Index

A

Acorn Squash
Vegetable and Wild Rice Stuffed Squash with Almonds 38
Braised Red Cabbage with Squash 42
Roasted Curry Acorn Squash Soup 135

Adzuki Bean
Ethiopian Style Pilaf 60

Almond
Maple Almond Granola 13
Longan Almond Barley with Apple Cider 19
Easy Lemon and Almond Ricotta 153
Coconut Protein Bars 157
Chocolate Protein Bars 158
Almond Protein Bars 158
Almond and Coconut Cookie Balls 160
Quinoa Almond Cookies 166

Apple
Cinnamon Walnut and Apple Bowl 12
Apple Cashew Granola 14
Apple Cinnamon Oats 66
Vanilla Oat Apple Crisp 159
Vanilla Apple Pie Smoothie 173
Almond Butter Apple Sauce 182

Artichoke Heart
Stuffed Tomatoes with Mint 76
Cauliflower Pea Pasta Salad 106
Spinach, Artichoke and Quinoa Dip 181
Artichoke and Feta Sauce 184

Arugula
Cannellini Salad with Orange and Fresh Oregano 115

Asparagus
Asparagus, Red Lentil and Leek Soup 25
Vegetables with Spicy Poppy Seed and Almond Butter Sauce 28
Indian Spiced Asparagus 36
Creamy Asparagus & Tofu Cubes 40
Fried Rice with Red Pepper and Asparagus 66
Penne with Asparagus and Carrot 94
Penne with Swiss Chard, Asparagus and Peanuts 95
Stir-Fried Noodles with Asparagus and Tomato 100
Asparagus-Onion Millet Stew 123
Fresh-Flavored Asparagus Soup 137

Avocado
Balsamic Glazed Strawberry and Avocado Toast 54
Raspberry Wheat Berry Salad 68
Mixed Greens Salad with Almond 109
Homemade Guacamole 186

B

Banana
Banana Flavor Peanut Butter Bites 9
Raspberry Banana Pancakes 14
Pecan Crunch Banana Bread 17
Peanut Butter, Banana and Cacao Quinoa 64
Seedy Buckwheat Porridge 64
Choco Almond Mousse Pudding 166
Raisin and Oat Cookies 166
Chocolate-Peppermint Banana Cream 167
Mixed Berry Pudding 169
Raspberry Acai Smoothie Bowl 172
Vanilla Fruit Smoothie 173
Vanilla Green Chocolate Smoothie 173
Banana Mint Smoothie 174
Banana, Peanut Butter and Chia Smoothie 174
Raspberry Banana Smoothie 174
Peanut Butter Creamy Banana Smoothie 174
Chocolate Peanut Milk Smoothie 176
Gingerbread Smoothie 176
Vanilla Banana Breakfast Smoothie 176

Basil
Easy Homemade Pesto 187

Beet
Tomato, Beet and Black Bean Salad 108

Black Bean
Black Bean and Chocolate Blender Muffins 10
Rice and Bean Tostadas 35
Black Beans and Brown Rice 44
Blackbean and Rice Enchilada Bake 51
Stuffed Poblano Peppers with Chipotle 58
Cajun Burgers 72
Orange Black Bean Taquitos 76
Avocado Black Bean Tempeh Nachos with Cashew Cheese 83
Mexican Black Bean Burgers 84
Cajun Beans and Brown Rice 89
Black Bean, Kale and Quinoa Salad 106
Pineapple Black Bean Salad 119
Black Bean Vegetable Soup 130
Black Bean Spread 184

Blackberry
Blackberry Cashew Granola Bars 20

Blueberry
Lemony Whole-Wheat Blueberry Muffins 20
Mung Bean Sprouts and Cabbage Salad 75
Blueberry Lychee Smoothie 172

Bok Choy
Bok Choy Stir-Fry 53
Penne with Bok Choy Béchamel 94

Broccoli
Broccoli Mushroom Breakfast Scramble 14
Fried Vegetables with Miso and Sake 36
Sweet Potato & Broccoli 40
Provencal Broccoli 42
Paprika Broccoli Casserole 52
Sweet-and-Sour Meatball and Vegetable 80
Broccoli Salad with Maple-Yogurt Dressing 108
Garlicky Broccoli Bisque 140

Brown Lentil
Maple Glazed Vegetable Lentil and Oat Loaf 46
Oats Lentil Loaf with Maple-Tomato Glaze 75

Brussels Sprouts
Baked Sweet Potato and Brussels Sprouts Walnut Salad 108

Butternut Squash
Slow Cooked Butternut Squash and Oatmeal 11
Spaghetti with Squash and Celery Sauce 96
Ginger Butternut Squash and Cauliflower Soup 127
Savory Squash-Carrot Soup 140

Button Mushroom
Buckwheat with Bow-Tie Pasta 31
Toasted Cashew and Mushroom Rolls 153

C

Cabbage
Cabbage Pilaf 32
Cabbage and Chickpea Pilaf 37
Spaghetti and "Meatballs" 95
Cabbage, Corn and Bean Soup 136
Stuffed Cabbage Rolls 159
Cabbage Alfredo Sauce 179

Cabbage Kimchi
Kimchi Noodle Salad with Peanut 103

Cannellini Bean
Veggie Green Goddess Sandwich 48
White Bean Stew with Saffron and Sage 78
Tuscan-Style Baked Beans and Polenta 83
Quick Caldo Verde with White Bean 86
White Bean, Pumpkin, Spinach and Artichoke Dip 181

Carrot
Potato, Lentil and Kale Soup 31
Slow Vegetable Roast 44
Carrot and Sweet Potato with Pine Nut 46
Curried Millet and Green Peas with Mild Harissa Sauce 49
Cinnamon Spiced Carrot Oatmeal Bowl with Pecans 68
Rice Salad with Date and Carrot 105
Carrot Date Salad with Walnuts 111
Hungarian Red Lentil Carrot Soup 126
Provencal Green Lentil Soup 137
Vegetable Spring Rolls with Peanut Dipping Sauce 150
Mixed Vegetable and Cashew Sauce 180

Cashew
Vanilla Walnut and Cashew Butter 18
Lemony Vanilla Pie Bars 159
Homemade Easy Cashew Milk 170
Raw Healing Pesto with Apple Cider 187

Cauliflower
Cauliflower and Chickpea Scramble 9
Grilled Cauliflower with Spicy Lentil Sauce 30
Curried Mixed Vegetable Soup 53
Garlicky Roasted Cauliflower and Potato Soup 57
Almond Noodles with Cauliflower 63
Chile Cauliflower and White Bean 90
Chinese Five-Spice Noodles 92
Cauliflower Linguine with Apricot 93
Cauliflower-Cream Pasta with Mint 93
Ponzu Noodle Salad with Black Pepper 101
Cream of Cauliflower Soup 135
Garlicky Cauliflower Wings 146

Chard
Quinoa Chard Olive Salad 109
Chard Salad with Creamy Tofu Dressing 114

Cherry Potato
Quinoa, Celery and Cherry Potatoes 70

Cherry Tomato
Taro Soup with Broccoli, Potatoes and Leek 128
Onion-Black Beans Vegetable Soup with Parsley 133

Chia Seed
Overnight Vanilla and Chocolate Chia Pudding 23

Chickpea
Homemade Falafel Chickpea Burgers 26
Chickpea Hummus Lettuce Gyros 28
Mashed Chickpea and Avocado Sandwich 30
Chickpea Bulgur Pilaf 32
Seasoned Roasted Beet and Chickpea Biryani 43
Chickpea Rolls 72
Easy Baked Chickpea Falafel 74
Chana Masala 77
North African Vegetables and Chickpeas 77
Lemony Chickpeas Salad 80

Ras El Hanout Chickpea 83
Mango and Chickpea Curry 84
Tomato Curry Chickpeas 84
Chickpea Couscous Salad 87
Chorizo Chickpea 87
Mexican Quinoa 90
Avocado, Chickpea and Vegetable Salad 113
Vegan Avocado Chickpea Salad 116
Chickpea and Artichoke Mediterranean Salad 117
Chickpea Salad with Cherry Tomato 117
Spicy Chickpea Quinoa Salad 118
Ginger Chickpea Cauliflower Soup 122
Spinach Chickpea Stew 124
Moroccan Chickpea and Tomato Soup 139
Baked Taco-Seasoned Chickpeas and Edamame 143
Vanilla Chickpea Cookie Dough with Pecans 156
Quick Hummus 168
Garlicky Roasted Red Pepper Hummus 179
Chickpea Avocado Guacamole 180

Chile
Homemade Mole Sauce 182

Coconut
Smoked Coconut Bits 164
Vanilla Carrot and Coconut Cake Balls 164

Collard Green
Garlic Sautéed Collard Greens 148

Corn
Burrito Bowl with Tortilla Chips 37
Blackbean and Rice Stuffed Peppers 49
Southwestern Mac and Black Beans 100
Blackbean Pasta and Corn Salad 107
Fresh Corn and Vegetable Salsa 111
Bean and Corn Salad with Almond Butter 114
Succotash Salad with Peanut Butter 116
Chinese Yam, Corn and Bean Salad 119
Corn and Potato Soup with Dill 132
Taro Bean Stew 137

Cranberry
Vanilla Cranberry Thumbprints Cookies 156

Cremini Mushroom
Polenta with Mushroom Olive Sauce 45
Creamy Garlic Mushroom Pizza 51
Black Bean and Mushroom Stew 73
Penne with Radish and Mushroom Sauce 97
Tempeh Onion Stuffed Cremini Mushrooms 152

Cucumber
Cucumber Bisque 140
Easy Chilled Pickles 145
Mixed Vegetable Wraps 147

D

Date
Nutty Date and Blueberry Muffins 12
Date Pumpkin Bites 60
Vanilla Seedy Granola 151
Nutty Lemon Oatmeal Cacao Cookies 157
Peanut Butter Protein Bars 161
Oat and Mint Brownie Date Bars 162
Pistachio and Coconut Ice Cream 168
Lemony Tahini Cream 170
Snow Pear Mint Smoothie 173

Delicata Squash
Stuffed Delicata Squash 47

E

Edamame
Edamame and Rice 74
Edamame-Radish Soup 125

Eggplant
Summer Ratatouille 25
Rice Stuffed Eggplant 37
Grilled Eggplant Slices 38
Creamy Eggplant Polenta Casserole 45
Spicy Savory Eggplant 48
Stir-Fry Eggplant Dengaku 49
Eggplant and Chickpea Pilaf 60
Tomato and Fava Bean Ratatouille 82
Penne with Potato and Eggplant 99
Roasted Eggplant, Carrot and Lentil Stew 136

Escarole
Escarole with Portobello 13

F

Fava Bean
Fava Beans with Olives 74

G

Garlic
Roasted Garlic Lemon Dressing 182

Golden Beet
Roasted Golden Beet and Tofu Curry 31

Great Northern Bean
Lime-Garlic Spread 185

Green Bean
Rice and Vegetable Stir-Fry 66

Green Chile
Chile Lime Chutney 144

Refried Lentil Pepper Dip   180

Green Jackfruit
BBQ Garlicky Jackfruit Sliders   25

Green Lentil
Lentils with Rice and Onions   69
Lentils and Eggplant Moussaka   79
Lentil Shepherd's Pie with Parsnip Crust   80
Lentil Pasta   82
Lentil Burgers   85
Lemony Lentil Salad   87
Mexican Chorizo Lentil   89
Lemony Lentil Cranberry Salad   116
Lentil Brown Rice Soup   138
Green Lentil Chickpea Stew   138
Green Lentil Mushroom Soup   139

Green Pea
Rice and Tofu Scramble   64
Baked Pasta and Peas   88

Guava
Guava Oatmeal with Yogurt   15
Overnight Oatmeal with Maple Syrup   21

H

Hazelnut
Hazelnut Choco Balls   160

J

Jalapeño
Roasted Jalapeño, Lime and Avocado Guacamole   153

K

Kale
Carrot Kale and Lentil Stew 28
Black Bean and Quinoa Bowl   66
Curried Kale Apple Slaw   107
Lemony Garlic Kale Salad   116
Baked Garlicky Kale Chips   166

Kiwifruit
Apple Granola Parfait   15
Breakfast Quinoa with Kiwifruit Compote   21
Fruited Pistachios Millet Salad   111
Kiwifruit, Black Bean and Rosemary Salad   118

L

Leek
Vegetable Broth   138

Lentil
Pesto Pasta with Lentils   102
Rice Salad with Cumin, Nutmeg and Lentil   110
Lentil Apple Salad 115

Lettuce
Vinegary Rice and Black Bean Salad   105

Lima Bean
Creamy Lima Beans Pasta Salad   114

Longan
Polenta with Longans and Dates   18

Lychee
Savory Tropical Green Smoothie   177

M

Mango
Mango Lime Salsa   110
Mango Choco Protein Pudding   165
Tropical Smoothie Bowl with Pine nuts   173
Mango Raisin Smoothie   177

Mint
Apple-Mint Soup 136

Mushroom
Mushroom Carrot Skillet   11
Mushroom and Quinoa Breakfast Cups   12
Mushroom Seitan Bourguignon   58
Cornmeal Polenta with Mushrooms 67

N

Navy Bean
White Bean Snow Pear Salad   85
White Bean and Barley Pilaf   88

O

Onion
Spicy Satay Sauce 186

P

Papaya
Papaya, Peach and Apricot Muesli   23
Mix Berries and Papaya Salad   116
Papaya Smoothie 177

Parsley
Cold Soba Noodles with Miso and Sesame Dressing   96

Peach

Maple Pine Nuts Granola   15
Breakfast Quinoa with Peach   18
Maple Granola with Peaches   19
Polenta with Peach and Dates Compote   19
Peach Kiwifruit Steel-Cut Oats   23
Easy Cold-Brew Peach Iced Tea   169

Peanut
Peanut Pasta Salad   103
Easy Slow Cooker Spicy Peanuts   168

Pear
Polenta with Seared Cranberry and Pear   62
Grains and Fruit Salad   106
Mixed Greens Salad with Orange   109

Pine Nut
Baked Pine Nuts Granola   17

Pineapple
Homemade Hawaiian Black Bean Burgers   26
Fried Rice with Pineapple   68
Pineapple Mango Smoothie Bowl   172
Orange Pineapple Smoothie   177

Pinto Bean
Baked Pinto Beans Taquitos   72
Pinto Bean Salsa   86
Spicy Tempeh   181

Plantain
Mango Plantain and Dates Cream   145

Pomegranate Seed
Pomegranate Ginger Sauce   186

Portabella Mushroom
Creamy Garlic Mushroom Gravy   144
Stuffed Portobello Mushrooms   32
Grilled and Marinated Mushrooms   34
Asian Style Stuffed Mushrooms   35
Fettuccine with Potato Mushroom Stroganoff   97

Potato
Scrambled Tofu with Potatoes & Bok Choy   13
Baked Potato Casserole   34
Healthy Twice-Baked Potatoes   34
Stuffed Yellow Bell Peppers   35
Broccoli Baked Potatoes   39
Potato Samosa Chard Roll   56
Homemade Pad Thai   92
Singapore Noodles with Tomato and Celery   99
Potato and Celery Lo Mein   101
Corn Carrot Zucchini Chowder   123
Potato Soup with Thai Basil   125
Garlicky Potato Leek Soup with Onion   125
Cabbage Vichyssoise with Mint   132
Red Bean Soup with Shallot and Thyme   133
Potato Soup with Tahini   134

Pumpkin
Winter Asparagus Salad with Toasted Hazelnut   113
Pumpkin and Cucumber Stew with Lime Juice   134

Purple Cabbage
Asian Veggie Slaw with Maple-Ginger Dressing   151

Purple Potato
Purple Potato and Lettuce Salad with Soy Sauce Dressing   107

R

Radish
Tuscan Radish Stew   128
Garlicky Vegetable Soup   139

Raisin
Salted Raisin Oatmeal   17
Congee with Raisin and Spices   17
Vanilla Protein Muffins   161

Raspberry
Raspberry Banana Muffins   10
Stovetop Raspberry Oatmeal   22
Spiced Sorghum with Almond and Raspberry   61

Red Bean
Pitaya Red Bean Salad   84
Red Bean Date Salad   85
Grilled Vegetable and Pineapple Salad   115

Red Bell Pepper
Garlicky Harissa Sauce   179

Red Cabbage
Soba Noodles with Vegetable and Peanut Sauce   27
Thai Rice Bowl with Peanut Sauce   63
Cabbage Salad and Almond Butter Vinaigrette   118

Red Kidney Bean
Veggie Quinoa Beans Soup   36
Kidney Bean, Barley and Broccoli Bowl   56
Italian Oats Rice Bean Balls   150

Red Lentil
Quick Cooking Red Lentil   82
Red Lentil Dahl   86
Mango Red Lentil Salad   88
Red Lentil Pasta with Pistachios   97
Noodles with Red Lentil Sauce and Peanut Butter   99

Red Potato
Radish, Potato and White Beans Salad   110
Warm Radicchio Potato Salad with Arugula Pesto   113
Pesto and Roasted Potato Salad   117
Zucchini Vegetable Soup with Tahini   138
Mashed Potatoes with Vegetable Gravy   147
Mustard Spiced Creamy Potato Salad   148

Rosemary Garlic New Potatoes 154

Romaine Lettuce
Black Bean and Rice Lettuce Wraps 67
Easy Basic Table Salad 118

S

Seitan
Seitan Sloppy Joes Sandwich 40
Baked Seitan Swirls with Mustard 143

Shiitake Mushroom
Thai Red Curry Fried Rice 62
Chickpea Soba Noodles in Kombu Broth 92

Snow Pear
Kiwifruit Muesli with Apple Cider 21

Spaghetti Squash
Baked Spaghetti Squash with Bok Choy 54
Baked Spaghetti Squash with Radish Sauce 55

Spelt Berry
Spelt Berry Longan Breakfast Cereal 22

Spinach
Spinach Pesto Quinoa Bowl 19
Blackbean Spinach and Rice Salad 27
Cauliflower, Spinach and Sweet Potato Lasagna 43
Spinach and Mushroom Pilaf 47
Taco Salad with Peanut Butter Dressing 79
Lemony Vegetable Salad 111
Moroccan Shepherd's Pie 162
Fruity Vitamin C Smoothie 172
Chocolate Avocado Smoothie 176

Split Pea
Split Pea Burgers 73
Sweet Potato Tofu Stew 133
Split Pea and Tofu Soup 135

Strawberry
Vanilla Strawberry Chia Seed Pudding with Chocolate 22
Strawberry Banana Smoothie 174
Easy Strawberry and Peach Vinaigrette 185

Sunflower Seed
Overnight Oats 70

Sweet Pea
Creamy Asparagus and Vegetable Stew 122
Homemade Deconstructed Malai Kofta 152

Sweet Potato
Rainbow Vegetable Breakfast Hash 10
Brown Rice Apricot Pudding 22
Sweet Potato and Zucchini 42
Sweet Potato and Cauliflower Pilaf 61
Vegetable White Bean with Sherry 88
Sweet Potato Quinoa Salad 105
Mushroom Sweet Potato Soup 124
Garlic Sweet Potato Gnocchi with Cashews 145
Garlicky Vegetable Burgers 148
Mashed Sweet Potato Bake 154
Sweet Potato Whole Wheat Cake 162
Vanilla Sweet Potato Pie Cream 167
Creamy Potato Oat Sauce 187

Swiss Chard
Stuffed Chard Rolls 160

T

Tangerine
Chocolate Cherry Oats 64

Taro
Taro Pie Oatmeal 20
Zuppa with Cucumber and Black-eyed Peas 85
Zucchini Taro Quinoa Salad 109
Quinoa, Cucumber and Taro Salad 110
Cherry Tomato Quinoa Tabbouleh 117

Tempeh
Mango Satay Tempeh 61
Lemony Marinated Tempeh 89

Tofu
Grilled Tofu with Mashed Potato Bowl 26
Marinated Mushroom and Tofu Scramble 52
Orange-Glazed Tofu Bowl with Brown Rice 57
Spicy Cajun Tofu 76
Smoked Tofu and Black Beans 78
Mint Larb Salad 114
Chilled Creamy Tofu Cheese 143
Sweet Tofu Cream 153
Tofu Sour Cream 184

Tomato
Celery Tomato Rancheros 9
Hummus and Date Bagel 15
Chickpea and Kidney Bean Stew 29
Baked Cucumber Stuffed Tomatoes 39
Lentil Mushroom Bolognese 39
Polenta with Creamy Tomato Sauce 45
Garlicky Tomato Carrot Soup 52
Carrot, Spinach and Bean Soup 53
Lentils with Rice and Macaroni 62
Quinoa-Stuffed Tomatoes with Cheese and Avocado 63
Black Bean, Tomato, Rice and Lentil Burritos 73
Mixed Bean Chili 75
Bean Chili with Lime and Jalapeño 77
Red Lentil Chili 78
Red Bean Gazpacho with Raisin 87
Baked Whole-Grain Ziti 94

Tomato Penne with Roasted Red Pepper Sauce 102
Soy Mince Spaghetti 103
Spiced Masoor Dal Tomato Stew 121
Vegetable Soup with Lima Beans 121
Tomato-Corn Chowder 129
Tomato Lentil Soup with Pine Nut 130
Corn-Tomato Chowder with Basil 132
Kombu-Tomato Broth 140
Tomato and Zucchini Soup 141
Homemade Shakshuka 144
Garlicky Red Pepper Farro and Kidney Bean Bowl 146
Quinoa Stuffed Peppers with Pesto 151
BBQ Sauce 184
Mexican Salsa 185

W

Walnut
Peanut Butter Chickpea Burgers 30
Baked Maple-Glazed Mixed Nuts 167

Watermelon
Easy Watermelon Lemonade 169
Strawberry and Watermelon Ice Pops 169

White Bean
White Beans Vegetable Salad 86
Provencal Beans & Cherry Tomato Salad 113
Asparagus Zucchini Stew with Rosemary 130
White Bean Hummus Stew with Mint 134
Lemon Chickpea and White Bean Hummus 147

White Potato
Quick French Fries 150

White Yam
Spiced Corn and Yam 67

Winter Squash
Miso-Glazed Winter Squash with Spinach 55

Squash and Peach Soup with Mint 126

Y

Yam
Yam-Carrot Bisque 128

Yellow Onion
Soy Mince Noodles 101

Yellow Squash
Roasted Vegetables with Whole-Grain Pasta 44
Summer Vegetable Pesto Casserole 55

Z

Zucchini
Spiralized Mixed Vegetables Lo Mein 27
Vegetable Enchiladas with Anasazi Bean Sauce 29
Grilled Veggie Kabobs 38
Zucchini and Cauliflower with Avocado 47
Zucchini and Kale Wrap 56
Indonesian Noodles with Tomato 93
Macaroni Zucchini Salad 95
Penne with Blackbeans and Bok Choy 96
Spaghetti with Lentil and Zucchini Ragu 100
Indonesian Noodle Salad with Lemon Juice 101
Udon Noodle with Zucchini 102
Bulgur, Kiwifruit and Zucchini Salad 115
Chestnut-Zucchini Soup 123
Lentil Stew with Maple Syrup 124
Noodle Soup with Mushroom and Sesame 126
Thai Potato Stew with Mint 127
Spicy Acorn Squash and Bok Choy 129
White Bean Stew with Hominy and Zucchini 129
Split Pea Asparagus Soup 141
Cheesy Zucchini Pancake 167

Made in United States
North Haven, CT
14 January 2023